SCRIMMAGE FOR WAR

A Story of Pearl Harbor, Football, and World War II

BILL McWILLIAMS

D1604331

STACKPOLE
BOOKS

Guilford, Connecticut

Published by Stackpole Books
An imprint of The Rowman & Littlefield Publishing Group, Inc.
4501 Forbes Blvd., Ste. 200
Lanham, MD 20706
www.rowman.com

Distributed by NATIONAL BOOK NETWORK
800-462-6420

British Library Cataloguing in Publication Information available

Library of Congress Cataloging-in-Publication Data

Names: McWilliams, Bill, 1933– author.
Title: Scrimmage for war : a story of Pearl Harbor, football, and World War
    II / Bill McWilliams.
Description: Guilford, Connecticut : Stackpole Books, [2019] | Includes
    bibliographical references and index. | Summary: "In late November 1941,
    two college football teams—Willamette University and San Jose
    State—set sail for Honolulu for a series of games with the University
    of Hawaii. The players found themselves caught up in the first days of
    the United States' war with Japan. They arrived home on Christmas Day
    after a dangerous journey back across the Pacific. Almost all of the
    players would go on to fight in the war. This book blends battle and
    gridiron—along with a strong dose of human interest, of college-aged
    young men unexpectedly caught up in the world war"— Provided by
    publisher.
Identifiers: LCCN 2019017670 (print) | LCCN 2019980509 (ebook) | ISBN
    9780811738675 (cloth ; alk. paper) | ISBN 9780811768733 (ebook)
Subjects: LCSH: Willamette University—Students—Biography. | San Jose
    State College—Students—Biography. | Pearl Harbor (Hawaii), Attack on,
    1941. | Football—Hawaii—History—20th century. | Football
    players—Oregon—Salem—Biography. | Football players—California—San
    Jose—Biography. | College athletes—Oregon—Salem—Biography. | College
    athletes—California—San Jose—Biography. | World War,
    1939–1945—Biography. | United States—Armed Forces—Biography.
Classification: LCC D767.92 .M429 2019 (print) | LCC D767.92 (ebook) |
    DDC 940.54/12730922794—dc23
LC record available at https://lccn.loc.gov/2019017670
LC ebook record available at https://lccn.loc.gov/2019980509

To Veronica Eileen McWilliams and Anna Bates McWilliams, two beautiful ladies, wives, inspirations, and loves in my life—for all they have sacrificed in support of the research, writing, and publishing of this true story.

*"Fight on, my merry men all,
I'm a little wounded, but I am not slain;
I will lay me down for to bleed a while,
Then I'll rise and fight with you again."*

"Johnnie Armstrong's Last Goodnight"
Stanza 18, Anonymous
From Dryden's *Miscellanies*, 1702

CONTENTS

Author's Note

READERS WILL SEE BOTH TRADITIONAL CIVILIAN AND TWENTY-FOUR-HOUR MILITARY DATE and timekeeping in this history. As an example, military dates are expressed as 19 December 1941 rather than December 19, 1941. With respect to time, on board a company-owned ocean liner, a typical morning clock time is normally expressed as 9:25 a.m. or 9:25 in the morning. On board a navy combatant such as the cruiser *Detroit*, or in an army air force airborne bombing mission, the same time will be expressed on a twenty-four-hour clock as 0925 hours. At 9:25 p.m. in the evening, military time will be 2125 hours.

When navy vessels are named the first time in the narrative, they are normally accompanied by hull numbers in parentheses immediately following the ships' names, which are italicized. Examples are the cruiser USS *Detroit* (CL-8) and the destroyer USS *Cummings* (DD-365). The acronym *USS* is "United States ship." Subsequent use of the ship's name in the narrative will drop the acronym *USS*.

Specific hull numbers are used to identify ships the first time the name is used in the text because, over time, ships' names are reused on newer ships of the same or similar type. A notable example in this history is the aircraft carrier USS *Hornet* (CV-8), which carried the sixteen army air force B-25 bombers, led by then Lieutenant Colonel James H. "Jimmy" Doolittle, on its flight deck in the historic 18 April 1942 bombing of Japan. The *Hornet* was sunk later in the war, and her name was given to another carrier produced in World War II, the *Hornet* (CV-12).

For readers unfamiliar with other navy, army, army air force, and marine terms and jargon, there are on-the-spot explanations throughout the narrative or at the bottom of the page where the term or jargon appears. Examples are two incidents involving a "windmilling engine" on B-17 bombers in chapters 13 and 19.

Note: If you wish to view additional images supporting this story but not depicted in this book, go to the author's personal website at http://www.west-point.org/users/usma1955/20315/SW.htm or, alternatively, to the following web address: https://theological -geography.net/?p=5507.

FOREWORD

SCRIMMAGE FOR WAR: A STORY OF PEARL HARBOR, FOOTBALL, AND WORLD WAR II IS A POWER-
ful, compelling, virtually unknown true story of football and war. Author Bill McWilliams
expands on his November 2011 book *Sunday in Hell: Pearl Harbor Minute by Minute*
through extensive research and numerous never-before-published photographs. He takes
readers through eleven days leading to the Shrine Bowl charity football game on Saturday
afternoon, December 6, 1941, in Honolulu, Territory of Hawaii. Fourteen hours later, the
Japanese attack on Pearl Harbor and numerous other targets on Oahu shattered our world
and plunged America into World War II.

Two champion West Coast football teams, the San Jose State College Spartans from
California, with twenty-five players, their head coach, team manager, photographer, and
yell leader, plus three others, and the Willamette University Bearcats from Oregon, with
twenty-seven players, their head coach, team manager, and publicist, plus twenty-two other
Salem citizens, were all beginning an incredible journey none would ever forget—one that
profoundly changed their lives.

On that infamous date, Sunday, December 7, the two football teams and their accompanying staff and fans were at first puzzled, along with all of Honolulu's citizenry, as they
witnessed, from a distance, incomprehensible, disastrous history and then became a part of
what they were seeing and hearing. Finally, in the devastating aftermath, they came face to
face with the stark, brutal reality of war and its effects.

In this historic tale, the two teams and their fans emerge in striking, never-before-told
stories as these young men and other civilians were ordered to evacuate Hawaii. They became
part of the SS *President Coolidge*'s already-full passenger complement. Another four hundred
evacuees, nearly all women and children—some of whom had lost husbands and fathers in
the attack—were sent home aboard the first World War II evacuation convoy from Honolulu to San Francisco. A small group of two converted former luxury liners escorted by two
navy combatant vessels began a perilous seven-day voyage through waters suspected of being
heavily patrolled by Japanese submarines.

But their safe return was only the beginning. In a look back at World War I, readers will
be taken on tours through training, the movement of troops to France, and seven days of
the brutal Battle of the Argonne Forest—the longest battle in American military history. It

began on September 26, 1918, and ended when the Armistice was signed on November 11. Readers will also travel overseas with the U.S. Army's "Wild West Division," the 91st Division, from Camp Lewis, Washington, for an intimate glimpse of the "War to End All Wars."

Subsequently, the story follows numerous World War II battles fought on the ground, at sea, and in the air in the European, Mediterranean, and Pacific theaters. Some will be familiar, others not, but all are stunning in their intensity and in revealing how they were seen by those who took part in the fight.

In Europe, we relive the 8th Army Air Force's daylight bombing campaigns, revealed through the eyes of the men of the famous 91st Bombardment Group (H), the men of the 324th's famed "Memphis Belle," and the group's 322nd Squadron over Berlin on December 5, 1944. We consider the "carpet bombing" in advance of the breakout at St. Lo following the D-day landings in Normandy. Then we see Operation Dragoon, the invasion of southern France on August 15, 1944, in which the 321st Bombardment Group (M), including its 448th Squadron of B-25 bombers, participated following months of strikes in Italy in support of ground campaigns there. Many other stories of men who witnessed and suffered the losses, found in missing air crew records and unit histories and letters home that carefully omitted the awful trials and losses endured, are revealed.

In the Pacific, we will see marine ground and air units on Funafuti Atoll, Betio Island, Tarawa Atoll, the Gilbert Islands, Guam, Kwajalein Atoll, Saipan, Tinian, and Eniwetok Atoll. The fierce sea and air battles over Rabaul's Simpson Harbor, navy and marine fliers' "Great Marianas Turkey Shoot," and the invasions of Japanese home islands Iwo Jima and Okinawa are vividly revisited. Operation Hailstone, Admiral Nimitz's crushing Pacific Fleet attack against Truk Atoll following the little-known marine high-altitude reconnaissance squadron's (VMD-254) extraordinary mission against the Japanese bastion there exhibits heroism in small, forgotten places. Another example of heroism in an obscure place is the Borneo campaign from May through early August 1945, drawn from the history of two 13th Army Air Force P-38L units, the 67th and 70th Fighter Squadrons flying out of bases in the Philippines, as World War II was finally coming to a merciful, abrupt end.

Throughout the book, readers are at the shoulders of the men who traveled to Hawaii in peacetime to play football for a worthy cause and enjoy an idyllic winter vacation in that fateful December 1941. Instead, they joined the first American victims and participants in an unimaginable event of great historic importance. Once having returned to the mainland United States, many of them became inspired "citizen soldiers" in a generation of Americans determined to fight through to ultimate victory over Fascist Italy, Nazi Germany, and the Japanese Empire. By virtue of Bill McWilliams's deep research and inspiring words, they should now become well known and never forgotten for their service and sacrifice.

Lieutenant General Wallace C. Gregson Jr.
United States Marine Corps (Ret.)

Part I
Inspirations and Reality

CHAPTER ONE

Voyage to a Dream

ON MONDAY, NOVEMBER 24, 1941, AT WILLAMETTE UNIVERSITY IN SALEM, OREGON, happy faces and big grins were everywhere, especially among twenty-seven players on the university's Bearcat football team. Their names had just been announced. They were leaving Wednesday, sailing from San Francisco on Thursday on the Matson Line's SS *Lurline* to Honolulu, on the island of Oahu, in what was then the Territory of Hawaii, where they were scheduled to play the University of Hawaii's Rainbow Warriors in the annual Shrine Bowl game. When the announcement came, planning was already under way for a Wednesday rally at Salem's Southern Pacific train station thirty minutes prior to departure.

At 10:00 a.m. on Wednesday, several hundred Willamette students, faculty, and the university band were joined by a number of Salem's citizens for the noisy, happy, excitement-filled rally at the station. Accompanying the team on Southern Pacific's "Klamath" were athletic director and head football coach Roy Servais "Spec" Keene, manager Dick Kern, and publicist Gil Lieser, plus twenty-two of Salem's citizens, including Mrs. Marie Keene; State Senator Douglas McKay, a close friend of the team's coaches, and his daughter, Shirley, a sophomore at Willamette; and Salem residents Mr. and Mrs. Harry U. Miller, Barbara Miller, Jack Hedgcock, Wayne Hadley (a senior at the university), Lorena Jack, Mrs. Waldo Zeller, Mrs. Charles O. Wilson, Mrs. Muriel Reynolds (wife of halfback Buddy Reynolds), Betty Byrd, Mrs. George E. Lewis, Mrs. Ray Waltz, Mrs. Gordon Moore (wife of guard Gordon Moore), Maxine Asheim, and Mr. and Mrs. W. H. Anderson. Also there were W. C. Henkle of nearby Dallas, Oregon, and N. G. Shafer of Kent, Washington.

Among those on the team drawn by Coach Keene's persuasiveness were freshman halfback Earl Hampton, a tough farm kid from Molalla, Oregon, convinced to play for him by mentioning the 1941 schedule, and two high school classmates and football teammates from Vancouver, Washington, High School, Ken Jacobson and Chuck Furno, with the promise that they too would play in Hawaii. The same promise lured guard Tony Fraiola to Salem, altering his plan to go home to New Jersey after he completed his hitch in the Marine Corps. Tackle Jim Fitzgerald was in spring football practice at the University of Oregon when

Ken Jacobson at the Salem, Oregon, Southern Pacific station, shortly before boarding the train on Wednesday, November 26, 1941, for Oakland, California, en route to San Francisco and Honolulu, Territory of Hawaii, with the Willamette University football team to play the University of Hawaii in the Shrine Bowl. (*Source*: KJC)

Keene mentioned the game in Honolulu and changed the direction of the new Willamette football recruit's life.

In Keene's remarkable run as head coach, his team had won fourteen and tied one of sixteen homecoming games, and in the period 1933 through 1938 they had won twenty-seven straight Pacific Northwest Conference games. The season of 1941 had been the Bearcats' best since Spec Keene began coaching at Willamette, with eleven of thirteen Northwest Conference first team all-stars soon to be selected from his team: ends Bill Reder and Marshall Barbour; tackles Martin Barstad, Neil Morley, and George Constable; guards Tony Fraiola and Gordon Moore, and backs Al Walden, Buddy Reynolds, Gene Stewart, and Ted Ogdahl.

The Bearcats, scheduled to play the University of Hawaii Rainbows on the first Saturday in December, were sailing on *Lurline* with another football team, California's San Jose State College Spartans. The Spartans, representing the college's more than three thousand students, having defeated the Bearcats 21–0 during the 1940 season, were scheduled to play the Rainbow Warriors the second Saturday in a police benefit game, with the two stateside teams playing one another in Honolulu on Tuesday, December 16, before their scheduled return voyage on *Lurline* three days later, for a December 24 arrival in San Francisco. The planned arrival would ensure that everyone on both teams could be home on Christmas Day.

Willamette fans at the rally and send-off after the team had boarded the train. (*Source*: KJC)

At San Francisco harbor's Pier 31 the morning of November 27, the crew of SS *Lurline*, the Matson Line's gleaming white ocean liner, were in the final stages of preparing her for another pleasurable, long-planned voyage to Honolulu, with a one-day en route port call, arriving Friday morning in the Los Angeles port at San Pedro.

The morning of the 27th, twenty-five members of the Spartan team were among the thirty-one people leaving San Jose by bus to the Matson line terminal in San Francisco. Accompanying the Spartans were Coach Ben Winkelman; manager Sebastian "Scrappy" Squatrito; yell leader Tommy Taylor; team photographer Bob McGaveren; Mrs. Ed Wenberg, wife of team co-captain and quarterback Ed Wenberg; and Lieutenant Dave Dorsey of San Jose, leaving the navy's nearby Moffett Field for assigned duty in Hawaii. The players were Bill Donnelly, Ed Wenberg, Gene Kasparovitch, Jack Galvin, Bob Hamill, Gray McConnell, John Brown, Walt Meyer, Ken Stanger, Don Allen, Hans Wiedenhoffer, Ken Bailey, Charles Cook, Wilbur Wool, Aubrey Minter, Bert Robinson, Bill Rhyne, George Foote, Paul Tognetti, Jack Lecari, Frank Minini, Fred Lindsey, Allen Hardisty, Chet Carsten, and Verne Cartwright. Most of the Spartans were between nineteen and twenty-one years of age. The oldest was Vernon Cartwright, who, on the voyage to Honolulu, was undoubtedly looking forward to celebrating his twenty-sixth birthday in the South Pacific on December 7.

The SS *Lurline* departing the Embarcadero, San Francisco, November 27, 1941, with the San Jose State College and Willamette University football teams, fans, and coaches on board. (*Source*: SJSULA)

The night prior to their departure, the Spartans played their final regular-season game at home in Spartan Stadium against a service team, the navy's Moffett Field Flyers, which, in a most unusual twist, was also coached by Ben Winkelman. Kickoff was at 8:00 p.m. Several former Spartans were stars on the Flyers, and typically, as with the Flyers, by season's end the Spartans had absorbed injuries adversely affecting their normal starting lineup, a fact noted as "banged up veterans" by the *Spartan Daily*'s student sportswriter in the November 26 issue. In spite of halfback Bill Rhyne's sterling performance before a crowd of 7,800 cheering spectators, a 22–13 loss to the Flyers sent them on their way to Hawaii with some season-ending pain—but looking forward to a restful vacation to mend and be ready for the December 13 game against the Rainbows. Their December 16 game against Willamette would give them a twelfth game in 1941.

While Coach Ben Winkelman outwardly expressed excitement similar to Willamette's Spec Keene about the talented athletes he believed would be drawn to the Spartans' football team by their return to Hawaii, he privately expressed some misgivings to his wife, who wasn't accompanying him on the voyage, misgivings she would later express as "a premonition."

Winkelman, who had played football at the University of Arkansas and was the first Razorback in the university's history to play professional football, was in his second year as head coach of the Spartans, and the 1941 team had garnered recognition as co-champions of the California Collegiate Athletic Association with a record of five wins, three losses, and two ties after winning the CCAA outright in 1940. On his young squad, none had been on the team in 1938, the last time San Jose had sailed to Hawaii to play the Rainbows, and few remained from 1939, when the Spartans were 13–0 under head coach Doug DeGroot, the only unbeaten season in the school's history.

Perhaps more noteworthy is the fact that behind Winkelman and his team in 1940 was a football legend, Glenn Scobey "Pop" Warner, who was now in his third season at San Jose State College as an "athletics consultant." He didn't go with the team to Hawaii this time, and he proved not to be that influential at San Jose State during the 1941 season. In 1939, he had brought to San Jose an extensive, marvelous collegiate football record as a player and coach—in a game to which he had introduced many innovative playing mechanics, including the screen pass, spiral punt, single- and double-wing formations, the use of shoulder and thigh pads, and helmets in red for backs and white for ends.

Since its inception in 1920, the annual invasion by mainland football teams to play the University of Hawaii had become the largest, most important, and most colorful sports spectacle in the Territory of Hawaii. A series of intercollegiate charity benefit games sponsored by the Aloha Chapter of the Shriners—the December sports contests between mainland schools and the Rainbows—had grown in popularity and attendance in every one of the twenty-one previous years, except 1931, when no games were scheduled.

The first of the three scheduled games in 1941 had become known as the Shrine Game, the leadoff, postseason event filled with good works and colorful history. The history of the Shrine Game, which spanned the beginning of what would become known in the United States as the golden age of football, included such notable colleges and universities as the University of Nevada, which sent their Wolfpack as the first visiting team and took the measure of the Rainbows, 14–0; Oregon; St. Mary's; Oregon State; Colorado; Colorado State; Washington; Washington State; Utah; Utah State; South Dakota State; Occidental College; the University of Denver; Oklahoma; Idaho; Brigham Young; California; the University of Southern California; Santa Clara; Drake University; College of the Pacific; San Diego State; the Green Bay Packers professional team; and more.

The first game this year was being played on the same day of the month as the first game against Nevada in 1920. The profits were for handicapped children. The police fund would receive the profits from the second game. Profits from the third game between the two West Coast teams were to defray the expenses for the two teams' travel.

It was late afternoon on November 27 in San Francisco when, in the U.S. Army's Hawaiian Department Headquarters on Oahu, the commander of army forces in Hawaii, Lieutenant General Walter C. Short, received a message handed to him by his chief of staff, which later became known as a "war warning message," from army chief of staff General George C. Marshall in Washington, DC. The same afternoon, a similar message to Admiral Husband E. Kimmel, commander of the Pacific Fleet, arrived from the chief of naval operations, Admiral Harold R. Stark, in Washington. The two highly classified messages gave carefully drawn guidance to the navy and army commanders of the Hawaii-based forces, stating that negotiations with the Empire of Japan had ended, unlikely to resume, and that hostilities could commence at any time. No offensive action was to be taken by American forces unless necessary for self-defense—that is, if the Japanese should strike the first blow. The messages also specifically cautioned against taking any action that would alarm the civilian populace.

By the time the messages were delivered to their intended readers in Hawaii, *Lurline* had already departed her San Francisco mooring en route overnight on her voyage for the Friday Los Angeles stopover in the port at San Pedro. Outbound, she glided beneath the Golden Gate Bridge, an engineering marvel that had been completed just four and a half years earlier, and entered the Pacific Ocean heading south along the coast.

Lurline, the last of Matson's great white fleet, had a storied history all her own. She began her regularly scheduled voyages to Hawaii and back following her January 12, 1933, maiden voyage from New York City, through the Panama Canal, and thence to Sydney, Australia; the South Seas; and her subsequent first entrance into San Francisco harbor on April 24, 1933.

Lurline's auspicious beginning included passenger travel by famed aviator Amelia Earhart from Los Angeles to Honolulu with her Lockheed Vega airplane secured on deck during the December 22–27, 1934, crossing. The voyage prepared her for the record-breaking Honolulu-to-Oakland solo flight she made in January 1935.

During the intervening years, the Matson line's reputation for gracious, relaxing travel soon stimulated a heyday of crack passenger trains, called "boat trains," carrying passengers from New York and Chicago to connect in San Francisco with liner sailings. *Lurline* attracted such Hollywood stars as William Powell, Carole Lombard, Jimmy Durante, Claudette Colbert, Myrna Loy, Frances Dee, and Shirley Temple, plus notable sports figures, including in one case a gentleman named Jackie Robinson, who was in Hawaii playing semi-pro football in 1941 after playing in the backfield of Pasadena Community College, and who following World War II became a national icon as the first African American to break into major league baseball, through the good offices of Branch Rickey and the Brooklyn Dodgers. Despite the difficulties of the Great Depression, the liners kept the popularity of travel to Hawaii high. On board among nearly seven hundred passengers were the two college football teams and accompanying coaches, managers, and a few fans. The Willamette University Bearcats from Salem, Oregon, and California's San Jose State University Spartans had finally embarked for their long-anticipated round-robin games with the University of Hawaii Rainbows.

As in the past, on this November 27, all passengers, except those unaccustomed to oceangoing travel and troubled by seasickness, learned in the first evening at sea that the food served on *Lurline* was top quality. On arrival in San Pedro the next morning, they could disembark feeling duly impressed, sightsee and shop in Los Angeles, and then board again to sail for Honolulu at 10:30 p.m. Willamette's freshman halfback, Earl Hampton, who had never seen the ocean before this voyage, was one of the few among the Bearcats who didn't suffer from seasickness. He was able to enjoy the food on the overnight jaunt to San Pedro and not lose weight on the voyage to Oahu.

Eighteen-year-old Shirley McKay, who began taking motion sickness pills when she boarded in San Francisco to avoid seasickness, chose to remain on board *Lurline* that day in San Pedro, while more passengers boarded for the voyage to Honolulu and the team members chose to see the city. On board with Shirley and her father was her boyfriend, the young man she would eventually marry, Wayne Hadley.

As for the Bearcats' Gordon Moore and his wife, Elaine, they hadn't taken a honeymoon, so they were taking advantage of the voyage, calling it their honeymoon, and Elaine was carrying a portable typewriter in her belongings. They had borrowed money from her husband's brother for her passage on the *Lurline*. They lived in an apartment above a mortuary in Salem, an unusual arrangement that permitted them to have housing and earn money. Elaine served the mortuary as a receptionist for funeral arrangements and services, and Gordon's responsibilities required him to pick up the deceased to be serviced by his employer, bring them to the mortuary, and, as he gained skill, assist in preparing bodies for storage and burial.

Among passengers boarding in San Pedro was Seaman First Class Ralph Ernest Poole from Milford, Ohio, who was returning to his assigned ship, the battleship USS *Arizona* (BB-39), from leave with his family after flying out of Chicago to the West Coast.

Willamette's Ken Jacobson, Chuck Furno, and Ted Ogdahl rented a limousine, toured Los Angeles, saw the famed hillside Hollywood sign, visited Grauman's Chinese Theater to see the movie stars' handprints in the concrete, and ate lunch at the Brown Derby Restaurant. Other teammates piled into taxis to take similar trips through a city few team members had ever seen.

Aboard *Lurline* outbound from San Pedro on Saturday morning, at first the 783 passengers brimmed with pleasure at the departure and ocean views, and with thoughts of lovely tropical islands—home for some passengers—while the men and women from Willamette and San Jose State had similar pleasant thoughts and conversations, envisioning the beauty of the islands that few from Willamette had ever seen, and football games filled with excitement.

Interest and participation in collegiate football had been strong and growing in Hawaii since 1920, at the beginning of the Shrine Bowl. The University of Hawaii was now to compete in three more games this exciting year, including the second annual Pineapple Bowl on New Year's Day, tentatively against Utah University. In the meantime, additional football excitement was stimulated on the island of Oahu, aboard ships in Pearl Harbor, and at sea the Saturday morning before the *Lurline* was under way, as thousands of servicemen and their families, as well as islanders, tuned in shortwave and amateur (HAM) radios to listen to the annual Army-Navy game broadcast from Philadelphia, Pennsylvania. Army's new head coach, a 1920 West Point graduate, but now the academy's first civilian coach in its history, was Earl Henry "Red" Blaik, who, along with Army fans worldwide, felt the sting of his team's loss to Navy, 14–6, in his first season with the Cadets. He had been a gifted multisport athlete as a Cadet, having graduated in 1917 from the University of Miami (Ohio)—"the coaches' factory"—where he played football for four years, and he had played end on the football team at West Point while Brigadier General Douglas MacArthur was the academy superintendent. As a Cadet, Blaik became a lifelong admirer and protégé of MacArthur's.

For her passengers now dreaming of paradise and football on an island where football was a year-ending highlight, the beautiful *Lurline* possessed all the comforts and luxurious surroundings of rattan furniture, strikingly attractive oil paintings, mother-of-pearl and inlaid wood paneling in public areas, and comfortable first-class staterooms furnished to match the public decor, plus a seasoned crew to offer everyone on board an unforgettable experience. Aside from the marvelous food, there were movies available in the evenings, a library and reading room, a swimming pool, an exercise room that included weight lifting, professional musicians and singers who provided floor shows, concerts and music for dancing in the Grand Ballroom, and relaxing lounges serving beer and cocktails.

The two teams could move about the ship freely, but due to cost considerations, their funding for the voyage relegated them to cabin-class staterooms, which didn't include bathrooms. Instead, they shaved, washed, bathed, and used the "heads" (toilets) in communal areas.

There were lounge chairs on deck and games such as shuffleboard. Inside were card games, and for the more daring, and those adults permitted, there were gaming tables and slot machines for gambling.

Coach Ben Winkelman had made clear to the Spartans, and to students at home before they left, that the vacation en route to Honolulu wouldn't be entirely free of workouts. He would have the team jogging around *Lurline*'s decks twice a day, with ample time available to make use of the weight-lifting equipment. Jack Galvin, San Jose State's right end, remembered Coach Ben Winkelman's daily putting his Spartans through light but vigorous workouts in spite of the rather limited space on *Lurline*'s decks. The remainder of the voyage passed rapidly, with the ship's purser and crew providing a whole range of social activities and professional entertainment to make the trip to Hawaii memorable.

In spite of the workouts directed by Ben Winkelman, Bert Robinson and Bill Rhyne found time to have fun and make light of the trip by having their picture taken holding a *Lurline* life buoy while posing on deck.

There were church services available on Sunday morning, and after dinner a movie, dancing, and, for adults (other than football players in training), champagne. While weather made the crossing somewhat rough, there was more than adequate opportunity to put aside the great Pacific's more uncomfortable side of winter weather. The worsening crisis in the Far East also drew little attention from excited passengers anxious to visit Oahu.

On Tuesday, the evening before *Lurline* arrived in Honolulu, there was the traditional Captain's Dinner, always a happy affair, which San Jose State's Jack Galvin recalled attending with his teammates. Singing during the dinner wasn't uncommon, but Lorena Jack ("Miss Jack" to Willamette's travelers and the team), while seated at the captain's table, wryly volunteered that their team couldn't sing.

Bert Robinson and Bill Rhyne holding a life buoy on *Lurline*, en route to Honolulu. (*Source*: KCC)

Tom Taylor, San Jose's head yell leader, began writing a letter, addressed to the office of the athletic director's office, Glen "Tiny" Hartranft, during the crossing and mailed it in Honolulu in time to be received on Thursday, December 11, and printed in the *Spartan Daily* on December 12. Tom's letter provided engaging accounts of the festivities on board ship—and a few less happy recollections of a crossing that was a "little rough," causing "each of us our spells of seasickness," mentioning "Paul Tognetti, John Brown, Mr. and Mrs. Ed Wenger and Aubrey Minter having felt the rock of the boat more than the rest of us, while Moe Hamill was the healthiest of all of us (although he did miss two meals)."

He went on to write, "All admit that never in our lives have we had meals to compare to the ones we're having on the ship. Fried chicken, steaks, capon, squab, with all the trimmings, and double orders if we want them." He wrote of a movie every day, dances at night, playing ping-pong and the slot machines, lounging in deck chairs, the team meeting girls traveling on the ship and dancing at night, "and a million other things."

He referred to the Captain's Dinner as "our Aloha dinner," writing, "The boys and I for once were all dressed up in dark suits—it's surprising to notice how many good looking boys there are on the team when they're all dolled up." He told his letter readers the team would be staying at the Moana Hotel in Honolulu with the team from Willamette University, and before closing, he pointed out, "Writing on a rocking boat makes it pretty tough, so excuse the scribbling. I will close now and will write another letter from the hotel in about a week," closing with "Me kea aloha nui oe, Tommy Taylor."

Then he wrote, "P.S.—Incidentally, we're going to have a band playing our school songs, and a rooting section to yell our yells, so don't worry—our team won't be without support. Once again—Aloha, and coach Ben sends his regards."

Then came one more brief paragraph: "Our trainer pro tem, Lt. Dorsey, who has been the life of the party while on board, wants me to add: Aloha nui loa ka kou. (Darned if I know what it means.)"

On Wednesday, December 3, the *Lurline* arrived from the second leg of her twice-monthly San Francisco–Los Angeles–Honolulu triangular voyage, carrying the normal passenger load, this time including the Willamette University and San Jose State College football teams. The two teams, with their coaches, cheerleaders, and small contingents of fans, along with the other passengers, received the traditional, warm Hawaiian welcome of band boys playing island music, leis, and hula girls before loading luggage on buses for the Moana Hotel near Waikiki, where both teams made their headquarters. Some of the Willamette men also received tall, round-topped straw hats similar to those purchased by others before leaving San Francisco. The visitors were welcomed by the Shriners, the University of Hawaii, Honolulu officials (including officers of the police department and at least one San Jose alumnus who was on the police force), and Luke Gill, a 1923 Oregon State graduate and University of Hawaii basketball coach and football co-coach, all with sports journalists looking on and asking questions, while visitors carrying their own cameras snapped pictures along with photographers from the Honolulu newspapers.

En route on late fall's rough seas, Willamette's freshman halfback, Earl Hampton, wasn't bothered by seasickness, but virtually all the other men on both the Bearcats' and the Spartans' teams, and many women, suffered mal de mer, while the coaches planned the afternoon of the arrival to restart more intense conditioning to finalize game preparations.

Typical of some of the more seriously affected by seasickness, Willamette quarterback Ken Jacobson lost six pounds along with nearly every meal he ate, in spite of the excellent food and the fact that the Willamette players ate their meals together. Coach Keene's wife, Marie, suffered even more. Ken Jacobson remembered that she was "real seasick," and according to Shirley McKay, Mrs. Keene slept on deck on a mattress nearly every night en route to stay near the ship's railings.

Among the welcoming party when the *Lurline* arrived were two former San Jose students and football players, Bill Bronson, who was in the army and stationed at Tripler Army Hospital, and Dick Hubbell, a former Spartan grid star and member of the Honolulu Police Department. Both were alumni of other schools but were anxious to see some of their former teammates and attend their football games.

Bill Bronson promptly wrote a letter to the office of the San Jose State athletic director, "Tiny" Hartranft, describing the team's arrival in Honolulu, unaware that yell leader Tom Taylor had done the same while en route from San Pedro. Received in the athletic director's office on December 10 along with a photograph showing some of the team members, *Spartan Daily* student sportswriter Peggy Richter published excerpts, along with other informa-

SS *Lurline* near Pier 10 in the port of Honolulu, one of the piers frequented by Matson's passenger fleet in the 1930s. The famed Aloha Tower is in the background. (*Source*: MNC)

tion, in the December 11 issue. Describing the "boys" in the picture as "disgustingly healthy" and telling of their arrival, Bronson wrote,

> *Wednesday night and all is well. The football team came in today, and I took the day off and went down to meet them. . . . I was surprised at how many of them I knew. Ken Bailey finally made it. He has wanted for years to make the trip with the team, and he finally got here. Yell leader, Tom Taylor, paid his way over, and all in all a good time was had by all. . . . When the boat came in to dock, they had a band playing and a broadcast of their arrival with words from the big shots that were on board, etc. A real nice Hawaiian reception.*
>
> *Since the San Jose team plays the police benefit game, the police took the job of making the boys at home. . . .*
>
> *He told of the police later loading them into cars at the Moana Hotel and taking them up to what they call the Pali. "It is a jumping-off place on a real high hill where the wind whips through so fast I could lean into the wind at about a 45-degree angle and not fall down."*
>
> *When we got there they passed out whole pineapples just picked off the bushes, cans of pineapple juice, coconuts, which you can crack open and drink the milk and then eat the pulp, and in general made the boys welcome.*
>
> *Then back to the Moana Hotel, the second best in the Hawaiian Islands. Not bad at all.*
>
> *I have my tickets for the game already and it is a good thing because they are sold out. I am really all thrilled about the game, the first one I've been able to get up any interest in*

for all season. Pardon me while I take time out for a war-whoop or two, because it really is swell to see people from home.

There was, in fact, other than the police benefit game against the Rainbows, a more fundamental reason for San Jose State players' association with the Honolulu Police Department. Not well known outside San Jose's college town community in 1941 was the fact that San Jose State College was among the earliest universities and colleges in the nation to include "police administration courses" in their college catalogs. The first year was 1931, and the objective of the two-year degree program was to provide a course of study, not theretofore offered, for the student planning to make police service his life work. The then San Jose State Teacher College's president in 1930, when the concept of police administration courses was first developed, was Theodore W. MacQuarrie, the same man who was president in 1941 and was eventually credited in 2005 with what became known as San Jose State University's Justice Studies Department. By the time the 1941–1942 academic year began, the course credit hours had grown from forty-one to seventy-two, and from a two-year to a four-year degree program with approximately seventy-five students in the "Police School."

As for the Willamette Bearcats, when Coach Keene and his team were greeted by the sportswriters who would cover Saturday's game, they were surprised to learn they were twelve-point underdogs in the matchup with the Rainbow Warriors, and they were determined to embarrass the local prognosticators by staging an upset. In answering questions posed by sportswriters, Coach Keene expressed the hope that a home-and-home contract could be signed with Hawaii, thus bringing the colorful Rainbows to Salem in 1942 and allowing the Bearcats to make a return trip to the islands in 1943. After the happy welcome, the two teams with their luggage left on buses for the Moana Hotel adjacent to Waikiki's famous beach—where both made their headquarters.

Front entrance to the Moana Hotel, Honolulu, Territory of Hawaii, December 1941. (*Source*: ESPNDF)

Over the preceding twenty-four hours, events brought these Wednesday headlines in American newspapers, though little notice was paid by the football contingents that had just arrived on the *Lurline*: U.S. DEMANDS JAPAN EXPLAIN INDO-CHINA WAR MOVES, PEACE TALKS ENDANGERED; TOKYO WARNED AMERICAN NAVY IN PACIFIC CAN SHOOT STRAIGHT; ALL U.S. MARINES OUT OF SHANGHAI; and BRITISH CHINA COAST SHIPS ORDERED INTO HONG KONG.

The Bearcats' Coach Keene conducted two hours of afternoon limbering up and signal drills on Hawaii University's Moi'li'ili Field at Honolulu Stadium, where in spite of their wobbly sea legs the team showed their zippy wide-open pass offense, while the Spartans' Coach Winkelman put his team through their paces in sweat suits on Punahou School's S. T. Alexander Field. On Thursday, both teams practiced twice, while on Friday, Willamette tapered off to a light workout prior to the next day's game. In between practices leading up to the Saturday game, time was spent on sightseeing trips, receptions, rallies, formal dinners, dances, and all that goes with bowl games, while at the hotel enthusiastic Willamette visitors put up an attractive display of Oregon products in the lobby.

"Boat Day" was in full swing at noon in Honolulu Harbor on Friday, December 5, when the *Lurline* prepared to sail to San Francisco on its twice-monthly triangular voyage there, then to Los Angeles, and then return. The ship's crew and port authorities efficiently completed a rapid, two-day turnaround for *Lurline*'s return voyage to the States.

While the two coaches were putting their teams through their paces on Thursday and Friday, Oregon state senator Douglas McKay and daughter Shirley were enjoying themselves immensely; at least Shirley certainly was, but the senator, following a Thursday radiogram to his wife of twenty-four years, Mabel, in which he said, "All well and happy," was already indicating his restlessness and desire to return home. His restlessness appeared first in a brief letter to his mother the same day; he then expressed similar feelings to Mabel and his second daughter, Mary Lou, on Friday.

Dec. 4, 1941

Dear Mother:

Well here we are enjoying the sun and swimming in this nice warm surf. This is really a great place to loaf.

Shirley was never so thrilled in her life. She is just walking on air and enjoying every minute.

We had a very rough trip over and most of the passengers were sick. Shirley was never sick but I didn't do quite that good, although I never missed a meal, and only lost one.

There is a real defense program here that has created a boom. Former W.P.A. [Works Progress Administration] workers are making $10–$15 a day and spending it every night.

The army is on the alert and is not worried about the Japs. People here think that if the Japs get tough we will blow 'em right out of the Pacific.

The *Lurline* is the only boat left on the Pacific carrying passengers and no one knows just when the Government will take her over.

Landing here was one of the most colorful sights I ever saw. The people are very friendly and welcoming a boat is an important job.

I'm sure we will have a wonderful trip but I think I'll also be ready to go back to work.

Tell the family hello for me.

Love from,
Douglas

Fri. 7:40 AM
Dec. 5-41

Dear Mabel & Mary Lou:

The clipper leaves at noon so will make a short report.

Shirley & I went shopping yesterday AM. In the afternoon we went swimming & loafed.

The Hostetler boy & Herr boy from Salem were here to see Shirley last night. They are in the Navy and are just back from Manila. Look fine but they are lonesome for Salem.

Irvin Hostetler (father of the boy) works in my shop. If you are down there tell Irvin we saw the boy. Herr's mother works at the Industrial Accident Commission. Phone 4171. Wish you would phone her & tell we saw her son.

This is a great place—I'm sitting beside an open window overlooking the beach and I can see the fleet putting out to sea. The Navy is not going to fool with Japan when they get orders. Its just too bad the War Lords of Japan have such a hold on their country.

I will be very glad to get back to Salem as I am tired of loafing already. The boat leaves today noon & we will leave on her next trip—I hope she makes it.

I don't expect to hear from you again for about a week and I'm sure I will be very lonesome. If I feel too bad I'll phone you—costs $7.50 which seems like an extravagance.

I just talked to Shirley but she says she has nothing to say. She is going to stay in this AM & press some clothes. Harry Miller & I are going down to the fish market and look around. Swim again this PM. This is the life—Wish you were here.

Several planes flying overhead now. The largest airport in the US is located here—Hickam Field.

Saw Elmer Hall yesterday. He is a Lt Col of Marines here. You know hes an old Oregon football player that married the Wooten girl.

Well there is just no news and it will soon be clipper time so I must stop.

Love to both of you,
Dad

Senator McKay and Spec Keene were close friends who had both graduated from Oregon Agricultural College, later renamed Oregon State College, in Corvallis, in 1917 and 1921, respectively. Both had served in France in World War I, with Senator McKay being a combat veteran in the Army of the United States' 91st Wild West Division in France where he had been seriously wounded, and Roy Keene in the 41st Division, a federalized National Guard Division, which had never entered combat as a unit, though it was the fourth division of thirty-three to arrive in Europe in World War I.

Quietly carried with Senator McKay on the trip was a letter of introduction addressed to Admiral Husband E. Kimmel, commander, Pacific Fleet, signed by Oregon governor Charles A. Sprague, in case Senator McKay had the opportunity to meet with Admiral Kimmel or might wish to avail himself of an opportunity to visit Pearl Harbor, where Admiral Kimmel's headquarters and housing were located. Perhaps while he was writing letters to Mabel he thought of the letter he carried from Governor Sprague, wondering when he might have the opportunity to meet the admiral—or wondering whether he should interrupt him in this time of increasing international tension.

‹—❦—›

This was the era of protective equipment for players that still left much to be desired in a fast, hard-hitting game involving well-conditioned, taller, heavier, faster, and more muscular than average men. Players wore black high-top shoes with hard cleats that screwed onto small metal bolts on the bottoms of the shoes, and leather helmets with snug fits—opening players to more serious head injuries—and no facemasks. At the beginning of the year, the National Collegiate Athletic Association Rules Committee had begun relaxing the limited substitution rules leading directly to two-platoon football, but it essentially continued to require players to go both ways—on offense and defense.

Sixty minutes of potentially exhausting playing time for players was not uncommon, and neither were injuries. Broken noses, lacerations requiring stitches, broken or knocked-out teeth, black eyes, and men knocked semiconscious or unconscious due to inadequate head protection were standard fare. "Iron man football," with a premium on coaches' unrelenting demands for physical conditioning, was a fitting description of the game that grew through the golden age of football. But the two teams about to engage in the 1941 Shrine Game grew up in that era and were accustomed to its rigors, and both had emerged with great respect for one another during the Rainbows' visit to the mainland in September. They scrimmaged the Bearcats at Willamette's Sweetland Field, a short distance south of Oregon's new capitol building.

The scrimmage, reported in the Monday, September 22, issue of the *Willamette Collegian* student newspaper under the headline "Cats, Hawaiians Stage Scrimmage," with the subheading "Both Elevens Well Matched," had occurred the previous Thursday, September 18, one day prior to the Bearcats' Friday-night season-opening game against a team from the Portland Army Airfield. Accompanying the Rainbow Warriors in the contingent of thirty-three was head co-coach Luke Gill, brother of Oregon State's "Slats" Gill and formerly assistant coach at Willamette.

The morning of September 18, the Rainbows were taken on a brief tour of Oregon's state penitentiary, the Oregon paper mill, and the relatively new capitol buildings. They then did most of the entertaining during a Lion's Club luncheon in their honor. The afternoon following the luncheon, the Hawaii gridders locked horns with the Bearcats in what Salem's *Oregon Statesman* newspaper described as "a lengthy scrimmage session" at Sweetland Field. The Bearcats came out of the practice session unscathed. The Willamette sportswriter described the scrimmage as a sneak preview, which "gave a definite indication that a real battle may be expected when the two elevens meet on the turf in Honolulu, December 6th." He continued, writing, "The Hawaiians, featuring a light, but snakey-hipped set of backs behind a not-too-light line, gave conclusive proof that they will be nobody's set-ups during the pigskin campaign."

After the scrimmage against the Bearcats, the Rainbow Warriors traveled north and played Portland University, the sole Catholic university in Oregon, in Portland's Multnomah Stadium on Saturday, September 20. After soundly defeating the Portland Pilots 33–6, the team, coaches, and entertainers traveled south to Stockton, California, to meet Amos Alonzo Stagg's College of the Pacific team on Friday, September 26, where they won 14–0 before returning home. In Stockton they had played and defeated a team coached by an American legend in collegiate football.

Stagg, born during the Civil War, in 1862, and graduated from Yale University where he was a divinity student, became another pioneering college coach in multiple sports, primarily American football. He entered the college head coaching ranks in 1890 at Springfield College and had come to the College of the Pacific in 1933 from Chicago University, where he had coached for forty years beginning in 1892. While with Chicago University's Maroons, he molded their football team into a national power, and like the younger "Pop" Warner, then consulting at San Jose State, he was not only a legend in his own time but also an innovator in the game, having originated such basic tactics in football as the man in motion and lateral pass, as well as some equipment. His iconic career included an appearance as himself in the 1940 movie *Knute Rockne, All American*, starring Pat O'Brien as Rockne, with Ronald Reagan playing the role of Notre Dame legend George Gipp.

With the December Hawaii-Willamette game now looming on the Warriors' home turf, *Honolulu Advertiser* sportswriter Andrew Mitsukado wrote in Thursday morning's paper,

Pregame mass bands at December 6, 1941, Shrine Bowl Game, Honolulu Stadium. (*Source*: KCC)

Roy "Spec" Keene has brought a tricky aggregation here for the annual Shrine benefit football classic.

The Bearcats use the man-in-motion considerably and also launch their attack from the short punt formation. They use a lot of reverses, spinners and fake spinners. Handling the ball well in the backfield, they fake effectively and unless the Rainbows are constantly on the alert, they may find the boys from the Northwest getting away for long gains both through the middle of the line and around ends.

Willamette combines a deceptive running attack with a substantial aerial offense. Buddy Reynolds and Gene Stewart do most of the passing with Bill Reder and Mervin Goodman on the receiving end. Besides being adept at dragging down passes, both Reder and Goodman are fast.

Buddy Reynolds, Ted Ogdahl and Chuck Furno are small, but fast and elusive. Furno is nursing a knee injury. According to Coach Keene, he did some running for the first time in some time yesterday afternoon at the Stadium where the Bearcats worked out. Stewart, who is one of the best passers on the squad is also a good ball toter.

If all these backs play up to expectations, the Rainbows will be hard pressed to stop Willamette.

The *Star-Bulletin*'s Loi'i Leong Hop commented the same day, "Al Walden, the kingpin of the Bearcat backfield, displayed plenty of charge as he lugged the ball on signal drills. Only 175 pounds, Walden promises to hit the line as hard as a 200 pound fullback."

On Thursday, the coaches disclosed their starting lineups. Co-coaches Luke Gill and Tommy Kaulukukul announced that the Rainbows would be fielding their strongest lineup in their Warner formation, the single-wing offense: Johnny Naumu at left halfback, Melvin

Abreu at quarterback, co-captain and Little All-American Nolle Smith at fullback, and Louis Collins at right halfback would form the backfield, with Kai Bong Chung at center, co-captain Chin Do Kim and Spencer Kamakana at guards, Unkei Uchima and Sadao Watasaki at tackles, and Lloyd Conkling and Hal Kometani at ends.

Coach Keene announced that his lineup would be Pat White at center, with Tony Fraiola and Gordon Moore at guards, co-captain Martin Barstad and Neil Morley at tackles, Bill Reder and Marshall Barbour at ends, Ken Jacobson at quarterback, Ted Ogdahl and co-captain Buddy Reynolds at halfbacks, and Al Walden at fullback.

On Friday, a luau was held in their honor, and the boys from Willamette, not used to fresh, exotic fruit this late in the fall (normally canned fruit only), ate too much of it and unfortunately suffered the fruits' debilitating gastroenteritis effects.

The newspapers urged fans to be in their seats by 1:15 p.m., when a parade of fourteen marching bands led by color guards with the flags of Hawaii and the United States would begin assembling on the football field, the marching order based on which bands had participated the most in the years since the event's inception. The marine band led the bands onto the field, and the Shriners' crack drill team entertained the crowd at halftime, as did the massed bands playing together.

When the kickoff came at 2:30, the crowd had swollen to an estimated 24,400, the largest in the event's history and just shy of the stadium's capacity of 25,000. Sophomore starting quarterback Ken Jacobson, representing a university of approximately eight hundred students, recalled that the Bearcats had never played before a crowd that size. Sweetland Field, the wood-frame stadium at Willamette, seated only five thousand fans. Marv Goodman was also awed by the size of the crowd: "I had never seen that many people in my life." Earl Hampton, a farm boy who attended a small-town high school and had never seen the ocean before he left Salem for the trip to Hawaii, had the same reaction when the team came on the field to warm up before the game. Among the crowd was an uncounted, large number of men in military uniforms—sailors, soldiers, and marines.

Giving away two inches in average height and six pounds per man in weight in this eleventh annual Shrine Classic, the Rainbows, with a 7 and 1 record, were favored by twelve points over the Bearcats. The men from Willamette University sported an 8 and 1 record and had clinched the Pacific Northwest Conference title while leading the nation's small colleges in total offense of 430.5 yards per game, 300.8 passing and 129.7 rushing. What's more, they outscored opponents 314 to 47 total points and held six of their nine opponents scoreless, placing them third in the nation on defense.

Before a stadium filled with excited football fans, the Rainbows and the Bearcats battled through a close first half, with Hawaii holding a slim 7–6 lead. As predicted, it was a wide-open game.

Hawaii won the coin toss and elected to defend the south goal, running with a stiff wind at their backs. Abreu kicked off, and Walden took it on his five yard line and returned to their twenty-five. The Bearcats wasted no time in opening up the game. Reynolds passed to Reder for fourteen yards and a first down at the Bearcats' thirty-nine. Reynolds passed again.

Incomplete. Walden off left tackle and made six, then failed to gain at center. Walden punted short into the wind and out of bounds on the Rainbows' thirty-five.

Hawaii's Collins, opening up their own offense, threw a long pass, which Ogdahl intercepted at the Bearcats' forty-six and returned eighteen to the Rainbows' thirty-six. After a long pass from Reynolds to Barbour barely missed, Walden made six at right tackle. Another pass from Reynolds failed, and Walden punted, angling out of bounds on the Hawaii twelve.

Nolle Smith made fourteen around left end to the Hawaii twenty-six. Abreu over right guard for four. Collins fumbled, and Smith recovered for a gain of three. Abreu tried at center but failed by inches. Abreu tried again but fumbled, hitting the line. Hawaii recovered but lost the ball on downs at their thirty-seven.

Walden made four at left tackle, and Ogdahl hit the same spot for two. Reynolds heaved another long pass to Reder, which was incomplete. An exchange of punts ended with Abreu booting out of bounds on the Willamette thirty-nine. Walden made three over left guard. Ogdahl then electrified the crowd, circling right end for fifty-two yards behind beautiful downfield blocking, and went all the way to the Rainbows' six-yard line, where he was overtaken by co-captain Nolle Smith. Walden at right tackle for one and a half yards, then swung wide at right end for a half yard to the four yard line.

With five and a half minutes left in the first quarter, Ogdahl, in a reverse from Walden, circled right end for the touchdown. Reder's placement for the extra point was wide, and the quarter ended with Willamette leading 6–0, though Willamette once again threatened late in the quarter.

Eleven minutes into a see-saw second quarter, the Rainbows scored after Reynolds fumbled and Uchima recovered on the Bearcats' nineteen. Nolle Smith made seven at left end and Hart two more when he slammed into the center of the line. Hart again over the right guard for four to the six, and a first and goal. Naumu made one at the right end, and Hart again slamming over left guard carried to the one-foot line. Hart then hit center for the touchdown, and Abreu kicked a perfect extra point to put the Rainbows up 7–6 with four minutes left in the first half.

Abreu kicked off to Willamette's eighteen. Taking the ball on the dead run, Walden returned brilliantly all the way to the Hawaii eighteen before he was tackled out of bounds by Naumu. Morley banged over center for five and a half, then again at left guard for no gain. A pass by Reynolds was intercepted in the end zone by Mun Kip Wong after it deflected off a Willamette player and then another Hawaii player. The touchback gave Hawaii the ball on their twenty. The Rainbows kept it on the ground and in six plays drove to their forty-one, where the half ended—with Hawaii still up 7–6.

The Bearcats, using short and long passes and multiple formations, including a man in motion off the single wing with an unbalanced line, had so outplayed the Rainbows that bettors changed the odds to favor them for the second-half finish; however, the first two and a half minutes of the third quarter once again altered the game's momentum.

Willamette kicked off defending the south goal. Fitzgerald booted the ball through the end zone to give the Rainbows the ball on their twenty. The Rainbows' ground game promptly exploded. Smith circled left end for twenty-six yards to their forty-six. Naumu slashed over right tackle but was stopped cold. Abreu through right end made eight. Hart broke through left guard for thirteen and first down on the Bearcats' thirty-three. Smith roared over left end for thirty-one, all the way to the Bearcats' two and a half before White brought him down. Hart made one at center and then punched over left guard for the touchdown. Abreu converted. Hawaii had opened their lead to 14–6.

Abreu, kicking into the wind, reached the Bearcats' eighteen, where Ogdahl ran it back twenty-two yards to their forty. Walden made six at left tackle; then he lost three over right tackle. Reynolds rifled a pass to Goodman for seventeen and a first down on the Hawaii forty. The Bearcats appeared to be on the move again, but Walden at left end lost two. A pass by Reynolds was intercepted by Naumu who lateralled to Smith—who fumbled. Fitzgerald recovered on the Hawaii twenty-seven. The Bearcats were again threatening.

A pass by Reynolds was incomplete. On a reverse at left end, Ogdahl gained nine. Walden broke through right guard for seven and a first on the Hawaii twelve. Walden at right guard gained one. A pass by Reynolds was incomplete. A pass by Reynolds to Ogdahl was incomplete. Then Hawaii blunted the drive when Smith intercepted a pass by Reynolds in the end zone for a touchback, with seven minutes to play in the quarter.

When Hawaii placed the ball in play at their twenty, Collins gained five at right tackle, then added four at center on the next play. Abreu slashed over left guard for eleven yards and a first down on the Hawaii forty. Collins then lost four at left tackle. Smith at left end made thirteen, missing first down by a foot. Abreu made two and first on the Bearcats' forty-nine. Collins picked up six at right end, and Abreu added five and a first down on the Willamette thirty-eight. Collins made three at right end, and Smith lost one at left tackle. On the next play, Smith, unable to get off a pass, picked his way around right end for nine yards and first down on the Bearcats' twenty-seven. Abreu couldn't gain at center. Collins passed to Smith for four yards. Another pass by Collins this time was intercepted by Barstad, who returned for two to the Willamette twenty-nine as the third quarter ended. Hawaii continued to hold their 14–6 lead, but the Bearcats were still in the game.

On the first play of the fourth quarter, Ogdahl at left end made eight to the thirty-seven. Walden hit right guard for one. Reynolds lost one at center, and Walden punted thirty-nine yards to the Hawaii twenty-four, where the ball was grounded. Smith made one at left end. Conkling on an end around lost two. On third down, Naumu punted into the wind, out of bounds on the Willamette forty-four.

Stewart lost three at left tackle. A pass by Stewart was incomplete. Another pass by Stewart was blocked by Smith. Stewart punted to the Hawaii twenty, but Naumu, in attempting to return, was tackled by Reder and gave up four yards to their sixteen. Hart made three. Then Naumu collected twenty yards around right end, giving the Rainbows a first down on their thirty-nine. Smith made three at right tackle and on the next play exploded over left tackle, all the way to the Bearcats' thirteen, where Ogdahl tackled and drove him out of bounds. It was a forty-six-yard gain, ending in another serious second-half threat by the Rainbows.

Collins stabbed at right tackle for one yard. Collins lost one but was offside on the play. Willamette refused the five-yard penalty in favor of the down. A pass by Collins was incomplete. Another pass, Collins to Smith, lost four, with Willamette taking over on downs at their own seventeen to apparently thwart the Hawaii threat.

Ogdahl lost four at right end. Stewart recovered the lost ground on a sixteen-yard pass to Ogdahl, giving the visitors a first down on their twenty-nine. Attempting a pass, Reynolds was tackled for a loss of four. The Bearcats, slow to set the next play in motion, were penalized five yards for delay of game. A pass by Reynolds was intercepted by Collins on the Bearcats' thirty-one and returned to their fifteen.

Hart over center made two. Naumu went to the one-yard line through left tackle and then scored through left guard. The score came with four and a half minutes to play. Abreu's point after attempt hit an upright and bounded back onto the field. Hawaii had opened their lead to 20–6.

Sensing that the game was out of reach, Coach Keene gave his freshmen some playing time. In the final minutes, halfback Earl Hampton ran three successive plays and a first down on the Bearcats' thirty-one-yard line to end the game—after Hawaii's Naumu kicked off through the Willamette end zone. On his first run from the twenty, at right end, Hampton made five. On the next play he fumbled, but he recovered with a loss of five yards. On the final play of the game, he slashed over left guard for eleven.

In the second half, the Bearcats had been unable to mount a consistent offense against a practiced, hard-nosed defense that included a game total of seven intercepted passes—by a pass defense noted for its weakness—and the Rainbows completely reversed their fortunes. The game's statistics more emphatically told the story of the Rainbows' dominance, though the stateside team acquitted themselves well. Hawaii's edge in rushing yards was 318–107, and their total first downs were 17–8. Though the Bearcats outgained them in passing yardage 65–28, with five catches in twenty-six attempts, the Rainbows' seven interceptions completely frustrated Willamette's wide-open style of play.

The Bearcats' coach, Spec Keene, offered no excuses for the loss and would have much work to do to prepare for their December 16 game against San Jose State. One effort they would certainly have to make was to acclimate to eighty-degree temperatures after coming from near-freezing temperatures in Salem. Sophomore halfback Chuck Furno had other thoughts: "I blame it on the trip. We hadn't been on land too long. It was a pretty rough crossing. Some of the guys lost a lot of weight. I could stand on the dock and get seasick." Sophomore quarterback Ken Jacobson said, "I think I ate only one meal I was able to keep down the whole time on the ship."

Marv Goodman had a different perspective: "We played both ways. . . . I played end on both sides of the ball. It was freezing when we left Salem, then we hit eighty-five-degree weather and we didn't last long." Earl Hampton remarked years later, "The Hawaiian boys were fast. I think we could have given them a better ballgame, if a number of our fellas weren't recovering from seasickness. I don't want to use that as an excuse, but think that certainly impacted the final score."

In the crowd watching the game were the San Jose State Spartans and their coach, scouting their two opponents. The happy Rainbow fans now looked forward to the next game, on December 13, while the Bearcats mentally began preparing to take the measure of the Spartans on the night of December 16.

Rushed preparation for the Bearcats' next game, ten days in the future, wasn't necessary. The Friday before the game had been "Boat Day" on Oahu and was the day the *Lurline* had departed for the mainland. Tomorrow was Sunday, a day off in Hawaii, a day filled with time for church services, recovery from parties and dances, picnics, and plans for guided bus and automobile tours of beautiful Oahu and its many tourist attractions. Ken Jacobson unfortunately had to stay in his hotel room that night while his teammates were enjoying Honolulu. He didn't feel well, having received a blow to his head when he fell backward onto the field's hard surface during the game and remaining on the sidelines for a time.

Tony Fraiola, an ex-marine and an older, more worldly team member who had once been assigned to Oahu while on active duty, told some of the Bearcats, including Earl Hampton, that he would take them to see the section of Honolulu where servicemen liked to go and acquaint themselves with "women of the night."

As for the Spartans' Jack Galvin, he and some of his teammates went out in the evening after the game, mixed with the public, and walked the streets of Honolulu. They were going to tour the island in two or three cars the next day, one of the cars belonging to a teammate's sister who lived on Oahu.

What none among the two stateside football contingents could possibly have known was that the catastrophic vise of a world war was closing round Oahu that night from the north, bearing down toward a 6:05 a.m., December 7, launch from 220 miles north of Oahu, in two waves of 183 and 167 aircraft, against numerous targets on the island and a date with infamy. They came from a Japanese naval force of six aircraft carriers, two battleships, two cruisers, and ten destroyers—a powerful, fast-moving carrier strike force the likes of which the world had never seen.

Scouting and screening in front of the strike fleet were three Japanese submarines, while twenty-seven more, five of them powerful, new submarines carrying a total of five midget submarines on their afterdecks, were closing from various directions. The midgets, carried on "mother boats" approaching Hawaii from the southwest, were to be launched a short distance outside Pearl Harbor, converging with the intention of entering the harbor from the south. The remainder of the Japanese submarines in the large offensive operation approached their assigned stations from the west, northwest, and north to Hawaiian waters, some with orders to later operate along sea-lanes between Hawaii and the West Coast of the United States. Three of the total were patrolling in detached support of the oncoming Japanese force, two initially far to the north in Aleutian Island waters and another in the South Pacific, and would arrive to join the force in their assigned missions.

Among their missions was one perhaps intended to be a final profound shock in the Japanese Empire's bitter surprise handed to the United States. Nine submarines to be positioned on stations off the U.S. West Coast were scheduled to surface on Christmas

Eve night near major port entrances and with their deck guns shell targets they had previously reconnoitered.

While the Imperial Japanese Navy's forces were closing from multiple directions that Sunday morning, American Vice Admiral William F. "Bull" Halsey's Pacific Fleet Task Force 8, with its carrier USS *Enterprise* (CV-6), three cruisers, and nine destroyers, was closing on their home port at Pearl Harbor from approximately 215 miles west of Oahu, returning from a mission to reinforce Wake Island's defenders with twelve marine F4F "Wildcat" fighters. Admiral Halsey and his command, also unaware of the Japanese fleet bearing down on Hawaii, at 0618 launched the first of eighteen Douglas Dauntless SBD-3 scout and dive-bombers from *Enterprise* to scout ahead of Task Force 8 and land at Naval Air Station Pearl Harbor on Ford Island.

And, converging on Oahu from the northeast, from the 38th Reconnaissance Squadron in Albuquerque, New Mexico, and the 88th Reconnaissance Squadron from Fort Douglas, Utah, bound for the army air force's Hickam Field, the Hawaiian Department's Bomber Command, and eventually for Clark Field in the Philippines, was a stream of twelve B-17 bombers, eight newer-model B-17Es, and four B-17Cs. They had departed from Hamilton Field, twenty-five miles north of the Golden Gate Bridge, beginning Saturday night at 2030 hours, Pacific time. Not only did the planes have no ammunition and their guns were still packed in Cosmoline, but they also carried only a skeleton crew of pilot, copilot, navigator, engineer, and radio operator, filling out the rest of the normal crew of nine with key squadron specialists such as crew chiefs, some maintenance technicians, the squadron flight surgeon, and a combat photographer—along with several aviation cadets acting as navigators—with crews totaling 104, including thirty-five officers, fourteen aviation cadets, and fifty-five enlisted men.

The Willamette and San Jose State football teams, their coaches, and all who accompanied them on the *Lurline* were about to witness, and then participate in, history—in the first and most disastrous American battle in World War II's Pacific theater—and the beginning of an abruptly and violently changed nation in a new world that would never forget the catastrophe the battle triggered.

CHAPTER TWO

Disbelief and Bitter Reality

AFTER A LEISURELY SUNDAY-MORNING BREAKFAST FOR SOME, AND THE PREVIOUS EVEning's lively, rapturous island life with its sensual music and dancing, the two football teams and all their accompanying coaches, cheerleaders, and fans were completely relaxed Sunday morning, preparing to spend the day sightseeing. Ben Winkelman and most of his twenty-five players were having breakfast shortly before eight o'clock. Moments later, some players spotted what looked like smoke to the west.

Jack Lecari recalled years later,

> *Even when someone said bombs were falling, we laughed at it. We had heard maneuvers were being held that weekend. Hmm, we thought, pretty realistic sounding maneuvers. A man then raced into the Moana Hotel and delivered the news. The Japanese are bombing Pearl Harbor. That convinced us something was up.*

But San Jose's Jack Galvin recalled when he arrived later for breakfast,

> *When I arrived for breakfast, the first thing I noticed was the absence of waiters for our tables. We went out on the deck and there were soldiers with rifles already deployed below the deck. We went on our planned tour in two or three cars but we didn't get to see much. We did see one airplane with a red meatball underneath its wing. A lot of people were simply walking up and down beside the roads.*

There was indeed something going on outside the Moana Hotel. But reality, wrapped in shock and disbelief, was coming slowly to hundreds of thousands on the island of Oahu, and to more than 132 million people in the continental United States. The eager visitors from Salem, Oregon, and San Jose, California, were especially totally unprepared for the fury that struck Oahu that day.

In residences and buildings with windows that afforded the smallest possibility of scenic views, with little or no accompaniment by delayed and muffled sounds, recognition of the unfolding, life-changing disaster was far more slowly comprehended than in Oahu's military cantonment areas, airfields, dining halls, aid stations, and hospitals, and especially in Pearl Harbor on board bombed, torpedoed, burning, and sinking ships. German-born Hans Wiedenhoefer, a member of the San Jose State Spartans' football team, was also having breakfast in the hotel with his teammates.

Nobody knew what was going on. Some of us thought it was maneuvers. Others saw spouts of water in the harbor and a waiter told us he figured somebody was shooting whales. A couple of us took a walk down to the beach and when we saw one of those big bombs hit the water we knew it wasn't whale shooting and hustled back to the hotel. One of those bombs hit in the water about a hundred yards from the hotel and another one demolished a building a block away.

He said the populace was calm, all went home quietly, and there was no confusion. But to distant witnesses, there was confusion, and plenty of it.

Bill Rhyne, halfback on the Spartan team, witnessed the same "big spout of water in the harbor" and overheard the explanation about whales spouting. "Later we went to the beach, but they wouldn't let us go into the water, and that afternoon we read in the paper of the attack. It was the first we knew of it."

Tom Taylor, the head yell leader who accompanied the Spartans, said, "I thought the attack was a dress rehearsal for M-day" (Mobilization-Day, a term commonly used in contingency war-gaming and planning). The team was preparing to take a bus trip around the island later when the attack began, and when the buses didn't show up, Coach Winkelman looked into it. He learned that all buses were being used by the military. This was the first he knew anything was amiss.

"It was quite awhile before we realized what was happening," the Spartans' star center, Wilbur Wool, said. "Then we only knew the islands had been attacked when someone told us. I don't know what the others thought then, but my first thought was about how I was going to get home."

More than one person posed the same question. How was anyone going to get home? None knew of the orders issued to the 1st, 2nd, and 3rd Japanese submarine groups. None knew the location of the Japanese fleet devastating the American air and naval forces on Oahu. Where might the ships be to take them home? What naval vessels would escort ships to take them through a Japanese fleet—wherever it might be—or Japanese submarines lying in wait for them? Willamette freshman halfback Earl Hampton and others believed they might be on Oahu for four months or more.

The Willamette University Bearcats' Coach Keene was with most of his team eating breakfast in the hotel. "We saw water splashing in the harbor and asked a waiter what it

Shirley McKay, daughter of Oregon state senator Douglas MacKay, both of whom accompanied the Willamette Bearcats to Honolulu for the Shrine Bowl game, photographed at the Moana Hotel in the period December 3–6, 1941, with Waikiki Beach in the background. (*Source*: KJC)

was." "It's a whale spouting," he said. "We all trooped out to watch it, treating it as a joke. We didn't know until late in the afternoon what had happened." The team saw planes dropping bombs in the water but thought it was U.S. Army and Navy planes practicing the "M-Day" maneuvers the islanders had been talking about so much.

Later, Coach Keene repeated,

No one became particularly excited. We didn't even know what was going on until almost five hours after the bombing started. Not even after we'd inspected a bomb crater two blocks from our hotel did we realize an attack had been made. We thought it was practice maneuvers by the army and navy air corps.

Jim Fitzgerald was next door having breakfast at the Royal Hawaiian Hotel when he saw the smoke. Locals seated nearby told him it was some kind of drill. When he went outside to the entrance of the Moana Hotel, soldiers were already present and beginning to impose martial law. A bus intended to take Willamette visitors on a tour of the island and a visit to the Shrine Hospital was there, and a "whole bunch of servicemen were standing outside the Moana." An officer told the driver to take the servicemen back to their base. The bus driver was actually arguing with him, but he did as he was told.

Sometime later, when it was clear there had been an attack and events seemed to have a momentum all their own, Coach Keene considered the possibility of food shortages—which prompted him to remove the display of Oregon products from the hotel lobby and take them to his room for safekeeping and possible future use.

Ken Jacobson has vivid memories of what was planned for the day and what happened. He recalled it was a brilliant Hawaii morning, and he was standing with teammates outside the Moana Hotel waiting for a bus to take them to a scheduled picnic on the other side of the island where University of Hawaii cheerleaders would be attending. The bus never arrived. As they waited, they watched what seemed like dozens of fighter planes in the distance like silver specks buzzing everywhere. The realistic military maneuvers seemed astonishingly complete: water spouts, puffs of smoke, and distant sounds of explosions. "It's kind of affected my whole life."

Irv Miller remembered, "We were having breakfast and I looked down the oceanfront toward the entrance to Pearl Harbor and could see these big gushers of water. It was some of the first bombs. The people at the hotel told us it was just a practice, some kind of maneuvers."

Shirley McKay recalled,

The first we knew something wasn't right—we were waiting for the tour bus in front of the hotel. When it pulled up to load, the driver opened the door, apologized and said "You can't get on board. The military is using the buses." And he drove off.

She became alarmed, but her father said, "Don't worry about it. We're going on a picnic this afternoon."

Senator McKay said,

We didn't know Hawaii had been attacked until we heard the president say so in his Washington, DC, broadcast, although we had seen planes dropping bombs and had put aside as "wild rumor" the story brought to the hotel by an eyewitness of fire on Pearl Harbor and Japanese planes overhead.

Indeed, Shirley encountered a near-hysterical woman staying at the Moana Hotel who said she had driven from a vantage point nearer the spreading inferno and was telling anyone who would listen of airplanes, explosions, and fire on the waters in Pearl Harbor. Shirley, who initially dismissed her remarks, would soon learn that this woman was clearly an energized witness of unimaginable, horror-filled events.

In the meantime, Elaine Moore, wife of Gordon Moore, had climbed up toward Punahou School to view the picturesque scene below her and was witnessing what she believed were military maneuvers over the island, until she concluded that an attack was indeed in progress. She began making her way back to the hotel and en route picked up a piece of hot shrapnel with some newspaper pages, wrapped it, and carried it back to their hotel room and placed it in their luggage.

Earl Hampton said, "I happened to be out in front of the hotel while it was going on. Down the street there was a big explosion about two blocks away. . . . We didn't know exactly what was going on until later, when we picked up news on the radio." Earl recalled the team had a luau. They had sunbathed on Waikiki Beach. They went to a dance. They had watched a live broadcast of the Webley Edwards radio show. Edwards was an Oregon State graduate, and that morning he was the first to broadcast the awful news.

While bits and pieces of the news filtered into the hotel by word of mouth as the day wore on, the visitors were unaware of the extent and seriousness of the Pearl Harbor disaster. Then someone turned on the radio in the hotel lobby.

Lorena Jack, also known as "Miss Jack," remarked facetiously, "The Japs must be after us." She was later shocked to learn that her facetious remark was a statement of fact. The rumor was no rumor, though, later in the day, fear-breeding rumors did run rampant.

San Jose's Hans Wiedenhoefer said, "A picnic had been arranged for the Spartans and some seventy-five box lunches were all prepared. Well, with the bombing, we just held the picnic right in the hotel, box lunches and all." Unknown to all the visitors, around the hotel where the two teams were staying, planned events to mobilize both the military and the civilian populace began and reached a feverish pace, along with rumors that spun out of control. The sources of all the rumors and other activities that would follow became clearer much later in the day.

The *Lurline*, which left Honolulu on Friday, "Boat Day," was seven hundred miles northeast of Oahu on Sunday morning. On board were 784 passengers, including socialite model Miss Marjorie Petty and University of Hawaii president Dr. D. L. Crawford, a record load

Steam schooner SS *Cynthia Olson*, attacked approximately one thousand miles northeast of the Territory of Hawaii on the morning of December 7, 1941, the first American flag–bearing merchantman sunk by the Japanese in World War II. (*Source*: UDML)

because the Matson line's SS *Matsonia*, already in San Francisco, was being converted to a troopship, leaving almost no transportation to the West Coast from Honolulu. *Lurline's* communications officer of the watch, "Tiny" Nelson, was listening intently to message traffic when the ship's chief officer, Edward Collins, entered the radio compartment. After exchanging greetings, Nelson's attention returned to his duties. Within seconds, the expression on his face abruptly changed, and he motioned Collins to read over his shoulder the message he was typing. He had begun receiving, and then answering, the first of a series of emergency messages from an American merchant vessel, the SS *Cynthia Olson*, a 2,170-ton steam schooner out of Tacoma, Washington, on December 1, carrying a load of lumber to Honolulu.

The *Cynthia Olson's* distress signals began at 0730 Hawaii time and reported that she was under attack by a surfaced submarine. Her radio operator signaled her latitude and longitude and indicated that her crew were swinging out lifeboats to abandon ship. On board were thirty-three merchant seamen and two soldiers. Based on the distress calls, which were also picked up by listening stations on the West Coast, Nelson was able to obtain a bearing and distance. The attack on the *Cynthia Olson* began approximately three hundred miles from *Lurline*, bearing 005 degrees—slightly east of due north from the liner. History would later reveal that Imperial Japanese submarine I-26 had struck the first blow against an American merchant vessel in the Pacific war and would become one of the empire's most notorious submarines of World War II.

The *Cynthia Olson* went down approximately two hours later, one thousand miles northeast of Oahu, and her crew and two passengers were never found. Approximately forty-five minutes after receiving the emergency signals, *Lurline's* Commodore Charles A. Berndtson, the ship's captain and Matson's passenger fleet senior officer, received word of another far more startling message relayed from Oahu: "AIR RAID, PEARL HARBOR." Nothing would ever be the same for the *Lurline*, her crew, or her passengers. She would not return to Oahu to bring more tourists to the island, nor bring home the bowl game voyagers from Salem, Oregon, and San Jose, California. Before the day ended, all on board would know that at least one enemy submarine lay between their ship and the safety of San Francisco Harbor.

Imperial Japanese Submarine I-26, the submarine later credited with sinking the SS *Cynthia Olson*. (*Source*: IJN)

Unknown to the two football teams, their coaches and fans, and all other guests and tourists on Oahu who would be scrambling to find a way home from the islands, this stunning incident foretold a period of alarming Japanese submarine attacks along the sea-lanes between Oahu and the West Coast and in the waters up and down the coast. Though coded "top secret," naval intelligence and operational submarine attack warnings were being broadcast to ships transiting the routes, as well as around the Hawaiian Islands and south toward Australia, and sketchy and often uninformed notice of them was taken in press reports, the details remaining cloaked in secrecy. The next day, in his address to Congress and the nation declaring war, President Franklin D. Roosevelt referred to the sinking without identifying the *Cynthia Olson* by name or where, specifically, the attack took place.

On board *Lurline*, after doing everything possible to shift into wartime operations—including a change of course, acceleration to flank speed of twenty-two knots, zigzagging while beginning the dash for home, instructing the crew to paint over portholes and windows to avoid showing light at night, confiscating and holding passengers' radios until arrival, calling in active-duty and former military men, and forming a watch and security detail—Commodore Berndtson called a meeting to brief all passengers at 5:00 p.m.

At 2:00 a.m. on the morning of December 10, Commodore Berndtson and his crew safely steered *Lurline* beneath the Golden Gate Bridge. At noon she joined her Matson sister ship, SS *Matsonia*, already handed over to the U.S. Maritime Commission to begin her rapid conversion to a troopship. In six days, the *Lurline*'s bright white exterior would receive multiple coats of admiralty gray, specifically intended to better hide her from the enemy. The outward change would be matched by dramatic changes inside.

All trappings of luxury disappeared, along with openness and the sweeping grandeur of a once-proud liner built for happiness and relaxation on the high seas. War was closing around her ever more tightly, while to the southwest of Oahu, three other ships that had received word of the attack on Pearl Harbor were on course for Honolulu: the American President Lines' SS *President Coolidge*, the U.S. Army transport *General Hugh L. Scott*—formerly the *President Pierce*—and the U.S. Navy's heavy cruiser USS *Louisville* (CA-28).

Launched in 1931, *Coolidge* was a luxury ocean liner, originally built with her sister ship, the *President Hoover*, for Dollar Steamship Lines. They were the largest merchant vessels built in the United States up to that time. In 1938, when Dollar Steamship Lines collapsed, she was transferred to the American President Lines.

The *Coolidge* was aimed at holiday celebrants seeking sun in the Pacific and Far East. During her time as a luxury liner, she broke several speed records on her frequent trips to Japan from San Francisco. Passengers had a luxurious experience on the ship, with spacious staterooms and lounges, private telephones in their staterooms, two saltwater swimming pools, and a barbershop, beauty salon, gymnasium, and soda fountain.

But not today. From this day forward, the word "luxury" would gradually disappear from the passengers' and crew's vocabulary. On board the ten-year-old, 21,936-ton liner, only fifty-four feet longer than the six-hundred-foot, sleek, faster cruiser *Louisville*, were missionaries; Manila businessmen; several scores of young Chinese believed to be en route to join others of their countrymen at army air force training centers; Russian and British diplomatic figures who had left China ahead of the renewed Japanese drive deep into that country; U.S. military and diplomatic dependents who had voluntarily left China, Japan, the Philippines, and other Southeast Asian countries on urgings of the State Department; an American businessman, John J. Waldron, a World War I veteran who had been in China for eighteen years, had developed a thriving carpet business, and by chance had left the Chinese capital for Shanghai to arrange for shipment of a $25,000 cargo of raw materials to America; and many others. A ship capable of providing service to a maximum of 988 passengers, *Coolidge*'s normal complement of 290 officers and men was expecting a reasonably routine voyage to Honolulu and on to San Francisco in spite of the tension in the Far East.

On board the smaller, slower *Scott*, the crew's outlook on the voyage was little different. The U.S. Army transport *General Hugh L. Scott*, built in 1921 and transferred to the army on July 31, 1941, and modified to carry troops, had made a prior trip to the Orient to reinforce the American forces in the Philippines and bring Americans home. The *Scott* arrived in San Francisco from Manila on October 31. At 535 feet in length and displacing 12,579 tons, she could carry up to 2,470 passengers and had been sent back to Shanghai on one more trip to evacuate Americans voluntarily leaving East and Southeast Asia.

On December 7, the three ships were on a northeasterly course of 051 degrees at a standard speed 16.5 knots, near maximum speed for *Scott*, when at 0815, on the bridge of *Louisville*, officer of the deck Ensign Henry F. Lloyd logged, "Word received of Japanese attack on U.S. territory and declaration of war on U.S. and Great Britain."

Speaking to a newspaper reporter in San Francisco eighteen days later, Milton McManus, the executive officer on board the *Coolidge*, told of the passengers' and crew's reactions to the news.

They first heard that the United States had declared war on Japan. "The boys in the crew thought that was elegant. We'd been waiting for it, ready for it, and now we were in it. Most of the boys were tickled pink." There was little worry at first. A good part of the crew consisted of Japanese-Hawaiians, but right off the bat they held a meeting, counted noses, and announced that they were 100 percent behind the captain. "Just tell us what we got to do," they said. "It'll be done."

And it was done. In a record-breaking effort, they camouflaged the entire ship in nautical gray in two days—two days while they were lunging through heavy seas in their race back home. They blacked out portholes, splashed paint over the decks and sides, and cut their radio-sending equipment out of commission. On board, life went on. Just before the ship crossed the international dateline, a Chinese mother gave birth to a little girl. The ship's officers were nominated as godfathers-in-general, and the ship's cook put on a celebration.

The SS *President Coolidge* and U.S. army transport *General Hugh L. Scott* would arrive in the port of Honolulu on a date and time known to only a few on Oahu. Like all information about ships' schedules, including their names, *Coolidge* and *Scott*'s arrival in Honolulu immediately became highly classified the day of the attack.

CHAPTER THREE

Attack!

ON DECEMBER 7, AT 7:48 A.M., ELEVEN JAPANESE FIGHTER AIRCRAFT, FROM THE FIRST wave of 183 raiders, began strafing Naval Air Station Kaneohe Bay on the windward side (northeast shore) of Oahu. Within minutes, dive-bombers, horizontal bombers, torpedo bombers, and additional fighters, in rapid succession, began striking other assigned targets with devastating effect: the army air force's Wheeler and Hickam Fields, Naval Air Station Pearl Harbor on Ford Island, the marines' Mooring Mast Field on Barbers Point, and the Pacific Fleet ships moored in Pearl Harbor, while additional fighters struck the same and various other targets, including Schofield Barracks, Honolulu's John Rodgers Airport, and vehicles on roads near military installations. The raiders' well-planned and well-rehearsed attack seemed to come from every direction of the compass, with the first bomb on Ford Island at 7:54 a.m. and torpedoes already in the water on both sides of Ford Island, tracking toward battleships, cruisers, and other types of larger vessels. From Ford Island at 7:58, a brief, hurried message was sent by the navy and relayed around the world. It would become one of the most famous messages ever dispatched: "AIR RAID, PEARL HARBOR. THIS IS NOT DRILL."

In Honolulu, at seventeen seconds past 8:04 a.m. on December 7, radio station KGMB interrupted a concert program to recall all army, navy, and marine personnel to duty. At 8:08 a.m. in Pearl Harbor, on the east side of Ford Island, one 1,765-pound bomb released by a Japanese high-level bomber penetrated the forward deck of the battleship *Arizona*, between the number 1 and number 2 heavily armored gun turrets—each of which housed three fourteen-inch guns—and plunged deep into the area of the ship's forward magazines, causing a huge, thunderous, and fiery secondary explosion. The blow sounded her death knell, and she rapidly settled at her moorings in eight minutes, with a veritable inferno on her forward half, midship to bow.

The overpressure from the explosion literally blew approximately one hundred crew members off the decks of the repair ship, *Vestal* (AR-4), into the water, including Commander Cassin Young, the ship's captain. Her bow pointed opposite the direction of *Arizona*'s and was

ISLAND OF OAHU, TERRITORY OF HAWAII
7 DECEMBER 1941

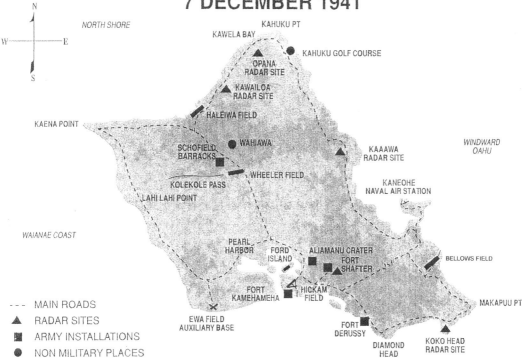

Island of Oahu, Territory of Hawaii, December 7, 1941. Diagram depicting main roads, radar sites, army installations, and nonmilitary places. (*Source*: USAF)

moored only eight feet outboard of that ship. *Vestal* suffered extensive port-side fire damage when heat from the fiery blast set surface paint and mooring lines afire—and three unidentifiable, severely burned bodies were later found on *Vestal*'s afterdeck.

Moored on the west side of Ford Island from the rapidly sinking and burning *Arizona*, where Pacific Fleet aircraft carriers were normally moored, was the old, pre–World War I battleship *Utah* (AG-16), which had been converted to a radio-controlled target ship in 1932 and in 1940 was modified again to become a training ship for antiaircraft gun crews. She was defenseless this day because she had just returned from a Saturday target mission, and all her guns and ammunition were stowed. At 8:12 a.m., listing heavily to port after she was struck in her thin-plated hull by two torpedoes, she snapped her mooring lines, capsized, and rolled almost inverted.

Forward of the *Utah*, toward the northeast, on the same side of Ford Island, the light cruiser *Raleigh* (CL-7) had also been struck by a Japanese torpedo bomber in the first moments of the attack, and her entire crew was struggling to keep their ship from suffering the same fate as the *Utah*, while on the east side of the island, the battleship *West Virginia* (BB-48), the victim of multiple torpedo bomber and level bomber attacks, was on fire and sinking, with her captain mortally wounded.

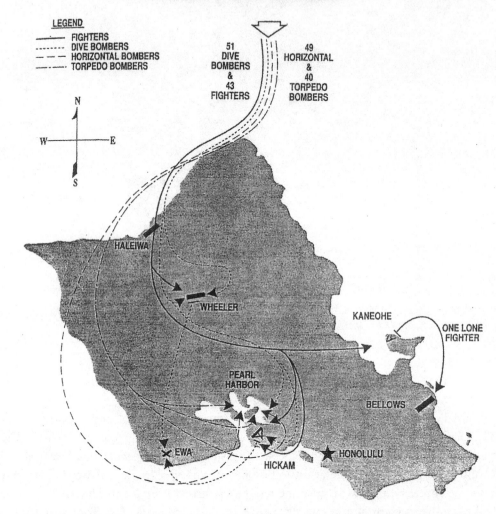

JAPANESE AIRCRAFT DEPLOYMENT FIRST ATTACK

LEGEND
——— FIGHTERS
········· DIVE BOMBERS
– – – HORIZONTAL BOMBERS
–·–·– TORPEDO BOMBERS

51
DIVE
BOMBERS
&
43
FIGHTERS

49
HORIZONTAL
&
40
TORPEDO
BOMBERS

N
W ——— E
S

HALEIWA

WHEELER

KANEOHE

ONE LONE
FIGHTER

PEARL
HARBOR

BELLOWS

EWA

HONOLULU

HICKAM

WHEELER, EWA, FORD ISLAND, AND HICKAM HIT BY DIVE BOMBERS.
PEARL HARBOR HIT BY HORIZONTAL, TORPEDO, AND DIVE BOMBERS,
43 FIGHTERS ESCORTED BOMBERS DOWN THROUGH CENTRAL OAHU, THEN
BROKE OFF AND ATTACKED ALL INSTALLATIONS EXCEPT HALEIWA.
BELLOWS HIT BY ONE LONE FIGHTER.

Japanese aircraft deployment, first attack. (*Source*: USAF)

Overhead photograph of Pearl Harbor, with Hickam Field in the upper left center, east of the harbor entrance; Ford Island in the center-right; and "Battleship Row" just east of Ford Island; overhead photograph taken in October 1941. (*Source*: NA)

Planes and hangars burning at Wheeler Army Airfield, Oahu, as seen from a Japanese navy plane, soon after the field was attacked on the morning of December 7, 1941. (*Source*: NHHC)

Torpedo planes attack "Battleship Row" at about 0800 on 7 December, photographed from a Japanese aircraft. Ships are, from lower left to right, *Nevada* (BB-36) with flag raised at stern; *Arizona* (BB-39) with *Vestal* (AR-4) outboard; *Tennessee* (BB-43) with *West Virginia* (BB-48) outboard; *Maryland* (BB-46) with *Oklahoma* (BB-37) outboard; *Neosho* (AO-23) and *California* (BB-44). *West Virginia*, *Oklahoma*, and *California* have been torpedoed, as marked by ripples and spreading oil, and the first two are listing to port. Torpedo drop splashes and running tracks are visible at left and center. White smoke in the distance is from Hickam Field. Gray smoke in the center middle distance is from the torpedoed USS *Helena* (CL-50) at the navy yard's 1010 dock. Japanese writing in the lower right states that the image was reproduced by authorization of the Navy Ministry. (*Source*: NPSAM)

At 8:15 a.m., just as radio station KGMB was beginning its second emergency broadcast, the battleship *Oklahoma* (BB-37) on the east side of Ford Island rolled on her port side, the victim of seven Japanese torpedoes. San Jose State's Wellington "Gray" McConnell and Spartan teammates Allen Hardisty and Charlie Cook had been out that morning on a drive with three University of Hawaii coeds and were returning them to their homes. They had a disturbing view of the bombing, watching from a hilly area overlooking Pearl Harbor from the north: "Planes were diving. We could see the battleship *Oklahoma* capsizing. It was horrible."

Months would pass before a full accounting of the attack victims' 2,403 dead (including 68 civilians) and 1,178 wounded could be made. With the passage of years and missing never found came the intensely studied, wrenching realization of 670 unknown, unidentifiable victims of the attack who were buried in 252 different locations on Oahu. Others were washed out to sea by the tides and finally declared missing, their remains never found.

Forward magazines explode on USS *Arizona* (BB-39) after she was struck by a Japanese armor-piercing bomb. At far right is the mainmast of USS *Oklahoma*, heeled over sharply to port thirty to forty degrees as she capsizes. Slightly to the left of *Oklahoma* are the forward turrets of USS *Tennessee* (BB-43), with the rest of that ship covered by the blast from *Arizona*'s explosion. At far left is the bow of USS *Vestal* (AR-4), moored outboard of *Arizona*. (*Source*: NA)

Station KGMB repeated their order at 8:15 and 8:30, and police and firemen were called at 8:32. The first reference to an actual attack came at 8:40. "A sporadic air attack has been made on Oahu. . . . Enemy planes have been shot down. . . . The rising sun has been sighted on the wingtips!"

Radio stations barked orders and warnings every few minutes. As time passed, announcements became more urgent.

The United States Army Intelligence has ordered all civilians to stay off the streets. Do not use your telephone. The island is under attack. Do not use your telephone. Stay off the streets. Keep calm. Keep your radio turned on for further news.

Get your car off the street. Drive it on the lawn if necessary, just so you get it off the street.

Fill water buckets and tubs with water, to be ready for a possible fire. Attach garden hoses. Prepare to take care of any emergency.

Keep tuned to your radio for details of a blackout which will be announced later.

Here is a warning to all people throughout the Territory of Hawaii and especially on the island of Oahu. In the event of an air raid, stay under cover. Many of the wounded have been hurt by falling shrapnel from antiaircraft guns. If an air raid should begin, do not go out of doors. Stay under cover. You may be seriously injured or instantly killed by shrapnel falling from antiaircraft shells.

At 10:00 a.m., mobilization of the Territorial Guard was ordered. At about 11:00 a.m., a radio announcement summoned all American Legionnaires. Within an hour, three hundred to four hundred veterans of the Spanish-American War and World War I assembled at their clubhouse.

Governor Joseph B. Poindexter, broadcasting over station KGU, proclaimed a state of emergency, and at 11:41 a.m., the army ordered the Honolulu commercial broadcasting stations off the air to prevent their beams being used to guide enemy planes—fourteen minutes after the first of four A-20s of Hickam Field's 58th Light Bombardment Squadron began taxiing out "to search for and attack a Japanese carrier reported south of Barbers Point." The four A-20s' launch, though an inspiring lift to witnesses at Hickam Field, marked the beginning of an uncoordinated, almost chaotic and futile December 7 search for the Japanese strike fleet by army air force, navy, and marine aircraft and ships of the Pacific Fleet. The enemy had vanished as they had come—without discovery or counterstrike by American forces.

Before the radio stations went off the air, the order recalling all service personnel had been broadcast by each station a dozen times; however, many residents didn't have their radios on, were indoors, or were quietly having breakfast and had no idea of the events in progress. The announcements summoned doctors, nurses, and volunteer aides; civilian workers of the army and navy; and employees of various firms. Motorcycles and trucks were called to first-aid stations.

When the radios went off the air, the silence was ominous, even more nerve shattering than the announcements, and led nearly everyone on Oahu to twist radio dials searching for more information. On police radio frequencies, they heard patrolmen being ordered to investigate a steady stream of alarming reports. For days thereafter, many radio sets on Oahu remained on. A week later commercial stations resumed their regular schedules, but in the meantime residents kept their radio sets on all the time, tuned to police broadcast frequencies—except when advised to turn to commercial stations for special announcements. Nine times KGU and KGMB returned to the air that first day, for periods varying from forty-five seconds to five minutes.

General Short, the commander of army forces in Hawaii, visited the governor at 12:10 to ask for martial law. He told of the damage at Pearl Harbor and the military airfields and of his fears that the Japanese would attempt a landing the next morning, aided by local saboteurs. He assured the governor that martial law was "absolutely necessary" to implement the orders which the military could enforce. While the governor had wide powers under the M-Day Act, he could enforce them only through civilian agencies, and their facilities would have been inadequate in the face of invasion or uprisings. Governor Poindexter was reluctant to relinquish control to the army, but he felt that conditions were so alarming that he must defer to the judgment of a military man. He promised General Short an answer in an hour and placed a telephone call to President Franklin D. Roosevelt in Washington.

The call went through at 12:40. Following instructions from the navy censor already on the job, the operator asked the governor, "What are you going to talk to him about?" She refused to complete the connection until a superior finally told her it was all right to let the governor talk to the president.

General Short and his staff feared an invasion, a fear heightened by the unknown location and strength of the Japanese strike fleet. According to contingency plans, army forces had gone immediately to full alert, while antiaircraft batteries began moving to their preplanned positions as soon as the attack began—but too late to augment fleet and airfield defense during the attack.

View of "Battleship Row" as probably seen by the crew of the *Nevada* (BB-36) when she steamed down the main channel during the Japanese raid. *West Virginia* (BB-48) is at the right, sunk alongside *Tennessee* (BB-43), with oil fires shrouding them both. The capsized *Oklahoma* is at the left, alongside *Maryland* (BB-46). Crewmen on the latter's stern are using fire hoses to try to push burning oil away from their ship. (*Source*: NPSAM)

JAPANESE AIRCRAFT DEPLOYMENT SECOND ATTACK

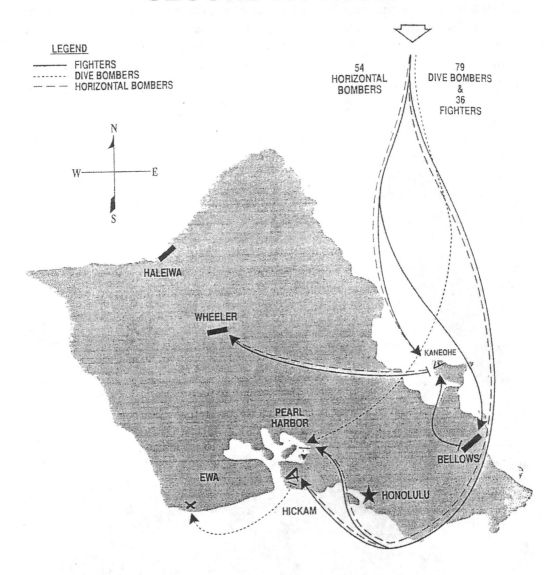

LEGEND
—————— FIGHTERS
· · · · · · DIVE BOMBERS
— — — HORIZONTAL BOMBERS

54 HORIZONTAL BOMBERS

79 DIVE BOMBERS & 36 FIGHTERS

HALEIWA
WHEELER
KANEOHE
PEARL HARBOR
BELLOWS
EWA
HONOLULU
HICKAM

WHEELER, KANEOHE, BELLOWS, HICKAM, AND PEARL HARBOR HIT BY FIGHTERS.
HORIZONTAL BOMBERS HIT KANEOHE, HICKAM, AND PEARL HARBOR AND STRAFED WHEELER.
DIVE BOMBERS HIT PEARL HARBOR AND STRAFED HICKAM AND EWA.

Japanese aircraft deployment, second attack. (*Source*: USAF)

As soon as the attack commenced, the 24th and 25th Division units came to full alert and began mobilizing to move into preplanned but unprepared positions to defend against possible landings by Japanese troops. On the higher ground behind Naval Air Station Kaneohe Bay and elsewhere along sections of coast considered likely landing areas by enemy troops, hectic preparations were under way to augment positions with civilian volunteers, filling sandbags while digging and reinforcing trenches, to strengthen defenders' gun emplacements and firing positions.

While the raid was in progress and frantic rescue and lifesaving medical works were under way in the harbor and surrounding areas, women and children in the military and civilian housing areas on the navy yard and at bases and airfields had begun wondering where to go and what to do, though many had been told to "stay inside—this is the safest place" when their husbands and other women, mostly in uniforms and uniform medical dress, rushed to their duty stations.

During the same period, schools on Oahu were ordered to close. The army and navy began moving and escorting military dependents off posts, airfields, and bases to safer areas where buildings and facilities such as the University of Hawaii, Kamehameha School, other high schools, and the YMCA could house them.

The Japanese second wave flew into a veritable hornets' nest of fleet air defense fire. View of Pearl Harbor looking southwest from the hills to the north. Taken during the Japanese raid, with antiaircraft shell bursts overhead. The large column of smoke in the lower center is from the *Arizona* (BB-39). Smaller smoke columns further to the left are from the destroyers *Shaw* (DD-373), *Cassin* (DD-372), and *Downes* (DD-375), in dry docks at the Pearl Harbor navy yard. (*Source*: NA)

At 4:25 in the afternoon came another announcement on the radio. The islands had been placed under martial law, and the office of the military governor of Hawaii had been assumed by Lieutenant General Walter C. Short, commanding general of the Hawaiian Department.

The governor's proclamation, in accordance with powers given him under the Organic Act, placed the territory under martial law and suspended the privilege of the writ of habeas corpus. It went further, requesting the commanding general to "exercise the powers normally exercised by judicial officers," the legality of which was to be debated for years. The general's proclamation told the populace:

> *The imminence of attack by the enemy and the possibility of invasion make necessary a stricter control of your actions than would be necessary or proper at other times. I shall therefore shortly publish ordinances governing the conduct of the people of the territory with respect to the showing of lights, circulation, meetings, censorship, possession of arms, ammunition, and explosives, the sale of intoxicating liquors, and other subjects.*

Shortly after martial law was declared and in the twelve days that followed, the two football teams and their accompanying coaches and fans were mobilized and became participants in the stunning turn of events that would forever change their lives and the lives of more than 132 million Americans.

One of Willamette's starting ends, Marv Goodman, recalled that he and a group of his teammates were sitting outside the hotel talking when an army car came by and stopped when one of the soldiers inside saw the players. The soldier asked, "Are you fellows mobilized?" When they said no, the soldiers went inside the hotel and found Coach Keene, and later the players were each issued World War I helmets, World War I Springfield 1903 rifles and bayonets—fixed on the rifles—and gas masks. The rifles, once issued, were "stacked" in the hotel lobby, undoubtedly under guard. Earl Hampton, who was inside the hotel at that time, also recalled Coach Keene coming into the hotel lobby with "some military personnel" and the stacked rifles with bayonets.

Coach Keene, accompanied by Senator McKay, called a meeting with the entire Willamette contingent, and McKay, who had been seriously wounded during World War I, began firing up the team, explaining the use of the rifles stacked inside the hotel. They were expected to learn how to use the M1903 World War I Gerund rifles.

Later, after the hurried orientation, there was one player, Gordon Moore, who didn't like the way his teammates were handling the rifles, and he spoke up, asking, "How many of you have ever handled or fired a rifle?" Only three, in addition to Gordon, raised their hands, and he recommended that everyone carry unloaded weapons, a recommendation agreed to in the beginning by the officers training them, but in the years ahead it would result in much teasing by his Willamette marine buddies.

This was the beginning of training for the two teams, who in next two days would have wartime missions assigned to them. They were told that local authorities were requesting the two teams' assistance. The players were also informed that they would have to help strengthen and man defensive positions on the beach that night. When McKay came back into the hotel, he said to Shirley, "There, I hope your friends don't kill each other." Among the Bearcats, Earl Hampton; Tony Fraiola, the experienced former marine; Gordon Moore; and Jim Fitzgerald, who had been in the army national guard, were the only four players who had experience handling rifles.

Marines were on the beach near the Moana Hotel stringing barbed wire. Earl Hampton said, "They told us that they were expecting the Japanese to attack the island and that Waikiki would be a likely place. They were digging trenches out on the beach and some of us were helping them." Willamette's sophomore halfback Chuck Furno, drafted with others to assist the marines, had left his freshly issued rifle at the hotel in the afternoon while he worked beside them. Earl Hampton learned that soldiers were digging and sandbagging trenches and firing positions near the hotel, and he recalled a night filled with the sounds of military vehicles moving through the streets. Like hundreds of others manning defenses on or overlooking beaches and other key areas on Oahu that first night—and the nights thereafter—every strange sound, such as breeze-rustled bushes or palm trees, was suspicious, if not frightening. The sound of distant gunshots was all too frequent, stirring even greater tension and sleeplessness. Marv Goodman said it was the longest night he ever experienced. Furno, told by marines that the Japanese would probably come that night, said, "We couldn't defend against anything. Why wouldn't they come?"

Chuck Furno, like many others on the two teams, was undoubtedly already beginning to think hard that first terrible day: "How am I going to get home? How in heck can I get word to my family that I'm OK, we're all OK, and we'll be home for Christmas, no matter what?" He would find a way. He was that kind of competitor and fighter. The answer came to him sometime between Sunday and Tuesday, December 9, after a lot of questions and answers, probably through the hotel staff: write a letter to his family in Vancouver, Washington, and get it on what everyone else eventually learned was the last Pan American Airways Clipper to leave Oahu in the wake of the Japanese attack, the Philippine Clipper. That aircraft, one of three Clippers caught airborne over the Pacific when the Japanese attacked, had made good its own desperate escape from across the international dateline at Wake Island on December 8 (December 7 on Oahu) and had come carefully but noisily to the Pan Am terminal in Pearl Harbor's Middle Loch to the west of Pearl City on December 8.

The Philippine Clipper, a Martin M-130 under the command of Captain John H. Hamilton, a lieutenant in the naval reserve, was en route, twenty minutes outbound from Wake Island, to Guam when the radio operator received the news about the attack on Pearl Harbor. Commander W. Scott Cunningham, the navy officer in charge of Wake, sent Hamilton a message suggesting he return to the island. Hamilton ordered the crew to dump about three thousand pounds of gasoline to get down to the maximum landing weight and returned—as Pan American's packet of emergency instructions directed. Among the passengers were a military mission, a Flying Tigers pilot, and a cargo of airplane tires, all destined for China.

On landing, about forty minutes after takeoff, Hamilton went to Cunningham's office while the aircraft was being refueled. Cunningham cleared him to take off again, subject to his orders, and suggested the crew take a patrol flight with F4F Wildcats escorting before leaving for Midway, which Hamilton agreed to do—with a 1300 hours takeoff. Commander Cunningham, an experienced aviator, laid out a plan that included escorting the Clipper with two F4Fs from VMF-211 and sufficient fuel for the Clipper to conduct the search and the flight to Midway with a reserve. The Japanese had other plans.

At 0710 that morning, 8 December, thirty-four Japanese Mitsubishi G3M Type 96 "Nell" land attack planes of the Chitose Air Group lifted off from the airstrip at Roi in the Marshall Islands. Shortly before noon they came in on Wake at thirteen thousand feet. Clouds cloaked their approach, and the pounding of the surf drowned out the noise of their engines as they dropped down to 1,500 feet and roared in from the sea. Lookouts sounded the alarm as they spotted the twin-engine, twin-tailed bombers a few hundred yards off the atoll's south shore, emerging from a dense bank of clouds. They attacked Wake Island just prior to noon, and within ten minutes the area was a shambles. (The raid at Wake was prior to 2:00 p.m. Hawaiian time, December 7.)

Hamilton, who a few minutes before the raid began had left Commander Cunningham's office, had just arrived at the hotel by car and due to construction had to walk when he looked up and saw the oncoming Nells. He ducked into one of the drainpipes and later recalled that they came in a nine-plane, close formation. The first nine started by machine-gunning the construction camp. The second nine began the bombing, dropping what appeared to Hamilton to be small bombs of about 150 pounds. He said, "The bombs fired the hotel, destroyed the Pan American buildings and dock, but didn't hit the Clipper. However there were 16 bullet holes in the plane. By good fortune no bullets struck a vital spot.

The garrison at Wake Island took a terrible blow in the air attack, which was to become a daily ritual. Receiving warning at 6:50 a.m. the morning of the Japanese attack on Pearl Harbor were the 1st Marine Defense Battalion, which numbered 449 men who had arrived on the island on August 19, followed by VMF-211's twelve F4F Wildcat fighters and their pilots delivered by Admiral William F. Halsey's Task Force 8 with the USS *Enterprise* (CV-6) on December 4. The garrison was still building its base and defenses and had not yet received its radar, which was still in Hawaii. Lacking radar, and with no revetments to protect the aircraft from bombs, the garrison immediately went on wartime footing, and it was decided to keep four of the twelve Wildcats airborne on patrol as a hedge against surprise attack. One two-plane section, Captain Henry T. Elrod and Second Lieutenant Carl R. Davidson, flew north, and Second Lieutenant John F. Kinney and Technical Sergeant William J. Hamilton flew to the south-southwest at thirteen thousand feet. Both sections were to remain in the immediate vicinity of the island.

Visibility was poor, and the four Wildcats failed to spot the Japanese aircraft. Seven of the eight Wildcats on the ground were destroyed. Worst of all, VMF-211 lost twenty-three men dead and eleven wounded, including two pilots killed, from among fifty-five total aviation personnel on the ground. No Japanese aircraft were lost. At one stroke, VMF-211 lost 75 percent of its aircraft and more than 60 percent of its personnel. Pan American's base suffered a knockout blow.

In the book *Pan American's Pacific Pioneers: The Rest of the Story*, Jon E. Krupnick recorded the "Report of Attack on Wake," written by John B. Cooke, the manager of Pan Am's Wake Island base.

After the bombing attack was over, I was bleeding some about the face and body, but a quick check assured me I had no injury of consequence.

I then left what was left of the building to see how others fared, proceeding directly to the hotel about a half block distant. This framed building of 40 rooms and spacious lobby and dining room was badly battered and one wing was already ablaze. Several minutes search revealed no one there and in leaving I noted what appeared to be all of the white Pan Am personnel on the dock or approaching it and the Clipper's engines were being started.

At first it seemed to me to be a bit cowardly to think of leaving, but there would have been no purpose in remaining. Every Pan Am building had been hit and several were burning. Power was gone and radio was gone, all was gone. The station had been rendered useless.

A check revealed 16 bullet holes in the Clipper, but miraculously, somehow, the gas tanks and engines were not damaged. To leave meant saving the airplane and ourselves so we left.

Thirty-seven of us [including crew members], plus fuel, made a terrific load for the Martin. The first try for takeoff failed, as did the second. For a third, the safety factor was nil as already the engines had been full throttled longer than cylinders ordinarily stand. But Captain Hamilton promptly taxied back for another try. This time he kept full speed the entire length of the runway. When the point had been reached where it was either take off or crash, the plane lifted and retained sufficient altitude to cross the island. We then skimmed the water for several hours. Necessarily, and to better avoid detection, at nightfall we took a respectable altitude that remained well aloft until we neared Midway, which we reached at midnight.

Ten Pan Am Chamorro employees from Guam were killed in the attack on Wake Island. As soon as the bombers left Wake and the damage assessment was complete, Captain Hamilton canceled the proposed reconnaissance flight and ordered the M-130 stripped of all extraneous equipment and cargo. With the passengers aboard, he lifted off for the 1,185-mile flight to Pan Am's blacked-out base at Midway. He was about forty miles from the base when he reported seeing two warships heading away from Midway, and when he landed just prior to midnight, he learned the island was shelled that afternoon.

They left Midway a little more than an hour later, this time with the destination of Pearl City on Oahu. For a time, they took a course toward the alternate landing area at Hilo, fearing they wouldn't be cleared to land at the Pearl City terminal. They were then informed the way was clear at Pearl Harbor.

The escape from Wake Island by the Philippine Clipper was one piece of good fortune in the midst of an attack that foreshadowed a far greater disaster for Wake Island's defenders fifteen days hence. Departing from Pearl City, Hawaii, the afternoon of December 9,

Captain Hamilton flew the Philippine Clipper under radio silence to Pan Am's base in San Francisco Bay, arriving on December 10. All except the crew and one company executive, Frank McKenzie, an airport maintenance engineer, were left at Honolulu, where they could be evacuated to the mainland by ship.

Chuck Furno's parents, Mr. and Mrs. Charles Furno, living at 1104 W. 13th Street, would receive his astonishingly positive letter on December 12, 1941, published in full in the Vancouver, Washington, newspaper the next day. It had arrived in San Francisco on December 10 aboard the last Pan Am Clipper from Oahu and was published under the headline "He'll Be Home for Christmas," with the subheading "Parents Receive Letter from Charles Furno Written since Pacific War Broke." The lead paragraph of the article explained that the letter was written on Moana Hotel stationery in Honolulu and was dated December 9.

Dear Folks:

Thought I'd better drop you a line and let you know that I am all right. Had a little scare Sunday but everything seems to be under control now. Don't worry about me because am fine and so are all the other fellows. Spec [Spec Keane, Willamette coach] is trying to get some of us jobs over here until we get home. Weather has been keen over here. Went in swimming yesterday and the water was neat.

This letter may not get on the Philippine Clipper which came in last night from Wake Island. I guess they bombed everything but their plane over there and they escaped. We sure have been getting lots of thrills that we didn't bargain for. I'm just hoping you get this letter because I want you to know we are in good hands and there is nothing to worry about.

Well, I will close now hoping you are as well as I.

Love to all
Chuck

P.S. Will probably be home on Xmas day as planned.

The Philippine Clipper arrived at Pan Am's Treasure Island terminal in San Francisco still carrying the sixteen bullet holes it received from the Japanese aircraft that attacked Wake Island.

Chuck Furno's letter left on the Clipper on Tuesday afternoon, not quite forty-eight hours after Chuck learned he had been mobilized to defend Oahu against a possible Japanese invasion of the island. That Sunday night a total blackout was in effect, and the military and the entire island of Oahu were on alert and tense, having been buffeted all day with attack-related announcements and frightening rumors, while at the Moana Hotel, throughout Honolulu, and especially at Punahou School—a school the Willamette football team would come to know well—the reality of martial law's meaning was slowly but relentlessly becoming clear.

CHAPTER FOUR

War and Martial Law Come to Punahou School

CHARLOTTE PEABODY DODGE, A 1902 GRADUATE OF PUNAHOU SCHOOL WHO LATER TAUGHT history, mathematics, and social studies at the school from 1906 to 1946, wrote this account of December 7 and the tumultuous days and war years on the school's beautiful campus:

Sunday morning was quiet on the campus, though breakfasters watched the "unusually realistic maneuvers." Mr. Hubert V. Coryell packed his bows and arrows and his targets and set out as usual for Sunday archery practice a Kapiolani Park. He and a dozen others, including a young naval lieutenant, got in some good shots before they were hailed by a passing service man as "darned fools," and then they heard his car radio blaring Webley Edwards' now famous announcement: "Attention everybody—Pearl Harbor is being bombed by the Japanese. This is not a war game; this is not a workout; this is the real McCoy. . . . All service men and defense workers report for duty at once. . . . Civilians, go home, get off the streets, keep calm." The lieutenant rushed off to his duty. Mr. Coryell went home and found campus people either watching from Rocky Hill, standing around in troubled groups, or glued to their radios hoping for further details. There were calls for doctors and nurses and there were one-way reports on the police band. Otherwise there was silence, and billowing smoke in the west.

A little before noon, while the usual paper bag luncheons were being distributed at Dole Hall, fires broke out on nearby McCully Street. . . . For the first time the danger seemed real, and close. Teachers and girls on the upper floors of Castle Hall packed their belongings and came downstairs dragging their mattresses for the night. The Red Cross unit was established in the basement. A few refugees from Hickam Field were being made comfortable in Rice Hall. The radio announced orders from the Military Government to close all schools and for complete blackout at dusk.

Campus men and boys met and organized into a guard for the night. ROTC rifles were without firing pins, but the officer in charge authorized teachers to arm themselves if they could. Some had only a stick, a length of pipe, or a plumber's hammer, but each man and boy patrolled a portion of the campus on four-hour watch. One teacher, with his two twelve-year-old partners, held up an armed "M.P." who proved to be searching for his wife among the refugees. At nine o'clock a terrific explosion broke windows in Montague Hall and Pauahi. An anti-aircraft shell had exploded on the lawn between the buildings.

But it was at 1:10 a.m. that Punahou's wartime fate was decided. Trucks from the Corps of Engineers rolled up to the main gate and Mr. Berger, guard in that vicinity, was informed that the Engineers were taking over the school equipment. Cooke Library, containing the school switchboard, would serve as headquarters. Before anyone could obtain the keys, impatient officers had broken a door and were moving furniture about, while more trucks and hundreds of men poured through the gates. Mr. Berger directed traffic with his flashlight, but otherwise the blackout was complete. Some damage was done during this panicky establishment of an army on top of a school, but rumors concerning harm to the library had little foundation. . . .

Just before dawn Mrs. Nina T. Brown received orders for breakfast for 750 men. She had to do her planning in the dark, for not a match could be struck until daylight, but the breakfast was forthcoming. Thereafter for weeks, an estimated 1300 persons filed past her cafeteria tables each meal. She managed the task alone for a few days, and then was put under the authority of a newly-arrived civilian, Milo Marchetti by name, who became head-man at Dole Hall. All the volunteer helpers, resident teachers and others, now became employees of the Hawaiian Constructors, classified as "kitchen help" and paid (eventually) at the lowest wage scale. It was hard work, with 8-hour shifts. Meal hours were strenuous and between-times there were hundreds of sandwiches to be cut and made. . . .

Dormitory children were quickly evacuated to the homes of relatives or friends, and workers filled all three residence halls. . . .

Meanwhile the campus swarmed with men of the Corps of Engineers whose offices were now located in the principal school buildings, while hundreds of "Hawaiian Constructors'" employees were living in Rice Hall. . . . Their trucks were parked on Alexander Field and at several other campus sites. Cooke Library served as headquarters and a subterranean bomb-proof passage connected it with the offices in Alexander Hall. Montague Hall was used for storage and Pauahi [Hall] was headquarters for the campus guards. . . .

Use of the campus by the army, in case of an "emergency," had been planned for months before and teachers had seen officers taking careful notes as they toured the buildings. Yet the occupation came, like the Blitz itself, without specific warning to trustees or administrators.

The reaction of Punahou School's Charlotte Dodge to the 9:00 p.m. explosion of an antiaircraft shell between Montague and Pauahi Halls on the night of December 7 was typical for the storm of antiaircraft fire in and around Pearl Harbor that night, believed initially by most who heard the fierce gunfire to be the result of a second bombing attack by the Japanese. Her reference to a nearby fire at McCully Street during the morning's air raid was at the intersection of McCully and King Streets, where it was later learned a five-inch antiaircraft round had fallen, done heavy damage, and started the fire.

Punahou School aerial photo, circa 1939. Note all the various buildings named in Charlotte Peabody Dodge's account of December 7, 1941, and the school's war years. (*Source*: PSA)

San Jose State's Hans Wiedenhoefer similarly related that "once during the second bombing of Honolulu, Aubrey Minter and Walt Meyer had to duck under a car to avoid flying debris from a bomb which landed too close for comfort."

Both nighttime incidents point to two misconceptions created by the shattering surprise attack and the fierce, explosive tension the raiders provoked among defenders and

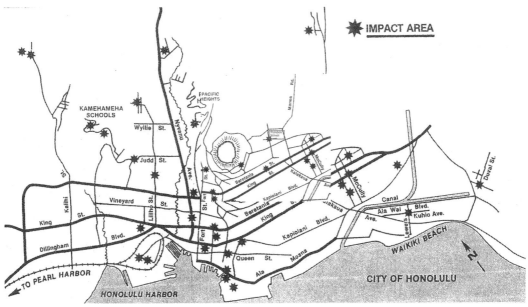

Cutout annotates location of Punahou School in the impact area, with rounds that fell near the entry gate to the school and at the intersection of McCully and King Streets. (*Source*: USASC)

Damage to a structure in Honolulu at the corner of McCully and King Streets, from falling five-inch antiaircraft round. Photo shows a volunteer fireman aiding a man on the roof by handing him a fire hose. (*Source*: USA)

Oahu's populace that first twenty-four hours. One misconception was that Japanese raiders "bombed Honolulu." Numerous thorough investigations by explosives experts, engineers, and subsequent historians have revealed that the Japanese didn't target Honolulu and didn't deliberately bomb the city or its suburbs. There may have been a small number of bombs jettisoned inadvertently or intentionally during airborne emergencies, but there were no planned attacks on the city. Instead, spent rounds from American antiaircraft guns during the morning's raid, fired from ships in Pearl Harbor at Japanese aircraft attacking from the northeast, east, or southeast, were falling into commercial and residential areas, and in waters along the beach, and exploding—adding to the fear, carnage, and damage inflicted on Oahu.

The second misconception was a "second bombing of Pearl Harbor" at night, which never occurred. Instead, a devastating friendly-fire incident occurred over Pearl Harbor the night of December 7, following the daytime search for the Japanese strike fleet. The incident occurred when six navy fighter aircraft from the carrier *Enterprise* (CV-6), returning from the delivery of twelve marine F4F Wildcat fighters to Wake Island, were diverted from their intended recovery on the carrier following a torpedo bomber's landing accident on the carrier's flight deck. Already low on fuel, the six fighters were attempting to land at Naval Air Station Pearl Harbor on Ford Island.

When night came, it multiplied the nagging fears of another attack. The tension was palpable. But there were other factors at work. Boiling anger, deep resentment, and a mounting fury laced with a determination to strike back. It was a fury that stretched all across the Territory of Hawaii, and when General Short issued a comprehensive set of orders accompanying the martial law announcement, the orders added more tension to the mix. The orders were printed in the *Honolulu Star-Bulletin*'s third extra that afternoon:

If you are ordered by military personnel to obey a certain command, that order must be obeyed instantly and without question.

Avoid the slightest appearance of hostility in words or act.

Certain enemy agents have been apprehended and detained.

Civilians who go about their regular duties have nothing to fear.

All citizens are warned to watch their actions carefully, for any infraction of military rules and regulations will bring swift and harsh reprisals.

Prisoners when captured, will be turned over to the nearest military patrol, military guardhouse, police patrol or police station.

Information regarding suspicious persons will be telephoned to the provost marshal at Honolulu 2948.

A complete blackout of the entire territory will go into effect at nightfall tonight.

Anyone violating the blackout by showing a light will summarily be dealt with.

All civilian traffic except in case of dire emergency, will cease at dark.

In this emergency, I assure you that the armed forces are adequately dealing with the situation and that each and everyone of you can best serve his country by giving his whole hearted cooperation to the military and civilian governments.

Further instructions regarding civilians will be issued as need arises.

Keep your heads and do your duty as Americans.

With radio stations silent, rumors started and remained rampant. People had been urged to stay off the phones to keep from jamming the lines. Literally thousands of men unaccustomed to routinely carrying or manning loaded weapons were now deployed throughout the island on full alert in fixed sentry or gun positions or on patrol. People working with the military in various areas on the island considered possible targets or vulnerable to landings by troops were digging bomb shelters or defensive positions.

Air-raid wardens patrolled nearly every city block in Honolulu, the ranks of the prewar group having been swollen by hundreds who had responded to radio appeals that morning. The youths of the Hawaii Territorial Guard stood lonely alert at twenty-five strategic locations.

The governor, the secretary of the territory, and the governor's private secretary grabbed a short rest at Washington Place. In his diary, Secretary Hite noted, "Dinner in dark pantry.

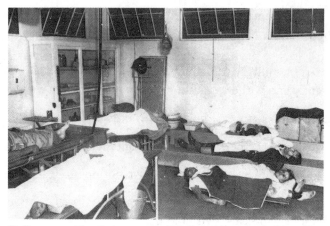

Civilian casualties lie in a makeshift first-aid center in Honolulu. Sixty-eight civilians were killed and thirty-five wounded, many by falling antiaircraft artillery rounds. (*Source*: USA)

Outside flares from Pearl Harbor plainly visible from Lanai. During the night machine guns on Punchbowl kept firing at planes."

At a plantation hospital crowded with civilian and service casualties, a nurse wrote of the night of December 7:

> *It was a strange experience indeed working through long black hours with feeble assistance of a blue-covered flashlight which cast a weird shadow on the faces of the patients already unrecognizable by the charred flesh and violet purple coloring of Gentian violet. We spent the night stumbling up and down corridors, sneaking in doors to prevent the escape of dim light from the heat cradles, feeling for feeble pulsations in temples or wherever flesh was intact. The only natural part of the strange night was the intermittent crying of babies in the nursery at times when they felt they were entitled to food regardless of bombings.*

While the fires on the sunken battleship *West Virginia* were extinguished before day's end, *Arizona*'s fires were still burning and eerily lit the harbor and the northeast portion of Ford Island, which further increased the tension that had been exacerbated by the onset of nightfall. A battered, chastened military, coming into the dark of night, was now deployed in fighting positions all across Oahu, on tense, full alert, an alert that now could best be described as "hair-trigger." As one officer on the damaged, hemmed-in battleship *Tennessee* explained, "If the Japanese decided to attack again the night of 7 December, the fire still burning on Arizona was a perfect guide for them."

As the six navy fighters from *Enterprise* entered the potentially explosive environment created by all that occurred during the day, no one could possibly learn which gun or ship fired the first rounds, but when the firing began, it was deadly. At 2101 hours, or 9:01 p.m., the battleship *Maryland*'s navigator, Lieutenant Commander Hugh W. Hadley, logged, "Aircraft with running lights approached ship in bombing position and not in landing position for Ford Island. All ships opened fire." At 2108, he recorded, "Commander Patrol Wing TWO ordered 'Cease fire.'" Two minutes later, CINCPAC—the commander in chief, Pacific Command—and Patrol Wing 2 ordered, "Disregard cease fire."

The countermanded order introduced confusion into already volatile circumstances. Astern of *Maryland*, *Tennessee*'s navigator, Lieutenant Commander Jasper T. Acuff recorded, "At 2104 commenced firing on planes crossing over ship. 2109 ceased firing."

When the six *Enterprise* aircraft approached Ford Island, the 251st Coast Artillery's Battery G was in position at the submarine base, with Battery H on Ford Island. At 2003 hours, seventy-five marines armed with ten .30-caliber and eight .50-caliber machine guns reinforced Battery H. At 2054 came the moonrise, beginning to add more light—and shadows—to the night. According to the 251st war diary, at 2115 both batteries, and undoubtedly the reinforcing marines, opened fire.

At 2049, the 25th Infantry Division, now deployed in its planned defensive sectors, sent a FLASH message to all division units: "Unidentified plane flying low toward Pearl Harbor. Received from Wailupi." Someone had reported sighting the inbound F4Fs. At 2103, with VF-6 aircraft passing near Hickam, another FLASH: "Enemy attacking Hickam Field." At 2106: "Enemy planes attacking Pearl Harbor." Then, at 2112, another message to the division: "No instructions regarding friendly planes rocking wings as means of identification. 5th Column tactics [sabotage tactics] suspected." At 2116, another FLASH message: "Enemy planes flying toward Schofield toward Newark. (and how!)" Then, finally, at 2128, FLASH: "To all stations; those are our planes trying to land—pass along to all sectors—this report from Navy."

The message was too late. Jack Leaming, the radioman-gunner from *Enterprise*'s VS-6, had been on the nine-plane search for the Japanese strike force that afternoon, was on Ford Island for the night in the unit's hangar, and had just been assigned a cot next to an ensign when the night exploded into furious gunfire. He grabbed his flight gear and ran for 6-S-7, his airplane. He recalled, "Outside every available machine gun and AA battery around was firing at some incoming planes. I arrived outside in time to see a plane crash and explode north of Ford Island. Then, another trying to land was fired [caught on fire] over the dry dock area and the pilot bailed out." The explosion north of Ford Island was Ensign Herbert H. Menges's F4F slamming into a house in Pearl City, then into a nearby gully. The plane Jack Leaming saw "fired over the dry dock area" was Ensign Eric Allen's.

Reported in numerous ship's deck logs, seen and heard from almost every area south of Oahu's mountain ranges, and from Honolulu to the southern and southwestern shores of the island, perhaps, if nothing else, the fierce reaction demonstrated that the enemy—if they chose to strike again—would probably have paid dearly, even though they wouldn't be attacking with aircraft running lights blinking.

Four of the six airplanes from Fighting Squadron 6 were down within five to eight minutes, three definitely shot down, resulting in the deaths of three pilots and the injury of a fourth. A fifth pilot attempted to land at Ewa, but his engine quit, probably due to fuel starvation or engine damage, and he parachuted to safety. With running lights on, the flight had apparently taken spacing in two sections, with the lead aircraft pulling ahead to make the low pass during the descending approach to Ford Island to give each section adequate spacing and lateral separation on landing roll-out on the wide runway. Unfortunately, taking space for landing, with two sections of aircraft on a low and slow, final approach, had just the opposite effect in terms of safety. The still-angry, hair-trigger hornets' nest of gunners observing their approach, guns armed and ready, could concentrate fire on each section, and on each airplane one at a time when the formation scattered. But that wasn't all. The storm of antiaircraft fire had other sad consequences.

Ironically, on board the USS *Argonne*, a repair ship moored with bow toward the northeast across the main channel to the east from Ford Island, there were two other casualties. At 2116, Seaman Second Class Pallas F. Brown, who that morning had narrowly escaped with his life from the capsizing *Utah*, was killed by a .50-caliber machine-gun bullet fired from somewhere to the west. The stray round passed through the port side of *Argonne* at frame 70, struck another *Utah* survivor, Seaman First Class W. A. Price, in the left arm before mortally wounding Pallas Brown.

San Jose State's Walt Meyer and Aubrey Minter were working with the police that night. Walt, speaking of what occurred, said, "Aubrey Minter and I had an experience the first night when we were on duty on the Pearl Harbor road that really was a thrill. We were stationed to tell motorists to turn off their lights [enforcing the blackout], and we saw a group of about six airplanes come over in pairs. We thought they were American ships, but soon the antiaircraft opened up. It was like a giant Fourth of July. We saw one of the planes go down."

Lieutenant Colonel Herbert H. Blackwell, an antiaircraft brigade executive officer, who after going without sleep for more than thirty-six hours following the attack then slept for a few hours Monday night, recalled the nights, the tension, and the anger in a letter home he began writing his family two days after the attack:

> *The first nights after the attack guards were posted everywhere, and it was extremely dangerous to go out at night, for fear of being shot. . . . Monday night I went to my quarters for a few hours of rest, and it sounded like a battlefield. Rifle and occasionally machine gun fire was heard on all sides, occurring about every one or two minutes. With much of the population here Japanese the threat of sabotage is great. However, these soldiers on guard were shooting on bushes when the wind would sway them, at any suspicious sounds, which may have been made by animals, etc. Whenever they heard or saw anything that did not respond to their challenge they shot at it. . . . Fortunately, so far as I know only one of our own soldiers has been shot, which I think is very remarkable. I shall be very glad when we have a little moonlight again.*

At 10:00 a.m., mobilization of the Territorial Guard was ordered. Formation of the Guard had been discussed ever since the National Guard was called to active duty in 1940. There was some doubt about whether the governor had the power to form one until he was given authority by the legislature in late October 1941. The University of Hawaii Reserve Officer Training Corps (ROTC) was called to duty, and its members became the nucleus of the Hawaii Territorial Guard. Other youths, including many from high school ROTC units, were rapidly enlisted, and by nightfall the guard numbered 35 officers and 370 men.

At about 11:00 a.m., a radio announcement summoned all the American Legionnaires. Within an hour, three hundred to four hundred veterans of the Spanish-American War and World War I had assembled at their clubhouse. One Legionnaire reported his early-morning activities as follows, bringing a bright spot of humor to an otherwise dark, confusing time:

Got out my Winchester rifle and 30 rounds of ammunition. Found to my dismay that I had forgotten how to load it. Started downtown, as I anticipated landing parties, parachutists and street rioting. Realized that I might be mistaken for a rioter or a guerilla myself, so went back home and got my old uniform out of the moth balls, on the theory that it would be helpful in reassuring some group of civilians, in case I should have to deal with any who were more excited and scared than I was myself. Couldn't find various items, and couldn't remember how to put on insignia. Got mad and bawled out the members of the household. Was told to go on out and fight the Germans instead of the women folks at home. The dog spied my Sam Browne belt on the lanai, and dragged it over to the guava bushes in the next lot to chew it at leisure. Recovered it and spanked the dog. Started downtown again and stopped in the Legion to find out what was best to do. There were already about 75 of the comrades there and more arriving every few minutes.

Two truckloads of men were sent to police headquarters for assignment to various duties, and another group helped at fires near the Legion clubhouse. By 4:00 p.m., organization had been completed, with each man assigned to an eight-hour watch. Most of the veterans were assigned guard duty. One detachment answered SOS calls and cared for dud bombs. Others helped the engineers, and some went to the waterfront.

Army intelligence, assisted by the Federal Bureau of Investigation, and police began arresting residents considered dangerous. Because one-third of the total population in the islands were of Japanese ancestry, internal security in case of war with Japan had long been a matter of official concern. Cards had been prepared with the names and addresses of Japanese suspects, and these were divided among thirteen squads of officers. Within three hours of the declaration of martial law, nearly all the Japanese suspects considered most dangerous were in custody at the immigration station.

There would be more taken into custody the next day, as security agencies, augmented by additional volunteers, expanded the net to include Caucasian suspects—practically every German or Italian alien in Hawaii, with the exception of the aged and infirm. San Jose State's Coach Winkelman, who contacted the Honolulu Police Department looking for a way home for his team, had already volunteered his team's assistance to the police after department members had taken team members in tow when *Lurline* arrived midweek. Now, after the attack, several participated in arresting Japanese aliens. A San Francisco member of the San Jose squad, former Lowell High School's Hans Wiedenhoefer, told of working with the police:

> Next day we joined the police force, were given steel helmets, arm bands and riot guns, and assigned to various police posts for eight-hour shifts along with regular members of the force. I was working with a Hawaiian policeman when we got a call to raid a place which had a powerful short wave radio set in it. It was pitch dark, there wasn't a light and you couldn't see the front of your nose.
>
> We closed in and found the radio equipment all right but four fellows we were supposed to nab weren't there. Apparently, two of them had been tipped off because we found a note from them warning the other two to beat it.
>
> The Hawaiian policeman told me I had better stay there and keep watch and then he left me. For a few minutes my knees knocked pretty hard, and when I heard somebody fooling around a window in the next room I just rushed in there, aimed and took a shot.

He said he couldn't tell whether he hit the target, but he said it felt pretty good to see several policemen come rushing up after he fired. Later, Wiedenhoefer and Gray McConnell, in company with a regular policeman, made four arrests. By the end of the day on December 8, 482 persons were in custody on Oahu—370 Japanese, 98 Germans, and 14 Italians.

San Jose State's twenty-one-year-old senior and Spartan right end, Jack Galvin, had a different experience riding in a police patrol car during the days the team assisted the police on Oahu. Riding one night during hours of blackout, the patrolmen received radioed orders to proceed to a residence where a woman was in labor and about to deliver a baby. Not long after they entered the home to assist, Jack suddenly found himself cradling the newborn in his arms. Totally surprised and ill prepared for such an event, he asked, "Now what do I do?"

On December 8, a day of deepening sadness, the funerals began, events the visitors from Oregon and San Jose, California, didn't observe or participate in directly. Army dead were buried in the cemetery at Schofield Barracks. The navy buried 328 in its plot at Oahu Cemetery in Nuuanu Valley, 18 at Kaneohe Bay, and 204 in a new navy cemetery that had to be established at the time by purchasing twenty-five acres at Red Hill, near Aiea. Calls for blood donations had already overloaded medical facilities where donations were being accepted.

For islanders and the military charged with defense of the Pacific bastion, mixed with all the loss, sadness, frustration, and anger about the visible dead and wounded were concerns for the missing. When the final count of dead and wounded was reached, 1,606 of the presumed dead were the missing who were finally declared dead. The missing were lost in the following categories: Army 3, Army Air Force 15, Marine Corps 66, and Navy 1,522. The greatest losses of missing occurred in the navy on the *Arizona*, followed by the *Oklahoma* and *Utah*, where, on the three ships, it was impossible to recover hundreds of bodies. The final death toll on *Arizona* was 1,177, including 73 marines and 1,104 navy; on *Oklahoma*, 14 marines and 415 navy; and on *Utah*, 58 navy, for a total of 1,577.

In Washington, DC, on the night of December 7, Secretary of the Navy Frank Knox had decided that he must go to Oahu to conduct a personal—but obviously official—visit to the island to determine the extent of the damage and, if possible, to find out why the Japanese had caught U.S. forces unprepared. After securing President Roosevelt's permission, he and a small party, including his aide, Captain Frank E. Beatty, departed Anacostia Naval Air Station, California, at the south end of San Francisco Bay on Tuesday morning, December 9, and arrived safely at Kaneohe Naval Air Station on December 11. Lieutenant Commander "Beauty" Martin, Kaneohe's commander, met the navy secretary at the seaplane ramp. Martin found the secretary friendly but intensely serious and eager to get to the bottom of the ugly business. He showed Knox and his party the devastated air station, the wrecked PBYs, the burned hangars, and the officers and men "trying to salvage something out of the wreckage."

Secretary Knox met Admiral Kimmel in Honolulu at the Royal Hawaiian Hotel, and they proceeded to the admiral's quarters. He invited Knox to stay with him, but the secretary politely declined in view of the "investigative nature of his visit." He had given orders "that he would not be the guest of any senior officer on Oahu."

The group from Washington observed an atmosphere of apprehension on Oahu. Captain Beatty, Knox's aide, described the Hawaiian command as "definitely security minded," with conversations "carried on in whispers" and "much glancing around lest their words be overheard." Post-attack shock was still evident among many, and everyone recognized the danger inherent in the island's exposed position. General Short deployed everything in the Hawaiian Department to stop a possible invasion. One top officer thought the attack had been a hit-and-run strike. A senior officer among the Hawaiian Department engineers "became almost paranoid about the Japs' return." He was "really quite obnoxious with his prophecies of doom."

The islands were far from alone in their anxieties. In Washington, Rear Admiral Richmond K. Turner, assistant to the chief of staff, United States Fleet, on December 9, in an operations message, informed Kimmel,

> *Because of the great success of the Japanese raid on the seventh it is expected to be promptly followed up by additional attacks in order [to] render Hawaii untenable as naval and air base in which eventuality it is believed Japanese have forces suitable for initial occupation of islands other than Oahu including Midway, Maui and Hawaii. . . .*
>
> *Until defenses are increased it is doubtful if Pearl should be used as a base for any except patrol craft naval aircraft submarines or for short periods when it is reasonably certain Japanese attacks will not be made.*

Pearl Harbor presented a grisly picture to Secretary Knox and his group of visitors, "the shambles of the Battle Line of the world's mightiest fleet." Foremost in their minds, however, "was the human loss and suffering." During the visit, they watched men remove bodies from the oil-covered waters while others worked briskly, "clearing up wreckage and preparing for another attack."

Later General Short met with Knox at Kimmel's quarters and talked with him for approximately two hours. He briefed the secretary concerning the status on Oahu before the attack and about the air strike, and he harped heavily on the fifth-column activities. Knox needed no convincing regarding Hawaii's Japanese. At the end of his trip he reported to Roosevelt, "The activities of the Japanese fifth columnists immediately following the attack, took the form of spreading on the air by radio dozens of confusing and contradictory rumors concerning direction in which the attacking planes departed, as well as the presence in every direction of enemy ships." In reality, the army and navy on Oahu required no Japanese assistance in generating confusing messages on December 7.

In contrast with misapprehensions about the local Japanese, the commands already had a good idea of the composition of the attacking force. Papers discovered on a Japanese plane that crashed indicated a strike force of six carriers, three heavy cruisers, and numerous auxiliary craft, including destroyers and other vessels.

There were questions and frank exchanges of answers regarding warning messages thought to have been transmitted to and received by the commands the night before the attack. Obviously these men were discussing no previously unknown dispatch that satanic forces withheld from its addressees. They were talking about the famous warning that General Marshall sent in association with Admiral Stark, not on the night of December 6, but which arrived shortly after noon on December 7 for one very good reason: the message from Tokyo upon which it was based was not received, decoded, and translated by the U.S. Army until the morning of December 7.

Admiral Kimmel was equally honest with Knox in other ways, and so was General Short. Both admitted that they had not expected an air attack and that the Japanese caught them unprepared and unawares. Kimmel had regarded a submarine attack as "the principal danger from a Japanese stroke without warning."

Knox's findings regarding the state of readiness to defend against a carrier strike seriously disturbed him. In a December 18 letter, he wrote, "It is simply incredible that both the Army and Navy could have been caught so far off first base. . . . They evidently had convinced themselves that an air attack by carrier born [sic] planes was beyond the realm of possibility, because they made no preparation whatever for such an attack." Believing in an American repulse of a nonexistent third-wave attack at "about eleven o'clock" on December 7, Knox was sure that had the defenders been ready, they would have beaten off the initial assault. (It's important to note that the "nonexistent third-wave attack" was the tragic friendly fire incident involving the six F4F Wildcat fighters from *Enterprise*'s VF-6 the evening of December 7.)

Kimmel was still commander in chief and still concerned with the war situation, and he could see some positives in the circumstance. The oil tanks had escaped destruction, as had his machine shops, what he referred to as his "Navy behind the Navy." And above all else, his invaluable carriers had escaped damage. On December 10, he sent a reply to Admiral

Stark's office, responding to Rear Admiral Turner's OPNAV message of the previous day, emphasizing that he and his command were ready for action:

Since the appearance of the enemy in this area, all tactical efforts with all available forces have been vigorously prosecuted toward locating and destroying enemy forces, primarily carriers. Our heavy losses have not seriously depleted our fast striking forces nor reduced morale and determination. Pearl must be used for essential supply and overhaul facilities and must be provided with additional aircraft both army and navy also relief pilots and maintenance personnel. Pearl channels clear. Industrial establishment intact and doing excellent work.

A gargantuan cleanup and repair task remained. Further devastation greeted Knox and his party on Ford Island, but the most painful sight of all were the hundreds of wounded at the naval hospital, some "so terribly burned and charred as to be beyond recognition." That evening, Thursday, December 11, Governor Poindexter joined the group at dinner in the blacked-out hotel, and they sat up most of the night discussing what they had seen and "planning for the morrow."

The next morning Knox visited the Hawaiian Department's command post for an extensive briefing. On this occasion he didn't "indicate in any way that he was not satisfied" with what Short had done. He spent about two hours at the command post, and after picking up casualty lists, photographs of the damage, and various Japanese souvenirs, Knox and his party left for Kaneohe that afternoon and shortly thereafter took off for the mainland. As soon as his plane touched down in Washington, he hurried to the White House. The original copy of his report carries the notation in Roosevelt's handwriting, "1941—given me by F.K. 10 P.M. Dec. 14 when he landed here from Hawaii. FDR."

CHAPTER FIVE

The Guards at Punahou School

On Monday, December 8, Willamette's Coach Keene volunteered the team to assist in guarding Punahou School, the just-established new home of the Hawaiian Constructors, who were under the supervision of the Army Corps of Engineers. Punahou, founded in 1841 as a school to provide a quality education for the children of Congregational missionaries, was founded one year prior to the Methodist-owned mission school that eventually became Willamette University.

In operations originally intended in 1834 to "educate and civilize" indigenous tribes in the Willamette valley in what first became Oregon country, on February 1, 1842, a board of trustees was appointed and a constitution and bylaws were adopted for the new school for children of settlers and named the Oregon Institute. Now, one hundred years later, Willamette's mobilized football team, for the second time in two days, received a wartime mission as America was entering World War II.

The next day, the players began preparing to stand guard at Punahou in their newly issued World War I helmets and an undisciplined semblance of uniforms, when some had never held a rifle in their hands—and others had held one for the first time the tense, fear-filled night after the Japanese attack—and had certainly never held loaded rifles with fixed bayonets. Transported to the school early the morning of December 9, where they remained through December 18, they were joined by mobilized Hawaiian Territorial Guard soldiers. Willamette's halfback Chuck Furno noted that they first started two-hour guard tours, then were off for four hours. Earl Hampton remembered it was "supposed to be four hours on and four off," but "it was more like six hours on and two hours off." Later, when the men complained of their inability to obtain sufficient sleep on that schedule, the tours were changed to three hours on and six off.

Headquartered and billeted in Punahou's two-story Pauahi Hall, not far from the barbed-wire main gate entrance to the campus, they prepared and were posted to their assigned sentry locations from the ground floor and slept upstairs on mattresses laid on the floor. Earl Hampton went on to say,

We marched a 700-yard route, one guy starting at one end, one at another. I marched the same route as Miller. Every time we got close to each other, we would talk really loud or even sing, so we'd know who was coming. There was some shooting going on. This was kind of wild country, and the wind was blowing at night, and the trash was blowing in the bushes. People would think there was something going on out there and fire away.

Some of their meals were at Dole Hall, where, on December 8, Mrs. Nina T. Brown and volunteers among resident teachers and staff began preparing meals for approximately 1,300 Hawaiian Constructors and their Corps of Engineers supervisors who came through their cafeteria each meal. The balance of the guards' meals consisted of sandwiches furnished by Mrs. Brown and her helpers.

During the period the football players were on guard duty at Punahou School, the inexperience of everyone involved in the duty exploded in a mishandled sawed-off shotgun incident involving one of the mobilized guardsmen. Willamette's quarterback, Ken Jacobson, described the incident: "We were sleeping in an upstairs room," he said. "One of the guardsmen had a shotgun. He set it down on the butt too hard, and it went off. Shot came through the floor into the room. Everyone raced upstairs to see if anyone had been hit by the errant shot. With great relief we found the shotgun pellets had penetrated the wood floor between two mattresses, harming no one." Undoubtedly, however, Ken and some of the men sleeping when the shotgun blast was fired were more than startled—if not by the blast, certainly by the commotion caused when guards about to go on duty came rushing upstairs to see that no one was hurt.

The Punahou athletic field becomes a parking area for military vehicles and a garden for plants to be used as wartime camouflage, c. 1942. (*Source*: USACE)

Temporary buildings constructed on the Punahou campus by the Corps of Engineers, c. 1942. (*Source*: USACE)

Ken remembered well how they were instructed to react while on patrol if approached by a person unknown to them: "Halt! Who goes there? Stand and be recognized." Halfback Gene Stewart remembered,

That guardhouse seemed the blackest spot on earth at night. . . . The toughest dive-bombers we faced were the Hawaiian mosquitoes. Were they ferocious! . . . We were ordered to shoot out any lights visible after 5 p.m. . . . Lots of shooting took place, but the only Willamette man to let fly with his rifle was Al Barrett. He banged away with his rifle at a fellow who wouldn't stop when challenged. The shot was wide.

Marv Goodman said, "I had about a block to patrol. . . . There weren't any traffic or lights, it was eerie. I had a round in the chamber. I really didn't know much about firing it. We were certainly projected into an atmosphere we weren't prepared for."

Two other teammates, Ted Ogdahl and Andrew Rogers, independent free thinkers at heart, decided to handle their guard duty frustrations differently. They decided to simply walk off the job and back to the Moana Hotel, where they reported to Coach Keene, probably seeking another form of duty that would allow them to remain at the hotel each night. Keene informed them that no rooms were to be had, and there was no money to pay for the rooms (if they were available) because of the ongoing emergency. They were to return to their guard duties—and they did, with no further comment except to tuck the incident away in their memories for future laughter.

"Honeymooning" Gordon Moore, used to working in and living with his wife, Elaine, in an apartment above a mortuary in Salem, had yet another experience. While he carried out sentry duties, Elaine and her portable typewriter found employment at Punahou—as a technician typing classified messages for the engineers' command, a new experience for her

64

as well. She didn't understand the code she was typing but wrote numerous messages all day long, every day.

A true perfectionist, she likely made few errors, but one night she made the mistake of running afoul of one of the Willamette sentries marching the Punahou campus perimeter. She was crossing the line of march heading toward the hotel when she heard a voice she immediately recognized as her husband's: "Halt! Who goes there? Come forward and be recognized." He was startled when she came forward in the darkness and announced herself: "It's me, Elaine." After the husband-and-wife encounter, she thought, "Good thing those rifles weren't loaded!" She didn't learn until much later that Gordon's rifle was in fact loaded.

Willamette freshman Glenn Nordquist, one of the men on guard with World War I–era equipment at Punahou School after manning a defensive position on Waikiki the night of December 7, was affected differently by his experiences than his teammates were. While walking his assigned post at the school, he had an epiphany. He promised God that if the team and all who came with them returned home safely, he would quit football, leave Willamette University, and become a minister. He steadfastly kept his word and lived the life he promised.

Shirley McKay recalled that her father, Oregon state senator Douglas McKay, who was a World War I veteran, helped to train the Willamette players in how to load, handle, and use their weapons before they began their duties at the school. Little did she or any of the players know how well Senator McKay was qualified to train them for sentry duty or impose military discipline as best he could. He had not gone into detail with the players about his World War I service.

As a young, extremely well-trained infantry lieutenant, Douglas McKay had arrived in France in July 1918 with the American Expeditionary Forces' 91st Division, the proud Wild West Division, and fought in the bloody Meuse-Argonne Offensive, going "over the top" beginning September 26 of that year until severely wounded by a German artillery or mortar round on October 3. After seven days of ferocious fighting, it was a round that killed three of the men in a patrol he was to lead, and nearly killed him, as he was briefing them prior to their departure from behind the hard-won line they had fought their way to, to gather intelligence for the next phase of the long-planned Allied offensive to end the war.

More than twenty-three years later, Ken Jacobson would remember receiving $5 a day in wages while serving twelve days in various duties, ten on guard, and accumulating $60 before their unexpected, short-notice voyage home. The women who accompanied the teams to Hawaii had different experiences that were to better prepare them for their wrenching voyage home.

Though they had come to cheer for Willamette and San Jose State and to enjoy Hawaii, the women who had accompanied the teams volunteered a day or two after the attack to assist in the hospitals. Most worked at the army's Tripler General Hospital, not exactly as Florence Nightingales, but rather as nurses' aides. When they arrived at Tripler the first day, they washed dishes left in the kitchen since the attack; began carrying trays of food, medicine, and bandages; helped feed and bathe the wounded; and assisted nurses in dressing wounds. They took the temperatures of men whose chief concern was their anxiety to get back and do some more fighting. Beginning Thursday morning on December 11, they were taken by Red Cross vehicles from the hotel to the hospital each day.

Willamette's "Miss Jack" had charge of a ward in the hospital, but even she wasn't exempt from tedious, difficult labor. She reported having made thirty-two beds in one day. Shirley McKay was assigned to a ward in Tripler with young children who had minor wounds and had been separated from their parents during the chaos of the attack. She took interest in a young Hawaiian boy she estimated to be about five years old. Shirley couldn't speak 'Olelo Hawai'i, a Polynesian language, and the child didn't speak English, was lonely and frightened without his parents, and was drawn to Shirley's attention and kindness. After about five days, the child's father, who had been frantically searching for the little boy, entered the ward and was tearfully overjoyed to learn that his son was safe and not seriously injured. Their reunion became a glowing memory for Shirley, one she carried all her life, and likely sharpened by her prior experiences and observations on the day of the attack.

On the first tense night of December 7, Shirley returned to her hotel room and was sharply aware of the enforced total blackout and the host of rumors and nagging fears that the Japanese might return with another air raid, or worse, an invasion of Oahu. She, and undoubtedly her father, knew there were Willamette team members who had dug trenches and fighting positions and strung barbed wire during the afternoon, and at night were manning fighting positions alongside infantrymen on Waikiki Beach in back of the hotel. In the black of night inside the hotel, with the nearby and distant outside noise of occasional gunshots, military vehicles, and troops on the move, she was tormented by large flying insects, and she found what seemed to be the only means of keeping them at bay: matches.

When she left her room for a meal in the hotel restaurant and walked down the halls between room entrances, where she was certain no light would escape, she decided to light a match to drive the insects away. The match seemed to work until the rifle-bearing military guard, who surprisingly was posted at the end of the hallway that first night, saw her approaching. He brusquely told her to put out the match. Frustrated by the nightly swarm of large flying insects after returning from work at the hospital, lighting the match going down the hall from her room became a nightly ritual. So did the guard's admonition: "Miss McKay, would you please blow out that match?!"

While the two football coaches and their teams' followers were deeply concerned about how and when they might return home, Spec Keene and Ben Winkelman, as well as others, were confronted with frustrating censorship restrictions in attempting to telephone university and college officials to at least let them know by any means that everyone was safe.

Newspapers and radio broadcasts in America were filled with stories about war and the Japanese attack on Pearl Harbor, all stirring fears for anyone stranded in Hawaii by the attack.

At San Jose State College, as early as December 8, rumors were circulating that the Spartans had been assigned to police duties in Honolulu. Athletic Director Glen "Tiny" Hartranft had attempted to get through to Ben Winkelman on Monday, December 8, but was unsuccessful—though the FBI, Moffett Field, and Matson steamship lines had cooperated with him in attempting to establish contact through their various channels. Ben Winkelman finally succeeded in sending a cablegram to Athletic Director Glen Hartranft on Wednesday, December 10, saying everyone was safe and confirming that the team had been assigned to police duties and was patrolling in downtown Honolulu.

The Spartans' circumstances sparked more questions and speculation about the scheduled game with Hawaii's Rainbow Warriors on December 13. Would the game be played as planned? Officials at the college first expressed confidence that the game would be played in spite of the attack, as would the December 16 game against Willamette. Surely the San Jose and Willamette contingents would have priority on the services of the *Lurline* in returning home at the scheduled time.

Everyone associated with the prospective games and return voyage home was completely unaware of events going on in San Francisco's harbor—the mobilization and conversion to troopships of the entire Matson passenger fleet after the Pearl Harbor attack. Clearly, however, San Jose State College officials learned early that there would be no shortwave radio broadcasts of the games, as amateur radio operators had already been informed and had in turn informed college officials that no broadcasts of the games would be permitted.

Undoubtedly after several earlier attempts, on the night of December 11, while the Willamette team and their accompanying fans were fully mobilized and heavily engaged in wartime "special" duties, Willamette's Coach Spec Keene was finally able to put through a telephone call from Honolulu to Oregon's Governor Charles A. Sprague. The clamp of censorship was fully in force, and the conversation brief, with subject matter extremely limited. The conversation was reported by the *Oregon Statesman* newspaper and briefly mentioned in the top left corner of the *Willamette Collegian*'s front page the next day. "Party all o.k. and fine. We are working on special duty. Please notify parents, relatives, and friends. Everything o.k." No mention was made about coming home. The newspaper reports, undoubtedly also mentioned in local news broadcasts, brought collective sighs of relief at the university and among all who read or heard the encouraging news.

But both teams' situation remained tenuous and uncertain at best. Until December 11, no one at home had heard or seen any reports at all, only rumors and reports from letters of their happy, pre-attack arrival in Honolulu aboard the *Lurline*. And certainly no one could say when or how the two contingents of travelers might return to the mainland.

On December 11, however, one highly respected gentleman who accompanied the Willamette team, Oregon state senator Douglas McKay, decided he would try writing home one more time, though there were no more Pan American Clippers known to be leaving Oahu for their home base at San Francisco Bay's Treasure Island.

But in the United States, Pan American's fleet of Clippers was already being mobilized to support the war effort with naval reserve officers, similar to the Philippine Clipper's Captain Hamilton, who flew home from Pearl Harbor to San Francisco on December 10 following the Wake Island attack. Such men were already qualified to continue flying operations in uniform. Military-flown shuttle flights to Oahu and back were already beginning, and Douglas McKay's December 11 letter did reach home while the two football teams remained stranded on the island.

Dec. 11, 1941.

Dear Mabel & Mary Lou:

I don't know whether there will be any clipper mail or not but I'll write anyway.

We are all well and happy. Plenty to eat & plenty of sleep.

This is a great experience & I would not have missed it for anything.

This ocean is so warm here that it is a pleasure to swim in it.

Look out for the business until I get home. Tell Robin 1. Cut down any possible expense. 2. Collect receivables like he never did before. 3. Get on a cash and budget basis except to those of good credit experience.

You had better check with them every day until I get home.

Go through all my personal mail and pay my insurance policies as they come due.

Keep cool and don't worry. I wish you were here.

Tell Barbara Earle to buy what feed my horse needs from D.A. White for I'm going to ride him a lot when I get home. She works at the Unemployment Commission.

Just heard that there may be a clipper out tomorrow so better drop this in the mail.

Good night.

Love,
Daddy

CHAPTER SIX

Orders to Evacuate

IN THE NAVY'S PACIFIC FLEET HEADQUARTERS AND THE ARMY'S HAWAIIAN DEPARTMENT, joint planning to evacuate military dependents and nonessential government employees and their dependents began imperceptibly after an October 31 memorandum from Secretary of the Navy Frank Knox arrived in Hawaii six days later, thirty-one days in advance of the Japanese attack. The result?

When December 7 came, there was no evacuation plan. But planning, preparing, and doing, heretofore virtually nonexistent, accelerated abruptly. The attack lit a blowtorch underneath navy and army staff officers, along with retired navy captain Max M. Frucht, the territorial representative to the U.S. Maritime Commission, who suddenly realized he had the additional duty of managing the evacuation thrust upon him.

The memorandum from Secretary Knox had instructed, "Have plans prepared for the evacuation of dependents of Navy service personnel, Navy civil service, and employees of Contractors engaged in Navy construction projects, from outlying bases under their respective jurisdictions." It went on to say, "When dependents of both Army and Navy personnel are present at the same base, coordination in planning will be obtained by means of a Local Joint Planning Committee, the recommendations of which will be forwarded through channels and reviewed by the War Plans Division of the Chief of Naval Operations." Neither on Oahu nor anywhere in the Territory of Hawaii's 14th Naval District had a local joint planning committee been activated when the Japanese attack occurred.

To complete an evacuation, the memorandum outlined the alternative means:

When appropriate, local plans should provide for: (a) utilization of returning troop and supply ships, acquisition of ships by charter or requisition; (b) the issuance of precautionary notices suggesting the return of dependents by available means prior to the date set for compulsory evacuation in order to avoid congestion and unavoidable inconveniences; (c) local evacuation in the event ships are not available; (d) limiting the amount of household goods that may accompany evacuees as necessary in case shipping space is limited, and storage of the remainder at Government expense until transportation is available; (e) dispatch notification to the Chief of Naval Operations at the time the evacuation is ordered, of the number of evacuees in order that funds may be made available for their transportation and reception; (f) alien dependents desiring to enter the United States should make application to the local American Consul for non-quota entry.

Secretary Knox also ordered,

The Commandants of the above mentioned Naval Districts and the Governor of Samoa should be directed to comment upon the desirability of evacuating dependents from stations under their jurisdiction. They should also comment upon the effect of failure to evacuate dependents by M-Day from the point of view of the defense, food, and water supply, hospitalization, morale, and freedom of action.

M-Day, abruptly, harshly delivered with no warning on December 7, had come and gone, and the need to evacuate Oahu had become far more immediate, complex, and difficult to manage. The incipient, pre-attack belief among the military commands on Oahu that the primary, if not exclusive, threat to Hawaii was sabotage following the outbreak of war had brushed away any sense of urgency to publish precautionary notices encouraging voluntary evacuation by dependents.

Now, after the devastating attack, the question had become—especially for stranded tourists—"How are we going to get home?" Despite the instantaneously prevalent and powerfully motivated feeling throughout the island of working together against a common enemy, fear and tension were now present in the questions hovering over tourists and others feeling stranded on the islands. The abrupt, massive relocation of dependents and others to safety from on or near military installations during and after the attack had been an additional rude shock, and a foretaste of things to come.

Adding to everyone's discomfort was the unadvertised but "word-of-mouth, spreading reality" that expended projectiles fired during the fierce antiaircraft defense had killed and wounded many in Honolulu and surrounding areas. While next time the enemy could deliberately attack Honolulu and all the other towns, as well as likely military targets, and everyone might—just might—have warning to take cover, the depressing thought of being killed by your own defenders' guns didn't help civilian or military morale.

The problem and the related questions now were these: How many are we going to have to evacuate to the mainland? Who are they? What are the priorities to be given in evacuating them? What and how much of their belongings can they take with them? How soon and on what ships are we going to send them? And how is all this to be funded? Short-notice, rushed, effective communication with many people, in the face of an immediate need for the utmost secrecy regarding ship movements, plus congestion and inconvenience, were a required way of life.

Placing announcements and press releases in newspapers and on the radio regarding ship departures and arrivals could result in ships being sunk and heavy loss of life. The phrase "loose lips sink ships," which later became more than a slogan, was deadly serious.

What's more, the brutal attack suddenly added to the list of evacuees. The more seriously wounded in the attack, along with accompanying doctors and nurses, as well as the widows and children of men killed and those still missing in action entered into the equation, all with higher priority than nonessential government employees, military dependents, and employees of contractors.

Tourists had come by sea on the vessels plying in and out of Honolulu from the mainland and points further east, including the two mainland football teams from San Jose State and Willamette University. En route from Manila by way of American Samoa, and due to arrive on the 16th, were the SS *President Coolidge* and the U.S. Army transport *General Hugh L. Scott*, escorted by the cruiser *Louisville*, the two American President liners already laden with passengers who had left further distant shores, many voluntarily returning to the United States.

Compounding the circumstances was the immediate and serious threat of Japanese submarines. This threat, expected if war broke out, first became evident an hour before the air attacks on Oahu and was punctuated forty minutes later with the reported attack on *Cynthia Olson* one thousand miles to the northeast, and then by the sinking of a Japanese submarine on December 10, later learned to be the I-70, north of Oahu, and the Matson Line's *Lahaina*, the latter on the 11th. The initial blows on the 7th were followed by a rash of increasing submarine attacks on navy task forces and on unescorted vessels in the shipping lanes between Hawaii and the West Coast—as well as in the waters adjoining Oahu and surrounding the islands.

A leisurely, planned, voluntary evacuation by single, unescorted, unarmed vessels was now out of the question. The Pacific Fleet suddenly had thrust upon it what undoubtedly had been part of contingency planning—all shipping to and from the mainland, and further toward American bases in the Pacific, had to be escorted by naval combatants with well-prepared and well-led antisubmarine capabilities. Fortunately, the navy was already improving those capabilities as a result of the Atlantic Fleet's support and assistance of the British, plus the Atlantic neutrality patrols undertaken earlier in the year.

Added to the immediate problem were the virtual destruction of all the navy's long-range patrol aircraft on Oahu and the termination of Pan American Airways' burgeoning civil air travel route from the mainland through Oahu to points in the Far East and the southwest Pacific. A small number of Pan American Clipper passengers from the two planes that had been forced to divert and turn around from their planned routes were now on Oahu, a small number of them seeking a way back to the mainland.

The afternoon of December 12, retired captain Max M. Frucht, whose office was on the seventh floor of the Aloha Tower in Honolulu, asked Mr. Randolph Sevier, the manager of the steamship department of Castle & Cooke Ltd., which ticketed commercial ship passengers, to make office space available for Frucht and his staff. Frucht asked for locations that would facilitate their management of the evacuation. Late that same afternoon, Sevier replied by letter, offering a fourteen-by-twenty-foot office space on the first floor, near Castle & Cooke's passenger department.

For the moment, the form of transportation to be furnished for evacuees was unknown, and Sevier advised Frucht to avail himself of the services of their passenger department.

Though Sevier seemed to acquiesce to Frucht's request, to satisfy his company's management procedures, he also wanted the retired captain's request and any other such requests to come from Rear Admiral Bloch, the commandant of the 14th Naval District, and suggested the wording to be used. The move continued to be held up by bureaucratic nonsense despite Admiral Bloch's written request to Sevier on December 14, worded precisely as Sevier asked.

Planning moved ahead, undoubtedly at a frantic pace in spite of the delayed move. But the delay exercised by Castle & Cooke, and acquiesced to by Frucht in the face of a full-blown crisis, was the first indicator of trouble ahead. Twelve days later Admiral Bloch's patience would run dry.

On December 12, Frucht had been given the estimated numbers of dependents to be evacuated to the mainland from both the army and the navy. On December 15, Frucht received revised numbers totaling an estimated ten thousand navy-related dependents, and General Short sent Lieutenant Colonel Casey Hayes to Frucht's office with revised numbers totaling 4,996 army-related dependents, which were passed to Admiral Bloch in a memo. The questions remained: Who would be the first to depart on orders, and what would be the assigned priorities?

While the evacuation planning was in progress, Japanese submarines were continuing their attacks. The night of the 14th, twenty-nine miles north-northeast of Oahu, off Cape Makapuu, the Norwegian freighter *Hoegh Merchant*, which had left San Francisco for Manila on December 8 and had been rerouted to Honolulu, stopped to await daylight before proceeding to the port. She carried 7,500 tons of general cargo, including 100 tons of explosives, and was struck by a torpedo on her starboard side, near no. 3 hatch. History would eventually reveal that the Japanese submarine that attacked her was I-4, captained by

Norwegian freighter *Hoegh Merchant*, commanded by Captain Einar Anderson, torpedoed by Japanese submarine I-4, captained by Commander Hajime Nakagawa, at 0355 hours the night of 14 December 1941. She sank at 0533 hours, according to the log of the USS *Trever* (DMS-16), which was standing by to assist after navigating to the area where flares had been fired, signaling distress. By 0658, *Trever* had picked up all thirty-five crew members and five passengers. (*Source*: NMF)

USS *Trever* (DMS-16), off Mare Island Navy Yard, June 16, 1942.
(*Source*: NHHC)

Commander Hajime Nakagawa. His crew found her in the dark, torpedoed her, and sank the stationary ship. Fortunately there was no loss of life when she was struck, and her crew of thirty-five and five passengers were picked up by the minesweeper *Trever* (DMS-16), which brought them into Honolulu the same day.

On December 15, with *Coolidge* and *Hugh L. Scott* one day from arrival in Honolulu, Admiral Bloch, already showing frustration, wrote to Admiral Kimmel, the commander in chief:

> *I propose to immediately start to evacuate the dependents of Navy and Marine Corps personnel in Hawaii.*
>
> *In order that I may have people available to go on the first transportation available, I request that you take necessary steps to have about 500 dependents of Navy and Marine Corps personnel attached to the Fleet register with the Transportation Office in the Navy Yard, giving their names, addresses, and other data that may be required in connection with this movement.*
>
> *I suggest that the first ones taken be on a voluntary basis and that all notices put out be so communicated as not to cause panic among dependents.*
>
> *At a later date, I hope to get an office established up town so that this registration can take place up there. At the present time this seems to be impracticable.*

On December 16, the day of *Coolidge*'s and *Hugh L. Scott*'s arrival in Honolulu, and the same day three Matson liners, including *Lurline*, all three now converted to troopships, departed San Francisco in Convoy 2005 bound for Honolulu, Bloch's chief of staff wrote a brief memorandum to go district-wide in the 14th Naval District:

> *Dependents of Navy Personnel desiring evacuation to mainland should register as soon as practicable with District Overseas Transportation Office, Pearl Harbor or with the Office of Captain M.M. Frucht, USN (retired), in the Castle and Cooke Building, Honolulu, T.H.*

By December 16, an evacuation order had been announced and received in all the civilian, navy, and army organizations affected by the order. On the same day, Frucht readied a press release for the 17th containing the order's key provisions.

Evacuation from Oahu to the Mainland will begin at once for all wounded who are able to travel, tourists, and dependents of Navy personnel, civil employees and defense employees, with priority in that order, it was announced yesterday by Capt. M.M. Frucht, U.S. Navy evacuation officer.

The number of persons to be evacuated was not disclosed. "Navy lists of wounded and personnel dependents have been completed," Captain Frucht said. "Tourists and family dependents of civil defense employees must register. There is a deferred list to include dependents employed by the government or on government projects, and dependents of employees who have permanent homes here."

Registration was to begin immediately, and evacuations would begin right away, Captain Frucht said. Frucht's telephone number was given as 66752.

The official notice issued from Captain Frucht's office follows in full:

The Navy Department has directed the evacuation from the island of Oahu to the mainland in the following priorities:

  1. *Wounded.*

  2. *Tourists.*

  3. *Dependents of Navy Personnel.*

  4. *Civil employees' dependents*

  5. *Defense employees' dependents*

Of the above categories the following will be placed on the deferred lists:

  1. *Dependents employed by government or on government projects.*

  2. *Dependents of employees who have permanent homes here.*

Persons coming in the second priority will register at the Honolulu Gas Company with Commander H.W. Boynton. Registration for the third, fourth and fifth priorities will be taken in the building of Castle and Cooke, Limited; in the Navy Housing Projects by Lt. Commander S.B. Wood, and in the Overseas Transportation Office, Pearl Harbor, by Commander Barrett. The registration will consist of obtaining the names of dependents, the local residence, household effects, if any, and whether they desire to leave as soon as convenient or wish to be placed on deferred lists for evacuation.

Similar sets of instructions went from the army's Hawaiian Department, telling department members and their dependents what must be done to obtain passage on ships evacuating army wounded, dependents, and civilian employees' dependents. The beginning of the evacuation, though far too late in planning, was gathering momentum, but there was much more to do—and much confusion. Because planning for the evacuation began barely thirty-one days prior to the attack on Pearl Harbor and had progressed hardly at all, Frucht and his staff, now trying to get organized, were being progressively overwhelmed by tasks needing prompt attention.

There were numerous additional considerations and details that had to be worked out in the last-minute crush and scramble to begin evacuating the more than twenty thousand who would eventually leave through the port of Honolulu, beginning with the departure of the first convoy on December 19.

There were many questions to be answered, such as how many people could be accommodated on each ship. The limitations for all the passenger-carrying vessels would be lifeboat and life raft capacity and the ship's ability to accommodate that number with sleeping areas, food, water, and life jackets. The *Coolidge* and *Scott* were already carrying passengers when they arrived on December 16, though some number would disembark because Hawaii was their destination. Ships arriving from San Francisco in the coming days, and which had been quickly converted to troopships capable of carrying increased passenger loads, would be disembarking all their passengers—the reinforcing troops, equipment, and supplies—and could accommodate far more than *Coolidge* and *Scott*.

How would the evacuation be funded? Who fit the definition of tourist and how was their passage to be paid? How much would be charged per person for the one-way trip? Who might have to pay their own way? What household effects could be shipped? Could pets go with their owners? Could automobiles be shipped? Individual appeals were already pouring in, some asking to be exceptions to the evacuation order, and others not on the priority list appealing because they wanted to escape the threat of renewed attacks. Some saw the tourist priority as a way out and were quite willing to fraudulently pose and apply as tourists.

Three new questions arose from the appeals and requests for exceptions to the evacuation orders: How should appeals and exception requests be submitted? To whom should they be sent, and who should decide and respond? As planning continued, the people and military commands on Oahu received another shock—though not entirely unexpected.

On December 17, in the midst of the frenetic efforts to plan and organize the evacuation's beginning, press releases revealed that all three senior military commanders, Admiral Husband E. Kimmel, commander of the Pacific Fleet; Lieutenant General C. Walter Short, the army's Hawaiian Department commander; and army air force Major General Frederick L. Martin, commander of the department's Hawaiian Air Force units, were being replaced. One officer would replace both Generals Short and Martin and was already on Oahu on the 17th conducting an investigation directed by General George C. Marshall when the announcement was made. He was army air force Lieutenant General Delos C. Emmons. The new commander of the Pacific Fleet would be Admiral Chester W. Nimitz, who didn't arrive until Christmas Day and would take command on December 31, 1941.

Army air force Lieutenant General Delos C. Emmons was already on Oahu on December 17, 1941, leading an investigation team dispatched to the island by General Marshall when he was directed to relieve and replace General Short, effective that day. (*Source*: USAF)

Admiral Chester W. Nimitz arrived in Pearl Harbor on Christmas Day 1941 and took command of the Pacific Fleet in a December 31 ceremony. (*Source*: NPSAM photograph 29)

CHAPTER SEVEN

The Enemy Below

A Precursor

IN THE TWELVE DAYS FOLLOWING THE JAPANESE ATTACK, OAHU'S VISITORS FROM SALEM, Oregon, and San Jose, California, were mercifully almost completely unaware of how exactly they were going to get home and the growing danger that stood between them and the safety of West Coast ports. Coach Spec Keene and Senator McKay had informed the entire Willamette contingent early on that the remaining football games were canceled and that everyone might be in for a lengthy stay on Oahu, but at the time of their expressed caution, the full extent of what they might face was unknown.

In the meantime, U.S. naval intelligence and fleet commanders were confronted with the need to make a prudent set of assumptions regarding their operations. Sizable Japanese submarine forces were on station in waters around the Hawaiian Islands, along the sea-lanes between Hawaii and the Philippines via Midway and Wake Islands, between Hawaii and Australia, and between Hawaii and U.S. West Coast ports, and were probably on or en route to stations off key West Coast port entrances.

At 6:50 a.m., sixty-four minutes before the Japanese raiders' first bomb struck Ford Island, a Japanese submarine—later determined to be one of five midget submarines launched from large modern "mother boats" (submarines) shortly before midnight—was reported fired on and depth-charged by the destroyer *Ward*, just outside the entrance to the harbor. Second, at 7:30 a.m. Hawaii time, aboard the San Francisco–bound *Lurline*, on the West Coast and probably to Pacific Fleet headquarters on Oahu had come the 7 December distress signal reporting an attack on the steam schooner SS *Cynthia Olson* approximately one thousand miles northeast of Oahu.

At 8:44 a.m., inside Pearl Harbor during the air raid, in an area west of Ford Island known as the Middle Loch, the destroyer *Monaghan* rammed, depth-charged, and sank a midget submarine that had slipped into the harbor before or during the air attack. At 10:04 a.m., as the last of the Japanese aircraft were departing for their carriers and the cruiser *St. Louis* was exiting Pearl Harbor, accelerating to twenty-five knots, two torpedoes

Destroyers *Chew* (DD-106) and *Ward* (DD-139) at Hilo Sugar Docks wearing their pre–World War II paint, the Territory of Hawaii, July 22, 1941. The training ship USS *Antares* (AKS-3), the minesweeper *Condor* (AMc-14), and *Ward* participated in identifying one or more Japanese midget submarines outside the entrance to Pearl Harbor early the morning of December 7, 1941, prior to the air raid. (*Source*: NHHC)

A Japanese midget submarine lies beached near Bellows Field the morning of December 8 on the windward side of Oahu. The midget's mother boat was submarine I-22. (*Source*: NPSAM)

fired by a Japanese submarine exploded against a coral reef approximately two hundred yards off the ship's starboard beam, an incident that gave her crew the ship's lasting affectionate nickname, "Lucky Lou."

Early the morning after the attack, the two-man crew of an army air force 86th Observation Squadron O-47B aircraft, already planning for a post-dawn patrol, was ordered to depart Bellows Field earlier than intended after the control tower reported "a strange object in the surf near the reef." Bellows Field, located on the northeast side of Oahu, was a new, expanding airfield, still under construction. Right after getting airborne in the dim early light, the pilot saw a strange and curious sight in shallow water near the beach, just west of the north end of the runway. It was a beached enemy midget submarine.

Then, in the twenty-four to forty-eight hours after the attack, patrols and task forces operating in the waters surrounding Hawaii reported a substantial number of known or suspected contacts with the undersea enemy, more than confirming the presence of possibly numerous enemy submarines. In the period from December 7 to 15, the *Enterprise* and its Task Force 8, operating to the south and southwest on December 7 and 8, and north through northeast of Oahu from December 9 to 15, recorded by far the largest number of enemy submarine contacts, compared to the Pacific Fleet's *Lexington* and *Saratoga* carrier task forces operating in widely separated areas during that same period.

Early the morning of December 10, Task Force 8's *Enterprise* aircraft separately attacked two enemy submarines caught running on the surface northeast of Oahu. In after-action reports, both pilots wrote of having observed near misses with their single dive-bomb passes but couldn't confirm sinking either submarine. Later that day, another *Enterprise* pilot attacked a surfaced enemy submarine in another dive-bomb attack. The submarine's failure to dive throughout the airborne attack convinced the pilot that the boat had previously been

USS *Enterprise* (CV-6) en route to Pearl Harbor, October 8, 1939. Photographed from the cruiser *Minneapolis* (CA-36). (*Source*: NA)

Japanese Submarine I-70, damaged in prewar collision.
(*Source*: IJN)

damaged. Both the pilot, navy lieutenant Clarence E. Dickinson, and radioman/gunner Thomas E. Merritt believed they sank the enemy boat, and it was subsequently reported as sunk—a report that history would eventually prove accurate. The submarine was I-70, captained by Commander Takashi Sano.

The end came in the early afternoon 121 miles northeast of Cape Halava, Molokai, Hawaiian Islands, at latitude 23 degrees, 45 minutes north, longitude 155 degrees, 35 minutes west. Lieutenant Dickinson, the pilot who had himself been shot down by swarming Japanese fighters over Oahu on the morning of December 7—costing the life of his radioman/gunner—had his opportunity for payback and succeeded. He struck with one dive-bomb pass, and the submarine sank, leaving four Japanese sailors in the water who later perished.

The next day, December 11, the Matson Line freighter *Lahaina* was sunk approximately seven hundred miles northeast of Oahu. On December 13 *Lexington*'s Task Force 12 encountered and repeatedly depth-charged an enemy submarine attempting to penetrate the carrier's escorting screen southwest of Oahu, unknowingly causing severe damage and the submarine's limping, surfaced withdrawal from the Pearl Harbor operation. Early on the morning of December 14 had come information that a submarine had sunk the Norwegian motor ship *Hoegh Merchant* in the channel between Oahu and Molokai.

On December 17 and 18, initially unknown to the navy, two more ships fell victim to submarine attacks, 200 and 150 miles south of Oahu. The first was another Matson Line freighter, the *Manini*, which sank in six minutes. The other, the American merchantman *Prusa*, went down in approximately five minutes. Both ships sank so rapidly that the crews hadn't time to send emergency signals, which resulted in grueling sea survival episodes for the two ships' surviving crew members.

Perhaps most important for the future of the visitors from Salem and San Jose was another unknown, but possibly suspected by naval intelligence, nine Japanese submarines

The Matson Line's freighter *Lahaina*, sunk by Japanese Submarine I-9 on December 11, 1941, about seven hundred miles northeast of Oahu. (*Source*: MNC)

that had been ordered to stations off the West Coast, from Cape Flattery in the north to San Diego in the south, to commence operations against shipping. On December 17, the same day the three senior army, army air force, and navy commanders in Hawaii were relieved of command, the first in a series of more than a dozen submarine attacks began off the mainland's West Coast.

CHAPTER EIGHT

A New Adventure

The Mixed Blessing

THE FIELD COMMANDERS AT HICKAM AND WHEELER, COLONELS FARTHING AND FLOOD, had all women and children evacuated. Some had already departed on their own in private automobiles, seeking the comparative safety of Honolulu or other outlying areas. At Hickam a loudspeaker blared, "Get all women and children off the base." Ira Southern and others helped search the houses and found women and children under beds, outside, or already preparing to leave. They boarded Honolulu Rapid Transit Company buses and trucks provided by the evacuation committee of the Major Disaster Council. Some evacuees moved in with friends. The remainder stayed at the University of Hawaii's Hemenway Hall, at public schools designated by the evacuation committee, in private homes of families who had volunteered to house them, and at other places such as plantation clubhouses and Hongwanji School in Wai.

On December 7, by the time the last of the Japanese aircraft had withdrawn toward their carriers, military dependents (many of them women and children) began fleeing from military installations in automobiles to the comparative safety of Honolulu. Throughout the day and night, trucks and buses with evacuees coming from Hickam and Pearl Harbor brought fear, rumor, and great uncertainty to others in the civilian population. The military had informed them that they had to evacuate to a safer area the afternoon following the attack. Numerous people from Hickam Field took a few personal belongings and went to Kamehameha School in a convoy of private automobiles escorted by the military. On arriving at the school, they settled into a boys' dormitory, and army air force civilian engineers voluntarily returned or were ordered back to work to begin inspecting damage at Hickam. Rumors were immediately pervasive, the first one being that Japanese paratroopers had landed. The effects of the immediate evacuations lingered while the threat of further attacks, real or imagined, continued.

On December 16, the *President Coolidge* and the *General Hugh L. Scott* arrived in Honolulu, escorted by the heavy cruiser *Louisville* (CA-28). When they arrived, *Coolidge*

82

and *Scott* were already carrying nearly full loads of passengers, including hundreds of voluntary evacuees from the Philippines, China, and elsewhere. Among the evacuees on board *Coolidge* were others from the Far East proceeding to assignments in the United States, such as Royal Leonard of the China Aviation Corporation, formerly personal pilot to Chiang Kai-shek; V. M. Zubilin, going to Washington to be third secretary of the Soviet embassy; Mrs. V. M. Zubilin; and J. Thyne Henderson, formerly first secretary of the British embassy in Tokyo, en route to Chile. An added surprise for children and other boarding passengers were two panda bears sent from Madame Chiang Kai-shek, a gift to the United States China Relief organization.

On arrival, the world cruise ship and her smaller accompanying American President Lines vessel were immediately placed at the disposal of the military on Oahu to transport navy and army wounded and other designated passengers back to the mainland—to the extent that the two ships could accommodate additional passengers. Two navy doctors on board as passengers were placed on temporary duty orders to tend to the wounded and were glad they could be of assistance.

Both ships were converted into semi-hospital ships. Bunks were added to sick bays. Crews gave up sections of their quarters for the wounded. Additional space for attack survivors was prepared in one of the steerage compartments. Cots lined the sides of passageways and filled the *Coolidge*'s spacious lounge, from which furnishings had been removed. The ship's nursery was likewise converted into sleeping quarters.

Cots filled staterooms, so closely placed that there was no room left for passage. Into the two ships' already overcrowded deck spaces on December 18 and the morning of the 19th were jammed additional scores of the hundreds waiting to leave the islands, including tourists; all but seven of the football players from San Jose State, the entire Willamette

The Presidents Line's SS *President Coolidge* photographed before she was purchased from the Dollar Line. (*Source*: NPSSFMML)

University football team, and the coaches and fans who accompanied both teams; many expectant mothers; widows and children of servicemen killed in the attack; and nonessential government employees and contractors and their dependents.

On the morning of December 18, at Pearl Harbor's naval hospital, in their ward uniform capes, blue felt hats, and blue sweaters, Nurses Ruth Erickson, Lauretta Eno, and Catherine Richardson waited for a driver to pick them up at their quarters. When he arrived and inquired of their destination, they still had no idea. They went by the officer of the day's desk and picked up their priority orders, which directed them to one of the piers in Honolulu. They were to go aboard the *Coolidge* along with a number of corpsmen from the hospital and prepare to receive 125 patients. Eight volunteer Red Cross nurses from the Queens Hospital in Honolulu were attached to the *Hugh L. Scott* at the next pier, preparatory to tending 55 additional army and army air force wounded. The navy nurses calculated *Coolidge's* medical supplies for a ten-day period.

The naval hospital brought the requested supplies on the 18th. Then came the nurses' arduous task of preparing beds for the patients, checking supplies, organizing nursing watches, planning meals for helpless men, positioning adequate medical supplies near the most critical cases, and the thousands of other details associated with such a tremendous first venture. On the *Coolidge*, Catherine Richardson took the 8 a.m. to 4 p.m., Ruth Erickson's duty ran from 4 p.m. to midnight, and Lauretta Eno was on from midnight to 8 a.m.

Early Friday morning, December 19, on the docks in Honolulu, final preparations were under way for the departure of the *Coolidge* and *Scott*, to be in the first convoy from Oahu to the mainland after war began, carrying evacuees to safety.

During that tense and fearful period, it was not known from hour to hour whether another attack might hit Hawaii. Yet out of the awful confusion, through the efforts of these hastily recruited Red Cross nurses under command of navy nurse Catherine Richardson, came final readiness for the arrival of the stretcher cases.

Beginning the same morning of the 19th, passengers watched from the ships and piers in stunned and solemn silence as the wounded were brought aboard. The approximately eight hundred passengers on the *Coolidge*, who had come from Manila and had heard of the Philippine capital's bombing as well as of the attack on Pearl Harbor and had gone through the en route transition from peace to war, until that moment hadn't seen the direct effects of war. They now confronted a far more sobering sight.

The services' commands decided that patients who would need more than three months of treatment should be transferred to the mainland. Ruth Erickson noted, "Some were very bad and probably should not have been moved." There were men hideously burned by explosions and fire. There were fracture cases wearing body as well as limb casts, as well as amputees. There were sightless men, their eyes covered with bandages.

They came to the piers in the navy's blue and army's tan ambulances. The thirty critically burned patients brought to *Coolidge*, and those with multiple fractures, were sent to the sick bay. The remaining ninety-five carried by the *Coolidge* were distributed in the lower-deck quarters already prepared. Wounded officers were placed in staterooms. Meanwhile, no doubt, similar preparations and patient loading were in progress on the *Scott*, which took aboard fifty-five stretcher cases in addition to approximately 150 army dependents and other civilians ordered to leave Hawaii.

Although all possible assistance was given by the ships' personnel, the responsibility for trying to keep the fearfully injured survivors alive until they reached adequate medical facilities was entrusted to seven navy doctors, the *Coolidge* surgeon, and eleven Red Cross and three navy nurses. Many of the remaining passengers, added to those who had arrived on the ships, received one to two hours' notice to board, though notification had begun on Thursday.

There were differing explanations and memories of why the two teams, their coaches, and their fans became passengers with the wounded on *Coolidge*, and specifically why the football players were to be directly involved in helping to assist and care for the wounded. Everyone who sailed on the *Lurline* and wanted to return home knew that Coach Spec Keene and Oregon state senator Douglas McKay, along with Coach Ben Winkelman, had been trying to find a way back to the States for the teams and their fans ever since the attack. For security reasons, orders to board the ships that morning had come to evacuees with no more than two hours' notice by phone and messengers to hotel rooms, restaurants, movie theaters, beauty shops, homes, apartment buildings, military units' headquarters, and dependents' quarters.

A small number among the San Jose State players believed that Coach Ben Winkelman had secured their team's passage home with an offer to assist and get them to the right pier in the port of Honolulu. Information circulated among members of the Willamette contingent indicated that Senator Douglas McKay and Coach Keene had negotiated an agreement with the *Coolidge*'s skipper to bring the team aboard for the voyage home in exchange for their helping to tend the wounded.

Coach Ben Winkelman had an entirely different problem with his football team than did Coach Keene, and when the Spartans boarded, they came from a different form of duty than the Willamette boys. During the final five days with the Honolulu Police Department, the players had participated in guarding key facilities in and around Honolulu, including some limited sentry duty at Punahou School, due to continuing fears of sabotage in connection with a possible landing of Japanese troops. Ben Winkelman had learned in the days leading up to the departure that seven of his team, all California boys, had decided to remain on Oahu, working in the police department. Heartened by their performance on duty, the chief of police told the boys he liked their work, and they believed the $165 monthly salary was difficult to turn down.

The Spartan coach acquiesced to their wishes in advance of the orders to board that morning. Wanting to do their part in the war effort were Fred Lindsey from Berkeley, Chet Carsten from Camino, Paul Tognetti from King City, Jack Lecari from Sacramento, Don Allen from Red Bluff, Ken Stanger from Pasadena, and Bill Donnelly from Ventura. Though not a shock to their coach and other team members, their decision would certainly be a shock to their parents and friends back home. Jack Galvin, who came home with the rest of the team, recalled, "To get aboard, to get passage, we had to sign a paper saying we'd help the women and children." In fact, events would prove that the boys from San Jose also helped with the wounded.

An eighth Spartan player, John Brown, went to the dock to see the team off and was talked out of staying, literally at the last minute, by team co-captain and center, Bob Hamill. The remaining Spartan team, and those accompanying them for the voyage home, now numbered twenty-four, including him, instead of the thirty who planned to return home.

For his part, Coach Keene divulged years later that some of his players expressed the wish to remain on Oahu and volunteer to serve in the military, but he refused their requests, saying they must discuss such matters with their families when they got home.

None of the three men leading the two contingents ever publicly discussed exactly how it all came about, which would probably have dispelled the differing views and memories. They were aware of the priorities assigned to the various groups of evacuees on the first convoy home—wounded and tourists being the first two groups, with the contingents from Willamette and San Jose clearly among the second group, along with other tourists on the island. Fortunately, compared to many others who entered the stream of evacuees eventually leaving the islands on voyages to the mainland, notification was relatively simple because all the two football contingents were staying at either the Moana Hotel or Punahou School.

At Punahou School, Ken Jacobson and his teammates had been told on the 18th that they were going to go by bus to "visit" Pearl Harbor, which, since the attack, had provoked increasing curiosity among all visitors to Oahu. But curious visitors and talk about the extent of the damage were definitely discouraged by the military. Military dependents and others being evacuated were instructed to discuss with no one the damage they had seen at Pearl Harbor. Security and censorship had become extremely tight. Events surrounding the abrupt scheduling of the two football contingents' voyage home later caused considerable speculation about why the Punahou guards' planned a bus trip to Pearl Harbor on the 19th, which was in fact the date of the *Coolidge*'s sailing. It's entirely possible that they were being alerted to be ready for a trip to Pearl Harbor as a cover story in order to avoid disclosing the *Coolidge*'s departure date and time—and to be able to bring them aboard in time for departure.

For the boys from San Jose State and Willamette, and for the *Coolidge* crew members, there would also be approximately four hundred women and children, the children ranging in age from infants to teens, who would need assistance, encouragement, and a calming influence in what could become a disastrous panic if a submarine was successful in a torpedo attack. There were women who were ordered to evacuate Oahu with their children six days before Christmas, on painfully short notice, leaving their husbands behind with little or no chance to say good-bye, men who were facing an elusive, implacable, and aggressive enemy. Worse, there were widows with children who had lost husbands and fathers. The great majority of the evacuees had no chance to call or write home and tell family they were OK and were coming home, and none of them, they would soon learn, had ever been placed in circumstances like the ones they were now facing. The sharp, painful reality would set in once they boarded *Coolidge* and *Scott* and were under way.

As for Christmas, there had been precious little time to think about it in the face of the continued night-and-day wartime footing, news of submarine attacks, local evacuations and dislocations, school closings, blackouts, troop and vehicle movements, almost constant military alerts, orders to evacuate, and the abrupt, terribly short notifications to report to dockside, although a few managed to think ahead to a possible Christmas at sea, in light of a voyage of unknown duration to an unknown destination.

The relatively small number of passengers coming from Manila on the two ships whose destination was Honolulu were perhaps fortunate. They didn't have to witness the boarding of the newest passengers in Honolulu, nearly all unaccompanied women and children, and later the wounded, the first sign of things to come on an island preparing for more war. First, on December 18, to passengers remaining aboard the two ships, came the signs of ships being converted to temporary hospitals. There were vehicles carrying doctors, nurses—including Red Cross nurses—and corpsmen and later unloading medical supplies and equipment. Then came the stream of army, navy, and civilian ambulances the morning of the 19th, bearing the wounded, with whom the passengers on board, including the boys and ladies from Willamette and Salem, would soon become acquainted.

The boys from Willamette and San Jose State were to learn soon enough that they would be assisting 125 wounded, which could mean, in the dire emergency of a torpedoing, helping them to lifeboat stations and into the boats. The wounded selected for the voyage home were those so severely injured as to require specialized care, such as the thirty severely burned victims, plus amputees, and the blind, all believed to be in sufficient condition to travel but also believed to require at least three months in the hospital. Unknown to the boys on the two football teams, the wounded on *Coolidge*—all navy and marines—would also include men with severe fractures, rendering them virtually helpless and requiring stretcher bearers—or, if no stretchers were available, two strong men to carry each one that crew members, corpsmen, doctors, and nurses couldn't carry to lifeboat stations—for which members of both teams practiced daily after they were en route.

CHAPTER NINE

Under Way

In Pearl Harbor on Friday morning, December 19, crew members on board other ships saw or later learned that two destroyers and a cruiser had left Pearl Harbor. The first was at 0933, the destroyer *Reid* (DD-369), whose captain was Lieutenant Commander Harold F. Pullen. The second, *Cummings* (DD-365), whose skipper was Lieutenant Commander George D. Cooper, got under way at 0939, and the 7,050-ton light cruiser *Detroit* (CL-8) followed at 0955.

At the outbound *Detroit*'s conn when she left Pearl Harbor was her commander, Captain Lloyd J. Wiltse, and on the bridge was her navigator, Lieutenant Commander R. E. Elliott. On leaving Pearl Harbor's Berth F-13, Captain Wiltse opened his sealed instructions. San Francisco was Task Group 15.2's West Coast destination.

At approximately 1100 hours, with the older, slower *Scott* leading *Coolidge*, the two ships were under way from Honolulu to rendezvous with *Detroit*, *Cummings*, and *Reid* just outside the harbor. Because of reported submarine activity in recent days, Task Group 15.2's route to San Francisco would be decidedly different. Maneuvering at various courses and speeds, the navy's three combatants were in formation with the two passenger carriers at 1158 hours, speed 15.5 knots, one knot slower than *Scott*'s maximum speed, on a westerly course of 267 degrees.

On board *Coolidge* and *Scott*, as soon as the ships left the harbor and while the two ships were maneuvering to join formation, passengers were served lunch, and not long afterward, they assembled on the promenade decks to receive the mandatory briefings at their assigned lifeboat stations—and the even more sobering instructions regarding the carrying, donning, and wearing of life jackets.

Typically, instructions were "Carry or wear of life jackets is mandatory at all times when moving about. We are at war, and this is not simply a drill. The winter seas will be rough at times. There have been reports of submarine attacks and submarines may be lying in wait. Should submarine alerts occur you will be ordered to don your life jackets. Be ready to don

Destroyer USS *Cummings* (DD-365), commanded by Lieutenant George D. Cooper, submarine screen for Task Force 15.2. Photo taken off Mare Island Navy Yard, March 4, 1942. (*Source*: NAPR)

Light cruiser USS *Detroit* (CL-8), command ship for Task Group 15.2, under command of Captain Lloyd J. Wiltse, convoyed *Coolidge* and *Scott*, departing Honolulu for San Francisco on December 19, 1941. Photograph taken off Mare Island Navy Yard, February 18, 1942. (*Source*: NAPR)

your life jacket at any time and move quickly to your lifeboat station if told. Follow the crew's instructions without question."

Following boat assembly and life jacket instructions, with ships now in the open sea, about eight hundred of *Coolidge*'s passengers were receiving their second and far more intense welcome into wartime sailing, this time clearly under threat of submarine attacks. While there was elation at prospects of going home, many, already somewhat affected by what they had just heard, were becoming reacquainted with the unpleasant, discouraging mealtime aftereffects of rolling and pitching decks. As if that weren't enough, as the day wore into night, they would feel the effects of repeated zigzagging, blacked-out ships with less than desired ventilation, and the beginning of mixed, unpleasant odors from seasickness, medications given to the wounded, and burned flesh oozing body fluids in spite of bandages and ointments intended to assuage the terrible burns some men had received.

There was yet another set of wartime instructions, followed by drills for the boys from San Jose and Salem—to learn which wounded Pearl Harbor survivors they were assigned to and would need to assist in moving to which lifeboat stations in an emergency. They were also asked to assist women and children in an emergency as well, particularly those who had lost their husbands and fathers in the attack.

Willamette football players outbound from Honolulu on the starboard (right) side of *Coolidge*, early Friday afternoon, December 19, 1941. Note Oahu's south shoreline in the background. The ship is on a westerly course. Also note the sober expressions of the players. With two hours' notice, they had come off of sentry duty at Punahou School to load on board *Coolidge*, where they now knew of the wounded on board the ship they would be helping to care for, that there was a serious submarine threat facing them for the voyage home, and that they were billeted in steerage. L–R are Ted Ogdahl, Cece Conner, Allan Barrett, and Charles Furno. (*Source:* KJC)

Detroit, with *Scott* and *Coolidge* in column, spaced eight hundred yards astern of the cruiser, with *Reid* and *Cummings* on opposite flanks, held their westerly course until 1314 hours; then the formation came further starboard to 310 degrees and began zigzagging using plan no. 33. They were entering the Kauai Channel and were beginning their passage between Oahu, to the east-southeast, and Kauai to the west-northwest. Always thoughtful, Ken Jacobson was soberly, and correctly, concluding that the convoy was taking a different route than normal, probably because of prior Japanese submarine activity.

If Japanese submarines on stations in the vicinity of Oahu sighted the task force, they apparently couldn't position themselves for attacks and didn't report its sighting. While there was no submarine alert given to the passengers that first afternoon, many knew why the ship periodically zigzagged and explained the procedure to others. To the uninitiated, zigzagging at first equated to a submarine alert.

At 1533, the zigzagging ceased, and four minutes later the five ships swung further right to course 015 degrees true, or fifteen degrees east of north. To reduce the likelihood of submarine attack, the task force was now positioned on a track approximately sixty-five miles west of the normally busy sea-lane leading from Oahu, through the channel between Molokai and Oahu, to San Francisco. At 1603, zigzagging resumed, ceasing nearly two hours later, when darkness had closed around Task Group 15.2. At 1700, while zigzagging was in progress, the *Reid* logged a friendly plane over the convoy, undoubtedly assisting the search for any signs of submarines while providing protective cover for the convoy. This was the first night out, and the task force hadn't experienced a submarine alert yet.

The Willamette and San Jose State football teams were berthed in steerage, along with a few crew members, a small number of the least severely wounded, and other passengers, who had given up their assigned berths in favor of the wounded. They had hammocks and some cramped bunks for sleeping. The women who accompanied the teams were in third-class cabins with Chinese, Turks, and others fleeing the war. Typical of the crowded conditions, Shirley McKay was in a third-class stateroom with seven other women.

The long, tense journey, and the last leg home for thousands, had begun, while ahead, off to starboard, over the horizon, the cruiser *St. Louis* (CL-49) and the destroyers *Smith* (DD-378) and *Preston* (DD-379), making up Task Group 15.6, were escorting Convoy 2005, the Matson Line's *Lurline*, *Matsonia*, and *Monterey*, carrying 9,918 troops, base course southwest, at 243 degrees, bound for Honolulu.

Approximately twelve hours behind Convoy 2005, sailing on a different route but also bound for Oahu, was Convoy 2004, six ships escorted by the cruiser *Phoenix* (CL-46) and destroyers *Cushing* (DD-376) and *Perkins* (DD-377). The two convoys were carrying the 34th and 161st Infantry Regiments, their artillery battalions and guns, ammunition, unit equipment and supplies, airplane parts and bombs, and a company of marines from San Diego. Also aboard were a fully loaded ammunition ship, plus two fully loaded navy oilers for offloading to storage tanks on Oahu.

Both the 34th and the 161st Regiments had originally been destined for the Philippines, but while en route, in San Francisco, they were diverted to reinforce the 24th and

25th Divisions on Oahu. The diversions expressed the American military's suddenly deepened fear of invasion and potential loss of Hawaii immediately following the Japanese attack on Pearl Harbor and the Hawaiian-based forces' failure to find the enemy's strike fleet.

The morning of the 21st, at 0700 hours, Task Group 15.2, composed of cruiser *Detroit* and the destroyers *Reid* and *Cummings*, escorting *Coolidge* and *Scott*, was holding steady on a northeast course, when the *Reid* left the formation to return to Pearl Harbor. When the destroyer left the formation, *Scott* held her position as convoy guide, with *Coolidge* astern, in column, destroyer *Cummings* on *Scott's* port bow, and the *Detroit* on *Scott's* starboard bow.

On board *Coolidge* and *Scott*, life was less than pleasant for the wounded and their attending nurses and doctors. Water had to be conserved. No bathing was allowed for able-bodied passengers. There was a movie in a blacked-out compartment the previous night, and the passengers, though crowded and still wrestling with the heavy sea's discomforts, were making the best of a difficult, tense situation. But the doctors and nurses couldn't avail themselves of the entertainment. Aboard *Scott*, Red Cross nurse Margaret Logan, later writing of her experiences and those of the navy nurses on *Coolidge*, described conditions that the nurses, corpsmen, and doctors faced tending the seriously wounded on both ships.

None of this small medical force had ever worked under such conditions, and most of them felt utterly helpless, exhausted, and desperate. It is possible that few of them ever expected to reach their destination.

As the ship pitched and rolled, neither medications nor food could be given properly to a majority of the patients. Feeding alone took precious hours that seemed to never end as nurses patiently forced drop by drop or spoonful by spoonful of liquids through the blistered and bleeding features of men completely swathed in bandages.

Of all passengers aboard, the missionaries probably offered the greatest assistance. They rotated twenty-four hours daily in helping to feed this tragic cargo. They sat for hours trying to calm the ones suffering from shock. They answered every call and could hardly have done more.

With an absolute blackout ordered throughout the ship at each sunset, the already overburdened ventilating system seemed to stop. Sweeping in nauseating waves down passageways and into every corner, the sickening mix of odors from putrefying flesh that oozed through bandages, medicines and antiseptics, food, unwashed bodies, and oil fumes often became too much for even the bravest of nurses.

Stumbling to the upper decks through cluttered passageways and up endless darkened ladders, they would snatch a few moments of solitude and breathe deeply of the salt air before hurrying back down to their work in the stifling confines of those too sick to know or care what happened.

Aboard *Coolidge*, the doctors, nurses, medics, missionaries, and numerous volunteer passengers faced conditions that were actually as difficult as (if not worse than) those described by Margaret Logan, magnified in part by sheer numbers, with 125 severely wounded. In the presence of the men they attempted to help, all who assisted struggled to hide their emotions and unflinchingly absorbed the wrenching sights, sounds, and smells that came from a large number who might never be whole again, while adding to tortuous, inner thoughts and an agonizing question: How will we ever rescue them if a Japanese submarine successfully attacks this ship?

There were many who volunteered to help the doctors, nurses, and missionaries with the wounded, among them the football players from Willamette and San Jose State, and the men and women who accompanied the teams. As many as six men at a time had to help gently turn the badly burned in their makeshift heat cradles to relieve pressure from lying in one position too long and hopefully avoid infection.

They talked with the wounded, attempting to lighten their burden and pain with pleasant memories or humor. They read to them; they wrote letters home to their parents, fiancées, or girlfriends and then read the letters to them; they fed them and helped move them when needed; and they carried among themselves difficult, unforgettable images and experiences.

Ken Jacobson and Chuck Furno, who were high school classmates and football teammates at Vancouver High School in Washington State and were in the Bearcats' backfield together, separately remembered participating in the same event because "we hung out together a lot." They helped carry one of the wounded down to surgery, possibly for a leg amputation. Chuck Furno helped feed the wounded and read to some of them. Ken and Chuck both remembered the heavy, sickening odor of burned flesh mixed with the smell of medications.

Shirley McKay, who slept in the *Coolidge*'s ballroom in her clothes and with her life jacket on the last two nights of the voyage to San Francisco, learned that some didn't want letters written home, fearing they wouldn't be accepted because of their devastating wounds. "They had been star football or baseball players and now had no arms." Echoing in her memory was the singing of Christmas carols at the Christmas Eve party.

Elaine Moore, Gordon Moore's wife, was one of those who volunteered to read to the wounded and write to their families for those whose hands were terribly burned and bound up. While helping such men, she encountered an extremely difficult experience with one of the badly burned men when a boat drill was called while she was comforting him. The terrified sailor grabbed her arm and piteously cried, "Don't leave us!" Elaine told Gordon of her experience, and he went to the *Coolidge*'s captain to tell him of the incident. Captain Nelson acted, ordering that ship crew members be assigned to stay with the wounded during boat drills so that they could be assured they wouldn't be abandoned under any circumstances.

Previously confined to steerage, word of the two football teams' dedicated assistance to the wounded and to evacuees from Oahu reached the *Coolidge*'s Captain Nelson, and he granted them "the run of the ship." In addition to the bright, energetic, and positive attitudes of the football players moving about the ship, additional levity arrived when passengers ordered to leave Oahu learned of Madame Chiang Kai-shek's two panda cubs on board, her gift to the United States China Relief Organization. During the day, when seas weren't too rough, to the delight of parents and their children who sailed on *Coolidge*, the pandas playfully performed like children themselves on the deck in the fresh salt air.

Ken Jacobson, who carried a camera with him, accumulated a remarkable collection of photographs depicting the Willamette football team's journey to San Francisco. Among his collection were delightful photos of Madame Chiang's pandas.

Quarters in steerage, SS *President Coolidge*. Photograph taken by Bert Robinson. (*Source:* KCC)

The morning of the 22nd, while cruiser *Detroit*, with destroyer *Cummings* in Task Group 15.2, continued their escort and screening duties, maintaining the starboard bow and port bow positions on *Scott*, with *Coolidge* in column astern of *Scott*, history later revealed that Japanese vice admiral Mitsumi Shimizu, from his command ship at Kwajalein, had ordered that the Christmas Eve shelling of targets on the West Coast be postponed until December 26. The order to delay the attacks came on the same day the headquarters of the Japanese Combined Fleet learned of the arrival of three American battleships, the *New Mexico* (BB-40), *Mississippi* (BB-41), and *Idaho* (BB-42), off the West Coast after transiting the Panama Canal.

Reacting to information later proved to be false, the order had the effect of concentrating most of the nine submarines south of San Francisco and sending three of them to intercept the nonexistent task group when most of the convoy traffic was transiting in and out of San Francisco.

Fortunately, the ordered Christmas Eve shelling never occurred. The order was later countermanded when submarine commanders raised doubts about completing the mission due to low fuel and their ability to successfully redeploy with the operation delayed two days.

Meanwhile, never aware of the original Japanese plan to attack West Coast targets, Task Group 15.2's commander, Captain Wiltse, held the convoy on course at 058 degrees, speed sixteen knots, bound for San Francisco. They were halfway through their voyage to San Francisco, and the commanders had been warned via highly classified messages of increasing

Ken Jacobson took a photograph of one of *Detroit*'s two Curtis SOC scout planes on December 23, 1941, after they were launched to search ahead of Task Group 15.2 for possible enemy submarines, ships, or aircraft while en route from Honolulu to the West Coast, December 19–25, 1941. The *Detroit* as yet had no radar on board, though the Pacific Fleet was modernizing, and the scouts served as the convoy's eyes and ears as much as possible. (*Source*: KJC)

submarine attacks off the West Coast. Given the acceptable weather and the fact that they were approaching an area of increasing threat, caution was an absolute necessity in defending the ships and people in the convoy.

While submarine attacks were in progress further south the morning of the 23rd, Task Group 15.2 was continuing on a course of 070 degrees, still holding 16.5 knots. On board *Detroit*, general quarters sounded at 0600, flight quarters at 0655, and at 0714 and 0721 planes were launched and flew on ahead of the convoy, watching for signs of enemy activity.

Detroit's Curtis SOC-3 bi-wing scout planes, with two crew members each, were the eyes of the great majority of the navy's combatants during the time of the Japanese attack on Pearl Harbor. The airborne scout planes substituted for both radar and sonar (the acronym for "sound navigation and ranging"), the still-primitive underwater submarine detection device invented by the British and given the acronym ASDIC (Allied Submarine Detection Investigation Committee), a detection system now common, sophisticated, and essential in today's antisubmarine warfare. Both radar and sonar were being phased into the Pacific Fleet when the attack occurred, but in December 1941, with priority given to aircraft carriers, battleships, and seaplane tenders, capability upgrades to date had not yet reached into the Pacific Fleet's cruisers and destroyers.

At 0840 hours, the relative calm aboard *Scott* and *Coolidge* abruptly changed when the destroyer *Cummings* signaled the convoy, "submarine contact, bearing 155 degrees true," approximately on the starboard beam of the convoy, and in the direction from which an enemy submarine might approach.

Cummings left the formation to investigate. *Detroit* immediately signaled evasive course and speed changes, and aboard the two liners the submarine alert brought orders for mandatory wearing of life jackets and more disquieting excitement to weary and harried passengers. Though the destroyer shortly reported the contact as apparently false, the passengers' worries weren't relieved. They were entering the final forty-eight hours of a perilous journey, a journey that few on *Scott* or *Coolidge* would ever forget, and the submarine attacks were continuing, capturing headlines up and down the West Coast, headlines above stories that would soon be read in Hawaiian newspapers and repeated on radios. Chuck Furno would say later, "We had heard about Japanese subs, and being below the waterline, we figured if the submarines hit us, we'd be dead, so we slept on deck the last three days."

Then came that bleak Christmas Eve, Wednesday, when the convoy had held an easterly course, keeping a sharp lookout, with all passengers ready at a moment's notice to react should an attack occur. *Detroit* launched no planes, and the convoy zigzagged only once, late in the afternoon.

Willamette's James Fitzgerald recalled in a commemorative video years later that on Christmas Eve night the sickening odor emanating from the wounded was so powerful he had to go out on deck to the ship's railing and throw up. He had gone into what he described as a stateroom where there were eight burn victims in bunks.

During the days and nights preceding Christmas Eve, an appeal to passengers on the *Coolidge* brought more clothes, books, magazines, and cigarettes than the wounded could use. There had been movies every other night, and dancing on alternate nights. Some passengers had taken swims in the ship's pools, despite the increasingly cold winter air. Games were played almost constantly. Barbers in the group volunteered their services free, giving shaves and haircuts. Every means available had been used to keep morale up, while during the days, when passengers were on deck, they watched the sea for telltale signs of periscopes. Danger lay like a pall over the ship, and at no time was vigilance relaxed.

Ironically, at the same time that circumstances seemed so bleak on Christmas Eve, in Salem, Oregon, Judge E. M. Page received an intimation that the Willamette Bearcats were on their way home. He had been trying for five days to get through by phone to the Moana Hotel to speak with Senator McKay and finally succeeded, only to learn that the senator had checked out four days earlier.

On this day especially, the passengers and crew, determined to keep spirits up and tension and fear at bay, held a Christmas party before the ship was darkened for the night. They sang the Christmas carols etched in Shirley McKay's memory and were able to give a few gifts, most of them prepared weeks prior. There was no candy or nuts for the children, and only a few toys that had been put on board at the last moment by busy Red Cross workers. There were far more children than gifts. While one *Coolidge* crew member later proudly described the party as "a Christmas party for history," a passenger described it as "sad." The attack had sent widows with children home on the two ships.

Not all was sad, however, as young men seriously wounded but not broken in spirit livened up the trip—and the party—with wisecracks and humorous banter. Almost all had shown improvement on the trip. Their cheerfulness deeply impressed the passengers. One young sailor whose right leg had been amputated above the ankle saw a friend whose left leg had been similarly amputated. He sent him a note that said, "How about a dance?"

The football players continued to lift spirits during the party. One had earlier made light of his being billeted in steerage, saying that if a torpedo hit the ship, it would come into his living room. The last blackout of the convoy came at 5:00 p.m., after the Christmas Eve dinner and party.

That night the doctors and nurses lost one of the wounded, an older seaman, Boatswain's Mate Second Class Alvin Albert Dvorak of Minneapolis, Minnesota. He had been badly burned and was losing intravenous fluids faster than they could be replaced. *Coolidge*'s destination now was San Francisco with 124 patients and one deceased.

Willamette's James Fitzgerald recalled the loss of the sailor with stunning clarity in a later filmed interview. James had a short time earlier been attempting to talk with the sailor, and he wasn't responding. One of the medics who observed the young football player's efforts to help came toward Fitzgerald, motioning and telling him he wanted to speak to him, then quietly said, "Leave him be. He's dying." Fitzgerald then described what occurred afterward, telling of teammate Gordon Moore, whose wife was in a third-class stateroom while he was in steerage with his teammates on the return voyage: "A teammate, Gordon Moore, who lived in an apartment just above a mortuary in Salem, knew all about how bodies were treated for burial, and told me the *Coolidge* had everything on board to do what was needed." Fitzgerald, who had been shocked to learn the sailor had died, then watched as Gordon Moore helped prepare Alvin Dvorak for transporting him home for burial, rather than burial at sea, "a memory as vivid as if it was yesterday."

At midnight, with *Cummings* still on the port bow of *Scott*, *Detroit* on the starboard bow at the same 1,500-yard distance, and *Coolidge* astern of *Scott*, Task Group 15.2 continued to hold its easterly course. At 0120 hours, the convoy entered heavy intermittent squalls and rain showers, with lowered visibility shrinking to one thousand yards, then eight hundred yards, until the *Coolidge* disappeared in the haze astern of *Cummings*.

Aboard *Detroit*, after the long, tense night, general quarters sounded at 0600. General quarters on *Detroit* began the wake-up from restless, almost impossible sleep on *Coolidge* and *Scott* and a flurry of activity. Passengers, told they were nearing the coast, knew the Golden Gate Bridge would soon come into view. At first light, army bombers from the Western Defense Command joined in escorting the convoy.

The early morning of Christmas Day brought relief to Red Cross nurse Margaret Logan, who was on *Scott* and later described what occurred on *Coolidge* that morning as the passengers began realizing they were near the end of a long, dangerous journey.

As a Christmas gesture, perhaps an expression of thanksgiving, there was a scramble to buy gifts for the wounded. All on board contributed something, from the lowliest cabin boy to the slightly rumpled official. The store on the *Coolidge* was bought out by breakfast time. Each patient and nurse received at least one gift—clothing, cigarettes, toilet articles, or some useful present.

At 0635 the electrical gang on the *Detroit* activated the degaussing coils that virtually eliminated the buildup of static electricity on the hull of the cruiser as it moved through the ocean's waters, a defense against possible magnetic mines left by the enemy. Twenty minutes later the watch sighted the Farallon lights six miles to the north, slightly aft of the port beam, and after signaling the turn to the convoy, it came port to 020 degrees. *Detroit*'s crew turned on her lights at 0721, followed immediately by the other ships in the convoy, and at 0755 the watch logged sighting the San Francisco lightship slightly east of north. Then came varying courses and speeds to enter the inland waterways. Task Group 15.2, soon to pass beneath the Golden Gate Bridge, was about to arrive home while Christmas breakfast was being served.

CHAPTER TEN

They Came from the Early Morning Mist

LONG BEFORE THE SHIPS DOCKED AT THE EMBARCADERO, HIGHLY CLASSIFIED, CODED MESsages had been received in the 12th Naval District, sent from Oahu's 14th Naval District, copied to the chief of naval operations in Washington, DC, telling the district commandant to plan for and expect the arrival of wounded and other evacuees from the attack on Pearl Harbor. Task Group 15.2's estimated date and time of arrival was communicated via encoded message as well, with information regarding the wounded and other categories of passengers on board the *Coolidge* and *Scott*. By the time the two passenger carriers docked, preparations were in place for handling them—and, as much as possible, for keeping tight secrecy on all the convoys transiting San Francisco.

Soldiers with rifles, sailors with pistols, and policemen closed off the area and kept the public, including reporters, behind wood barricades set up two to three blocks from the Embarcadero. In advance of their arrival, ambulance after ambulance rolled onto the piers. Army trucks arrived, laden with stretchers.

Already painted admiralty gray, the two ships with their escorting navy combatants came like ghosts gliding out of the morning mists from their passage beneath the Golden Gate Bridge. *Cummings* had pulled ahead of the convoy to enter the channel into San Francisco Bay, followed by *Detroit*, and the larger *Coolidge* moved ahead of *Scott*. Passengers topside who first glimpsed the Golden Gate and the San Francisco skyline for the first time in weeks felt safe. Everyone on board the ships was elated to be home at last. As they approached the Golden Gate, cheerful choruses of "California, Here We Come" again echoed among some of the *Coolidge*'s passengers. Years later, Shirley McKay Hadley's voice wavered when she remembered people singing "California, Here We Come" as they drew near their destination and passed beneath the Golden Gate Bridge. "We knew we were finally back where we should be."

The two escorts left *Scott* and *Coolidge* as the larger ships slowed and turned toward their moorings at the Embarcadero. *Detroit* anchored at Berth No. 1, San Francisco Bay, at 1015, after *Cummings* came into Berth No. 4 at the San Francisco anchorage at 0950.

Ken Jacobson photographs *Coolidge*'s passage beneath the Golden Gate, Christmas Day, 1941, after she pulled ahead of *Scott* to enter San Francisco Bay. (*Source*: KJC)

Passengers on *Coolidge* and *Scott* were asked to wait until the wounded going down the gangway were taken off the ships before they disembarked. The city's health director, J. C. Geiger, had dispatched four emergency hospital ambulances to rush any critical cases that might need immediate blood transfusions to the San Francisco Hospital blood bank. Red Cross nurses and workers, more angels of mercy, arrived to help and to take charge of the large number of civilian evacuees the ships carried. They were a welcome, cheerful sight bringing fresh donuts and coffee. Taxicabs were allowed through the barricades but were kept at a distance while the wounded were taken off the ships. Reporters, in writing their stories, were forbidden to name the ships in print or in photographs, what time they arrived, or when they might depart.

In the cold, drafty air, the grim task of unloading the casualties began, a slow, steady procession of men swathed in bandages, flat on their backs on stretchers, carried down the gangways and gently lifted into waiting white navy and tan army ambulances. Minutes after the ships docked, some of the wounded were on their way to local hospitals. No sooner did one ambulance load and pull away than another pulled forward to receive its patients.

Though local civilians and newsmen had to stay behind the barricades and couldn't get near the wounded, one reporter asked a policeman to describe what he had seen. "I saw them. I saw what bomb blasts and shrapnel did. I saw what were once fine, husky lads. And it hit me, like a Joe Louis punch in the pit of the stomach." There were young women waiting there, and one of them asked a sailor on guard at the barricade, "Do you know whether Johnny Thompson is aboard? He was an aircraft gunner . . . or something." "I don't know nobody," the sailor said and moved on.

Some of the navy ambulances went on ahead to Mare Island. Simultaneously, the long task got under way of transferring other navy patients not needing emergency care to two lighters—ferries on which cots had been set up. They were being taken to the Mare Island naval hospital, accompanied by the nurses who came with them on the *Coolidge*. Transfer to the first ferry was complete close to noon, and the trip up San Francisco Bay to the Napa River and Mare Island began, with the second following at about 2:00 p.m.

In the meantime, passengers went down the gangways to a city more than well prepared to meet and assist them. First came children, some with their mothers, some alone. They were the families of navy and army men, some of whom had been killed in the attack. Set up on the docks were canteens to give hot coffee to the women and hot chocolate to the children while they waited in the cold morning air to process through customs. Mrs. Philip A. Coxon and her Red Cross workers greeted them and began providing warm clothing for children clad in clothes too thin for mainland climates.

After the women and children cleared through customs, the Red Cross nurses and workers escorted them to waiting automobiles that whisked them to various quarters where they found Christmas cheer, candy, and toys for the children. If additional clothing was required, they got exactly what they needed from Red Cross supplies. If boys needed sweaters, they received sweaters. If girls needed dresses, they received dresses. Two layettes were provided for two babies born on board the ships.

Through the combined efforts of the Red Cross and the National League for Women's Service, the latter an organization created during World War I, stations had been set up, and an organization had been completed for getting evacuees to relatives or friends. The Women's City Club and Hospitality House in Civic Center were ready to aid navy wives and children. The Western Women's Club and the Women's Athletic Club were prepared to perform similar services for army evacuees. From Mrs. Alvin Wade, assistant hostess at Fort Mason, came an urgent appeal for volunteer nursemaids and women to care for evacuated children.

Civilian passengers needing assistance went to the California School of Fine Arts, where they were fed, clothed, and cared for. Any civilians ill or injured were taken to hospitals by city ambulances. Soon evacuees were dispersing to the city's hotels, to the homes of friends, or to the many stations established for them.

There was intermittent drizzle. Taxicabs had received numerous calls and were unable to keep up with the demand, thus causing some waiting and extended transportation delays for some of the evacuees leaving individually for other destinations.

Both football teams and all who came home with them quickly cleared through customs when they disembarked. Coach Keene hurried off the ship ahead of those with Willamette and called Mrs. Prince Byrd in Salem. He said, "Our entire party just docked here. In fact, it isn't even off the boat yet." He asked Mrs. Byrd at once to notify all parents, friends, and immediate relatives of members of the party. Mrs. Byrd did as he asked and later in the day told an *Oregon Statesman* reporter, "This is the outstanding Christmas of my life." On hearing the news, Mrs. Mabel McKay, wife of Senator McKay—and Shirley's mother—added, "It made a swell Christmas of it."

Following his call, while the joyful news was spreading in Salem and among families, friends, and relatives, Coach Keene wasted no time setting up train reservations on the

Southern Pacific "Beaver" for a 6:00 p.m. departure for the overnight ride north—toward home and a belated holiday. They had to cross the bay from the Embarcadero on a ferry to catch the train from Oakland. His team and all who were returning to Salem with them had been fortunate for more than one reason. Travel by train on Christmas Day was lighter than normal, which facilitated the short-notice reservations in spite of the rapidly changing wartime conditions.

Coach Ben Winkelman, the eighteen players who sailed home on the *Coolidge* with him, and the four people accompanying them to Hawaii and back were elated when they passed beneath the Golden Gate Bridge and arrived dockside just before noon, one day later than originally planned when they departed San Francisco on November 27.

One slight disappointment did occur when they disembarked from *Coolidge*. Army officials confiscated photographic equipment valued at more than $400 and containing a few aerial combat scenes, carried by the Spartans' team photographer Bob McGevren. Afterward, they handed him a receipt. They also confiscated copies of any newspapers evacuees carried home from Oahu in an effort to avoid giving away information to frighten the American people about the disastrous effects of the Japanese attack. Not until Elaine Gordon arrived home in Salem did she remember the piece of shrapnel wrapped in a Honolulu newspaper in her luggage. When she did, she came forward to authorities in Salem to give them the newspaper. By that time, the paper's contents were of no concern, and Elaine was able to iron out its wrinkles and years later give the newspaper to her daughter, Carolyn, as a family keepsake.

Arriving with Coach Winkelman were Manager Sebastian "Scrappy" Squatrito, Mrs. Ed Wenberg, yell leader Tommy Taylor, Bob McGevren, and players Ed Wenberg, Jack Galvin, Dene Kasparovich, Bob Hamill, Gray McConnell, John Brown, Walt Meyer, Vern Cartwright, Ken Bailey, Hans Wiedenhoefer, Wilbur Wood, Charlie Cook, Frank Minini, Aubrey Minter, George Foote, Billy Rhyne, Bert Robinson, and Allen Hardisty.

The last information college officials or the team's families and friends had heard, their entire Spartan contingent had arrived safely on Oahu, and all were safe following the attack but were stranded with no further word forthcoming on when they might come home. Their last known status was revealed in letters written by Ben Winkelman, Tommy Taylor, and Bert Robinson shortly after they arrived on Oahu before they were all stranded by the Japanese attack. Their departure on the *Coolidge* had been on extremely short notice, and with phone access sharply limited and tightly censored, none were permitted to apprise people when they were coming home—or that they were coming home at all.

Some people scattered in all directions from San Francisco, traveling by plane, train, and bus to reach home and anxious families in time for Christmas. Hans Wiedenhoefer, the San Francisco boy who graduated from Lowell High School, didn't need to board the bus back to San Jose and beyond. He undoubtedly was the first home, after Coach Winkelman, Hans, and the entire San Jose contingent were cornered by reporters wanting to know all they could find out from the team about their voyage to play a football game that never occurred—and particularly all about their experiences while stranded on Oahu and during their voyage home. Hans, more than all the rest, had stories to tell—and he gladly told them, as did a few others.

Afterward, the remainder who were heading toward San Jose climbed aboard a Greyhound bus, which dropped off several en route near their homes. They came with no warning, bringing joy to all those who hadn't been told of their "Christmas presents." Like Jack Galvin—who got off the bus in Redwood City and walked a considerable distance from Bay Shore Boulevard up a road to the front door of his home, where he knocked before entering—most would completely surprise their family members and friends when they arrived on Christmas Day. Jack's family was eating Christmas dinner when he surprised them.

The rest of the bus passengers were in San Jose at the Seventh Street Varsity House at 4:30 p.m., the same time the docks were finally cleared in San Francisco. The first to greet the team was the dean of men Paul Pitman, followed by more reporters from the *San Jose Mercury Herald*, who asked questions similar to the ones asked by San Francisco newspaper reporters. Dean Pitman said, "This is really Christmas!" Team member Vern Cartwright agreed and said, "We didn't think we'd get back for years."

Commenting on the seven players who stayed behind in Honolulu to accept full-time jobs with the police, Coach Winkelman said, "The police department wanted men, so some of the boys stayed." He spoke of the team's high morale throughout their stay in Hawaii and the "marvelous organization" of the police department and reported that Honolulu's chief of police, W. A. Gabrialson, was impressed with the police service of the seven men and had prevailed upon them to stay on at a salary of $165 a month. They joined a former teammate, Dick Hubbell, who had received an appointment to the department the previous year. Coach Winkelman also told reporters that he had served on police duties and that all expenses for the trip, despite the fact that the team played neither of its two scheduled games, would be taken care of by the Honolulu Police Department and university officials. He likewise reemphasized that the team spent their last five days with the police, on guard duty at key installations rather than on patrols.

Safely at home, some of the players told reporters they were already thinking of enlisting in various branches of the armed services. Bill Rhyne mentioned the marines, while Charlie Cook believed he was headed for the air corps. Co-captain Bob Hamill pointed to the air service as well, unless police service was ruled more important.

Within fifteen minutes after the team arrived at the Varsity House, friends and relatives began descending on the house to claim players and take them off to private homes for the holiday.

CHAPTER ELEVEN

Rolling North to Home and a Joyful Welcome

THOSE TRAVELING TO THE VARSITY HOUSE IN SAN JOSE AND HOMES IN OTHER NEARBY California towns had much less distance to travel than the fifty-one people who had to take the train north to Salem, Oregon, and Willamette University.

The first step was to get the whole contingent, with all its baggage and football equipment, across Oakland Bay to board the train on time, which they did. Christmas evening, while they were still en route northeast toward Davis, California, on board the Southern Pacific "Beaver," Salem's *Oregon Statesman* sports editor, Ron Gemmell, phoned the Davis station asking that Coach Keene be paged to answer his call. At Gemmell's request, the Southern Pacific stopped the train in Davis, and Coach Keene got off and returned his call.

"Hello. We're all together and all fine. We'll arrive in Salem at 1:59 [p.m.] tomorrow. We came over on steerage in a troopship, with the boys attending wounded soldiers and sailors on the ship." He went on to quickly explain what their reactions were, what they were doing when the Japanese attack began, and what they had done in the intervening period before returning in the convoy. "There was happiness in Keene's hurried, 'See you tomorrow,' as he rang off to catch the train," wrote Gemmell for the *Statesman*'s Friday edition.

Excitement was building in anticipation of the party's arrival on Friday, while later Thursday night Southern Pacific agent F. E. Taylor, traveling with the Willamette contingent, informed the *Statesman* that passenger trains were running about three hours late. Howard Maple, assistant football coach at Willamette University, after learning of Taylor's remark, said, "A gala reception for the returning Bearcats is planned if definite time of their arrival can be ascertained far enough in advance."

The Associated Press forwarded a complete list of arrivals in San Francisco, which included everyone who had departed for Hawaii, except for two who bought tickets planning to remain in Hawaii: Mrs. Charles O. Wilson and Maxine Aasheim. On the return, the Willamette party "adopted" two travelers, Mrs. Lyle Buck and her four-and-a-half-month-old daughter, Thelma Veronica, who were on the *Coolidge*, on their way from Peking, China, to McMinnville, Oregon, to be with Mrs. Buck's parents, Mr. and Mrs. Lyle Clevinger.

Traveling on Pullman cars with top and lower berths made up for sleeping the one night en route—and meals served in dining cars—the Willamette party's overnight train ride to Salem was both restful and fitful after their seventeen days on Oahu; their involvement in the stunning aftermath of the Japanese attack; a long, emotion-filled voyage to San Francisco; and the anxious rush leaving *Coolidge* to board the Southern Pacific "Beaver." Excitement, elation, and joy over their safe return home was tempered by sober reflection and conversation about what they had been through, seen, and done during a terrible time filled with sadness and other wrenching emotions. The thoughts racing through their minds were undoubtedly the same thoughts the men and women from San Jose State came home with in the hours and days of Christmas 1941.

Some quietly thought to themselves, "There were many, probably thousands, in uniform among the huge crowd at the game—I wonder how many died or were seriously wounded the next day." Willamette's James Fitzgerald and Marv Goodman did, and repeated their questions many times in the years to follow. Undoubtedly some wondered whether any of the desperately wounded on *Coolidge* were in the stands watching the game that day. "I wonder how long the war will last." "What should I do?" "What are you going to do?" "Will you join the armed forces? Which service? Or will you continue at Willamette, wait and see what happens, or wait to see if you're drafted?" "Will you join right away, so you can choose the service you prefer?" "Will you try to finish school before joining the armed forces?" All their questions would be answered by choice and circumstance, but for now they knew they were coming home safely.

The disastrous Allied defeats preceding their temporary wartime mobilization on Oahu between December 7 and 19 continued while they were en route home. Prior to December 7, from newspapers and radios they had heard the endless stream of news about the defeats of nations with which the United States was now allied by virtue of its entrance into the war. From Eastern and Central Europe, the Balkans, Scandinavia, and North Africa; from on and under the Atlantic Ocean and Mediterranean Sea; and from the fierce German Blitz in the skies over England, the news had come for more than two years.

Now, after December 7, from the Japanese Empire's rapid and brutal onslaught in Asia; the air and seaborne attacks on Pearl Harbor and the Territory of Hawaii, Midway, and Wake Islands; the landing of Japanese troops in Hong Kong, the Philippines, the South Pacific, and Southeast Asia; and the Japanese submarines' presence along their route to San Francisco, with successful attacks and sinkings of American vessels off the West Coast and in Hawaiian waters, came an avalanche of bad news and bitter reality about the conflagration now sweeping the globe—World War II.

Wake Island had fallen while the two teams were en route home, practice and rumor-spawned air-raid drills were in progress up and down the West and East Coasts day and night, and an inadequately prepared America was rushing ground, air, and naval forces to defend the West Coast, while, unknown to the general public, quickly forming convoys that left San Francisco on December 16 and 17 were carrying the army's 34th and 161st Infantry Regiments. Originally intended for the Philippines, loaded with the two regiments were all their supplies, guns, equipment, and ammunition, plus badly needed aircraft parts, bombs, and other supplies to reinforce and resupply Hawaii-based naval, ground, and air units. Three additional ships from San Diego joined the three in the second convoy en route, including two fully loaded navy tankers and an additional transport carrying marines and their command elements.

During the same desperate period, the American armed forces diverted another heavily loaded, seven-ship convoy carrying three National Guard artillery battalions with all their guns, supplies, and ammunition, together with army air force units and their aircraft, bombs, and ammunition, to Australia. Also originally intended for the Philippines, this latter highly classified convoy, personally authorized by President Franklin D. Roosevelt, designated "Operation Plum," and later called the "Pensacola Convoy," had departed Hawaii on November 29, a scant four days before the *Lurline* arrived in Honolulu carrying the happy and excited contingents from Willamette University and San Jose State College.

This would be the beginning of a long, incomprehensively destructive war, the most destructive war in human history, an unforgettable worldwide disaster. But there would be some more temporary happiness and celebration for the Willamette University Bearcats and San Jose State College Spartans and their fans before war would close around and swallow their lives and drown their stories in the endless stream of the war's battles and a worldwide cloud tinted red by blood and darkened with sorrow.

A large, noisy, cheering crowd of approximately one thousand people from Willamette and the university's hometown, roughly one-thirtieth of the city of Salem, including the Willamette band and cheerleaders, lined the tracks and loading platform when the train arrived. Their "war veterans" were safely home from Hawaii and the shattering, disillusioning Japanese attack on Pearl Harbor.

The excitement swept through the crowd, urged on by the Willamette band's fight songs and cheerleaders' yells, marking the beginning of a welcome home and a groundswell of pride mixed with a sense of relief and other emotions the likes of which few had ever witnessed at Oregon's capital city train station. Gone was the sting of defeat on the University of Hawaii gridiron. This was a much greater victory, at least temporarily parting the dark clouds of war the Japanese Empire had spread across the great Pacific Ocean and around the world.

There were parties in their honor and endless questions from faculty, students, friends and relatives, townspeople, and newspaper and radio reporters while the nation was accelerating a massive wartime mobilization. At both San Jose State College and Willamette University, there were requests and invitations to the Pearl Harbor returnees to tell of their experiences, these travelers-turned-observers and participants in a shattering, historical event.

At Willamette, first were welcome-home parties and talks involving women who had accompanied the football team. During the Christmas holidays, Betty Cooper hosted a luncheon party in her home on Salem's Broadway Street in honor of Shirley McKay. Attractive decorations of holly and red tapers were on the luncheon table for the nine women, and in the afternoon Shirley told of her experiences in the war zone.

"Welcome Home" was the theme of a buffet supper for Shirley McKay, at which Mabel McKay, Shirley's mother, was hostess. The supper preceded an informal evening. Holiday decorations were used on the table and about the rooms, adding to the festive occasion for the fourteen attending.

On Monday, January 5, 1942, Miss Jack—Lorena Jack—held the rapt attention of one hundred girls at a sorority house meeting as she told of her experiences and impressions of her trip to Hawaii. Starting with the time the train left the depot in Salem and finishing with the party's arrival home again, she related everything she thought would be of interest to the girls. The leis that were given to visitors, the large bushes of double poinsettias, and the abundance of fresh fruit were among the things that attracted her attention, she said.

A Wednesday, January 14, article in San Jose State College's *Spartan Daily* and two articles in the January 23 Willamette University's *Collegian* indicated a small amount of all the curiosity spreading in Oregon, Washington, California, and beyond the first month and a half of the war about the Bearcats and Spartans football teams and their voyage to Hawaii and back.

At San Jose State College, while team members were asked and did share their experiences following a January 14, 1942, *Spartan Daily* article, "Gridders to Tell of Island Attack," team members seemed less inclined to tell of their experiences on Oahu and during their emotion-filled voyage home on the *Coolidge*. An expression of their reluctance was in the words of San Jose's Sebastian Squatrito, the team's manager and a sports reporter for the *Spartan Daily*. On his return nearly a month earlier, he was asked by the anxious head of the journalism department to produce a story. Squatrito's response: "The games were canceled, so there was no story."

Spec Keene and various members of the Bearcats team who traveled to Hawaii were in great demand as speakers before chambers of commerce, Kiwanis clubs, and other public gatherings. During the weeks following the New Year, Coach Keene spoke before the Portland Chamber of Commerce, Capitol Post No. 9 of the American Legion, the Salem Anglers Club, the Portland Rotary Club, and as guest speaker at the annual banquet given each year in honor of the football team at Portland University.

Others who told of their experiences were Ken Jacobson and Chuck Furno, who spoke on radio station KVAN, Vancouver, Washington, where the two men had been elementary and high school classmates and football teammates before they graduated from Vancouver High School in 1940 and entered Willamette University. Another member of the team, Pat White, was a guest of American Legion Post No. 1 of Portland.

An additional article in the *Collegian*'s January 23 issue, under the tongue-in-cheek headline "Scalping Doesn't Worry Stew; Accepts Chemawa Coach Job," spoke to the past and future for the boys of Willamette's 1941 Bearcats. The article disclosed that the Washington Redskins of the National Professional Football League had notified Gene Stewart on his return from Honolulu that he had been drafted by their organization. The Bearcats' sterling season had drawn that kind of attention to the team and its stars. A senior on the 1941 team, Gene was notified that he had been hired as the new athletic director at Chemawa Indian School, succeeding Doug Olds, a past graduate of Willamette.

But the past and present, along with happiness, glowing memories, and the future, seemed about to vanish. Then came the letters, similar letters signed and sent on the same date,

JAN 7 - 1942

My dear Dr. Knopf:

I am sure you have heard by now of the fine part a squad of athletes from your school played in bringing to this country the first detachment of wounded from Pearl Harbor. Just the same, I would like to share with you and your students a portion of the report turned in by the senior Naval officer aboard the Merchant vessel used to evacuate these brave victims of Japanese treachery. This officer, a Captain in the United States Navy, writes:

"On board, as passengers, were the football squads of Willamette University and San Jose College, in Honolulu for games with the University of Hawaii at the time of the Japanese attack.

"These men, under their respective coaches, volunteered in case of emergency to rescue and place in the ship's boats the seriously wounded men. They drilled at their assignments. In addition, they volunteered to and did feed such wounded as were unable to help themselves. They promoted good morale among the patients in many ways.

"I consider the services rendered by these young men to be very commendable".

No words of mine can add to the sentiments expressed in that brief extract. Both on behalf of the Navy and myself, however, I can express appreciation for the willingness with which these fine young athletes instantly offered their aid in time of danger. That is the spirit which I believe now dominates us all, and which with God's help will carry us to ultimate victory.

Sincerely yours,

Frank Knox

To "Spec" Keene we
owe our deepest
gratitude. His fine
leadership made possible
such commendation.

CARL SUMNER KNOPF

PRESIDENT
WILLAMETTE UNIVERSITY
SALEM, OREGON

Copy of original 7 January 1942 letter of commendation from Secretary of the Navy Frank Knox to Willamette University president Dr. Carl Sumner Knopf, PhD.

January 9, 1942, from Secretary of the Navy Frank Knox to the respective presidents of San Jose State College and Willamette University, Dr. Theodore W. MacQuarrie and Dr. Carl S. Knopf, arriving January 12.

Unknown to all who had excitedly sailed on the voyage to a dream, Secretary Knox was on Oahu during the dark days immediately following the Japanese attack, as those who had first dreamed of paradise and football then voluntarily began serving their nation as young, inexperienced citizen soldiers, policemen, nurses, and nurses' aides in those first days of World War II, wondering if or how they would ever get home. Undoubtedly, when Secretary Knox was doing his preliminary investigation of the disaster that befell the American armed forces, Hawaii, and especially the Pacific Fleet, he learned of the two football teams, coaches, and fans stranded on Oahu. Then he learned of them in different roles, roles he marked in the annals of two of America's many marvelous schools of higher learning.

The stories and legacies of the two teams and their followers are now coming alive as they leave us, one by one, nearly all gone but gradually revived, briefly told, retold, and spread slowly following World War II, almost entirely in magazine and newspaper articles, and finally, many years later, in a brief National Football League narrated video shown on television with commentary. Stories, legacies, a football game never to be forgotten, and a return from hell.

Part II

Duty, Sacrifice, and Honors

CHAPTER TWELVE

Mobilization and Accounting

THE ATTACK ON PEARL HARBOR PROVOKED A PROFOUNDLY RIGHTEOUS ANGER AMONG THE American people. A wave of patriotic indignation over Japanese duplicity and brutality swept the country. Isolationism virtually evaporated as a public issue, and all political parties closed ranks in support of the war effort.

On 11 December 1941, the United States declared war on Germany and Italy, the same day that the two Japanese allies had announced earlier that they were at war with the United States. Indeed, in retrospect, despite the immediate tactical success the Japanese achieved at Pearl Harbor and in the six months afterward, the attack proved to be a monumental blunder. Allied with Nazi Germany and Fascist Italy after signing the Tripartite Agreement of 27 September 1940, Japan, firmly seated in the brutal triumvirate of the new totalitarians of the twentieth century, had fully unleashed the dogs of war in the Pacific. To this day, World War II remains the ultimate measure of worldwide catastrophe and the most destructive war in human history, having taken an estimated sixty million lives.

Early the following month, President Roosevelt dramatized the magnitude of the effort the war demanded by proclaiming a new set of production goals—60,000 airplanes in 1942 and 125,000 in 1943, 45,000 tanks in 1942 and 75,000 in 1943, 20,000 antiaircraft guns in 1942 and 35,000 in 1943, half a million machine guns in 1942 and as many more in 1943, and 8 million deadweight tons of merchant shipping in 1942 and 10 million in 1943.

Vanished were the two illusions that America could serve only as an arsenal of democracy, contributing weapons without the men to wield them, or, conversely, that the nation could rely solely on its own fighting forces, leaving other anti-Axis nations to shift for themselves. "We must not only provide munitions for our own fighting forces," Roosevelt advised Secretary of War Henry L. Stimson, "but vast quantities to be used against the enemy in every appropriate theater of war." A new Victory Program boosted the army's ultimate mobilization goal to ten million men, and the War Department planned to have 71 divisions and 115 combat air groups organized by the end of 1942, with a total of 3.6 million men under arms. As army planners had predicted back in the spring of 1941, the

United States now seemed destined to become "the final reserve of the democracies both in manpower and munitions."

In response to the attack on Pearl Harbor and declarations of war against Japan, Germany, and Italy, the United States mobilized armed forces and a war production base like none ever seen in the history of the world. With the 1940 census reporting a population of slightly more than 131 million, America built the mightiest seagoing fighting force in the history of the world, consisting of forty aircraft carriers, twenty-four battleships, and twenty-four thousand aircraft, manned by 3.3 million men, plus a marine corps of 480,000 men. By June 1944, the number of men and women in uniform had swelled to its peak of more than twelve million, and by war's end more than sixteen million had served in the armed forces.

Complementing the two-ocean power of the U.S. Navy, Marine Corps, and Coast Guard, the nation's shipbuilding industry produced an incomparable sealift capability. When the war began, the United States had only about 1,340 cargo ships and tankers. Despite the loss of 733 merchant ships of more than one thousand gross tons prior to the September 1945 victory over Japan, the number of ships controlled by the War Shipping Administration grew to 4,221 with a deadweight tonnage of 44,940,000. Liberty ships and Victory ships comprised the great majority of additions to the merchant fleet, with approximately 2,400 being Victory ships (with another three hundred built in Canada), an improved and faster cargo carrier constructed beginning in 1942.

This vast fleet of merchant ships carried the materials and men needed for victory to all parts of the world. Between 7 December 1941 and the surrender of Japan, 268,252,000 long tons of cargo left U.S. ports. About three-fourths of this cargo was carried in ships controlled by the War Shipping Administration. Imports during the war ran to 70,652,000 tons of dry cargo and 35,118,000 tons brought back in tankers. A large part of this cargo was carried on ships defended by navy armed guards. From the outbreak of war to 30 November 1945, more than seven million army personnel and more than 141,000 civilians were transported overseas—plus navy men and marines not counted in these totals. The great majority was carried in army and navy transports and merchant ships.

The navy armed 6,236 of these ships to the end of World War II. Of this number, 4,870 were U.S.-flagged ships, 244 were U.S.-owned but under foreign flags, and the rest were foreign-owned and foreign-flag ships. Armed Guards were placed aboard nearly all of the 5,114 U.S.-owned and U.S.-flagged ships.

The Japanese attack on Pearl Harbor and the Philippines resulted in a significant but temporary loss of strength for the U.S. navy and initially placed the navy in a defensive posture in the Pacific. The only weapon system immediately available to take the war to the enemy was the U.S. submarine force. President Roosevelt's prewar decision to conduct "unrestricted submarine warfare" in the event of hostilities with Japan hastened the wartime success. Throughout the war, the growing U.S. submarine force was employed in attacks on Japanese merchant shipping as well as on Japanese fleet units when the opportunity presented itself. In both of these tasks, the American submarine force was aided by Magic intelligence derived from broken Japanese codes. The Japanese navy, with Mahanian intellectual roots, prepared tardily and insufficiently for an undersea onslaught not directly related to the "decisive battle" like those the empire had waged in wars past. The American navy won a spectacular victory.

The Death of Imperial Japan's 7 December Carrier Strike Force

Not one Japanese ship or submarine involved in the attack on Pearl Harbor survived World War II. Following the loss of the first midget submarine to the guns and depth charges of the destroyer *Ward* outside the harbor early the morning of 7 December, the first major submarine sunk was I-70 on 10 December, the victim of Lieutenant Clarence Dickinson's dive-bomb attack launched from the carrier *Enterprise*. The first Japanese surface vessel lost was the carrier *Soryu*, at 1910 hours on 4 June 1942, in the Battle of Midway, followed fifteen minutes later by the sinking of the carrier *Kaga*.

Akagi and *Hiryu* were also sunk at Midway. They were the last of four veteran Pearl Harbor carriers sunk at Midway. The final two Pearl Harbor carriers, *Shokaku* and *Zuikaku*, were at the Battle of the Coral Sea but missed Midway and remained in operation until the United States was deep into its strategic offensive in 1944. The *Shokaku* was sunk 19 June 1944, during the Battle of the Philippine Sea by the submarine *Cavalla*, operating from Pearl Harbor. The *Zuikaku* was sunk off Cape Engano by American carrier aircraft on 25 October 1944.

On 15 June 1944, after Vice Admiral Jisaburo Ozawa's failed naval Battle of the Philippine Sea, in which the Japanese lost five hundred aircraft, Vice Admiral Chuichi Nagumo, who commanded the carrier strike force at Pearl Harbor, and his army peer, General Yoshitsugu Saito, attempted to defend the island of Saipan against the American assault. On 6 July, in the final stages of the Battle of Saipan, Nagumo committed suicide, not in the traditional method of seppuku, but rather by a pistol to the temple. His remains were later found by American marines in the cave where he spent his last days as commander of the Saipan defenders. The Japanese posthumously promoted him to admiral.

The last survivor of Admiral Nagumo's 7 December carrier strike force was the heavy cruiser *Tone*. She was caught and sunk at her moorings at Kure, in the Inland Sea, in the great raid of 24 July 1945 when American and British carrier groups put 1,747 of their aircraft over the Inland Sea, its bays, its harbors, and its islands.

On 18 April 1943, by coincidence Easter Sunday and the first anniversary of the Doolittle Raid, in a mission designated Operation Vengeance, Admiral Isoroku Yamamoto, commander of the Combined Fleet and architect of the Japanese attack on Pearl Harbor, was killed on Bougainville Island in the Solomon Islands when his Mitsubishi G4M "Betty" transport bomber was shot down by army air force P-38G aircraft flying out of Henderson Field on Guadalcanal.

On 14 April, the U.S. naval intelligence effort code-named "Magic" intercepted and decrypted orders alerting affected Japanese units in the I-Go operation—the disastrous Japanese withdrawal from Guadalcanal—to a morale-building tour of the units by Yamamoto.

Information was passed to President Roosevelt, who requested that Secretary of the Navy Frank Knox "get Yamamoto." Admiral Nimitz consulted with Admiral Halsey, and

Vice Admiral Chuichi Nagumo, who commanded the Carrier Strike Force at Pearl Harbor, and his army peer General Yoshitsugu Saito attempted to defend the island of Saipan against the American assault. On 6 July 1944, in the final stages of the Battle of Saipan, Nagumo committed suicide. The Japanese government posthumously promoted him to admiral. (*Source*: NHHC)

Admiral Isoroku Yamamoto, Imperial Japanese Navy, was killed on Bougainville Island in the Solomons 18 April 1943, by coincidence Easter Sunday and the first anniversary of the Doolittle Raid on Tokyo, when his Mitsubishi G4M "Betty" transport bomber was shot down by army air force P-38G aircraft flying out of Henderson Field on Guadalcanal. Portrait photograph, taken during the early 1940s, when he was commander in chief, Combined Fleet. (*Source*: NHHC)

because navy fighters hadn't the range to carry out the mission, it fell to the army air force's 339th Fighter Squadron, 347th Fighter Group, 13th Air Force. In a near perfectly planned and flown mission assigned the eighteen aircraft in the 339th, Yamamoto's aircraft was intercepted and shot down after a two-hour-and-nine-minute flight to the planned intercept point. (Ten of the pilots came from the other 347th squadrons.)

A "Killer Flight" of four P-38s led the low-level mission fifty feet above the wave tops to a point short of the intercept where the remaining fourteen, which included two spares, climbed to eighteen thousand feet and provided top cover against expected reactions by Japanese Zeroes flying top cover for the two Bettys. The mission proved to be the longest intercept mission of the war. Both Bettys were shot down, the second carrying members of Yamamoto's staff. But the war's road to that point for the Allies had been long and hard.

The shattering truth of World War II for America was the staggering casualties. In 1,364 days of war beginning on 7 December 1941 through the Japanese surrender on the deck of the battleship *Missouri* on 2 September 1945, America suffered 435,399 dead and 670,846 wounded, a total of 1,106,245—an average of 811 per day, with an average of 319 dead per day.

Among the dead were 78,976 Americans missing, later declared dead. In the twelve-month period beginning in June 1944, when America and its Allies were on the offensive in every theater of war, America suffered casualties averaging sixty-five thousand per month, killed, wounded, or missing. Only the nation's nineteenth-century Civil War, when Americans bitterly fought one another, surpassed World War II in the number killed on both sides.

THE FATE OF THE SHIPS ON WHICH THE BEARCATS AND SPARTANS SAILED

The Matson Line's SS *Lurline*, which took the Willamette and Spartan contingents on their Voyage to Paradise, shortly thereafter, with her sister ships *Matsonia* and *Monterey* in Convoy 2005—in the first troopship convoy to leave the West Coast after the war began—brought 9,918 troops with all their equipment, supplies, and guns to reinforce units in Hawaii.

The same ships then carried the first full load of evacuees, 3,504—the great majority women and children, including fifty-seven wounded on *Lurline* with 1,807 other evacuees, and a lesser number on *Monterey*—home from Hawaii in the period 26–31 December 1941.

Lurline and her sister ships all survived the war with distinguished records of service—along with Matson's fourth great passenger liner of that era, SS *Mariposa*, the sister ship of *Lurline* and *Monterey* not mentioned in this work. Table 1 tells of the liners' magnificent wartime contributions to the nation and its armed forces.

After *Lurline*'s postwar conversion and rebirth as a luxurious ocean liner, still under the direction of Captain Charles A. Berndtson, she would later be shown in a closing scene in the movie *From Here to Eternity*, the 1953 film that won six Academy Awards, including Best Picture. To this day, images of her can still be found on the internet, at https://www.youtube .com/watch?v=qsUOQWGgVWc and https://www.youtube.com/watch?v=0gbEAbhSJtg.

The light cruiser *Detroit* (CL-8) and the destroyer *Cummings* (DD-365) both survived World War II with distinguished records of service.

Table 1. Distinguished Wartime Records of Matson Liners

Vessel	Number of Voyages	Miles Steamed	Total Passengers Carried	Total Meals Served
Lurline	31	388,847	199,860	9,322,706
Average/voyage		12,544	6,447	300,732
Matsonia	33	328,301	163,732	6,526,524
Average/voyage		9,949	4,962	197,773
Monterey	26	328,490	170,240	8,663,471
Average/voyage		12,634	6,547	333,210
Mariposa	29	414,589	202,689	10,571,670
Average/voyage		14,296	6,989	364,540
Grand Total	119	1,460,227	736,521	35,084,371
Average/voyage		12,271	6,189	294,827

After the attack on Pearl Harbor, where *Detroit* escaped damage, she completed her convoy duties, which extended into 1942. She then sailed from San Francisco on 10 November 1942 for Kodiak, Alaska, to become flagship for commander, Task Group 8.6, and patrol between Adak and Attu to prevent further enemy penetration of the Aleutians. On 12 January 1943, she covered the unopposed landings made on Amchitka to gain a base from which to cut the Japanese supply line, and, after repairs at Bremerton in February and March 1943, she returned to patrol duty to intercept reinforcements trying to reach the Japanese garrisons on Kiska and Attu. In April she bombarded Holtz Bay and Chicago Harbor on Attu, returning the next month to join in the assault and capture of the island. In August she took part in the bombardments of Kiska, then covered the landings on 15 August, which revealed that the island, the last outpost held by the Japanese in the Aleutians, had been secretly evacuated.

Detroit remained in Alaskan waters until 1944, operating with the covering group for the western Aleutian bases. In June 1944, she saw action with Task Force 94 during the bombardment of shore installations in the Kuriles. She sailed from Adak on 25 June and, after repairs at Bremerton, arrived at Balboa on 9 August to serve as temporary flagship of the Southeast Pacific Force. She patrolled on the west coast of South America until December.

Clearing San Francisco on 16 January 1945, *Detroit* arrived at Ulithi on 4 February for duty with the 5th Fleet. She acted as flagship for the replenishment group serving the fast carrier task forces until the end of the war and entered Tokyo Bay on 1 September. *Detroit* continued to direct replenishment operations for the occupation fleet and, in addition, the repatriation of Japanese to the home islands from Pacific bases. She left Tokyo Bay on 15 October for the States with returning servicemen on board as part of Operation Magic Carpet, the massive sealift bringing Americans home from World War II. *Detroit* was decommissioned at Philadelphia on 11 January 1946 and sold on 27 February 1946.

Detroit received six battle stars for World War II service.

When the Japanese attacked Pearl Harbor on 7 December 1941, the destroyer *Cummings* (DD-365) weathered bombs, which fell ahead and astern, receiving only minor casualties from fragments, and sortied on patrol almost immediately. From 19 December 1941 to 4 May 1942, *Cummings* escorted convoys, including Task Group 15.2, between Pearl Harbor and San Francisco, then sailed between Suva, Fiji Islands, and Auckland, New Zealand, from 9 June to 13 August on similar duty.

After overhaul at San Francisco, *Cummings* escorted a convoy to Noumea and Wellington, New Zealand, in November 1942, then began patrol and escort missions for the Guadalcanal operation from bases at Espiritu Santo and Noumea until 17 May 1943, when she sailed to Auckland, New Zealand, for a brief overhaul. Returning to Noumea on 4 June, *Cummings* screened transports to Auckland in July, then served at Efate from 5 August until 4 September.

Overhauled on the West Coast again, *Cummings* joined Task Force 94 to patrol off Adak, Alaska, between 1 and 16 December before returning to Pearl Harbor on 21 December. Assigned to the 5th Fleet, she sortied on 19 January 1944 for the Marshall Islands operations, accompanying the carriers for air strikes on Wotje and Eniwetok until 21 February. *Cummings* sailed from Majuro 4 March for Trincomalee, Ceylon, where she rendezvoused on 31 March with British ships for exercises. She sailed on 16 April with British Force 70 to screen during air strikes on Sabang, Sumatra, on 19 April, then returned to Ceylon until 6 May, when she cleared for Exmouth Gulf, Australia. With British Force 66, she sortied on 15 May for air strikes on Soerabaja, Java, and then left the British forces and returned by way of Sydney to Pearl Harbor.

Arriving at San Francisco on 7 July 1944, *Cummings* sailed on 21 July to escort President F. D. Roosevelt embarked in the cruiser *Baltimore* (CA-68) to Pearl Harbor, Adak, and Juneau. The president and his staff came aboard on 8 August for transportation to Seattle, and upon arrival there, on 12 August, President Roosevelt broadcast a nationwide address from the forecastle of *Cummings*.

Departing Seattle on 13 August 1944, *Cummings* joined Task Group 12.5 at Pearl Harbor for an air strike and shore bombardment of Wake Island on 3 September. With the 3rd Fleet, she joined in the bombardment of Marcus Island on 9 October, then screened the escort carriers as they launched the supporting air strikes on Luzon, Cebu, Leyte, Samar, and Negros during the Leyte landings and gallantly engaged the Japanese in the decisive Battle for Leyte Gulf. She took part in the bombardment of Iwo Jima on 11 and 12 November, and then she returned to Saipan on 21 November for local duty.

She interrupted this duty to join in the repeated strikes on Iwo Jima from 8 December 1944 to 19 March 1945, when she supplied fire support for the invading troops. She was stationed off Iwo Jima, occasionally escorting convoys to Saipan and Guam until the end of the war. Her duties included local convoy escort and control duty and the important air-sea rescue work that accompanied the intensified strikes on Okinawa and the Japanese home islands. She supervised the occupation of Haha Jima on 9 September, then sailed from Iwo

Jima on 19 September for San Pedro, California; Tampa, Florida; and Norfolk, Virginia. *Cummings* was decommissioned on 14 December 1945 and sold on 17 July 1947.

The USS *Cummings* (DD-365) received seven battle stars for service during World War II.

The destroyer *Reid* (DD-369), which participated with the cruiser *Detroit* and the destroyer *Cummings* in Task Group 15.2 during the first forty-six hours of escorting the *Coolidge* and *Scott* from Honolulu to San Francisco from 19 to 25 December, was less fortunate despite her distinguished World War II service.

During the attack on Pearl Harbor, *Reid* fired at the Japanese planes, and her group of destroyers downed one. After the attack, *Reid* patrolled off the Hawaiian Islands, Palmyra Atoll, and Johnston Island in December. In January 1942, she escorted a convoy to San Francisco. Following patrol off Hawaii, she steamed to Midway Island and then twice escorted convoys from Pearl Harbor to San Francisco.

Departing Pearl Harbor on 22 May, *Reid* steamed north to bombard Japanese positions on Kiska Island, Alaska, on 7 August. She supported landings at Adak, Alaska, on 30 August and sank by gunfire the Japanese submarine RO-1 on the 31st. After transferring five prisoners to Dutch Harbor, Alaska, she patrolled near New Caledonia, Samoa, and the Fiji Islands during October and November.

Departing Suva Harbor, Fiji Islands, on Christmas Day 1942, she escorted army troops to Guadalcanal before guarding a convoy to Espiritu Santo, New Hebrides. In January 1943, she bombarded several enemy locations on Guadalcanal.

After patrols in the Solomon Islands, *Reid* provided radar information and fighter direction for landings at Lae, New Guinea, on 4 September. While supporting landings at Finschhafen, New Guinea, on the 22nd, she downed two enemy planes.

After patrol and escort duty off New Guinea, she sailed from Buna Roads, New Guinea, to escort troop transports to landings at Arawe, New Britain, on 15 December 1943. She protected landings at Cape Gloucester, New Britain, on the 26th and at Saidor, New Guinea, on 2 January 1944. She guarded landings at Los Negros Island, Admiralty Islands, on 29 February and at Hollandia, New Guinea, on 22 April. Her guns supported landings at Wake Island on 17 May, at Biak on the 27th, and at Noemfoor Island, New Guinea, on 2 July.

Departing Pearl Harbor on 29 August, she supported air strikes against Wake Island on 3 September. After patrols off Leyte, Philippine Islands, in November she steamed to Ormoc Bay, Leyte. She supported landings there on December 7 and escorted the damaged *Lamson* (DD-367) toward Leyte Gulf.

Escorting reinforcements for Ormoc Bay near Surigao Straits in the Philippines on 11 December 1944, *Reid* sank in approximately two minutes after being hit by two of seven kamikazes. One of the landing craft (LSM 42) accompanying the force of seven destroyers picked up more than one hundred of her crew members, many seriously wounded, and 103 others lost their lives in the violent explosions and rapid sinking.

Reid received seven battle stars for World War II service.

Neither *Coolidge* nor *Scott*, which made up the first convoy to San Francisco from Honolulu, survived the war. The *Hugh L. Scott* met her end at the hands of a German U-boat in waters off North Africa during Operation Torch, America's first major offensive operation across the Atlantic against the Axis Powers.

The *Hugh L. Scott* was taken over by the navy on 14 August 1942; converted to an attack transport in Hoboken, New Jersey; and sailed to join Task Force 34 in Norfolk, Virginia. After loading troops and equipment for Operation Torch, the invasion of North Africa, the task force sailed on 24 and 25 October for the coast of Morocco. Assigned to Task Group 34.9, Center Attack Group, *Scott* arrived off Fedhala, Morocco, on November 8.

The *President Coolidge*, sinking on 26 October 1942 after hitting two mines while traversing the Scorff Passage into Segond Channel, Espiritu Santo Island, New Hebrides. Troops of the 172nd Regimental Combat Team, the 43rd Division, climb down ropes and cargo nets to escape as the ship lists to port at a rate of about one degree per minute. Some are fortunate to be taken to shore by lifeboat or raft, while others must swim. Two men lost their lives in the tragic accident, which could have been far worse had it not been for the actions of Captain Henry Nelson, his crew, and the disciplined response by the officers and men of the 172nd RCT. (*Source*: NA)

The evening of 12 November, after offloading her troops and cargo, she was riding at anchor in Fedhala Roads when the German submarine U-130 slipped in among the ships and fired five torpedoes at three transports. All torpedoes hit their targets, and they burst into flames. Tasker *Bliss, Scott*, and the *Edward Rutledge* (AP-52) were U-130's victims. The crews abandoned all three, and the *Rutledge* and *Scott* sank shortly. The *Bliss* burned until 0230 the next morning and then sank. Casualties among the three ships were eight officers and fifty-one men.

On 26 October 1942, in the Pacific, while the major naval battle of Santa Cruz was in progress three hundred miles north, another drama was taking place at the island of Espiritu Santo. The former American President Lines' magnificent cruise ship, SS *President Coolidge*, converted to a troopship following the attack on Pearl Harbor, and with the *Hugh L. Scott*, the first to carry evacuees from Honolulu to San Francisco after the attack, was carrying 5,050 army troops, 50 navy armed guards (members of deck gun crews assigned to defend merchant vessels), and Signal personnel, plus 340 ship's crew, when she struck two mines in a defensive minefield and sank in ninety minutes.

Bound for Espiritu Santo in the New Hebrides Islands from Noumea, New Caledonia, Captain Henry Nelson's ship attempted to enter Segond Channel from the east through Scorff Passage rather than from the south between Acore Island and Tutuba Island. The tragic accident came thirteen weeks after the destroyer *Tucker*, a Pearl Harbor survivor, fell victim to another minefield at the south entrance to Segond Channel while turning north from Bruat Channel. The two mines that *Coolidge* struck were part of a barrier of mines intended to block enemy penetration of the anchorage and huge staging base through Scorff Passage.

Though the *Coolidge* was a great loss to the Allied cause, the incident was intensely controversial and later the subject of three courts of inquiry. Captain Nelson averted a major disaster by acting quickly after the two mines exploded, the first on the port side beneath the engine room at 0935 hours. The ship maintained forward momentum, and thirty seconds later the second mine blasted the starboard bottom plates amidships, also near the engine room. After rapidly obtaining sketchy damage reports, he correctly concluded that he was going to lose the ship. He ordered all watertight doors closed, followed by "hard right rudder" to take advantage of the headway to turn the ship directly into shore and beach her in shallow water. At 0938 the ship struck the coral ledge fifty meters from the shore, and Captain Nelson immediately called, "Abandon ship!"

Miraculously, in the next ninety minutes, all but two men escaped the sinking *Coolidge*, which heeled to port, capsized as she was going down, and slid stern first down a steep bank toward deeper water. The first was fireman Robert Reid, who was working in the engine room and was killed by the initial mine blast. The second was Captain Elwood J. Euart of the 103rd Field Artillery, attached to the 172nd Infantry Regiment aboard, who was the troop mess officer on duty in the enlisted men's mess hall and personally checked the clearing of the area when the alarm sounded.

On arriving at his abandon-ship station, he learned of men trapped in the hold and went there. By lashing himself to the low end of a rope, he was able to hold tight enough for men to climb up it to safety, even though the ship was listing badly. Finally, as he attempted to climb up, almost vertically by that moment, with the help of a few men at the other end of the line, the ship sank very quickly. "For his unselfish, heroic action and with utter disregard for his own safety, Captain Euart conducted himself far above and beyond the call of duty, saved countless lives and gave his life that others might live." So stated the citation accompanying the posthumous award of the Distinguished Service Cross.

The evacuation of more than twenty thousand dependents and nonessential personnel from the Territory of Hawaii continued into the fall of 1942, fortunately with no losses of en route passenger carriers or escorting combatants, while the buildup of American forces in the Pacific continued at an accelerated rate.

World War II's Effects on Collegiate Football

The Japanese attack on Pearl Harbor and America's massive mobilization had a profound effect on collegiate football, as well as on every other facet of American life. The war initially drained college campuses of athletes and the ability to financially, and in terms of people available, support intercollegiate athletics. Football, the acknowledged "manly sport" that had long before the war been an active part of competition between military units, garrisons, and posts, quite literally joined the armed forces, with armed services' teams—excluding Army and Navy, the service academy teams—appearing in national rankings in 1943 and 1944. In the period 1941–1943, nearly every member of the Willamette and San Jose State teams eventually donned military and other service uniforms to serve their nation, with many of them fighting in the great battles across the Atlantic and Pacific Oceans.

Top ten national rankings in 1943 included Iowa Pre-Flight at no. 2, Great Lakes at no. 6, Del Monte Pre-Flight at no. 8, and March Field at no. 10. Army and Navy, whose long-standing, popular collegiate rivalry dated to 1890, had figured in national rankings off and on preceding World War II and remained in the national spotlight during the war. Navy ranked no. 4 in 1943 and 1944, while Army was no. 11 in 1943 and won the mythical national championships in 1944 and 1945 and in 1946 was undefeated. That year, under Coach Earl H. "Red" Blaik—a 1920 academy graduate who resigned his commission in 1922 and was recalled to active duty as an army lieutenant colonel during the war—they shared the national title with Notre Dame after their "Game of the Century" 0–0 tie in New York City's Yankee Stadium.

The abbreviated season of 1943 at Willamette and 1942 at San Jose State College and the University of Hawaii marked the beginning of a full three-year football "time out" at the three institutions—until the nation's veterans returned home to continue their lives, educations, and, in many cases, further participation in collegiate sports. Thus, following the war, campuses were once again swelled, this time by the flood of returning veterans with the added incentives of the "G.I. Bill" to obtain or complete educations. As a result, generally, with the exceptions of some privately endowed colleges and universities, campus populations resumed growing with the nation's population.

As examples, in 2015 San Jose State University and the University of Hawaii would both compete in Division IA football, in the Mountain West Conference, against teams such as the University of Nevada; the University of Nevada, Las Vegas; Colorado State; Boise State; Utah State; Fresno State; Wyoming; the Air Force Academy; and San Diego State, while Willamette University, a privately endowed university, eventually entered a growing National Collegiate Athletic Association, Division III system, and continues to compete in Division III in the Northwest Conference.

On Oahu in those fateful December days, the 1941 football teams of San Jose State College and Willamette University had been at first involuntarily mobilized, and subsequently they voluntarily joined the millions of "boys" who were forced by circumstances to grow up quickly. At the earliest, bloody beginning, as witnesses and participants, where "uncommon valor became common," they were two small groups of men and women who earned everlasting recognition and commemoration among an entire generation of Americans whose love of country, sense of duty, and willingness to sacrifice quite literally saved their country—and civilization.

CHAPTER THIRTEEN

Changed Directions in Life

"IT [THE ATTACK ON PEARL HARBOR] AFFECTED THE TRAJECTORY OF ALL THEIR LIVES," said Debra Fitzgerald, an attorney in Alaska, whose father, James Fitzgerald, was a Willamette player. "Not only the bombing, which was shocking and dramatic," she added. "What was a more lasting impression was having to care for the wounded on the way home. My dad was 21; they were all just kids."

In the same interview with journalist Frank Marqua of the Santa Rosa, California, *Press Democrat*, Debra Fitzgerald recalled seeing a picture of some of her dad's team aboard the *Lurline* when the two teams were leaving San Francisco on 27 November 1941. "Their youthful enthusiasm was hard to miss." Yet in the Willamette team's season photograph, she described him as looking somewhat like a thug. James Martin Fitzgerald had been in spring football practice at Oregon University when persuaded by Coach Keene to enter Willamette and play on the Bearcats' Hawaii-bound team, and he went on to become an attorney and judge in Alaska after the war, serving in state and federal courts for nearly fifty years before retiring in 2009 to live in Santa Rosa, California.

During the war, Willamette's James Fitzgerald and Charles Furno and San Jose State's Hans Wiedenhoefer served in the Pacific theater, as did Willamette's Andy Rogers, Buddy Reynolds, Ted Ogdahl, and Native American Gilbert Cecil Conner, all in the marines, except for Furno, who flew P-38L's in the Philippines, a fighter-bomber in the army air force. Fitzgerald flew as a radioman/ventral gunner on bombing missions in the big, heavy, slow, single-engine TBF and TBM Avenger torpedo bombers beginning near Espiritu Santo, the largest of the New Hebrides Islands, which now comprise the nation of Vanuatu. Ironically, in Pacific waters surrounding Espiritu Santo rested the hulk of the *President Coolidge* during the entire period James Fitzgerald was flying combat missions in that part of the world. His, Andy Rogers's, Buddy Reynolds's, and Ted Ogdahl's wartime experiences could fill a book with powerful emotions involving battle and close encounters with death.

The great majority of the San Jose State and Willamette players served in the military. Those who were accepted enlisted. What moved them to enlist varied widely, but Willamette's

Andy Rogers shed some light on at least one reason enlistments were high—most wanted to avoid being drafted, because when Selective Service numbers were called, the draftee hadn't a choice as to which service to enter and would enter at the lowest level of responsibility and commensurate grade (rank), such as private or seaman.

How were some of the men at Willamette able to wait to the last minute to avoid the draft? Irving E. Miller, a backup halfback in the 6 December game against Hawaii and one of Andy's Bearcat team members, was married, and his wife, Marcella, served as secretary on the local draft board. She had knowledge of the Selective Service numbers of the local boys being called up and, of course, the numbers of local boys nearing call-up. She would phone and tip them off when their numbers were approaching the top of the list. It was a surreptitious means of taking care of the local boys to avoid a "no-choice" service experience and provide them with options as to the services the boys might desire—not an uncommon practice throughout the nation.

Many members of both football teams saw combat over the next three and a half years, in both the Pacific and the Atlantic–European–North African–Italian campaigns. One Spartan, center and co-captain Robert Hamill, saw action in three wars: World War II as a bomber pilot flying B-25 combat missions in the European theater, where he was shot down twice; additionally in the 1948 Berlin Airlift; and then in Korea and Vietnam as a base commander. He died in 2002, three days shy of his eighty-fourth birthday.

The square-jawed San Jose player, German-born Hans Wiedenhoefer, who had assisted the Honolulu police and federal investigators in arresting suspected Japanese spies immediately following the attack on Pearl Harbor, had a Forrest Gump–like experience. He was in the marines in the Pacific theater on the island of Iwo Jima on Mt. Suribachi's slopes, and he reached its highest point later in the day after five marines and a navy corpsman hoisted an American flag atop the bitterly contested mountain. The hoisting of the American flag on Suribachi became a world-famous photograph and the subject of the Marine Corps' Iwo Jima Monument in Washington, DC. The Battle of Iwo Jima was the bloodiest battle in marine history and one of the nation's bloodiest in the Pacific war. Journalist Frank Marqua is researching and writing a biography about Hans Wiedenhoefer.

Jack Galvin, right end for the Spartans, who found himself helping to deliver a baby in the mother's home while on patrol with a policeman on Oahu one night following the Japanese attack, graduated with a major in art. He then enlisted in the marines and served as a cartographer in American Samoa for most of World War II. On returning, he entered education and primarily taught art in high school. He died in April 2012 in Citrus Heights, California, at age ninety.

REUNION AND HONORS IN SAN JOSE

In 1991, each stateside 1941 football team had its own gathering to mark the fiftieth anniversary of the event that changed their lives. After several days of reunion activities, on Saturday afternoon, 16 November, in San Jose, seventeen Spartans still living at that time were given a tailgate party before the San Jose State University's football game against the

University of Hawaii Rainbow Warriors. Once they were seated in the university's stadium for the 1:30 kickoff, they were named as honorary captains of the Spartan team. During a halftime ceremony on the field, as part of the fiftieth anniversary remembrance of the Japanese attack on Pearl Harbor, they were honored and given an ovation by the crowd.

The game proved exciting as the two teams fought to a 35–35 tie, with San Jose State missing a forty-eight-yard field goal attempt five seconds before the final whistle, the third field goal attempt the Spartans missed in the game—in an era of collegiate football before rule changes provided for overtime periods to break ties.

In an article dated November 16, 1991, in the *San Jose Mercury News*, writer Dan Hruby recounted a number of recollections shared by the 1941 team. Among them was former halfback Bill Rhyne of Redding, California, who at age sixty-nine was a retired teacher and coach. Another was Gray McConnell, sixty-nine, a semiretired moving company employee who was the only survivor of the three players who had witnessed the capsizing of the USS *Oklahoma* during the attack, the other two—Allan Hardisty and Charlie Cook—when they were on a picnic with three University of Hawaii coeds. John Brown, a retired food products salesman, and an eighth man who almost remained with seven others to serve in the Honolulu Police Department, told how co-captain Bob Hamill, on the dock while preparing to embark on the *Coolidge*, had persuaded him at the last minute to come home with the rest of the team, leaving behind police uniforms John had already ordered. After he returned home on the *Coolidge*, he enlisted in the army air force and served five years.

Over the years, considerable curiosity had grown about the seven Spartans who remained on Oahu to work with the Honolulu police. Not everyone was eager to go home following the Japanese attack. Fred Lindsey and Ken Stanger, who became friends later in life when they both worked at Fremont High in Sunnyvale, joined the Honolulu police force. Stanger, a retired principal from Lynbrook High School, California, in his November 1991 recollections provided to Dan Hruby, said, "The military governor soon froze everyone in their jobs, a freeze that lasted two years." Fullback Fred Lindsey stayed five years. Halfback Paul Tognetti married a local girl and stayed in Hawaii permanently. Joseph Allen, Chet Carsten, and Jack Lercari stayed for varying periods, as did Bill Donnelly, who tragically died of a ruptured appendix thirteen months later.

Paul Tognetti was a sophomore quarterback for San Jose State. In *An Era of Change: Oral Histories of Civilians in World War II Hawaii* (University of Hawaii, Manoa), Tognetti told interviewer Joe Rossi in 1992, "So I was there with my little riot gun and hoped nothing would come in. And martial law was declared. Everybody had to be off the streets. And the Marines were on the waterfront, and anything that moved, their machine guns went all night." Tognetti, who remained in Honolulu, some years later, at ninety-one, said in his oral history interview, "After about a week, the word got around, 'Hey, any of you guys want to stay here?' And some of us got together and said, 'Hey, let's stay here.' And we joined the police force."

At the reunion before the Hawaii game in San Jose, Jack Lercari repeated what most of the seven who had stayed and served in the Honolulu police had said. The wages were an incentive to stay. "I had been making 36 cents an hour working on a farm at home," he told the *San Jose Mercury News*. "We were offered $166 a month to stay. Good money at that time." Five of those who stayed eventually made it back to the mainland—the exceptions being Paul Tognetti and Bill Donnelly. Most of the five went into education.

Lindsey and Stanger both became teachers and coaches. Born a week apart in 1920, they died within a year of each other, Lindsey in 2004 at eighty-three and Stanger in 2005 at eighty-four.

Lercari turned to coaching and teaching at Camarillo High School in Ventura before he went on to coach at Menlo College. He died in 2009 at eighty-nine. Joseph Allen returned to his hometown of Red Bluff, serving in the fire department for more than fifty years. The fire department training center is named in his honor. He died in 2006 at eighty-seven.

KENNETH C. BAILEY, "LITTLE PEARL HARBOR,"
AND THE MEMORIAL CHAPEL AT SAN JOSE STATE

The Spartan football team's experiences in their voyage to Hawaii and eventual return on Christmas Day in 1941 became one of many stark reminders that San Jose State College's students, graduates, and faculty would pay a heavy price in the war years ahead. As a result, the college dedicated its 1942 annual, *La Torre*, to the men and women in the uniform of the armed forces of the United States.

San Jose's Kenneth Cecil Bailey was born at Marshfield, Oregon, on October 22, 1921, the son of Wilber E. and Latitia N. Bailey. In 1925, the family returned to San Jose, California, and Kenneth attended the Pala School, east of San Jose near Alum Rock foothills, for

Four of the nine on the San Jose State College wrestling team. On the left, Dave Hines, killed in action during World War II, a close friend of Bert Robinson; third from left, Kenneth Bailey, also killed in action in a German bombing raid on ships in the harbor of Bari, Italy, on 2 December 1943. (*Source*: SJSULA)

the first three grades. The rest of his grammar school education was under the tutelage of his mother at the Lakeside School on the Black Road above Los Gatos. The first two years of his secondary education were spent at the Los Gatos High School. During his junior and senior years, he attended and lived at the Montezuma School in the mountains above Los Gatos.

In 1938, he entered San Jose State College, majoring in philosophy and psychology, with the ultimate objective of preparing for the ministry. He was active in YMCA work, leading a group of "Friendly Indians" in Los Gatos, and in the youth work of the Presbyterian church. In college he was a member of the freshman and varsity football teams, and during his last quarter, he contended as a heavyweight wrestler for the school.

After graduating from San Jose State in 1942, he enlisted in the army on 18 August, was inducted on 1 September, assigned to the Quartermaster Corps, and sent to Camp Lee, Virginia, for training. On 2 January 1943, he entered officer candidate school at Camp Lee. On receiving his commission three months later, he was assigned to Fort Knox, Kentucky, for mess officer training. From there it was back to Camp Lee, where he was transferred to the transportation corps and assigned duty as a cargo security officer, working out of the Cargo Security Detachment, New York Port of Embarkation.

In this capacity he made two Atlantic convoy crossings from New York to Liverpool, England, then requested a more dangerous assignment. The next crossing was from the port of Philadelphia, on the Liberty ship *John L. Motley*, which was heavily loaded with ammunition and high-octane gasoline. From Philadelphia, the *John L. Motley* sailed to Lynnhaven Roads, Virginia, where she joined Convoy UGS-22, which left Lynnhaven on 25 October 1943, bound ultimately for Bari, Italy, arriving on 28 November via Oran, Algeria, and Augusta, Sicily. The evening of 2 December 1943, she was moored among twenty-nine other ships of American, British, Polish, Norwegian, and Dutch registry—in a brightly lit harbor operating at full capacity to expedite the unloading of supplies supporting Allied forces engaged in the battle for Rome. The adjoining port city held a civilian population of approximately 250,000.

Bari, a British-controlled and managed port on the lower, southeast Italian (Adriatic) coast, had inadequate air defense, and no Royal Air Force fighter squadrons were based there, while fighters within range were assigned to offensive, bomber-escort duties, not port defense. Ground defenses were ineffective. All this in spite of the fact that the port was a major transshipment point for the British 8th Army and other Allied armies prosecuting the Italian campaign.

On the afternoon of 2 December, Luftwaffe pilot First Lieutenant Werner Hahn made a reconnaissance flight over Bari at twenty-three thousand feet in a Messerschmitt Me 210. Because he received no ground fire, he made a second pass, then turned north for home. His report resulted in altered plans involving Luftlotte 2, commanded by Luftwaffe general field marshal Wolfram von Richthofen, a cousin of the famous World War I fighter pilot, Manfred von Richthofen, who was killed during that war and became known by many students of military history as the "Red Baron."

Richthofen had offered Bari to his boss, Field Marshal Kesselring, as an alternative target to the one being considered—the 15th Air Force airfields at Foggia, Italy, seventy-five miles north. Richthofen believed that crippling the port might slow the advance of the British 8th Army. His assessment proved prophetic.

The 15th Air Force was building up after being activated in November, and its headquarters were moving into Bari. Its commander, army air force Major General Jimmy Doolittle, the internationally known leader of the sixteen carrier-based B-25s against Japan in April 1942, had just arrived in Bari one day earlier. The Germans, certain the Allies would expect that any raid on the port would come from the north, planned a route that would bring them into the target from the south. The result was a total surprise and a disaster for the Allies, so destructive that it would later earn the title "Little Pearl Harbor."

The attack began at 1925 hours (7:25 p.m.) when two or three German aircraft circled the harbor at ten thousand feet, dropping Duppel (thin foil strips) to confuse Allied radar. Flares were also dropped but weren't needed due to the harbor's being well illuminated. The bomber force of 105 Ju-88 A-4s came in at low altitude to stay below radar and was able to bomb with great accuracy. Arriving on schedule, Flight Lieutenant Gustav Teuber, leading the first wave of bombers, could not believe his eyes. The scene below was too good to be true—brilliantly lit, cranes lifting cargo from ships' holds, and the east jetty crowded with ships.

The raid lasted twenty minutes that seemed to inflict horror for an endless duration, with sunk and burning ships spread throughout the devastated harbor. Windows were shattered

Memorial chapel marble walls, containing 3,095 names of the missing, including Kenneth C. Bailey, San Jose State graduate in the class of 1942 and member of the Spartans' 1941 football team, killed in action in the harbor at Bari, Italy, the night of 2 December 1943. The inscription on the chapel wall reads, "HERE ARE RECORDED THE NAMES OF AMERICANS WHO GAVE THEIR LIVES IN THE SERVICE OF THEIR COUNTRY AND WHO SLEEP IN UNKNOWN GRAVES." (*Source*: ABMC)

seven miles distant by explosions on two ammunition ships. A sheet of burning fuel spread over much of the harbor when a bulk fuel pipeline on a quay was severed and the gushing oil ignited. The burning fuel engulfed otherwise undamaged ships.

Seventeen merchant ships carrying more than thirty-four thousand short tons of cargo were sunk or destroyed, three of which were later salvaged. Five of the seventeen were American, including the *John L. Motley*. Seven more ships were heavily damaged, among them three American. Casualties were one thousand merchant seamen and military killed, and an estimated one thousand civilians killed. Eight hundred more were hospitalized.

All eight American Liberty ships suffered crew losses: the *John Bascom* lost four merchant seamen and ten navy armed guards (navy men who manned defensive guns on merchant vessels) killed; the *John L. Motley*, thirty-nine merchant seamen and twenty-four armed guards killed; the *Joseph Wheeler*, twenty-six merchant seamen and fifteen armed guards killed; the *John Harvey* lost her entire crew of thirty-six merchant seamen, twenty-eight armed guards, and ten army men; and the *Samuel J. Tilden*, ten merchant seamen, fourteen American military, and three British military. Additionally, there were casualties on the damaged *Lyman Abbott*, *Grace Abbott*, and *John M. Schofield*.

The *John L. Motley* was moored to the east jetty with her anchor down and stern lines to the jetty, and reportedly had forty-five merchant seamen and twenty-eight navy armed guards to man ship defense guns. She listed no army cargo security officers on board, but oddly, only one or two other American merchantmen moored in the harbor mentioned having cargo security officers on board. Alongside her was the SS *John Bascom*.

At approximately 1940 hours, ten to fifteen minutes after the raid began, the *Motley* was struck by a bomb that hit the no. 5 hatch, setting the deck cargo and the cargo in the hold afire. The flames burned through her mooring lines, and the ship drifted down on the jetty and exploded with a tremendous roar. She blew up when she was only about fifty feet from the *John Bascom*. The force of the explosion caved in the whole port side of the *Bascom*, sinking her immediately. *Motley* reported thirty-nine of her crew members lost and twenty-four navy men killed, with the only survivors being men who were on shore when the Germans struck.

To compound the disastrous surprise of "Little Pearl Harbor," one of the American ships, the Liberty Ship *John Harvey*, was found to have carried a secret cargo of two thousand M47A1 mustard gas bombs, each holding sixty to seventy pounds of the agent. This cargo had been sent to Europe for retaliatory use if Germany carried out its threatened use of chemical warfare in Italy.

The agent spilled into waters already contaminated with oil from other damaged vessels, which became an ideal solvent for the sulfur mustard, but symptoms of mustard poisoning—blindness and chemical burns—didn't first appear to the medical staff until about twenty-four hours later. Of 628 bombing survivors, sixty-nine would die within two weeks.

While there was an attempt at first to conceal news of the secret cargo and its effects, it was impossible. There were too many witnesses, forcing the Allies to fully explain what had occurred.

Bari harbor, shut down for three weeks, didn't resume full operation until February 1944, which did in fact have a serious impact on the pace of the ground and air campaigns in Italy.

When Second Lieutenant Kenneth C. Bailey was not found after the attack, he was determined to be missing in action and was eventually declared killed in action on 2 December 1943. He was posthumously awarded the medal of the Order of the Purple Heart "for military merit and for wounds received in action resulting in his death." Because his body was never recovered, his name is listed among 3,095 names on the Tablets of the Missing (white marble walls) inside the memorial chapel at the Sicily-Rome American Cemetery, Nettuno, Italy. The cemetery is located thirty-eight miles south of Rome.

In 1944, Kenneth Bailey's parents, Mr. and Mrs. Wilbur E. Bailey, sent a letter to then president of the San Jose State College Alumni Association, Charles Hillis, which sparked the idea of a chapel dedicated to the military men who served their country during World War II. The letter read in part,

There are many gold stars on our Spartan service flag. Many more will be added. . . . Nothing that we who are left can do will bring these young people back or ease their sacrifice. For us it is possible only to keep their memory alive and let their sacrifice not be forgotten. . . . We wonder if a more fitting tribute could be offered to those who will not return than a moderately small chapel, nonsectarian, of appropriate architectural beauty, dedicated to the memory and to preservation and promotion of the finest qualities of the life they have laid down.

Mr. and Mrs. Bailey's 1944 letter was accurate in foretelling the sacrifices the San Jose State College students and faculty of the World War II era would make. Of the 4,108 who would eventually serve in the armed forces, 204 would have gold stars on the four service flags. The flags were eventually moved from the Morris Dailey Auditorium and placed in the completed memorial chapel. Some years later they were removed and now are stored in the university archives. Among the flags was a fifth flag with a single gold star honoring President Franklin D. Roosevelt, who died of natural causes in Warm Springs, Georgia, on April 12, 1945, before World War II ended.

A prompt and favorable response to Mr. and Mrs. Bailey's letter came to Hillis when he presented the suggestion to the administrative officers of the college, the Alumni Association, and subsequently the faculty, the student body, the San Jose State College Patrons, and community civic organizations. Funds were solicited from students, alumni, faculty, and friends of the college. The school began fund-raising in 1944 and hoped to raise $50,000 for the building, with any extra money to go toward artwork and other items to beautify the memorial, which was meant to be "a permanent symbol of the spiritual values that are the foundation of American democracy."

In 1949, the site was selected and architects were employed to draw plans. The ground-breaking ceremonies took place at 11:30 a.m. on Saturday, June 17, 1950, during Alumni Homecoming. On May 17, 1950, Mr. Paul M. Pitman, the dean of men, had written a

San Jose State College memorial chapel, north elevation. (Photograph courtesy of Bonnie Montgomery, San Jose, California, historian and researcher)

response to a query from Mrs. Hattie G. Davis of Noble, Missouri, a Gold Star mother whose son, Maurice Edwin Davis, was among the 204 men from San Jose State lost in World War II, inviting her to attend the groundbreaking ceremony. He informed her of future plans and reminded her of a previous request for memorial letters about sons lost by all Gold Star families.

His response also explained construction plans, with particular emphasis on what was planned for the building's cornerstone:

> *Since we hope to lay the cornerstone in the Fall, I trust that you will not fail to send us the biography I have requested. We want to seal it in the cornerstone as a permanent symbol of our indebtedness and our gratitude.*

Letters had in fact been sent to next of kin for all 204 lost in the war, asking that memorials be sent to the dean of men, Mr. Pitman, to seal in the cornerstone. Mr. and Mrs. Bailey sent a fifteen-page, single-spaced, typed letter to their son, simply titled "In Memoriam," a beautiful, loving tribute to his remembrance.

The completed chapel was dedicated March 28, 1952. At 3:30 p.m. on Saturday, June 7, 1952, a moving nondenominational dedication ceremony was held in the chapel. Although often referred to as the Spartan memorial chapel, the building is not for a specific religion but a place where all students can go to be spiritual. The undated program in which Mr. and Mrs. Bailey's letter is quoted succinctly described the chapel's purpose:

Memorial Chapel, a monument to the College men who died for their country in World War II, honors all students, faculty and alumni who served in the Armed Forces. It stands as an enduring reminder of the ideals for which they gave their finest efforts and often their lives.

VICTOR ALBERT "BERT" ROBINSON, B-17G PILOT, BASED IN ITALY

The Spartans' Bert Robinson, right halfback and one of twenty-three lettermen on the 1941 team, was a B-17 pilot in the army air force's 419th Bombardment Squadron, 301st Bombardment Group, 5th Bombardment Wing, 15th Air Force. The 301st was stationed at Lucera Air Base, Italy, where Robinson arrived on 25 July 1944, after completing his state-side pilot training.

Lucera Air Base was approximately ninety miles north of the British-managed port at Bari, Italy, where Kenneth Bailey, Bert's football teammate and member of the San Jose State College wrestling team, was killed in action on 2 December 1943.

Bert flew fifty-one combat missions in the 301st during World War II. His period of service in Italy ended when he returned to the continental United States on 25 February 1945. During the period when he was flying his fifty-one missions, the 301st was flying against numerous heavily defended targets in Italy, Germany, and France, plus targets in Poland; Hungary; the oil fields in Ploesti, Romania; Yugoslavia; Austria; and Czechoslovakia. The 301st additionally flew long, one-way missions in which they landed in the Soviet Union, turned around, and flew missions on the way back to their bases in Italy.

Bert, as he was known to his teammates, classmates, and friends, was born the youngest of five children, two girls and three boys, in Campbell, California, on May 24, 1922, where he grew up and attended schools through high school graduation and from there entered nearby San Jose State College the summer of 1939. On returning from Honolulu and his Pearl Harbor experiences with the Honolulu police, he completed his junior year and enlisted in the Army of the United States in San Francisco on 31 August 1942, and was called to active duty on 8 April 1943.

On the day he was to leave home for active duty, his father, a Spanish-American War veteran who was educated at the Colorado School of Mines and worked in a hardware store, came with him to the on-campus recruiting center at San Jose State College, and with a group of San Jose State graduates and students also called to active duty, Bert walked from the recruiting center to the train station, his father walking with him observing the proceedings and wishing him well before his departure.

Bert was bound for Monterey, California, where they were processed with physical examinations and received numerous orientation lectures and tests prior to his departure for Santa Ana, California, where he entered pre–flight training as an aviation cadet. Dave Hines, a close friend in his class and captain of the San Jose State wrestling team, was with him as far as Monterey, where they would go separate ways, Bert into the army air force, Dave eventually into the army's famous 82nd Airborne Division.

From Santa Ana, Bert entered primary pilot training at Visalia Army Airfield, California, and flew with civilian instructors in the PT-22. There he collected a memory he would vividly recall in a voice recording in 1988 as a humorous incident while flying with his instructor. In telling of the incident, he carefully explained to whoever might listen to the recording just exactly how to enter a loop, an aerobatic maneuver that the instructor first demonstrated. "Push the nose down to pick up enough [specified] speed to pull the nose up [past the vertical and continue over the top, inverted,] and pull through into the upright position." Now it was Bert's turn to try. Everything seemed to go well as Bert completed the loop, until he heard nothing from the backseat. Repeated calls to his instructor through the airplane's rudimentary speaking tube received no reply. Not until they landed did he learn that his instructor had "blacked out," according to his instructor, "due to prop wash."

For those unfamiliar with flying, the instructor had fibbed, and his modest student forty-five years later chose not to divulge that the strapping former collegiate football player, Bert Robinson, had caught his instructor off guard with the vigor of his back-stick pressure, which abruptly exerted excessive g-forces on his unprepared instructor and "blacked him out."

On completing primary pilot training at Visalia, Bert was assigned to Chico Army Airfield, where he completed basic pilot training in the BT-13. There he learned more advanced and demanding flying, including formation flying, which improves three-dimensional hand-eye coordination and situational awareness. While at Chico he was surprised to encounter his former head football coach at San Jose State, Ben Winkelman, who had entered the army when San Jose State closed down their collegiate football program after the war started and was assigned ground duties as an officer in the army air force.

In basic training, student pilots were given the opportunity to request the type of aircraft they wished to fly when they completed flight training. Bert, like many others, wanted to go into fighters, but he believed the demand far exceeded opportunities, so he requested night fighters, aiming for the P-61 Black Widow, for example. No luck. Instead, he was sent to Douglas Army Airfield, Arizona, for two-engine training in the AT-17, called by army air force pilots the "Bamboo Bomber," from where he would likely go into other, multiengine aircraft. While in training, he collected two additional incidents he remembered vividly in his 1988 recorded recollections.

The first was less serious, potentially, than the second, but it illustrated the two student pilots' willingness to fly low and take risks while "having fun," activities frowned upon by senior officers and flight supervisors. While criticism and authoritative prohibition are merited in such routine self-supervised training, of such mettle and independence is born the American airman, soldier, and sailor who has inborn, or trained into them, the willingness to take responsibility and leadership, with all the inherent risks, under the most extreme circumstances. And what did Bert and his "student cohort" do?

They observed a freight train below, moving on nearby railroad tracks, and decided to "buzz the train," which after all might be a type of target they would attack in combat. To someone unfamiliar with the term "buzz," one meaning it has, particularly among pilots and people in the aviation industry, is to fly by or over at very low altitude, preferably at high speed, to draw attention and reaction. And they did all three.

As they flew past the engine pulling the train, they observed the engineer casually eating his lunch next to his open window on the engine cab, with an apparent cup of coffee resting on the steel window frame. When they roared past in their speeding "Bamboo Bomber," they so startled the engineer that he knocked his cup of coffee out the window. Undoubtedly, there was laughter inside the cockpit as they together decided it would be unwise to make a second pass on the now wide-awake freight train crew—who might read the serial numbers on the aircraft the next time around and advise the army air force of the aircraft's number, and the pilots' hazardous behavior of "buzzing friendly citizens."

The next incident Bert recalled about the "Bamboo Bomber" in his 1988 recording, while humorous, could have been disastrous—but, again, Bert and his accompanying student pilot both escaped discovery and their commander's irritation for a series of fuel-control errors that came perilously close to a completely unwelcome and most public reality.

The Cessna AT-17 had two fuel tanks on board, with electrically driven fuel pumps that fed the plane's two engines but were designed interconnected to feed either engine. The fuel system design required the pilots to activate toggle switches to pump fuel from the two tanks to the engines one at a time. There were red fuel-low warning lights in the cockpit to tell the pilots it was time to switch to the other tank before running the engines out of fuel.

In this instance, the two student pilots saw the red warning light come on and switched on the second fuel pump, but they evidently didn't pay close attention to the fuel quantity indicators on the instrument panel, which undoubtedly were giving indications of trouble ahead. They were on their way back to base when suddenly the second fuel-low light came on. It was time to land quickly or get into serious trouble and have to attempt landing with both engines dead—completely dry of fuel. Not a happy circumstance no matter how many engines the airplane had.

It was also time to declare an emergency, but with a careful choice of words that didn't reveal low fuel as the reason for the emergency. Declare it they did, with both engines still operating, but shortly thereafter the engines quit, one at a time. Now near desperation, they asked the tower to clear all aircraft out of the traffic pattern so they could land unimpeded, believing they were close enough and with enough altitude and speed to safely "dead-stick" the plane onto the runway. They were ready to accept the consequences if they landed short with empty fuel tanks.

In one final move, Bert reached for and turned on the switch for the fuel tank believed first to have been dry. Both engines quickly came to life, and they landed as though nothing had happened, taxied into the parking ramp, shut down the engines, filled out their airplane's flight and maintenance log, and walked away. They certainly had done one thing right that saved them from far more serious trouble: when that first red fuel-low light came on, they immediately switched to the second fuel tank, leaving enough in the first tank to restart the windmilling engines and land safely. No one ever said a word to them or asked any questions, not even the men who refilled the fuel tanks.

In February 1944, Bert graduated from pilot training, received his wings, was commissioned a second lieutenant in the Army of the United States—reserves on active duty—and given thirty days' leave with orders to report to Hill Field near Salt Lake City. Hill Field was an air depot, with Wendover Field on the border between Utah and Nevada as a sub-depot where B-17 and B-24 transition training was in progress. Bert's transportation to Salt Lake City was by motorcycle, with three junior officers on board wearing their officers' uniforms—a humorous and most unusual sight.

While transitioning into the B-17 as a copilot at Wendover, the first of three phases of B-17 training, he was assigned to a crew he would primarily remain associated with throughout his combat tour and for many years after the war ended.

The second phase was in the 328th Army Air Force Base Unit, which provided replacement training in B-17s and B-24s at the 3rd Air Force base five miles northeast of Gulfport, Mississippi. When he and the crew completed that second phase, they traveled to Dalhart Army Airfield, Texas, in the northern part of the Texas panhandle for combat crew training. But they were unable to complete that phase in the 333rd Bombardment Group in Dalhart and were returned to Gulfport. The B-29 forces, with larger, heavier aircraft, were destined for the Pacific theater of operations and needed the longer runways at Dalhart.

During the final phase of his B-17 combat crew training, six weeks in length, he took another motorcycle trip, this time from Gulfport to New Orleans, and had an accident that fortunately wasn't debilitating, and he was able to complete his training on schedule. When the training was complete, the crew, having been together in training for approximately five months, was ordered to Langley Army Airfield, Virginia, to pick up a new B-17, a G-model, to fly overseas to their combat assignment. From production lines were coming a steady stream of 8,650 of this last and most technologically advanced version of all the Flying Fortress heavy bombers produced in World War II. The modifications gave the crews the ability to strike PFF targets. (PFF is an acronym for "Pathfinder Force," a form of radar navigation bombing through overcast skies, developed and improved as the war in Europe progressed toward its climactic end.) The 301st was flying B-17Gs, the latest model, which had been modified and improved, with a "chin [gun] turret" remotely controlled within the aircraft, and carrying the latest radar equipment, with crew training to do PFF bombing—all of which gained a consequent reduction of required crew members from ten to nine.

Copilot Bert Robinson and his aircraft commander, Bill Wilson, and their B-17 crew were about to begin the first half of an extraordinary journey into war. From Langley Field they flew to Bangor, Maine, and on to Newfoundland, where the aircraft commander was handed sealed orders they would open after they were airborne on what they probably believed was the final leg to Europe. Another surprise. The next destination was Lajes Field on the southeast coast of Terceira Island, Azores, a group of nine Portuguese-owned islands of volcanic origin 972 miles due west of Lisbon, Portugal. The long flight over the Atlantic, a new experience for the crew, caused them to wonder about navigator Bob Schlarb's ability to take them to their island destination in the middle of the Atlantic Ocean, but he proved that his skills shouldn't be doubted. Bert recalled, still with obvious pride, in his 1988 recollections that "our navigator split the runway."

Bob Schlarb, navigator, "split the runway" after a long flight over the Atlantic from Newfoundland to Lajes Field. (*Source*: KCC)

Then came the second surprise. Touchdown on the runway at Lajes brought a startling noise they had never heard in the big bomber. They had touched down on metal matting, which created an abrupt noisy rattle that decreased in intensity as the landing rollout slowed. They were among a stream of more than 1,900 American aircraft passing through Lajes since a 1 December 1943 negotiated agreement between the British Royal Air Force and the U.S. Army Air Force that governed the base's wartime operation, consistent with international agreements with the Portuguese government.

From Lajes, their next leg was into Marrakesh, French Morocco, where the crew visited the empty palace of Sultan Mohammed, who had gone into exile earlier in 1944 following his increasingly evident support of nationalists seeking gradual independence from French and European colonists, a status finally secured through negotiation eleven years after the war ended.

From Marrakesh, they flew to Tunis, Tunisia, on the northern coast of Africa, landing for stopover and refueling at an army air force base controlled by Air Transport Command, after the 12th Air Force had used the base to complete its 1943 Italian campaign and moved its headquarters and entire command to Italy. The field at Tunis eventually became known as Tunis-Carthage International Airport. From there it was on to Rome, from where, in the fourth week in July, they flew their final leg into Foggia, home of the 15th Air Force and the subordinate 5th Bombardment Wing, a few miles from their 301st Bombardment Group base at Lucera.

Bill Wilson, Bert, and their crew arrived at Lucera Air Base, about ten miles from Foggia, on 25 July 1944. The next day, the 419th Bombardment Squadron, the squadron to which they would be assigned, lost three aircraft among a total of eleven lost by the 301st Bombardment Group in a mission against the Wiener Neudorf aircraft factory, just south of Vienna, Austria. The 301st was the last group in the 15th Air Force stream of bombers targeted against Wiener Neudorf that day. The group's losses were devastating.

During the 18, 19, and 22 July missions to Memmingen, Germany; Munich, Germany; and Ploesti, Romania, the group had lost three more aircraft for a total of fourteen combat losses in one month, constituting a staggering, approximately 25 percent combat loss in one month, with virtually the same loss rate in the 419th in one day.

The group normally had fifty to sixty aircraft total in its four squadrons and were putting up an average of twenty-five aircraft per mission in July, with each squadron normally sending an average of five to seven of their thirteen to fifteen planes. But this day would be far different for many reasons, with the 301st sending twenty-eight aircraft airborne beginning at 0730 hours, following an early get-up and breakfast and a 0430 hours mission briefing.

This was to be a major 15th Air Force effort against the Wiener Neudorf aircraft factory, with the 301st B-17s included among a force of 495 bombers, B-17s and B-24s, escorted by 322 fighters. After the mission briefing, as was the routine, transportation was to their aircraft by trucks for pre-mission crew get-acquainted sessions for those who were "made-up crews" or "fillers" on the crews. After the 301st launched their twenty-eight aircraft, two returned early because they had to air abort.

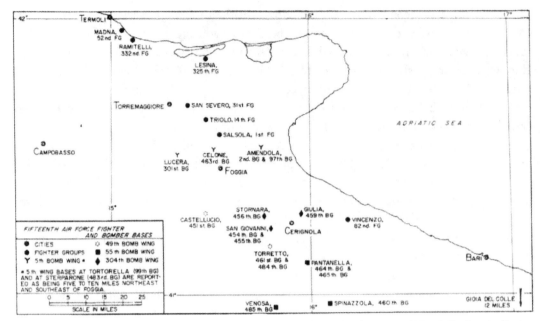

Map, 15th Air Force bases: Amendola (2nd BG), Celone (463rd BG), Cerignola (97th BG), Foggia (2nd BG, 463rd BG), Lucera (301st BG), Manduria (68th RG), Maricianise (97th BG), Sterparone (483rd BG), and Torotella (99th BG, 483rd BG). (*Source*: USAF)

Twenty-six aircraft from the 301st arrived at the point that fighter attacks began at approximately 1100 hours, sixty miles from the target and lasting about fifteen minutes. The loss of eleven aircraft on one mission constituted a shattering loss approximating 42 percent of the 301st Group's entire force in a single mission. Additionally, the group lost two more aircraft to accidents in July, one a ditching in which all crew members were picked up, and a second in which the fully loaded B-17G lost engines on takeoff and crashed, with only four surviving crew members.

Whether Bert and Bill Wilson's crew were aware of it or not, the 419th's 26 July mission probably directly influenced their assignment to the squadron. Further, it would take time to reconstitute the group's strength, and replacement crew members, such as twenty-two-year-old Bert Robinson and all those younger than him, would have to grow up rapidly in ways they never dreamed.

For the uninitiated coming into the 419th on 25 or 26 July 1944, immediately before or after the staggering losses on 26 July, the "scuttlebutt," filled with accurate descriptions, stories, and rumors of what was seen and heard that day from the men fortunate enough to have survived and returned, undoubtedly carried lifetimes of memories of courage, bravery, and heroism tinged with terrible images.

A photograph taken of eight of the ten-man crew commanded by Bill Wilson when they arrived in Foggia has standing, left to right, Robert C. Schlarb, navigator; Victor A. "Bert" Robinson, copilot; William S. Wilson, pilot; and Richard I. Hodder, bombardier, and

Bert Robinson with eight of ten B-17 crew members, 2 August 1944, L–R standing, Bob Schlarb, Bert, Bill Wilson, and Dick Hodder; front, Bill Sanders, Lee Isenagle, Terry Sanders, and Don Lape. (*Source*: KCC)

in the front row, William A. Sanders, waist gunner; Homer I. Isenagle, lower ball-turret gunner; Terry A. Sanders, tail gunner; and Donald E. Lape, radio operator. Two men not shown in the photograph were engineer Edgar W. Schlittenhart and gunner Frederick R. Prehn.

On the mission to Wiener Neudorf, the group had encountered 100 to 150 enemy fighters. Nine of the eleven lost were to fighter attacks, and two were reported lost in a midair collision, although later investigation revealed that one of the aircraft had gone out of control during the fighter attacks and collided with another, prompting an explosion from which only three of twenty crew members survived. In a cryptic special narrative report, the crew debriefings described the German fighter tactics and results on both sides:

ENEMY RESISTANCE
Fighters: 100 to 150 e/a [enemy aircraft] mostly Me 109's and FW 190's were encountered between 47 deg 32'N, 15 deg 42'E and the target. 75 to 100 made direct attacks on our formation. Fighters came in level in a straight line alternating above and below vapor trails until they came within range. Then the top line of planes went higher and came in at 6 o'clock. The bottom line came in low at 6 o'clock. The four end planes came round low and high and came in at 3 and 7 o'clock. Attacks made by e/a in groups of three or four seemed to concentrate on one plane at a time. After making passes from the rear, e/a would cut back and make attacks from 11 o'clock, both high and low. Me 109's were painted dark brown color, almost black. Me 210's observed were painted green.

B. Flak: Intense accurate heavy flak, both barrage and tracking types, was encountered in the target area.

Crews, at an altitude of 24,500 feet, were unable to observe gun positions because the target area was obscured by clouds due to an undercast and the intensity of the air battle. Flak damage among returning aircraft resulted in three minor and one major injury to personnel, and crews claimed twenty-three victories against the attacking fighters: destroying six Me 109s, sixteen FW 190s, and one Me 210, with two FW 190s probable and two FW 190s damaged.

Over a period of years, the recollections of men who survived that mission, historians' research, and further inquiry by grieving family members have added far greater depth and a much sharper reality to all that happened in the 26 July 1944 air battle as the 301st Bombardment Group's formation approached their target at Wiener Neudorf, Austria.

Kenneth P. Werrell, on page 179 of his 1991 book *Who Fears? The 301st in War and Peace, 1942–1979*, presents some of the facts, the 301st history provides more, and surviving aircrew members' recollections provide additional insight, recollections which also illustrate the relative scarcity of observations and facts normally summarized in mission debriefing reports transmitted to the 5th Bombardment Wing and the 15th Air Force.

The 353nd Squadron's pilot, Second Lieutenant Otto M. Rinderknecht, among his nine-man crew, in Fortress 42-31652, were the first to fall and were last seen at approximately 1105 hours by witnesses to the loss on 26 July, after Rinderknecht had to shut down an engine. The shutdown was "because . . . we started throwing oil from one engine," as described two years later by the radio operator, Technical Sergeant James A. Edwards, a filler and radio operator/gunner on the crew who had never flown with them previously. The pilot feathered the propeller, couldn't keep up with the formation, and began falling back from the group. Edwards, continuing in his statement, said, "We flew over some flak and got a few holes in us. The pilot asked for a heading to Switzerland and got it." The flak cut

The 301st, lined up, taxiing out for takeoff on a mission, Lucera Air Base, Italy. (*Source:* KCC)

an oxygen line to the ball-turret operator, setting the line on fire. Edwards, who had moved from his radio-operator position to man one of the waist guns on the run-in to the target, explained that the other waist gunner attempted to put the fire out but wasn't successful, and the ball-turret gunner had to get out of the turret and move up into the radio room. Edwards said, "We were shot up and had to bail out." The two fighters were part of the 100 to 150 fighters rapidly closing on their much larger target, the 301st Group, the last group in the stream of B-17 bombers that day.

The copilot, Second Lieutenant Robert J. Sutton, recalled following his repatriation from POW status after the war that three crew members were killed outright by the fighter attacks and never got out of the aircraft. German POW records confirmed that six were captured, and three of the six were wounded and placed in German POW camp hospitals. In a subsequent statement, Lieutenant Sutton expressed the firm belief that the ball-turret gunner was killed outright by a German fighter's 20 mm cannon shell before the aircraft broke up, stating, "I found and identified half his body on the ground. I wrapped it in a parachute and the Austrians buried him." He added that Second Lieutenant Roland V. Parker, the navigator, saw the bombardier, Second Lieutenant Daniel H. David, slumped over in his seat, and also believed he was killed by a 20 mm cannon shell and went down with the plane. Sutton further expressed the belief that waist gunner Corporal Jesse L. Taylor suffered the same fate, killed by a 20 mm cannon shell and never got out of the airplane.

The oncoming German fighters aiming for the trailing 301st Group immediately tore into the last squadrons in the 301st and downed three more Fortresses, all in the 419th Squadron. The first to fall in the German onslaught was First Lieutenant Alonzo I. Martin's plane, 42-102915, with a crew of ten, followed by Second Lieutenant Charles Starling's 42-31523, named "Bar Fly," both of which fell with engine fires and fires inside their aircraft, going into a spin before breaking up.

From Lieutenant Martin's plane, witnesses saw four to six chutes, with none seen from Starling's Fortress. Further investigation of the status of Martin's crew revealed that four men survived, were captured, were held in German POW camps until the war's end, and then were repatriated; five were killed in action, and one was declared missing and subsequently declared dead.

The ten crew members of Lieutenant Starling's Fortress surprisingly fared slightly better, in spite of eyewitness reports of no chutes and the aircraft's explosion. Five men were killed in action, and five survived, were captured, and were repatriated after the war.

Former First Lieutenant James P. Lilligren, 419th Bombardment Squadron (H), pilot of Fortress 42-31625, wrote a biographical piece years later that provided important insight into the cause for the high loss rate that July day in 1944. The 15th Air Force mission plan included P-51s to escort the bomber force, and for reasons debriefing aircrews and historians could not know, the fighters didn't rendezvous with them. The absence of the planned fighter escort clearly made circumstances far worse for the 301st Group.

The German fighters faced no resistance in forming and reforming to launch their repeated attacks throughout the sixty-mile running battle into the target area. The mutual support afforded individual bombers within their formation was effective and did take its toll on the German fighters, but the mutual support couldn't inhibit the rapid reforming to launch repeated attacks. Second, the fighters' ability to maximize their positioning to use their well-planned tactics—two, three, or four fighters attacking one bomber from multiple, three-dimensional directions—was made even more devastating by the use of both .50-caliber machine-gun and 20 mm cannon fire in their attacks, achieving maximum damage as rapidly as possible to each bomber selected for attack.

More poignantly, James Lilligren's piece also vividly recalled his and his crew's desperate struggle to bail out of a fatally damaged aircraft that "was hit by many 20 MM and 50-caliber shells setting the nose section on fire as well as the left wing. It seemed the entire aircraft was on fire. I later learned from the pilot of another B-17 that the entire tail section was shot off our plane." Author Kenneth Werrell, describing the loss, wrote that "Lilligren's ship was hit in the right wing, he had the vertical stabilizer almost completely shot off and had one engine on fire. It was last seen burning and spinning with three to four chutes visible." Lilligren wrote, "Of the ten members of the crew, only four survived. In addition to the Engineer, who bailed out immediately, my Radio Operator bailed out but was badly burned, one Waist Gunner made it and me." After the German fighters downed three Fortresses from the 419th, they continued chewing up the 301st from the rear toward the lead squadron in the group, the next five from the 32nd Squadron.

First Lieutenant Ralph C. Delonney's 44-6168 was the fighters' next victim. According to one survivor, "the plane was all full of holes, you could see the sky almost any place." With the plane on fire and out of control, he bailed out, one of two survivors of the crew. The 32nd Squadron's Second Lieutenant John L. Sullivan, pilot in 42-102913, had fires in one engine and the fuselage and completed a roll before it exploded. No chutes were seen. First Lieutenant Robert J. McManaman's 42-32107, First Lieutenant Richard H. Luebke's 44-6189, and Second Lieutenant Leo J. McDonald's 42-3157 fell in succession, all leaving the formation on fire. Three chutes were observed after McManaman's bomber stalled. From Luebke's aircraft, seven chutes were observed, and from Leo McDonald's aircraft, which fell in a spin, only one chute was observed.

As the German fighters continued forward, attacking in the 301st, from the last two to fall came the worst casualty reports. The 352nd's Second Lieutenant David T. Kerr, in Fortress 42-30385, was hit in the no. 4 engine, setting the right wing and cockpit on fire. The aircraft stalled, went out of control, and collided with First Lieutenant Ernest F. Howell Jr.'s 42-102929, also from the 352nd. An explosion ensued, killing all but three on board the two aircraft, each with ten-man crews. Lieutenant Kerr's aircraft was last seen by witnesses at 1118 hours, about eighteen miles south of Vienna, Austria. Two survived from Lieutenant Howell's crew, and one from Lieutenant Kerr's crew. He was Technical Sergeant Ernest L. Marlin, the radio operator/gunner. The two survivors from Lieutenant Howell's aircraft were Technical Sergeant John A. La Rosa, radio operator/gunner, and Staff Sergeant Wayne W. Hammond, waist gunner.

Unquestionably, Bill Wilson, Bert Robinson, and their crew met men within their new squadron that had been shocked and devastated by the 26 July losses in the 419th Squadron and 301st Group. It could not have been a pleasant welcome to either organization the last days of July 1944 after a long journey into war. Bert's first letter home from Italy was written 30 July, and of course he made no comment whatsoever or gave even a hint of what the entire crew had learned since their arrival.

30 July 44
Italy

Hi Folks—

Just a line or two to give you my permanent (for a while anyway) address.
    Hope everything is swell with you. Should be getting our back mail before long.
    Had a shower and clean clothes on today so really feel swell, & clean for a change.
    Roach is in the same group as me though in a different squadron, and lives just a few hundred feet away from our tent.
    Think I'll like the squadron and group. It's the second oldest bomb group, so has a lot of experience to pass on to it youngsters.
    Well, I haven't much to say at present as everyone can plainly see, so might as well close. Hello to everybody.

Love
Bert

Fortunately, August was considerably better.

When the month of August ended, the 301st Bombardment Group, commanded by Colonel John F. Batjer, reported flying twenty-one accredited missions, consisting of 553 sorties, and dropped a total of 1,435.625 tons of bombs, ranging in support of the invasion of southern France, Operation Anvil, later called Operation Dragoon, to the oil fields in Ploesti, Romania. Mission reports didn't indicate the number of aircraft put up per mission, but the average number of sorties was slightly more than twenty-six bombers per mission. By month's end, the group had lost four aircraft.

Strikes on targets in southern France began on 2 August, in advance of the 15 August landings, and the boys of the 301st described on that date and continued to talk about in the monthly summary what a "mad scramble they had on the morning of the invasion and how planes were all over the sky. They, sweatin' out our own planes more than the encounters of flak or fighters that may have been met at the beaches."

The first mission of the month was against Le Puzin oil storage, France, on 2 August. The group encountered no flak, while four Me 109s made a pass at the formation over the French coast on return but proved not to be aggressive. Bert flew his first combat mission with Bill Wilson and his crew—as a copilot in the group and 419th Squadron that day. The 301st suffered no losses over Le Puzin but the next day lost a 352nd Squadron aircraft to flak, with three other aircraft receiving minor flak damage, while attacking the Ober-Raderach Chemical Works at Friedrichshafen, Germany. Crews reported no fighters encountered, with moderate, inaccurate, heavy flak encountered over the target.

The aircraft number was 44-6284; the pilot and aircraft commander was First Lieutenant Edward R. Simon. He and his crew of nine apparently bailed out after being hit by flak, but waist gunner Staff Sergeant William "Gil" Sultan was killed in action after his plane went down during the bombing run. He is buried at the Florence American Cemetery, Florence, Italy.

Bert Robinson's flight log is not available, but examination of his period of service and the existing policies in heavy bomber groups suggest that on average he was flying missions approximately every third day. Bert had determined he was going to fly as many missions as he could, as rapidly as he could be scheduled. His duty period at Lucera and the January date on which he completed his fiftieth mission, 20 January, reinforces this conclusion regarding the frequency of his combat missions.

The 301st flew its next mission on 6 August, against the marshaling yard at Portes Les Valences, France, a mission in which Bill Wilson, Bert, and their 419th crew undoubtedly participated. Again, the 301st suffered no losses, but the next day was far different, when one aircraft was reported downed by flak, with another missing, both from the 32nd Squadron. Three returning aircraft had major damage, and sixteen had minor damage, in addition to the reported loss of two aircraft. Crew debriefings reported 10–15 enemy aircraft in the target area, and the mission aircraft had four encounters, coming in from all around the clock, but most coming in at six and seven o'clock, with one bomber crew claiming an Me 109 probably destroyed. But flak was the major killer that day, as it most always was in raids deep into Germany.

The target was Blechhammer Synthetic Oil Plant, Germany. It was designated a special mission, and the commander of the 32nd Squadron, Lieutenant Colonel Leslie W. Holman, an experienced, highly decorated combat commander, was the mission leader for the B-17s against the heavily defended target.

There was far more to the mission than was specifically known to crews other than the crews briefed to fly it—although scuttlebutt about missions to that particular target was generally well known. They were lengthy (eight to eight and a half hours), exhausting, and difficult, with heavier losses than normal.

On 4 May 1944, the 15th Air Force had been authorized to attack oil refineries at Ploesti, Romania, beginning a bombing offensive that would contribute greatly to the defeat of Germany. To accomplish this, the 15th established three objectives: (1) destroy the Romanian refineries at Ploesti and Bucharest; (2) destroy twelve natural refineries in Central Europe; and (3) eliminate the synthetic oil refineries at Brux (one of the three largest producers of gasoline in Europe), Blechhammer North, Blechhammer South, and Odertal (where 22 percent of the synthetic oil was produced, and where the Blechhammer/Odertal area was defended by twenty-five flak batteries). Blechhammer was also a World War II home of prisoner of war (POW) camps and forced labor camps.

The Germans were already in trouble with diminishing oil supplies for their war machine, having seen their captive Ploesti, Romania, oil production complex being battered relentlessly by the 15th Air Force for just over a year, since the courageous but costly 1 August 1943 low-level raid by 176 B-24Ds codenamed Operation Tidal Wave. Bert mentioned in general terms the infamous 1 August 1943 mission in his 1988 recorded recollections.

The Germans of necessity were supplementing their oil needs with synthetic oil and had built heavy concentrations of antiaircraft defenses to protect their production complex at Blechhammer. The 15th Air Force, which included a heavy bomber force of six B-17 groups and fifteen B-24 groups, each with fifty to sixty bombers, was now well equipped to achieve those objectives and began a campaign of large raids that employed both types of heavy bombers in separate formations with different times over the targets. The raid of 7 August was an example.

Flying one of the newest, PFF-equipped B-17G aircraft in the 301st Bombardment Group, 32nd Squadron, serial number 44-8001, Lieutenant Colonel Holman's crew included a highly trained "Mickey," as PFF operators were called. Second Lieutenant Norman E. Klein augmented the normal nine-man crew when weather would likely require bombing through overcasts. First Lieutenant John W. Kelly was copilot; Major Arthur L. McAdams, navigator; First Lieutenant Raymond A. Patterson, bombardier; Technical Sergeant Gene I. Micinski, engineer/gunner; Staff Sergeant William E. Caldwell, tail gunner; Technical Sergeant Linden Davis, radio operator/gunner; Staff Sergeant Bill H. Wright, waist gunner; and Sergeant Norman R. Adler, waist gunner.

Immediately after bomb release, Holman's aircraft was severely hit by flak in no. 4 engine, the right outboard engine, as reported in a statement written and signed by copilot Lieutenant John W. Kelly. The engine was lost and on fire, and several other fires were reported inside the plane. The whole fuselage was completely filled with smoke. Colonel Holman gave the command to the crew to prepare to bail out, but according to Kelly,

four (4) of the crew apparently decided the situation was too critical, so they jumped. The pilot or myself did not know about this until after the target area was cleared. I did not see the chutes, but according to a waist gunner in another plane, they chuted out okay.

Staff Sergeant Donald H. McColskey, the waist gunner in aircraft 42-97706, on 001s right wing, essentially verified Lieutenant Kelly's external observations of the flak hit on no. 4, but added, "I saw the Tail Gunner come out, his chute opened about 300 feet below us, then three (3) men come out of the front escape hatch, and I watched all their chutes open. The chances for survival of these men is very good." He went on to state the geographical coordinates noted when the men bailed out.

As soon as Lieutenant Colonel Holman became aware no. 4 engine was on fire, he had to redirect his attention to the emergency on board his aircraft and would have commanded,

"Fire, feather no. 4," while ensuring the designated alternate mission leader was taking hold of the mission leader's responsibilities—which would probably have been automatic as soon as the second in command saw the leader peeling out of the formation with an engine on fire. In the meantime, Lieutenant Kelly would have immediately taken action to both feather the engine and activate the engine's built-in fire suppressant system, a system that sprayed a heavy blanket of carbon dioxide inside the engine cowling to attempt smothering the fire. A fire in an aircraft engine of any type will eventually become catastrophic if it can't be suppressed or blown out in a rapid, accelerating descent. Had the fire on no. 4 not been put out, it would have spread and eventually caused wing failure or, worse, a massive explosion of ordnance or a fuel tank.

The result of the flak hit and ensuing engine fire, thick smoke inside the aircraft, rapidly executed emergency procedures, and preparatory command to bail out as 8001 peeled out of the formation to return to base were the bailouts of Major Arthur L. McAdams, navigator; First Lieutenant Raymond A. Patterson, bombardier; Technical Sergeant Gene I. Micinski, engineer/gunner; Staff Sergeant William E. Caldwell, tail gunner; and Technical Sergeant Linden Davis, radio operator/gunner, who were all listed on a casualty questionnaire completed by First Lieutenant Norman E. Klein, the PFF operator.

Assuming all four men survived, they probably became POWs, a fate another 32nd crew experienced, save one eighteen-year-old on his first combat mission in aircraft 42-31886, Private First Class Walter Drogt of Houghton Lake, Michigan, who was a trained turret gunner, but was flying his first mission as a waist gunner on this mission and was wounded before bailout and capture by German soldiers.

Other experienced leaders on the mission to Blechhammer on 7 August included First Lieutenant Gerald Bauer, who was on his fiftieth mission, was Private First Class Drogt's aircraft commander on Drogt's first combat mission, and would complete his combat tour, meaning he could look forward to a near-term return stateside. He was flying aircraft 42-31886, named "Amazing Mazie," leading two other aircraft in his element in the first wave of bombers.

The bombing altitude was twenty-three thousand feet. Three miles from the target, shortly after German fighters attacked, Lieutenant Bauer shut down the no. 4 engine and feathered the still windmilling propeller. (When an engine fails or is shot out, the propeller almost invariably continues to turn, driven by the airspeed and airflow as the aircraft continues to fly, but one or more additional steps must be taken to avoid loss of the aircraft. The engine's big, three-bladed propeller must be "feathered," accomplished by electrically activating a hopefully undamaged motor within the large engine, which "feathers"—streamlines—the three blades in the aircraft's slipstream. If the attempts to feather the propeller fail, the huge blades continue to windmill, acting as three large barn doors creating enormous drag on the aircraft. The inevitable results are decreasing airspeed, progressively increased power required of the other three engines while speed continues to decrease, continued loss of altitude just to maintain safe flying speed, and the virtual impossibility of safe return to base, even if every effort is made to reduce aircraft weight. The likelihood of overheating and failure in one or more of the remaining three engines increases with the use of maximum power in an attempt to slow or level the descent, with low airspeed and decreased cooling airflow over the big engines.)

Statements written by aircraft commanders Second Lieutenants Archie D. Staley and Leo F. Villarubia, who were from First Lieutenant Bauer's squadron and who were on the left and right wings, respectively, of "Amazing Mazie," provided some indication of why the aircraft failed to return. According to Lieutenant Villarubia,

> *Just before the target, 886 began to lose altitude and drop back from the formation . . . dropped his bombs before the target and turned for home. I attached myself to the tail end of the second wave and dropped bombs on them [meaning his bombs were released when the second wave released their bombs]. After the target, 886 and 357 [Staley's aircraft] cut inside our rally [turn/rejoin angle] and joined the tail end also. 886 was still going down now with #3 and 4 engines feathered. I stayed with the formation and left 886 and 357 just north of Bratislava. There is a chance of a forced landing and possibly a ditching and a fair chance of survival for the crew. No parachutes were seen and it is my belief that all crew members were aboard at time last sighted. When last sighted plane was about 15,500' still coming toward home.*

Lieutenant Staley's statement varied somewhat from the statement submitted by Lieutenant Villarubia.

> *Airplane #42-31886 was leading our three ship element. Approximately 3 miles before the target, he feathered #4 engine. Immediately after the target, he feathered #3 engine. He could not maintain altitude, going from 23,000 over the target to 14,500' five miles west of Bratislava. During this time, #3 was unfeathered for about two minutes, then feathered again. I communicated by radio and he said it was no good. He threw out all loose equipment. We left him five miles west of Bratislava at 14,500', flying an airspeed of 115 and losing 300' per minute. When last seen he was at 48 degrees 10' N 17 degrees 00' E on a 195 degrees heading. There is a good chance of a forced landing, also a possibility of ditching. There is a good chance of survival as there was no other damage to the ship visually. No one bailed out of the plane while it was still in sight.*

All crew members on 886 bailed out an unknown distance south-southwest of Bratislava, became POWs, and were repatriated after the war.

But the torment of the four who bailed out of 8001 over the Blechhammer area wasn't finished if they were captured. There began in the period 21 January–2 February 1945 an event remembered simply as "the March," a forced march of approximately ten thousand POWs by German SS guards. From the Blechhammer area came about four thousand POWs and another six thousand from sub-camps to the concentration camp Gross-Rosen to avoid their being freed by Allied armies closing in on the heart of Nazi Germany from the east and west. During the twelve-day march, there were about eight hundred prisoners who were unable to walk any farther or tried to flee; they were shot by the SS. Those who survived the march were sent to Buchenwald, one of numerous infamous slave labor, POW, and death camps in Nazi Germany.

On 10 August, the 301st and other groups flew a mission against Ploesti, Romania's Romano Americano Oil Refinery, with the 301st the last in the stream of attacking formations. This was Bill Wilson's, Bert's, and their crew's first mission to the heavily defended oil refineries. Flak was moderate to intense and accurate for the groups ahead, but the 301st mission leader, on hearing what was ahead, rallied the group to the left and caught minimum flak. No planes were lost, but one returned with major damage and four with minor damage.

On 12 August, the group struck gun positions in the Savona area, Italy. Again, there were no losses reported, but flak was debriefed as slight and inaccurate at the target, although three aircraft had major damage and four minor damage. On 13 August, the group struck gun positions in the Genoa area, Italy, with no fighters encountered and slight, accurate flak over the target. Six aircraft received minor damage. On 14 August, the 301st hit gun positions in the Toulon, France, area in preparation for the next day's landing of troops in the south of France. Debriefings revealed intense, heavy flak in the target area and no enemy fighters sighted; one aircraft received major damage and nineteen minor damage. Crews reported seeing ships in Toulon Harbor laying down smoke screens.

On 15 August, the group bombed a specific beach area, no. 231, near St. Tropez, France, in support of Operation Dragoon, the invasion of southern France. Target time was in advance of troop landings. There were no fighter attacks observed, and only three bursts of flak were seen. On the 16th, the group attacked Grenoble Railroad Bridge in France, with no fighters or flak observed and no damage to the aircraft. Photographs of the target indicated heavy, concentrated coverage. On the 18th, the group again struck the Americano Romano Oil Refinery at Ploesti, Romania. Crews described the flak as intense, accurate, and heavy in the target area, with no fighters encountered. Sixteen aircraft had minor damage, and two received major damage.

On 20 August, consistent with the 15th Air Force campaign plan, the 301st attacked the Oswiecim Synthetic Oil and Rubber Works, Poland. Crews reported that twelve enemy aircraft, Me 109s and Me 210s, were observed twenty-five miles south of Budapest, Hungary, but escorting P-51s drove them away from the formation. There was a possibility the enemy fighters could have attacked follow-on bomber formations. Moderate, inaccurate, heavy flak was encountered over the target. It appeared that two or three batteries were firing at the same time, as groups of eight to twelve bursts would explode simultaneously. Minimum flak was encountered unexpectedly above Oswiecim, Poland. Minimum flak was also encountered over Budapest; however, all 301st aircraft returned, eleven with minor flak damage.

Two days later, on 22 August, the 301st Group was one of at least two groups that attacked the Odertal Oil Refinery, Germany. Debriefings reported that the 301st encountered between ten and fifteen German fighters in the Vienna area. Attacks were made from four to seven o'clock and came in low, level, and high. They first attacked one of the other groups, then closed in on the 301st but had very little success on their passes—although one B-17 from another group was seen to go down due to the fighter attacks. Crews of the 301st reported two Me 109s and two FW 190s destroyed and one Me 109 damaged. Slight, inaccurate, and heavy flak was encountered at the target, and slight, inaccurate flak was observed at Gyon. Five aircraft returned with minor flak damage, and two had minor damage from fighter attacks.

The next day the 301st bombed an industrial area and south marshaling yard in Vienna, Austria. No fighters were encountered, while the formation encountered moderate to intense, accurate flak over Vienna, which was especially intense over the marshaling yard. Flak caused minor damage to eighteen aircraft, with major damage to two.

On 24 August, the 301st Group struck air defense installations at Pardubice airdrome, Czechoslovakia, sending 26 planes in a 15th Army Air Force mission of 158 bombers and 7 fighters that dropped 381 tons of bombs.

Twenty FW 190s were encountered by the 301st at 1251 hours in the target area. They made two passes but were then driven off by a very effective escort. The force encountered no flak at the target. All aircraft returned with no damage. Results and defenses encountered were virtually identical the next day when the group bombed air defense installations at Brno, Czechoslovakia. An empty shell case caused minor damage to one aircraft.

While the mission on 24 August was measured as a success, en route to the target a tragic accident occurred at approximately 0900 hours, resulting in the loss of 419th Squadron aircraft 44-6364, "Smiling Elsie," and five crew members in the Adriatic Sea, including the pilot, Second Lieutenant Stanley A. Peterson. Standard operating procedure for mission aircraft en route to targets was, within a designated area, preferably over waters such as the Adriatic Sea, to spread out the combat formation a sufficient distance to test-fire their guns prior to re-forming to proceed to their targets. In this instance, a tragedy ensued. A burst of fire from a 301st gunner testing his .50-caliber guns struck an engine on Lieutenant Peterson's aircraft, and it caught fire.

Lieutenant Peterson was unable to put out the fire and ordered the crew to bail out over water. He completed calls to Air Sea Rescue and attempted to ditch the aircraft in order to get rubber boats to the crew. While maneuvering to ditch the aircraft, it was observed to explode as it entered the water. One crew member, who had stated he was the ninth to bail out, said he counted eight parachutes in the air before he descended into the water, and the pilot was still in the aircraft when it exploded. A British Air Sea Rescue boat picked up five crew members that survived "Smiling Elsie's" loss. Five perished, including Lieutenant Peterson, who posthumously received the Silver Star for valor, the Distinguished Flying Cross, the Purple Heart, and the Air Medal with an Oak Leaf Cluster. The navigator, Second Lieutenant Alex Eisenstein, was killed, as were Staff Sergeant Clifford A. Gustafson, gunner; Staff Sergeant Frank J. White, radio operator/gunner; Sergeant John M. Curtin, gunner; and Second Lieutenant Stanley A. Peterson, pilot.

On 26 August, the 301st struck the railroad viaduct at Borovnica, Italy, encountering neither flak nor fighters, with all aircraft returning absent any damage. Continuing the air campaign against German oil production on the 27th, the group hit Blechhammer North, Germany. Flak was very accurate and intense, especially as the mission leader began a rally to the right. All aircraft returned, three with major flak damage and thirteen with minor damage.

On 28 August the mission was against the Moosbierbaum Oil Refinery, Austria. Intense and accurate flak was encountered at the target, but no fighters. Seventeen aircraft returned with minor flak damage, and six had major damage. The group put up twenty-eight aircraft on this mission, and all but one dropped bombs as planned, with two jettisoning one and a half tons each to keep up with the formation, releasing the other half of their bomb load as planned. One aircraft jettisoned three tons of bombs between the IP (initial point) and the target, feathered an engine, and left the formation. (Note: An IP is a point on the map, usually a well-defined geographical landmark that can also be seen on radar, used to align the formation for a straight, precise, known distance and time run-in to the target to help ensure bombing accuracy.)

On 29 August, the target was the Czegled marshaling yard, Hungary, with the last two squadrons encountering slight, inaccurate, and heavy flak in the target area. One aircraft had minor flak damage on return. Again, no fighters were encountered. The final mission for August 1944 was on the 30th, against the Novisad main marshaling yard, Yugoslavia. Flak at the primary target was slight and inaccurate, and no fighters were encountered. Nevertheless, aircraft returning included two with major damage and eleven with minor damage.

During August, Bert Robinson undoubtedly became aware of the oncoming European winter weather, which would reduce the number of missions the 15th Air Force could fly in their bombing campaign. He and Bill Wilson had immediately learned of the heavy losses the group and the 419th Squadron endured on 26 July, which sharply reduced the number of aircraft and crews available for group-assigned missions. Both units were seeking to recover combat strength. Both men were also seeing that it was virtually impossible to fly with the same crew all the time, and other opportunities existed to fly with other groups because combat organizations mutually supported one another to complete their respective missions. Further, there were unplanned events that entered in the mission and flight schedulers' equations, most notably aircraft losses, brief crew member illnesses, emergency leaves, variable rest and recuperation leaves, the number of in-commission aircraft available to the group and each squadron, and required training for various disciplines represented in each crew. The result was that they flew with varying crew members that came from within the 419th, other squadrons within the 301st, and perhaps other B-17 groups within the 5th Bombardment Wing.

Bert and most everyone else flying missions were oriented toward completing their combat assignments by reaching the fifty-mission threshold as soon as possible, although there were men who sometimes volunteered to stay longer, but they were invariably looked at carefully by flight surgeons and commanders before permission was ever granted to do so. Thus Bert sought additional opportunities to fly missions at a steady rate that would both increase his skills and complete his combat tour as soon as practical. There was one other important, near-term result of his drive, sense of duty, work ethic, and rapidly increasing pilot and leadership skills—Bill Wilson early on permitted him to take more responsibility in flying missions and recommended him to be upgraded to first pilot, which meant he would also be an aircraft commander by 11 September. This was the date on which he wrote his parents the following letter and casually mentioned he was a first pilot.

11 Sept. 44

Hi Folks—

Time to write a few lines again I reckon.

Just got a letter from Helen, seems to like it OK back there, and it seems like everyone is treating them swell.

Hope everything is swell with all of you at home. How is Uncle Ben?

Incidentally, got a letter from Hal Sonntag and he sends you his regards as always. Haven't heard from Dave or Del, and haven't had a chance to see Mark Kennedy here yet.

Incidentally again I got your package with the light plugs, which are fine. Thanks very much.

Also incidentally once more, I am now checked out as a first pilot.

Listening to Bob Hope now, so it's hard to concentrate on both.

Saw another kid from school the other day.

Pop, did I ask you to send me some sweat socks? If not, will you put some in with something sometime when you send something?

Not much news otherwise, everything is fine here, hope the same there.

Love,
Bert

While winter weather would soon be a factor in Bert Robinson's missions, and the 301st would fly only sixteen accredited missions in September, five less than in August, there was also a pronounced change in the comparative average number of planes the 301st launched per mission in August and September, going from twenty-six per mission in August to thirty-three in September. Sorties were 553 in August and 534 in September. Bombs dropped in September totaled 1,435.625 tons in August and 1,196.447 tons in September.

While the prize question of the month was "Where's the Luftwaffe?" because no encounters with German fighters took place the whole month, and only two Me 109s were seen from a distance, there was no question about flak. Thirty crew members were missing from three aircraft counted lost, two men were killed, and twelve more were wounded aboard returning aircraft. As one of the 301st gunners remarked, "Jerry may be out, but those flak guns sure as H— aren't!"

There was a group change of command the last week of September, with Colonel Batjer leaving for a new assignment in Bucharest, Hungary, and Lieutenant Colonel John D. Moorman as his replacement, who came into the 301st from the 5th Bombardment Wing.

An Oklahoma native, he attended schools there before entering West Point and graduating four years later in 1938. After receiving his wings at Kelly Field in 1939, he was assigned to Panama, returning in 1942 and serving with the 2nd Air Force as a group commander throughout the period of that air force expanded training program. In March 1944, he was sent to Italy. He was married, the father of a boy and a girl, who remained at home with their mother in Colorado Springs, Colorado.

The September summary history narrative also noted that the month "saw much assembling and ceremony with the award of many decorations to the officers and men for extraordinary heroism, superior leadership, and disregard for personal safety." The writer listed officers and men who received decorations, including Lieutenant Colonel Leslie W. Holman, the first Oak Leaf Cluster to his Distinguished Flying Cross (DFC) for leading the 7 August mission against Blechhammer, Germany, when his aircraft was heavily damaged by flak, four key members of his crew bailed out, and he and his copilot, First Lieutenant John W. Kelly, safely led all their 301st Group aircraft to base, except one missing and presumed down. Three other officers received Oak Leaf Clusters to their DFCs. Five officers, including the outgoing group commander, Colonel Batjer, and two enlisted men, received Silver Stars. Twenty-nine officers and men were decorated with the DFC, and six enlisted men earned the Bronze Star.

Then the monthly summary turned to losses. Two men on returning aircraft were killed in action, Staff Sergeant Jack D. Farmer and Sergeant Paul E. Tilite, both by flak on 10 September in a mission against targets in Vienna, Austria. Five officers and one enlisted man were wounded, all by flak on the same mission, while two other aircraft were shot down by flak, with all aboard declared missing. Two more officers and four enlisted men total were wounded in missions on 17, 18, and 20 September, with three in the mission of the 21st.

Twenty 301st Group crew members were declared missing in the two aircraft lost over Vienna, Austria, on 10 September, with another ten reported missing as a result of the 12 September mission over Lechfeld, Germany. Downed on 10 September were B-17Gs 44-6353, pilot and aircraft commander Second Lieutenant Gail E. Stubbs, 32nd Squadron, and 44-6348, pilot and aircraft commander Second Lieutenant Kenneth A. Wisner, 352nd Squadron. Fortunately, statements from crews who saw the two airplanes going down said they saw parachutes in both instances, and in the case of 6353, all ten crew members were recorded as having received POW medals.

Coincidentally, on board Lieutenant Stubbs's aircraft, 44-6353, as the engineer/gunner was Staff Sergeant Donald H. McCloskey, who, on the 7 August mission as a waist gunner on another 32nd Squadron aircraft that was flying on the right wing of Lieutenant Colonel Leslie Holman's mission-lead aircraft against the synthetic oil refinery at Blechhammer. He had seen and reported the four parachutes when four key crew members had bailed out with no order to bail out of Colonel Holman's aircraft shortly after his no. 4 engine was hit by flak, setting it on fire. There were two witnesses to the loss and possible crew status of 44-6353, and one or both observed the use of parachutes, but the unit history makes no mention of how many parachutes were seen among the ten possible. The time of aircraft loss was reported as 1035B (meaning the local time at Lucera).

Last sighted going down as a result of flak seven minutes later was 352nd aircraft 44-6348. There were three witnesses to the airplane's and crew's status while the aircraft was going down, and again, parachutes were observed, but available records didn't indicate how many. Closer examination of crew records, however, revealed that all ten men became POWs.

One more group combat loss in September was a 32nd Squadron aircraft that occurred on the 12th, with no details available in the unit history to explain what happened or the status of individual crew members. The September combat losses ended on 12 September in spite of the fact the group flew missions against Blechhammer oil refineries, Germany, again on the 13th; Salamis, Germany, on the 15th; the Budapest marshaling yard, Hungary, on the 17th; the Belgrade railroad bridge, Yugoslavia, on the 18th; back to the Budapest marshaling yard on the 20th; the Debreczen marshaling yard, Hungary, on the 21st; the Munich industrial area, Germany, on the 22nd; and the Brux oil refinery, Czechoslovakia, on the 23rd. The missions Bert Robinson flew as pilot and aircraft commander in September 1944 were increasing his skills as both a combat pilot and a leader for the crews with whom he flew and were preparing him for successful completion of his tour of duty during the 15th Air Force's air campaign against Nazi targets.

Still recovering from combat losses in July and August, the group received seven complete crews and nine new aircraft fresh from the factories during September, bringing the group an operational capacity of fifty-three crews and fifty-eight aircraft. It is important to note that the fifty-three crews still totaled less than desired to operate at optimal capacity going into October. During the same month of September, however, the historian noted that the linemen had been kept quite busy since no added ground personnel were assigned to take care of the increase in crews or aircraft. Left unsaid was the clear indication that this was not a desirable circumstance.

The narrative summary also noted that the weather had been of considerable detriment to flying as well as morale. Winterization of the base had begun in earnest in September, including raising the runways, and new construction was under way, with new S-2 (intelligence) and S-3 (operations) offices and a large group briefing room in progress, which would double as a theater. Plans for huts and stone houses were off the drawing board, and the summary humorously described each squadron area as looking "like the Federal Housing Program back home."

Not only was this bit of humor inserted in the narrative, but another, lighter note was also included in a section titled "NOW IT CAN BE TOLD":

Quite a number of our personnel have unquestionably become members of the Lonely Heart's Club, now that the WAC's have moved from this vicinity.

During their stay here, our clubs were opened and dances were held once or twice a week and too, there were quite a few picnics and beach parties that took place these summer months.

But with their parting, it neatly puts us back in the hole with a board plastered over it.

The 301st experienced sixteen combat losses in the period from September to December 1944: three in September, one in October, five in November, and seven in December. October began the weather cycle limiting missions over occupied Europe, with the total of accredited missions numbering thirteen, many of them accomplished by PFF bombing. Attacks were against such industrial targets as Blechhammer, Brux, Klagenfurt, Innsbruck, Munich, and Vienna, with bombs totaling 411.43 tons showered on Nazi targets.

There were 339 operational sorties, primarily into Germany, totaling 2,443 hours of operational flying, and for the second successive month no enemy fighters were encountered. Flak remained aggressive and heavy, costing the group one man killed in action, three men wounded, and one nine-man crew missing. As the month of October drew to a close, the influx of replacement aircraft and crews began causing other problems for the group. Aircraft numbered sixty-six, with fifty-seven crews adding to operational capacity at the end of the month, while in the same time period the frequency of accredited missions was falling, resulting in crews being able to fly fewer missions. The impact of increased restrictive weather and decreased missions was somewhat offset by an increase in the average number of group aircraft put up each mission to thirty-three. Yet aircraft maintenance and housing were becoming matters of concern, coming hand in hand with morale as potentially a major problem—aggravated by numerous forecasts of the war's end.

Commanders were already seeing it as obvious that the approaching winter months would make it impossible to fly all, or even 50 percent, of the existing aircrews. They foresaw the need for flight training when weather permitted and class work on the ground to both occupy a part of crews' available time and uphold combat effectiveness when called upon to fly missions. What's more, winter evenings were going to be long and dull until other, appealing activities could be found to pass the time constructively.

While it was important to keep aircrews occupied constructively, it was absolutely vital that outlets for ground personnel also be available, because they were being stretched, laboring longer to service the increase in aircraft and crews. The group was moving to meet their problems with clubs, classes, and organized recreation, while the new Morale Services for the special orientation of the airmen, was working closely with the Special Services staff.

The newspaper, *Bombs Away*, which had been dormant after its original startup in St. Donet, Africa, in May 1943 and had ceased when overcome by preparatory events for the Italian landings, now began operation in October 1944. The group newspaper was under direction of Lieutenant Crane McAtee, Special Services officer, and Lieutenant Richard H. Goldstone, group personnel officer, with staff editors from each of the squadrons. Every page of the first issue of *Bombs Away* was printed in the group's October history. They were confident their newspaper would be stiff competition for the army's *Stars and Stripes*. The paper's new masthead boasted the names of those enlisted men who aided the return of *Bombs Away*.

The same month, beginning 27 October, and also explained in the paper, the group formed a male chorus, which began meeting Friday evenings, with transportation services provided from squadron orderly rooms, voluntary participation in religious activities of the men's choosing, and other diverse secular venues.

Exchange programs with other army units began, one example attested to in *Bombs Away* involving Lieutenant Howell L. Pos of the 353rd Squadron, who had recently returned from the 5th Army front after spending four days of duty with the infantry. He volunteered and signed up as a tank driver but wound up in the infantry, and he gave a full account of his activities. Among his observations were how he was met by an infantry colonel along with a first sergeant from another bomb group on a similar exchange and was given a jeep and directions to the headquarters they were to report to, five miles behind the front lines; vivid descriptions of artillery exchanges at night while attempting to sleep; murals of German army life painted on the walls by a German soldier before the Germans were driven from the area a few nights earlier; the quality of meals for men on the line, which he was surprised to learn "were better than ours"; and how one soon learns how to recognize which shells are enemy and which are friendly—especially since the first night he and everyone else had to evacuate their quarters due to incoming German rounds.

Organized sports also received big play in *Bombs Away*, with competition between squadrons in the 301st and between groups. Basketball competition got under way, with Bert Robinson quickly making his mark on the 419th Bombers team, "paced by Lt. Vic Robinson . . . crushed the 726th Rattlers (a B-24 outfit) by 44 to 19. The first half was rough and tumble with both teams literally fighting for the ball. The bombers were tougher and at the whistle [half] were out front 13–7."

The flight surgeon's "Care of Fliers" report for the month of October disclosed twenty-three disorders due to flying, amounting to 328 days lost on the sick report, indicating an average recovery time of fourteen days per man. There were ninety-nine other disorders not due to flying, totaling 659 days lost on the sick report, an average recovery period of six and a half days per man. The increase in disorders not due to flying was caused primarily by the wet season and approaching winter, with the accompanying rise in nose, throat, and lung irritants. A total of 138 flying personnel received rest leaves during the month, totaling 851 days, or 6 days per man. (The rest leaves were undoubtedly leaves granted for what became known in the military as rest and recuperation, or R & R—mentioned by the flight surgeon in the next paragraph of his monthly report—to such places as the island of Capri, off the southwest coast of Italy.)

During October, 127 airmen departed upon completing their tours of duty in the theater, and 35 crew members were recommended for rest and recuperation in the Zone of the Interior (the continental United States).

The flight surgeon summarized environmental sanitation remaining at its previous satisfactory level, and the health of the command as a whole remained excellent. He next listed killed, wounded, and missing in action:

KILLED IN ACTION
Flight Officer ROBERT E. FOX, 29 October
(In the 352nd Squadron, killed in the mission against the Munich, Germany marshaling yard)

WOUNDED IN ACTION
First Lieutenant JOHN J. GALE, *29 October*
(In the 352nd Squadron, in the mission against the Munich, Germany marshaling yard)

Staff Sergeant RUSSELL L. MC DONALD, *12 October*
Sergeant VERNON E. KADEL, *12 October*
(Both men were wounded during the mission against the Belogna, Italy bivouac area. S/Sgt. McDonald was in the 353rd Squadron and Sergeant Kadel was in the 419th Squadron)

The following named officers and enlisted men are listed as missing in action from an operational mission against the Florisdorf oil refinery, at Vienna, Austria on 13 October, 1944:

SHAPIRO, *Irving D., 1st Lt., Pilot*
SHUMAKER, *David M., 1st Lt., Co-Pilot*
MCELLIGOTT, *Thomas F., 1st Lt., Navigator*
BEAR, *George H., 1st Lt., Bombardier*
DEBSKI, *Francis J., T/Sgt., Engineer/Gunner*
JOHN, *David, T/Sgt., Radio Operator/Gunner*
HAGAN, *Martin R., S/Sgt., Left Gunner*
MAYBERRY, *William P., S/Sgt., Right Gunner*
BERGERHOFER, *Albert, S/Sgt., Tail Gunner*

The 12 October mission that resulted in two men being wounded encountered moderate to heavy, inaccurate flak in the target area, with one aircraft returning with major damage and fourteen with minor damage.

There were two missions on 13 October. One was against Blechhammer South oil refinery, Germany. No aircraft were lost, but eight returned with minor flak damage. The other was to Florisdorf oil refinery, Vienna, Austria, where the one October combat loss occurred.

There were at least three witnesses to the loss of the 353rd Squadron's B-17G aircraft number 44-6363, piloted and commanded by First Lieutenant Irving D. Shapiro on the 13 October mission against the Florisdorf refinery. During the mission debriefing, crews stated that flak was encountered at the target and described it as intense, heavy, and accurate. In addition to the loss of Lieutenant Shapiro's aircraft, three returned with major damage and nine with minor damage. The aircraft felled by flak was last seen at about 1134 hours, base time, when visibility was very poor.

Though there were slight differences in the statements signed by the three witnesses on 15 October, there was fundamental agreement on major points. The formation was in between layers of clouds, the lowest believed to be about twelve thousand feet, the second layer approximately twenty-five to twenty-six thousand feet. The aircraft took a direct hit on the no. 3 (right inboard) engine just prior to or immediately after bombs away, and the propeller came off. The aircraft immediately turned right, out of the formation, descending under control. First Lieutenant Louis N. Baxter, bombardier on aircraft 44-6382, piloted by First Lieutenant Louis P. House and flying in the 1-2 position, reported seeing a large hole in the right side of the aircraft, near the copilot's seat, and a "small fire" in the no. 3 engine, and he expressed his belief that "the crew had an excellent chance of getting out." Lieutenant House's copilot on the same aircraft, Second Lieutenant David C, Brown, saw the loss of the propeller, and according to him, "the ship then dove down and to the right out of the formation." Technical Sergeant George D. Tucker, left gunner on aircraft 42-32105, flying in the 1-3 position and piloted by Second Lieutenant Robert A. Carrod, stated, "The propeller flew straight up. Looked like the ship peeled off to the right. No chutes were seen. A/C not on fire."

The crew of nine on 44-6363 were all captured, but the tail gunner, Staff Sergeant Albert Bergerhofer, was wounded and hospitalized by the Germans. He later was declared killed in action, while all other crew members were repatriated after the war.

The 301st flew seventeen accredited missions in November, seventeen in December, seven in January 1945, and twenty in February, the month Bert Robinson was ordered to return to the United States.

November missions continued to hit flak-heavy defended targets, resulting in an increase in combat losses to five in the month, two from the 352nd Squadron and three in the 353rd. Targets included Rosenheim, Germany, twice, once against an oil storage area on 4 November and the second against a marshaling yard on the 22nd, and Blechhammer, Germany, twice, on the 13th and 20th, both against oil refinery targets. Oil refinery targets at Vienna, Austria, were struck on 5, 7, and 18 November, and the 301st returned to Vienna a fourth time on the 19th to hit an oil storage area; oil refinery missions were sent against Linz, Austria, on 15, 24, and 30 November; on the 6th the group struck an oil refinery at Moosbierbaum, Austria; on the 7th was a strike on a marshaling yard in Maribor, Yugoslavia, then another marshaling yard in Salsburg, Austria, on 11 November, and coming back to Salsburg on the 17th and targeting an oil refinery; and strikes against transportation centers in Novipazar and Prijepolje, Yugoslavia, on 16 and 18 November.

The 353rd Squadron's first loss occurred on 7 November, B-17G aircraft 44-6263, piloted by Second Lieutenant George R. Kulp with a crew of ten. Parachutes were observed, and the plane was last seen to crash at approximately 1221 on the mission to the marshaling yard at Maribor, Yugoslavia. All ten were listed as missing but were captured and returned after the war.

The 352nd Squadron's loss of B-17G aircraft 42-97738 occurred on 13 November in a strike on a Blechhammer, Germany, oil refinery, with no information available, due to weather, as to what occurred. The pilot was First Lieutenant Wayne A. Wendt of Kalispell, Montana. Storms were briefed to be present in the route of flight. Witnesses observed nothing of substance to assist in understanding why the aircraft went down. The 301st history records were incomplete except for notations indicating that two crew members survived and returned home.

On 15 November, the 352nd lost B-17G aircraft 42-97728 during the oil refinery strike at Linz, Austria. The pilot and aircraft commander was Second Lieutenant Albert H.

Mitchko among a crew of ten. Strong winds were encountered all along the mission route, and weather was deemed the reason for the loss. First Lieutenant Joseph V. Morgan, a group duty officer, the sole witness of the plane's loss, received an SOS message relayed from 728 by a ground station at 1042 hours. Lieutenant Morgan's statement, signed on 17 November 1944, further explained that six PB-17G aircraft of the 301st Group took off at one-minute intervals from 0720 to 0724 hours to bomb Linz Tank Works, Linz, Austria. These aircraft were not flying formation and were to bomb individually. In the statement, Lieutenant Morgan explained further that the SOS message timing kept duty officers from determining whether the aircraft was returning early or was still en route to the target. Since they gave no position during the SOS, it was impossible to plot their position from the briefing navigator's flight plan.

The two survivors were Staff Sergeant Roy T. Patterson of Tyler, Texas, engineer and top turret gunner, and Second Lieutenant Harry P. Hillhouse of Birmingham, Alabama, navigator.

An oral thirdhand account of the aircraft loss came many years later from Larry D. Patterson, son of former staff sergeant Roy T. Patterson, who had passed away in February 1997. Over the years, Larry had spoken many hours with his father about his World War II experiences. It is a story of survival under desperate circumstances and credits Roy Patterson's survival to the crew's navigator, Second Lieutenant Harry Hillhouse, who literally kicked him out of the aircraft when it was spinning out of control and Patterson froze, refusing to bail out at the navigator's escape hatch.

What Roy Patterson probably didn't remember in discussing his experiences with his son was that on 4 September 1945, after his return to Tyler, Texas, he had written a statement to the army air force in which he recalled the loss of the airplane and all he could remember about the other crew members.

Roy Patterson had told his son that he was on his fourth mission and he was assigned to a crew and airplane that was not his because their gunner was sick. During the flight, one of the four engines quit. The tail gunner told the pilot that the engine was losing oil, but the pilot replied back that he would get it to restart. The pilot then told the bombardier to find some kind of target to get rid of the bomb load, which he did. The pilot did not feather the engine, and in a short time the engine seized up, causing the huge, completely stopped, three-bladed propeller to produce an unacceptable drag on the airplane and a virtually unstoppable loss of speed, resulting in a stall and out-of-control spin. Larry's father fell out of the top turret down to the emergency hatch below him and kicked it open. Roy Patterson then froze over the hatch, and the next thing he knew, the navigator, Second Lieutenant Harry P. Hillhouse, kicked him out of the airplane. There followed an incredible story of the use of his emergency "belly chute" to safely land after parachuting at what he believed was twenty thousand feet, capture by a civilian with a shotgun, being isolated in a small enclosure for about six to eight weeks, eventual turnover to a German soldier, months of internment in a Stalag Luft (German) POW camp, then being forced to march and countermarch in midwinter for five to six months as German guards moved west to attempt to first evade the oncoming Soviet Army and then avoid capture by the Western allies moving toward them, before the German guards gave their prisoners their guns, some asking to be shot, or fleeing.

Roy Patterson's 4 September 1945 statement explained that they were flying at thirty-one thousand feet to stay above stormy weather. The oil line on the no. 2 engine broke. The pilot never got the prop feathered in time, and the windmilling propeller caused the plane to lose altitude and enter the storm. He stated that there was also something wrong with the instruments, and the aircraft was being "thrown around bad." The pilot called over the interphone telling the crew not to get excited—he still had control. Patterson decided to put on his parachute anyway. He had just gotten it on when the airplane went out of control, and Patterson concluded it was in a spin. The centrifugal force slung him against the escape hatch, and he heard someone scream, "Get the hell out of here." Patterson released the escape hatch and went out of the aircraft. Due to weather conditions, he was not able to determine whether anyone else got out, and he never heard anything more about any of the crew until he got home and learned that parents of the crew had been communicating. He wrote all of them after he returned, and all he knew was that everyone was still missing in action.

On 14 November 1945, at Goodfellow Field, San Angelo, Texas, then first lieutenant Harry P. Hillhouse wrote a statement regarding the loss of 728 and all he knew regarding the other nine men of the crew a year earlier. He stated that the aircraft and crew were on a single-plane, delayed-action bombing mission to Linz, Austria—meaning they were on a "lone wolf" type mission against a single target with delayed-action fuses on their bombs. They were airborne at 0730 hours at Lucera, Italy, and at approximately 1130, while returning from their target, engine trouble developed in the no. 2 and no. 4 engines. He further stated that blizzard and icing conditions were prevalent, and at approximately thirty-two thousand feet the plane nosed over into a power spin. The pilot gave the orders to bail out over the interphone system and by means of the alarm bell.

Lieutenant Hillhouse went on to write that at that time none of them had their parachutes off, and he had difficulty getting out of the plane due to g-force pressure (in the spin) and gravity. He managed to crawl to the navigator's escape hatch and got his feet out in the slipstream and was drawn out of the plane. At the time he left the plane, the only other crew member who had bailed out was the engineer, Staff Sergeant Roy Patterson. All other crew members were in the plane when Hillhouse left it. He estimated the altitude of bailout at sixteen thousand feet.

He landed on the southwest side of a cliff on top of the Grossglockner Mountains and slid five thousand feet in a northwest direction down into the valley at the base of the mountain. He didn't see the plane crash from where he landed. Three impassable mountains obstructed his view. He was alone in this vicinity and stopped at an Austrian farmhouse. The next day he was picked up by the Gestapo.

Nothing else changed over the many years following the war, and the other eight crew members on 728 were eventually declared killed in action.

The 353rd Squadron lost B-17G aircraft number 44-6549 and six of its nine crew members to a midair collision with another 353rd aircraft, number 42-97910, when the 301st

Group was returning from a mission against the Florisdorf oil refinery, Vienna, Austria, on 18 November. The collision occurred about five minutes prior to the group formation's passing over the coast of Yugoslavia to cross the Adriatic Sea en route to Lucera. Weather wasn't a factor in the crash. The stunning collision in clear air with unlimited visibility cost the lives of all but three crew members, who were returned to base after successfully bailing out over friendly territory. There were several other witnesses to the midair collision in addition to the three crew members who survived the tragedy: Technical Sergeant David D. Ellison, togglier (in effect the bombardier on the B-17G), from San Antonio, Texas; Sergeant Vernon P. McKinley, engineer, from Whiting, Indiana; and Sergeant William E. Grinstead, waist gunner, from Albin, Wyoming. Men in other aircrews who submitted statements included Second Lieutenant Edward W. Lahr, navigator, whose aircraft, 42-97910, was flying the 3-3 position, in 301st combat box formation; Sergeant Walter F. Stiever, tail gunner on aircraft 42-32105, flying in the 3-2 position; and Staff Sergeant Joseph (NMI) Mena, tail gunner on 44-8161, flying the 2-1 position. (On the author's personal website, within the chapter 13 photographs, see the diagram of the twelve-plane combat box formation, which was normally flown by the B-17 groups in the 15th Air Force.)

The sequence of events described by the witnesses not on board 6549 were as follows: Second Lieutenant Albert L. Luster was the element lead in the third element of the lead squadron in the 301st's mission that day when his no. 2 engine (left inboard) began losing oil, causing him to feather the engine as he dropped back and down from his lead position in the element. Second Lieutenant Edward W. Lahr was the navigator in aircraft 42-97910, in the 3-3 position (on the right wing of 6549) when the aircraft

dropped back out of the formation and we were moving over into the 3-1 position. I heard someone say over the interphone "Pull it up, pull it up!" About the same time I heard a thump. We were not as yet in the 3-1 position when the accident occurred, but saw an airplane slipping away to the right, noticed no. 3 prop missing and no. 2 windmilling. There was a hole through the navigators flight deck about 8" wide and the width of the airplane, apparently caused by the prop of A/C No. 44-6549 cutting through. There was a hole in the right side by the escape kit. Our position at the time of the accident was 43 degrees 35 minutes North, 16 degrees 15 minutes East. After check of the damage, we decided to try for the base, which we easily made. No. 4 engine was leaking oil. When last sighted, A/C No. 44-6549 was in a spin and 3 parachutes were seen to land on the Yugoslavia Coast.

Sergeant Walter F. Stiever, tail gunner on aircraft 42-32105, flying in position 3-2 (on the left wing) of Lieutenant Luster's aircraft, provided another view of what occurred. He stated that his pilot called him and told him to watch where aircraft 6549 was going, that he had one prop feathered and was dropping back. Sergeant Stiever watched the airplane drop to the rear of 32105 (his aircraft). He then observed aircraft 44-97910 cross over the top of him, and when he was right above him, 6549 came up underneath and his tail got in the prop of 97910. The entire tail was broken off of 6549, and the plane rolled over and went into a spin. Stiever further stated that he saw three parachutes open, and then saw the plane crash in a small town, and it might have hit a building in the town.

One other crew member in the lead aircraft in the second element, which was to the left of both the lead and third elements in the box formation, gave yet another perspective of what occurred. Staff Sergeant Joseph Mena, tail gunner in aircraft 44-8161, flying the 2-1 position, recalled seeing 6549 pulling out of the formation to feather its no. 2 engine, which was leaking oil. He saw aircraft 42-97910, in the 3-3 position, pull out of the formation with him about five minutes before reaching the Adriatic coast. After 6549 feathered its prop, it started to come back into formation, moving back toward the 3-1 position. Then, as it was in direct line with his aircraft, a little low, 97910 started to come in, trying to take the element lead position, and in doing so came directly above 6549. He believed he saw 97910 come down on 6549, as it was almost in its level flight (proper position as element lead, the 3-1 position). Approximately five minutes before the coast on their way back to base, he saw only one parachute come out of the airplane and watched the aircraft until it hit the ground and exploded. (It is important to note that standard operating procedures undoubtedly stated that if an element lead dropped or fell out of a combat formation, one of the two wingmen in the element was designated to succeed as element lead and would move into the element lead position to provide continuity in leadership.)

Each of the three surviving crew members of 6549 had harrowing experiences attempting to bail out of the spinning aircraft. Technical Sergeant David D. Ellison recalled that he bailed out at about five thousand feet after struggling to salvo the escape hatch, assisted behind him by the engineer, Sergeant Vernon P. McKinley, whose chute opened at approximately five hundred feet. People around where he landed told him five chutes came out of the plane. Of the five, one failed to open or didn't open completely. The waist gunner, Sergeant Grinstead, stated that he bailed out between ten thousand and fourteen thousand feet and said he understood the people when they indicated that four parachutes were seen and one didn't open.

The 301st Group's fifth and final November loss occurred on 25 November 1944 in a mission ordered by the 15th Air Force. The 353rd Squadron received the single-ship night mission, flown by aircraft 42-97685 and commanded by the pilot, First Lieutenant Charles A. Govatsos of Milton, Massachusetts. The planned altitude of the mission was eighteen thousand feet with time on target planned for 0330 hours (3:30 a.m.) on an oil refinery in Linz, Austria.

In a brief summary written after the war, Lieutenant Govatsos recalled and summarized what occurred prior to and on the mission. He and his crew were formed as a crew in Tampa, Florida, and arrived in the 301st Group at Foggia in October 1944. The weather for the mission was expected to be a complete overcast all the way to the target. About an hour before reaching the target, the sky cleared, the aircraft was hit in its no. 1 engine by flak, and the prop could not be feathered. The engine caught fire, and Govatsos and his crew had to bail out at 2:00 a.m. on the border of Austria and Yugoslavia.

He landed in a small village in the mountains and in about five hours he was found by Tito's underground and later was joined with other crew members. The navigator and bombardier were POWs of the Germans. The underground was well organized and explained how they were going to walk the crew members out. Govatsos caught dysentery and had to stay in a small village for a few days. His radio operator stayed with him, as he could speak German. Later they joined another group and walked back to a site where a C-47 landed in a field and picked them up on 27 December 1944. He had been missing thirty-two days.

Bombardier Second Lieutenant Novello A. Gubitosi and navigator Second Lieutenant Arthur R. Moran, both captured by the Germans, were repatriated after the war, while all eight of the remaining crew were returned to Foggia and reunited in January 1945. Some flew additional missions before returning home safely from the war.

The seventeen 301st missions flown in December were all once again hazardous, especially in terms of antiaircraft fire, which continued unabated while Germany's Luftwaffe was being decimated over the German heartland by the Allies' relentless bombing and fighter campaigns—from the east and the west—following the 6 June landings in Normandy, while the Soviet armies and air forces drove ever deeper through Europe from the east. The result in 15th Air Force operations was the continued almost total absence of German fighter attacks on bombers throughout the final months of 1944 and into 1945.

The 301st historian summarized the beginning of December operations by describing the two types of targets attacked that month: oil and marshaling yards, beginning with the 2 December 15th Air Force mission against oil refineries in Blechhammer, Germany, with 162 B-17s and 195 B-24s, 276 of them dropping 568 tons of bombs on the primary target. The 301st launched forty aircraft, but only fourteen B-17s from the 32nd and 419th squadrons hit the primary target, achieving limited results due to poor radarscope identification. The 15th Air Force noted that only one Me 210 was seen, and one crew member in a straggling bomber with three engines running rough spotted three Me 109s within five hundred yards. The German fighters turned toward the bomber but then flew off, apparently inhibited by the army air force escort. It was on this mission that Bert Robinson took actions that earned him a Distinguished Flying Cross.

En route to the primary target, he learned that his engineer/gunner, Ed Schlittenhart, whose crew position was right behind him, had forgotten his oxygen mask, a discovery made when Bert commanded the routine oxygen check by the crew while the formation was climbing toward "crew, masks on, oxygen required" altitude. He had previously told his crew that any man who forgot his oxygen mask would have to suck on the hose the rest of the mission. The mistake wasn't to be a reason to abort the mission, and since that time, it became routine to have an extra mask on board in the event that a crew member made such an error. But on this mission, no extra mask could be found. Thus Schlittenhart dutifully did as his aircraft commander ordered. He "sucked on the hose." Nevertheless, the procedure wasn't foolproof in preventing hypoxia, and Bert remained concerned about the safety of his errant crew member.

Bert and his crew were among the fourteen 301st bombers to hit the primary target that day, and after they dropped their bombs and were turning in formation to go home, more serious difficulties began. On 4 December, apparently already told he would receive a Distinguished Flying Cross for his actions, Bert wrote in his own words what happened next:

I told the copilot to take over and turned to see if Schlittenhart was okay. I had all of the tubes and wires connected and couldn't turn far, but I could see he was slumped over. I didn't realize it, but I had pulled out the wire to the crew intercom, and couldn't tell them we were going down. I motioned to the copilot to go back and put Schlittenhart on the hose again. I turned back in my seat and pulled back on the throttles to start a rapid descent. We started going down [using his hands to describe how big planes go down to lower altitude, as they do by turning in formation], banking from side to side, sliding on one wing and then the other, trying not to look as if we were in trouble.

Regulars on my crew stayed in place and waited to see what was going on. The radio operator (not a regular) grabbed his chute, got to the waist door to bail out. My two waist gunners grabbed him and sat on him and told him to wait. The tail gunner waited at the exit door and buckled his chute on.

When we got down below ten thousand feet, I leveled off and turned around to see that Schlittenhart was coming around. The copilot was giving him pure oxygen.

At that point I started to radio to find a group of 17's that were starting to descend on a return trip. We eased up under them to the rear and went into a space with that group. Turns out it was our group! They had been surprised to see us bank out and surprised to see us back in formation.

We gradually caught up with our squadron. They were slowly coming down (lower RPMs to conserve fuel) as we were slowly going up to meet them.

Bert later once more showed his modesty and unassuming ways when he wrote home mentioning the Distinguished Flying Cross in a letter: "Don't pay any attention to all the 'baloney' along with it—that stuff goes on every day. . . . And like I told you with air medals, Mom, don't go spreading it all over the place, because it's mostly routine stuff. OK?"

Meanwhile, as Bert and his crew flew on toward Blechhammer, Germany, another bomber from the 419th was lost.

About an hour and a half after takeoff, First Lieutenant Eugene Tillotson's 419th Squadron Fortress 44-6186 began leaking fuel from his no. 2 engine. After trying unsuccessfully to feather the propeller, he asked permission to leave the formation to make an emergency landing on an island on the other coast of the Adriatic, but a new major who had just come to the squadron denied the request.

Finally, Tillotson broke from the formation, but by this time the leak had worsened and one engine caught on fire. The crew spotted and headed toward a convoy intending to bail out nearby, but there was now fire inside the aircraft. The pilot ordered the crew to bail out. Six men got out, and others went into the Adriatic with the downed bomber. Despite mountainous waves, a British boat picked up four crew members after they had been in the water for approximately forty-five minutes.

In spite of this account, surviving crew members' statements and the finding of two bodies suggest that possibly nine of the ten crew members successfully bailed out, but not all nine survived in the water. Second Lieutenant William N. Ferguson of Windsor, Missouri, bombardier; Master Sergeant Robert M. Noel of Mackville, Kentucky, lower turret gunner; Sergeant J. D. Grigg of Inola, Oklahoma; and Technical Sergeant John H. De Hart of Beaumont, Texas, survived. Second Lieutenant Ferguson, Sergeant Noel, and Technical Sergeant De Hart wrote statements that not surprisingly differed in what each man observed during their harrowing escape and bailout over rough seas from a burning B-17.

Lieutenant Ferguson's statement read in part,

> *After about an hour and a half of flying I noticed a strong smell of gasoline fumes. The ball turret gunner called out the number two engine was leaking gas. We turned back toward base and about fifteen (15) miles from the coast the engine caught fire. The pilot gave the order to prepare to abandon ship. The navigator and I put on our chutes and waited at door for order to bail out. About thirty (30) seconds the order came and I opened the door and stepped out of the plane. After my chute opened I looked back and counted four chutes but then lost sight of plane. A few seconds later I again saw the plane, which had just pulled out of a dive about 200 feet from the water.*

Sergeant Noel didn't comment on the number of chutes he observed, instead explaining the manner in which the engine fire on the no. 2 engine occurred, the fact that heavy smoke was inside the airplane when he bailed out, his struggles to free himself from his chute once in the water, and his approximate thirty minutes in the water before he was picked up by an escort vessel.

Technical Sergeant De Hart insisted that he counted nine chutes "dropping toward the water" and ended his statement with "It is my opinion that all but the pilot got out of the plane, as I am sure I saw nine (9) chutes, including my own. I was picked up by an English cavette [corvette] after about an hour in the water."

December missions included three to Linz, Austria, two to oil refineries and one to marshaling yards; four to Blechhammer, Germany, all against oil refineries; two to Regensburg, Germany, both against oil refineries; two to Moosbierbaum, Austria, against oil refineries; two missions against oil refineries in Brux, Czechoslovakia; one against an aircraft factory in Klagenfurt, Austria; one against an oil refinery in Odertal, Germany; and one against a railhead in Castelfranco, Italy.

On 15 December, Bert wrote a letter home and expressed some mild exasperation with his mother over her apparently repeated belief that the Germans were about to quit fighting. His emotions probably also reflected the hazards and losses the 301st and 15th Air Force continued to endure in the bombing campaigns over Nazi Germany and the Balkans.

15 Dec '44

Hi Folks—

Got two letters from you today. Not much to write, but will answer some of your questions.

Yes, I think I get most all your letters, but the length of time enroute varies, from 6 or 8 days to over a month at times. These were mailed Nov. 17 and 19th.

Mom, you always say surely the Germans will fold up now. Lord knows we all wish they'd fold tomorrow and it's possible they might. But it's also possible that they will have to fight through to the last of Berlin. You probably read in the paper about someone in Italy being short of ammunition, also in France. Also of Patton's Army stopping their advance because of fuel shortages. The guys up at the fronts are fighting just as hard now as they were a year ago, and it will be just as tough or tougher this winter, and nobody over here likes to think of people assuming the war is over. It is all over except for the fighting. I hope they fold tomorrow Mom, but I don't think they will, and let's don't keep assuming the Krauts are all through fighting, even though we wish it, OK?

Of the seven losses the 301st suffered in December, three were from the 419th Squadron, the second on 17 December against Blechhammer North oil refinery. The pilot and aircraft commander was Second Lieutenant Michael J. Kearns; the aircraft number 42-32104, named "St. Francis," was carrying a crew of ten. All six B-17 groups in the 5th Bombardment Wing were committed against the target, with target time of 1200 hours. The aircraft was last seen at approximately 1230 hours about twenty-one miles southeast of Blechhammer. It had fallen back from the formation for reasons unknown; it reappeared and attempted to rejoin, but it fell back again and disappeared.

All of the ten-man crew were eventually captured by the Germans. The copilot, Second Lieutenant David M. Jones of Shamokin, Pennsylvania, evaded capture for a time. The togglier, Technical Sergeant Leo J. Dyga of Muskegon, Michigan, was wounded prior to capture, was hospitalized by the Germans and recovered, and was repatriated after the war, as were eight other crew members. Sergeant Alvin J. Ellin, tail gunner, of Norton, Virginia, was shot to death—murdered—by a German SS police, Sergeant Swittaj, shortly after his capture on 17 December 1944.

The facts surrounding the aircraft's loss were explained after the war by returning crew members, and the tragedy and bitter irony of Sergeant Ellin's murder emerged from a number of sources, including crew members, German POW documents, and sympathetic Polish citizens who marked Sergeant Ellin's burial site, according to them, after his killers attempted to hide their crime by burying him next to a barn.

The German document stated,

The crew bailed out by parachute. One man being captured A.J. ELLIN was shot by the police Sgt. Swittaj at the attempt to escape. According to statement of physician the death was afflicted by a bullet through the abdomen. . . . Ellin was buried at the cemetery of Jawischowitz district of Bielitz—grave location between mortuary (tool booth) and hedge—on 20 December 1944 at 1700. 1 polish gravedigger and the police master (police post Jawischowitz) attended the burial.

According to his features E. had a Jewish appearance. No pictures of the grave were taken.

The copilot, Second Lieutenant Jones, reported after the war that Polish citizens in the vicinity who aided Jones in evading capture informed him that Gestapo agents had shot and killed one crew member upon landing. The name of the crew member killed was unknown to Jones until his arrival in the States. Correspondence with the engineer, Sergeant E. Tinley, informed him that he had seen Ellin unconscious or dead on the ground still in his chute harness, with four bullet wounds. Lieutenant Jones understood the Polish language fairly well and believed that what the people in the vicinity reported was true. All the crew members were armed with pistols, but Ellin was still in his chute harness and Jones could not see why he was shot resisting arrest. Details Lieutenant Jones picked up in that region led him to believe that the Gestapo in that area were particularly ruthless.

An unidentified crew member submitted a casualty report with a Polish newsman's (United Press) piece in a 6 November 1945 Polish newspaper, restating the name of Sergeant Ellin's killer and saying that he shot Ellin once in the back and shoulder and that the Germans tried to hide his body by burying it behind a barn, but the Poles found it and marked the spot. Sergeant Ellin's parachute was "full of blood" and was thrown in front of the other eight crew members then in custody at the Jawischowitz police station, Poland. There is no evidence that Sergeant Ellin's killer was ever held to account.

The final 419th loss was on 29 December in a raid against the Castelfranco Waneto Locomotive Depot, Italy: B-17G 44-6652, carrying a crew of ten men. Two direct flak hits in the ball turret, bomb bay, and radio room areas at twenty thousand feet, over the IP (initial point) to run in to the target but shot down by antiaircraft fire. The men were hit shortly after they made a routine oxygen check. The aircraft went into a steep dive and spin and exploded. The aircraft was last seen at 1200 hours. The pilot was First Lieutenant Lyle C. Pearson of Mankato, Minnesota. Six members of the crew returned after the war, all former POWs. Three were declared killed in action, while one other was declared missing in action but was eventually declared dead.

Astonishingly, the navigator, Second Lieutenant Arthur J. Frechette Jr., who was pinned in the aircraft when it went into the spin, was blown out of the aircraft. He remembered regaining consciousness at approximately three thousand feet and attempting to pull the ripcord on his parachute. Eyewitnesses said his parachute didn't open, but he survived the fall—landing on a snow-covered downslope side of a hill. His injuries included broken legs, arms, and ribs.

Killed in action were engineer gunner, Sergeant Farrell B. Haney; lower turret gunner, Staff Sergeant Charles A. Williams; and waist gunner, Staff Sergeant Mitchell

Vuyanovich. Missing in action and later declared dead was radar operator/gunner, Staff Sergeant Robert J. Halstein.

On 4 January 1945, the 301st launched thirty-one aircraft on a major strike against a railroad marshaling yard in Verona, Italy. Eight aircraft were from the 32nd Squadron, seven from the 352nd, eight from the 353rd, and eight from the 419th. On 8 January, the 301st target was a marshaling yard in Linz, Austria, with two other marshaling yards in Vienna, Austria, on 15 January and Brod, Yugoslavia, on 19 January.

Then, on 20 January 1945, came coffee and donuts for Victor Albert "Bert" Robinson. After his fiftieth mission, this one against an oil storage area in Regensburg, Germany, he flew one additional mission, undoubtedly on 1 February 1945, against Moosbierbaum oil refineries, a mission in which two 419th aircraft were lost.

The first 419th aircraft to be lost on the same mission on 1 February 1945 was B-17G 42-97736, piloted by Major Frank J. Muskus and carrying a crew of ten, last seen at 1237. Eight of the ten men survived the loss and returned following the war after being carried as missing in action. One, Technical Sergeant Hayward S. Alexander, radio operator/gunner, of Los Angeles, California, was declared killed in action, and Staff Sergeant Walter L. Stupak, gunner, of Bear Lake, Pennsylvania, was missing in action and later declared dead. As it happened, First Lieutenant Robert C. Schlarb, the navigator, of Pittsburgh, Pennsylvania, was also on 42-97736. Bob had been on Bill Wilson and Bert Robinson's crew when they flew their aircraft from Langley, Virginia, to Foggia and Lucera, Italy, in July 1944 and had astonished his fellow crew members with his navigation skills when he guided them to a safe arrival at the Azores airfield on the long journey into war. He bailed out of 42-97736, was captured, and remained a POW until the war's end, but he returned home, as did the rest of the eight crew members featured in this chapter.

The second 419th aircraft lost was B-17G 42-32100, nicknamed "Ragged But Right," apparently lost to antiaircraft fire and last seen and contacted by radio at 1242. Witnesses from two different aircraft stated that right after bombs away, the formation was scattered, and by the time they got together, aircraft 32100 was missing. A short time later they heard a radio call stating that he had two engines out and he was going to try to make it to Russia to bail out. Several other planes called him to wish him good luck. All ten crew members returned from the war, with one, Sergeant Edward A. Leonetti, waist gunner, a POW.

Since Bert's arrival in the 419th Squadron that July, the squadron had lost nine aircraft as of 1 February, the equivalent of nearly 75 percent of their aircraft, and, in spite of replacement aircraft and crews that were delivered to Lucera and the four squadrons of the 301st, the number of aircraft lost from this squadron is one perspective and illustration of the odds of any one man against surviving fifty missions for a safe return home.

Of the eight men pictured in Bill Wilson and Bert Robinson's original crew, radio operator Donald E. Lape arrived a corporal in July 1944 and went home a technical sergeant. In 1945, Sergeant Homer L. Isenagle, lower ball-turret gunner, and Staff Sergeant William A. Sanders, waist gunner, both returned from the war. Sanders went back to his home in Blakely, Georgia, where he took a job at Wynn's Department Store and worked for thirty-eight years.

He married Marjorie Houston, and they had three children, Barbara, Andy, and Jack. He passed away on August 13, 2010, at the age of eighty-eight.

Tail gunner Staff Sergeant Terry A. Sanders also returned home safely in March 1945, as did Second Lieutenant Richard L. Hodder, bombardier, wearing the silver bars of a first lieutenant and wearing a Distinguished Flying Cross and three Air Medals with three Oak Leaf Clusters.

First Lieutenant William S. "Bill" Wilson, Bert's aircraft commander on the flight to Italy, also returned home in February 1945. The last mission Bill and Bert had flown together, in command of different aircraft, was to Regensburg, Germany, when afterward Bert carried a broad smile while he drank coffee and ate donuts and a photographer snapped his picture for a press release back home. But there was another memory attached to the mission. He stated that the formations had to make three passes at the target before successfully releasing their bombs, a practice never approved by crew members, who frequently and audibly expressed outbursts of profanity when they had no choice but to "ride along" on missions when bomb runs were aborted for any reason.

On Thursday, 8 March 1945, the *Campbell Press* newspaper printed an article about Bert's twenty-one-day furlough after completing fifty-one missions, republishing the photograph of his fiftieth-mission cup of coffee, saying he stopped in Berkeley to visit relatives and a buddy who had preceded him home and whose furlough was just concluding.

Bill and Bert remained in contact after the war until Bill passed away in 1986. Bert carried many of Bill's recollections in his memory and mentioned them when he recalled his army air force service on the December 13, 1988, recording.

In that recording, he covered numerous recollections and vignettes recalled by him and Bill Wilson, memories not previously mentioned. In the summer of 1944, his closest friend from San Jose State, Dave Hines, after whom he later named his only son, and who is seen in the photograph of the San Jose State wrestling team with Kenneth C. Bailey, came to Lucera to visit Bert. Bill Wilson remembered that Dave, who was in the 82nd Airborne Division and later was killed in action, looked very "spifty" and clean in his uniform, and he slept on their floor, while the aircrew members who lived there looked "very grungy." When Bert spoke Dave's name on the recording, his emotion over Dave's loss, which he didn't learn about until after the war, was noticeable.

As to living conditions, they were primitive, but they were undergoing steady improvement in the six-plus months Bert was there: "Food ('Chow') was decent. We lived in tents with walkways of steel matting, and stoves fueled by 100 Octane aviation gas. There was one explosion and fire in another tent, with no injuries." But he noted that the inventive tent mate who had put their stove together had done so carefully to avoid a similar disaster. He also recalled the intramural basketball he played at Foggia. On the lighter side, he told of his R & R to the island of Capri and a special party at the Lucera officers' club, where an officer too well inebriated fell in a slit trench—normally identified as an open latrine.

Bert mentioned that he twice attempted to get into P-38 fighters right after arriving in the 15th Air Force, but the squadron commanders turned down his requests, saying the practice was stopped after two other bomber pilots crashed in such attempts. He pointed out that their formations were frequently escorted by fighters, often P-51s. (The famed 332nd Fighter Group "Red Tails," the Tuskegee Airmen, were in the 15th Air Force, based at Ramitelli.) He said the 301st flew two support missions during the invasion of southern France, code-named Operation Dragoon, saying that on the second mission they got "a good hit." He remembered that his first mission was to the Ploesti oil fields near Bucharest, Hungary, but he was careful to explain that it wasn't the infamous low-level mission of 1 August 1943, when B-24s took terrible losses. He recalled that most of their missions were at altitudes from twenty-three to twenty-eight thousand feet, the highest being at thirty-five thousand feet, where Bill said aircraft handling was somewhat "mushy" or "sloppy"; yet he pointed out that the B-17 flew better than the B-24s at higher altitudes.

Bert began his return home on 22 February 1945. Before he started his roundabout trip to the United States, the long, tortuous, twelve-day march of Nazi-held allied POWs, among them thousands of Americans who were army air force, had ended on 2 February. He traveled by Air Transport Command, flying from Naples to Casablanca, then to an intermediate stop, where he was watching a John Wayne movie, *Tall in the Saddle*, when passengers were called to their aircraft to fly across the Atlantic to Brazil. From there they flew to Jamaica and then on to Miami, Florida.

On returning to the continental United States, he began flying C-54s in the Air Transport Command out of Long Beach, California. While flying out of Long Beach, he had the opportunity to meet and have beers at nightclubs with such celebrities as the former cowboy movie star Bob Steele, who came out of the silent-film era, and Sons of the Pioneers leader, Bob Nolan, whom he regarded as more personable and friendly. He also garnered flying time in B-25s, taking note of the fact that Bill Wilson had been in an experimental B-25 flying training program before coming into B-17s, in which pilots were training for four-engine aircraft—a program that seemed more successful in rapidly training pilots into B-17s and B-24s.

Bert's football skills were already well known when he enlisted in the army air force. When he returned from overseas, he found that his services were of interest to the commander of the Air Transport Service, who wanted to establish a football team representing the command, headquartered at Nashville, Tennessee. He was stationed in Nashville in the 559th Base Unit when, as a result of the nation's demobilization, he was relived from active duty on 23 October 1945. His base of separation was McClelland Field, California.

Bert recognized in his postwar travels back and forth across the United States that he had missed the opportunity to begin playing football at San Jose State College in 1945 if he had chosen to stay on the West Coast, but he made up for his supposed error by playing on the Spartans' 1946 team after being released from active duty.

On September 28, 1946, the Spartans played a home game against the Willamette University Bearcats, making up for the 1941 game they couldn't play on December 16 that year because of the Japanese attack on Pearl Harbor. They thoroughly trounced the Bearcats 44–6. Several of the 1941 Bearcats were on opposite sides of the line of scrimmage that year, including Bill Reder, Pat White, Chuck Furno, Ken Jacobson, Marv Goodman, and Paul Cookingham.

Late in the 1946 season, the Spartans flew in a chartered airliner to Moscow, Idaho, to play the University of Idaho Vandals. The weather was difficult as they approached Moscow after dark, so difficult that the pilot was apprehensive about attempting to land and, knowing that some of the men on board had flown in combat and that one had flown a number of hours as an army air force transport aircraft pilot, quietly sent word into the passenger compartment asking whether anyone had any experience flying the C-54 type of army aircraft and might be able to assist in landing at Moscow. Word got to Bert, and he went forward into the cockpit without saying a word to anyone. Years later, onetime teaching colleague Dave Cripe at Campbell High School, California, repeated the story told to him by Bert.

The San Jose State College head football coach came forward into the cockpit and was startled to see Bert sitting in the captain's seat, flying the aircraft in their approach to land at the Moscow-Pullman Airport, at night, with the field illuminated by car headlights. They played the University of Idaho in Moscow the next day, October 19, 1946, and won 26–14.

Bert capped off his San Jose State football career helping the Spartans to a January 1, 1947, 20–0 victory over Utah State in the Raisin Bowl, played in Fresno, California, the school's first postseason appearance in the continental United States. Sportswriters in attendance voted Bert the game's outstanding player.

He was the youngest of five children and earned his bachelor's and master's degrees in physical education at San Jose State College. He was a physical education and driver's education teacher and basketball coach for more than thirty years at Campbell High and Prospect High in nearby Saratoga, California.

While attending San Jose State after the war, he met and began dating a lovely young lady he married on September 18, 1946, Sydney Smith, and they raised two children, a son, David, and a daughter, Kathleen, who adored her father and contributed so much in telling his story in this book. Her love for her mother was no less, stating, "She was an art major at San Jose State." She further elaborated saying she was an "amazing artist and homemaker," whose art went through many phases in which "she dabbled in all mediums, but much of her work was oil pastels and pencil," adding, "I have many treasures hanging in my house as do other family members. She did sell her work at art shows," and, "Towards the end of her life she made watercolor cards of Sierra Nevada wildflowers that were very popular with Echo Lake cabin owners, where she and my dad had our family cabin."

Bert Robinson's participation in athletics and graduation from San Jose State earned him induction into the San Jose State College Sports Hall of Fame, in both football and basketball, sports in which he earned letters three years, plus one year in baseball. But basketball was the sport he became most noted for when he returned to Campbell High School following his initial, two-year coaching and teaching job, 1947–1949, at Bakersfield Junior College, California. While there, he coached basketball and assisted in coaching football. His basketball coaching in Bakersfield resulted in his being listed in the college's archives as having an "All Time Coaching Record Year."

Victor A. "Bert" Robinson, assistant football coach, Bakersfield Junior College, California, during the period 1947–1949. (*Source*: KCC)

A prize athlete at Bakersfield Junior College was a football player named Frank (Francis Newton) Gifford, a star who had graduated from the town's high school and sought an athletic scholarship at the University of Southern California (USC) but was informed that his grade point average was too low. The news didn't stop him.

He entered the junior college, played one season, and was named to the Junior College All-American team while making the grades needed to enroll at USC. At USC, he was named an All-American athlete and player, graduating in the class of 1952. In the 1951 season he ran for 841 yards in 195 carries.

From USC he went on to far greater football glory in the professional ranks with eight Pro Bowl selections, six times All-Pro selection. He was on the New York Giants' 1956 National Football League (NFL) championship team and was the United Press International (UPI) NFL Most Valuable Player (MVP) the same year, the Pro Bowl MVP in 1958, and the UPI Comeback Player of the Year in 1962, and he was named to the NFL 1950s All-Decade Team. The New York Giants subsequently retired his jersey, number 16, and he was inducted into the College and Pro Football Halls of Fame. Over the years, Bert Robinson would talk of his admiration for Frank Gifford, as witnessed at Bakersfield Junior College, long before he made football history and later became a sports broadcaster, mainly during NFL games on CBS and later NBC.

Nevertheless, at Campbell High School, before he retired in 1983 at age sixty, Bert would become associated with another memorable future professional athlete—Craig

Morton—who played basketball under Head Coach Bert Robinson, along with Jack Schraub, both of whom went to the University of California and were later drafted to play football with the Dallas Cowboys. Craig played quarterback in the professional ranks eighteen years total, at Dallas, with the New York Giants, and with the Denver Broncos. Jack Schraub was selected by the Cowboys as an end, fifth in Round No. 13, with Craig Morton selected as quarterback, fifth in Round No. 1.

Heavily recruited out of Campbell High School, Craig Morton accepted a scholarship at the University of California where he was a three-year starter and won All-American honors his senior year. With his first-round selection to the Dallas Cowboys and the fifth overall in the 1965 professional draft, he came under supervision of legendary coach Tom Landry and led his team to Super Bowl V in 1970. After a brief period with the New York Giants, Craig joined the Denver Broncos in 1977, and in his first season he led Denver to their first-ever Super Bowl appearance. His performance that season, 1,929 yards passing, fourteen touchdowns, and a 12-2 regular season record, earned him the American Football Conference's MVP and the NFL's Comeback Player of the Year. Craig Morton was inducted into the Broncos Ring of Fame in 1988, the College Football Hall of Fame in 1992, and the University of California Hall of Fame in 1992.

Both of these men, Craig Morton and Jack Schraub, remained close to Bert and Sydney Robinson for the rest of the Robinsons' lives.

Kathy Carver's mother died on July 16, 2007, and both men spoke at her funeral. She and Bert had been married sixty-one years when she died. When Bert Robinson died on September 14, 2008, both men spoke at his funeral, and Jack Schraub sat with Bert's family every day in the room in which Bert died. Kathy and all her children sat with him that week and took turns holding his hands, urging him to "let go" while he continued to fight against the acute leukemia that eventually took him.

There could be no more loving tribute than that which Kathy Carver gave at her father's memorial services, which were held in what had been the Campbell High School gymnasium. The gym had been "his house," and for the ceremony its bleachers were filled with the high school's former students and athletes Bert had taught and coached for so many years.

My Dad

Hi, I'm Kathy, Bert's daughter. Thank you for coming to honor my dad. You all probably know I grew up in a little house about a mile away from here, but this was my dad's big house, and everyone here is a part of his family. So welcome home.

As a little girl, I clearly remember his unconditional love, the safety of his hugs, and the strength and calm he brought to our home. One of my fondest memories was often finding my mom and dad dancing in the kitchen after dinner. I would squeeze between them and climb up on my dad's feet to soak up some of that love. We played hide and seek in the house, and no matter how many times I hid behind the curtain on the window seat, he always acted surprised to find me there. We also played an indoor chase game, where he would chase me through the house and then switch directions to catch me off guard. I can remember when I started getting nervous not knowing where he was going to come from, he would stop and stretch out his arms so I could leap into them. We would laugh and laugh and then start over again.

As I grew older, I began to realize that he was no ordinary dad. I began to realize he was no ordinary man. As I look back and trace my memories, I understand more and more what a rare human being he was. He loved his family with all of his heart. My mother was the light of his life, and he cherished her every day. My brother Dave held a front row seat in his heart. In fact my dad saved his last smile for my brother. His grandchildren were his joy, and his great grandson, Nicholas, became the apple of his eye. His nickname for all of us was "Precious" and if you lingered at all after saying good-bye to him you could catch him looking up to the Heavens and saying "Thank you, God." And to all of his other sons and daughters, his athletes and students, you were a part of his family, our other brothers and sisters. He loved you very much. He remained a champion to his last moment, taking care of others before himself, making sure we knew he was going to be OK, holding on to say goodbye to each loved one as they came to his bedside.

So how can you possibly find words to describe the character of my dad? There really are none that don't pale in comparison to the man. You just had to have known him to understand. This is a man who had no enemies, a man who would put a smile on your face with his quick wit and never failing sense of humor. His courage led him to be a war hero, yet his sensitivity could bring him to tears over a nostalgic song or picture.

I just know that I am one of the most blessed people on earth to have learned from the best, just how you should live your life. I am going to try to make him proud. It warms my heart to know that he is at peace in Heaven. He is probably coaching some basketball team and telling some kid to "never give up the baseline." Jack, you get a break for a while.

And what makes me the happiest, is knowing he'll be dancing with my mom in the kitchen tonight.

Thank you all for helping us celebrate my dad's wonderful life.

CHAPTER FOURTEEN

Above and Beyond the Call of Duty

On Saturday evening, September 28, 1991, following the Bearcats' season home-opening 34–21 victory over Spokane, Washington's Whitworth College Pirates that afternoon, Willamette University held its first annual Athletics Hall of Fame banquet in Cone Fieldhouse. The university's president gave the opening remarks to all in attendance.

Welcome to this inaugural Athletic Hall of Fame banquet. I am delighted that Willamette, as a part of its Sesquicentennial, is establishing an Athletic Hall of Fame. This gives the university an opportunity to commemorate the athletic achievements of many outstanding men and women who have distinguished themselves as Willamette athletes, coaches or staff.

Willamette University's philosophy—small but excellent—describes not only the institution's academic programs, but also its reputation in athletics. At Willamette, academics have always come before athletics. But the university's athletic programs have been valued as an important part of developing skills and character.

Thank you for joining us this evening to recognize and honor the charter members of Willamette's Athletic Hall of Fame. I congratulate this elite group of inductees for their extraordinary accomplishments at the university and beyond. For those entering because of their service as coaches, I also extend my gratitude to them and their families for the dedication they have displayed in molding the lives of so many young men and women at Willamette.

Jerry E. Hudson
President Willamette University

On the final page of the program for the stirring, happy occasion is found THE PURPOSE OF THE HALL OF FAME.

The purpose of establishing the Athletic Hall of Fame is to formally recognize outstanding contributions to the heritage and tradition of Willamette University's intercollegiate athletic program.

It is the intent of this Hall of Fame to honor and preserve memory of those athletes, teams, coaches and others whose achievements have brought recognition and honor to the University and its athletic program.

Criteria for selection not only includes achievements while at the University, but accomplishments in the sports world later in life. Athletes must be out of school 10 years before becoming eligible for selection.

Each inductee will receive a plaque, which includes a photograph and citation highlighting the accomplishments of the inductee. A duplicate plaque will be displayed in a glass case adjacent to the west end of Cone Fieldhouse, near the main entrance.

As President Hudson explained in his welcoming remarks, Willamette University's inaugural Athletic Hall of Fame was an important event in the university's sesquicentennial celebration, concentrated on athletic achievements, and was separate and apart from the 1941 Bearcat football team's powerful story of mobilization for defense in the Territory of Hawaii and the additional life-changing experiences team members and others encountered on their voyage home.

Among sixteen inductees in the Hall of Fame's premiere class were two key figures on the 1941 Bearcat team, both deceased before 1991, Coach Roy Servais "Spec" Keene and Tillman Theodore Ogdahl, a star on both the 1941 and the 1942 teams, captain, and All-American halfback on the 1942 team. Ted, who returned wounded and highly decorated from heroic service during World War II, completed his education; began coaching at Grant High in his hometown of Portland, Oregon; amassed a sterling record there; and finally returned in 1952 to become head football coach for twenty years and head coach in track and field for thirteen years at Willamette, as well as the winningest coach in Willamette history, having surpassed the marvelous record of his mentor and the "father of Willamette athletics," Spec Keene. Nevertheless, Spec Keene's and Ted Ogdahl's recognition in the premiere Hall of Fame class was just the beginning of a rising tide of honors accorded the 1941 Bearcat football team.

In a Saturday, December 7, 1991, article in the Salem, Oregon, *Statesman Journal*, reporter Reid English chronicled in more than one story the 1941 Willamette Bearcat football team's fifty-year reunion at Honolulu's Moana Hotel, a reunion that coincided with the nation's fiftieth-anniversary remembrance of the Japanese attack on Pearl Harbor. Nineteen of twenty-one surviving team members attended.

The reunion was filled with emotion-charged memories of an anticipated grand time of two more football games at the end of an illustrious 8 and 1 season and sightseeing on an island most had never seen before. Incredibly, the good, warm memories almost vanished fifteen hours after the final whistle of their first scheduled game in Honolulu against the University of Hawaii's Rainbow Warriors. This was to be much more than a reunion. They had witnessed, and then become involved in, the event triggering America's shattering, bloody descent into the catastrophe that was World War II—the Japanese attack on Pearl Harbor.

Team members and wives attending the reunion were Ken and Velda Jacobson, Chuck and "Zip" Furno, James and Karin Fitzgerald, Pat and Ruth White, Marshall and Jean Barbour, George Constable, Gene and Pat Stewart, Earl and Connie Hampton, Tony Fraiola (resident of Kaneohe, Oahu), Cece Conner, Dave and Bea Kelly, Irv and Marcella Miller, Marv and Gloria Goodman, Bob Bennett, Wally and Dorothy Olson, Andy and Dottie Rogers, Wayne and Shirley Hadley, and Glenn Nordquist.

The reunion, crammed into a few brief days, brought happy memories of Willamette University, a championship team's camaraderie, a marvelous football season, and then a dream vacation voyage to an island paradise where they would be greeted warmly—in spite of some unwanted seasickness en route. There were parties, entertainment that included sensuous Hawaiian music and dances, and football practices and preparations for the first game, scheduled for Saturday, December 6, 1941, the first Saturday afternoon of that fateful month.

The memories and conversation undoubtedly included their immediate, yet involuntary-made-voluntary, willingness to serve in defense of an American territory most had never previously seen, service during and after their stay on Oahu that others were to see as duty, and a well-performed, courageous, and heroic, yet unavoidable head-on collision with the brutal realities of war—as witnessed on Oahu then seen closely and personally at sea.

Willamette University 1941 Bearcat football team fiftieth reunion photograph, taken at Punahou School, December 7, 1991.
Back row: Ken Jacobson, Earl Hampton, Wally Olson, Marshall Barbour, Andy Rodgers, George Constable, Marvin Goodman, Bill Kelly, Bob Bennett.
Front row: Irv Miller, Glenn Nordquist, Gene Stewart, Chuck Furno, Jim Fitzgerald, Cecil Conner, student at Bunal. (*Source:* KJC)

They had witnessed war's brutality on the island and in the faces of 125 severely wounded Pearl Harbor survivors on board the *Coolidge*. Thirty of them were horribly burned, and there were other evacuees who made indelible impressions on both football teams, including some Pearl Harbor widows with their children, plus numerous other evacuees, mostly women and children, abruptly leaving paternal family members behind while sailing for San Francisco through waters patrolled by Japanese submarines. And for all who attended the reunion, it would ring in memories of lives changed and a lengthening trail of tears and blood as World War II progressed—then afterward lives of service earning renewed and far deeper meanings than expected.

Shirley (McKay) Hadley and her husband, Wayne, longtime avid supporters and contributors to Willamette University and its football teams, who came to Oahu with the team in 1941, set up and coordinated the reunion. First came a reception at the Moana Hotel on Friday, December 6, followed that night by a reunion banquet, with Willamette president Jerry Hudson, an official from the University of Hawaii, and Willamette alumni living in Hawaii as special guests. Team member Earl Hampton was master of ceremonies at the banquet, and another team member, Reverend Glenn Nordquist, gave the invocation and benediction.

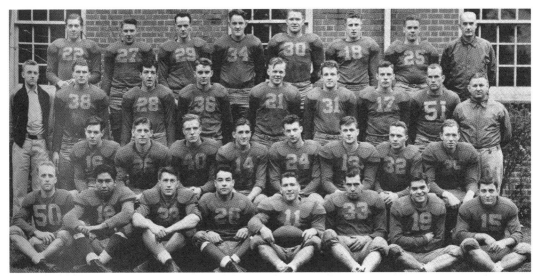

The 1941 Willamette University Bearcats football team: (front row, from left) Irv Miller, Cecil Conner, Pat White, Tony Fraiola, Al Walden, Jim Fitzgerald, Buddy Reynolds, Chuck Furno, (second row) Earl Hampton, Bill Reder, Martin Barstad, Ted Ogdahl, Jim Burgess, Gene Stewart, Glenn Nordquist, Wally Olson; (third row) Dick Kern (manager), Paul Cookingham, George Constable, David Kelly, Ken Jacobson, Allan Barrett, Marshall Barbour, Clarence Walden (no relation to Al Walden), Assistant Coach Howard Maple; (back row) David Kurtz, Robert Bennett, Gordon Moore, Andrew Rogers, Neil Morley, Marv Goodman, Carrel "Truck" Deiner, Coach Roy S. "Spec" Keene. (Note: David Kurtz, Clarence Walden, Carrel Deiner, and Coach Maple did not make the trip to Hawaii.) In 1997, the team was inducted into the Willamette University Athletic Hall of Fame. (*Source*: MOHLAWU)

Earl, on a first day typical of fifty-year school reunions, remarked that he hadn't seen Glenn or another teammate, Judge James M. Fitzgerald, since 1942. Oregon senator Mark O. Hatfield, a graduate of Willamette, and for whom the university library is named, was a special guest during the reunion and was awarded a certificate of commendation signed by Secretary of the Navy Henry L. Garrett III for each team member. In handing out the commendations, Senator Hatfield was contributing to the surviving team members' recognition, similar to Secretary of the Navy Frank Knox, who sent letters of commendation to the presidents of Willamette University and San Jose State College in January 1942 after the two teams returned home on the *Coolidge*.

On Saturday, December 7, the attending team members and their wives rode a bus for a sightseeing tour of the island and a picnic, just as was planned fifty years earlier when, because of the upcoming Shrine Bowl Game, they had planned to visit the Shriners' Hospital, a visit that never occurred because of the Japanese attack. Among the stops they made on Saturday was at the National Cemetery of the Pacific in the Punchbowl, and Punahou School, where the team was quartered and had stood sentry duty round the clock for ten days in December 1941 just prior to the team's short-notice departure on the *Coolidge*. Finally, they were to see Pearl Harbor, as they had intended all those years ago.

Instead, on this December 7 day, fifty years later, they toured Pearl Harbor as special guests in a motor launch in which they were sheltered from the sun as they eased past the quays where great ships had been moored on "Battleship Row" that terrible morning in 1941, and stepped from the launch onto the silent, somber *Arizona* Memorial, where the first 1,177 names of the ship's casualties were originally inscribed in the white marble walls. They listened in silence as a park ranger, acting as a docent, described the *Arizona*'s tragic end so long ago, stories of crew members lost in the ship's violent explosion and sinking, surviving crew members' heroism and valor that day, and the memorial's origin, while reminding them of the various highlights they had seen in a documentary film in the visitors' center theater before they stepped aboard the tour boat. It was a day and time, Pearl Harbor's fiftieth anniversary, when Oahu and Pearl Harbor were nearly overwhelmed with visitors, which included Pearl Harbor's survivors and family members, who were marking the event in their own lives.

Unquestionably, if any who had taken the November 1941 voyage on the *Lurline* had met and spoken with Seaman First Class Ralph Earnest Poole during the crossing and gazed in reverent awe at the marble inscriptions in the memorial fifty years later, they wouldn't have remembered him. But that Saturday in 1991, there, etched among the 1,177 in gleaming white marble, was his name. He had perished in the great ship's terrible end four days after the *Lurline* arrived carrying the visiting football teams, their coaches, and others accompanying them.

Might Earnest Poole have attended the Bearcats' football game on Saturday, December 6, 1941? Perhaps he did, especially if he had become aware of the two teams traveling with him on the *Lurline*. But no one will ever know.

On Monday the reunion ended, and everyone said their good-byes. The coordinator, Shirley Hadley, when interviewed by phone, told the *Statesman Journal* reporter that on the first day the attendees would break into three groups on Monday. "Some will visit the other islands for three days, some will stay in Honolulu and some will come home."

In the reunion book put together and furnished to each attending team member and his family, there are unforgettable personal and group photographs taken at each of the reunion locations visited. At the end, there was a lone photograph on the final page of two people who were obviously a still-in-love couple, Marshall Hall "Mush" Barbour and his wife, Jean, telling of his death on January 21, 1992, just six weeks following the joyous reunion—and reminding anyone who read the caption under the photograph that he was a bomber pilot in World War II.

Though the reunion partings included a tinge of sadness and there was shock when "Mush" Barbour died shortly thereafter, others who attended would not survive much longer either, though their stories continued to reemerge, along with more honors and the justifiable growth of the team's legend.

In the intervening years from 1991 to 1997, Dick Weisgerber, Willamette class of 1938, an assistant coach under Spec Keene during the 1941 season with a distinguished career in football after he graduated from the university, entered the Hall of Fame in the 1993 class. Marvin Goodman, a starter as a freshman on the 1941 Bearcats, and who after World War II returned to play football for the Bearcats' 1946 team, was awarded the Jack Dempsey Adam Hat Trophy for the most outstanding athlete at Willamette his senior year and was inducted into the 1994 Hall of Fame class.

On Saturday, September 13, 1997, the evening following the Bearcats' season-opening home football game against the California State University–Humboldt Lumberjacks, a team located in Arcata, California, Willamette University held its annual Athletic Hall of Fame Banquet.

The Bearcats had started the season with a bang in a 42–14 win over a Division II team. After the reception and attendees' movement to their seats, Willamette University's interim president, Bryan Johnston, provided welcoming remarks to the banquet attendees, this time in Putnam University Center on the campus. As had become the custom, he repeated the welcoming words of years past and recited the purpose of the Willamette Hall of Fame. Then came the introduction of the master of ceremonies, Buzz Yocom '49, and the invocation by the Reverend Paul Jewell '53, followed by dinner. Interim president Bryan Johnston then rose to review Willamette's athletic heritage. The presentation of 1997's eight inductees followed, each introduced by a designated individual, four of whom were Willamette graduates.

Two of the individual inductees were Wayne '42 and Shirley '44 (McKay) Hadley, inducted for meritorious service. Their Hall of Fame citation stated,

Wayne and Shirley Hadley had their first date at a Willamette football game. For the last 58 years, they have known and given support to Bearcat players, coaches and teams throughout the Northwest. The Hadley's were even in Honolulu at the "Pearl Harbor" football game in 1941.

Besides volunteering to help with tournaments, track meets, and baseball stadium groundwork, Wayne used his co-ownership of Capitol Chevrolet to provide team transportation for occasional road trips. Wayne and Shirley truly are a great example of alumni support for athletics at Willamette.

Prior to 1997, Willamette had inducted three teams into the university's Hall of Fame, two football teams and one basketball team. Both football teams, 1960 with an 8–0 record, and 1968 with a 9–1 record, were coached by 1991 Hall of Fame member Ted Ogdahl. Ted's 1968 football team entered the Hall of Fame in 1993, and his 1960 team entered in 1995. The third team in the Hall of Fame was the 1938–1939 basketball team, in the 1994 class, with a 29–6 won-lost record.

And in 1997, the legend, which had faded in and out of a dim and sometimes totally darkened limelight for fifty-seven years, reached its bright summit. Introduced by a gentleman named Al Lightner, who showed the team photograph with all its names and read the citation:

The 1941 football team, led by Hall of Fame head coach Roy S. "Spec" Keene, was special in two ways:

1. On the gridiron, the Bearcats forged an impressive 8–2 record, including six shutouts.

The Bearcats easily won the Northwest Conference title that season, outscoring their five opponents 218–7.

The 1941 team includes past Hall of Fame selections Ted Ogdahl, Marvin Goodman, Dick Weisgerber (assistant coach), and Keene.

Willamette had eleven of the thirteen players on the NWC first-team all-star unit: ends Bill Reder and Marshall Barbour; tackles Martin Barstad, Neil Morley, and George Constable; guards Anthony Jo Fraiola and Gordon Moore; and backs Al Walden, Buddy Reynolds, Gene Stewart, and Ogdahl.

2. Less than a day after Willamette lost a 20–6 contest against the University of Hawaii in Honolulu, Pearl Harbor was bombed by Japanese forces, leading to the United States' involvement in World War II.

The football teams from Willamette and San Jose were both in Hawaii to play a series of games with the U of H called the Shrine Bowl.

After the bombing, Keene volunteered his players and male supporters for ten days of guard duty at Punahou School, while the women on the trip were sent to a navy hospital as nurses' aides.

Most of the Willamette contingent left Hawaii nearly three weeks after the attack, arriving on the ocean liner President Coolidge in San Francisco Bay on Christmas Day.

From that day forward, more and more attention and individual recognition came to the dwindling numbers of team members. From an article published in the July 25, 2000, issue of Salem, Oregon's *Statesman Journal*, written by reporter Dan Meisler, came the revelation that the 1941 Bearcats football team's story was to receive national attention, but the attention would be brief. In an interview with the *Statesman*'s reporter, Earl Hampton offered his thoughts: "I would think it would be a major event in football history." The *Statesman Journal* published the article because the NFL Films producer, Peter Frank, who had heard the story at the war memorials in Honolulu, was in town working on the eight-minute documentary it would air in the series NFL Films Presents.

Frank, in his interview with Meisler, told what occurred after he learned of the 1941 Bearcats' voyage to Honolulu and back, saying he "pitched the story to Steve Sobol, host of the series . . . and got the go-ahead. The piece should air this November or December." The documentary aired that fall, was recorded, and was subsequently issued on a DVD in February 2006. Since the airing of the 2000 documentary by NFL Films, there have been a number of occasions in which the sadly dwindling number of team members have been recognized and honored at Willamette.

The latest was at a home football game against Pacific Lutheran on November 12, 2011, one day after Veterans' Day, when Ken Jacobson, Earl Hampton, and Chuck Furno were recognized and honored by the university community and fans attending the game. Earl and Chuck Furno have since left us.

Ken Jacobson, Earl Hampton, and Charles Furno at the 2011 Willamette University Homecoming Football Game with Pacific Lutheran on November 12, 2011, where the university honored the 1941 Bearcat football team. (*Source*: CSFFC)

The three present that fall day in 2011 were among the last few surviving members of the 1941 Bearcats football team, and they were being honored as men who became veterans the afternoon of 7 December 1941 when they were mobilized as a result of the declaration of martial law in Hawaii. They added to their quietly long-ago, dim but growing legend attending to and helping serve and assist the 125 severely wounded on board the SS *President Coolidge* during a tense voyage from Honolulu back to San Francisco, 19–25 December— through waters patrolled by Japanese submarines. Then, even more quietly, the vast majority of both the San Jose State and the Willamette football teams entered their nation's armed forces and served in the most destructive war in human history.

Now their exploits and contributions to their families, communities, fields of endeavor, and nation live on. Following are selected true stories that highlight the Bearcats' legacies following their 1941 voyage to paradise.

CHAPTER FIFTEEN

Leaders with Quiet Knowledge and Experience

ROY SERVAIS "SPEC" KEENE
College Interrupted by World War I, Service in France, Graduation, and a Lifetime
in Physical Education and Coaching Athletics

BORN ON A FARM ON JULY 1, 1894, NEAR THE SMALL TOWN OF HOPEWELL, OREGON, SOUTH from Salem, eight miles downriver, on the river's west side, Roy S. "Spec" Keene grew up in the state's capital city. He graduated from old Salem High School in 1915, where he immersed himself in athletics at an early age, earning thirteen letters: four in football as an end, four in basketball at center, four in baseball as a pitcher and shortstop, and one in track as a sprinter.

To the writer who interviewed Spec Keene for a September 1964 article in the Oregon State College *Stater* magazine, titled "Seventeen Proud Keene Years"—an article about his seventeen years as athletic director at OSC (now Oregon State University)—he spoke of what motivated his love of athletics and coaching: "I guess I went into coaching because I liked athletics and working with growing kids."

During the same interview, he told of his prep days at Salem High School, divulging one other keepsake, the nickname "Spec." "Leon ('Doc') Barrick ... gave me that," Keene recalled. "It happened one day when I was playing shortstop and he was at first base. He told me my throws looked like 'specks' coming at him. Isn't that a heck of a way to get a nickname?"

His high school prep accomplishments attracted attention outside of Oregon. Kansas State Teachers College in Pittsburgh, Kansas, which became a full-fledged four-year institution in 1913, was interested in his athletic abilities, but Keene and his Salem High School teammate, Bill Reinhart, chose Missouri Wesleyan in Cameron, Missouri. Reinhart's cousin, Bill Pixlee, was the football and basketball coach at Missouri Wesleyan, and both stayed with him during their first year in college.

One year in the Midwest was enough for both, and they returned to Oregon, with Roy going to Corvallis, to the Oregon Agricultural College, and Reinhart to Eugene, to the University of Oregon. A year later, the two of them joined the National Guard in Salem. Years later he explained to a newspaper reporter how the decision to join the Guard came about.

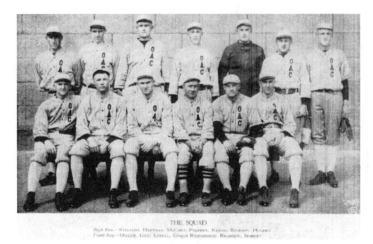

Oregon Agricultural College 1920 baseball team, Roy Keene standing in black shirt. (*Source*: OSULSCA)

He was having so much fun at school in Corvallis that he hadn't thought about enlisting, but his Belgian-born mother changed that when he came home for a weekend. "Son," she said, "don't you know there's a war on?" He added, "When your mother tells you that, it's all you need. I went down the next day and signed up."

Spec entered the Oregon Agricultural College in Corvallis in the late summer of 1916 and graduated in 1921 with a degree in animal husbandry, five years interrupted by nineteen months in military service during World War I.

He played class basketball his first three years at OAC, was a pitcher on the varsity baseball team all four years, was chosen the baseball team's captain in his junior year, and chose to bypass varsity football and basketball because he had ambitions to play professional baseball. He was in the Varsity "O" (lettermen's) Association his last three years and was student body president his senior year. During his time as student body president, he formed the committee that put in motion plans for the Memorial Union, the college's first student union building.

Additionally, he was active his last three years in the Withycombe Club, an animal husbandry club; was president of the Kappa Sigma Nu fraternity his second year; was president of the Phi Delta Theta fraternity his junior year; was on the Student Affairs and Social Committees his senior year; and was in the Vigilance Association in his junior and senior years, an association that actively supported and pursued the concept and practice of the college's honor code. And in between all the student activity, he entered active duty in the Army of the United States during World War I when the National Guard's 41st Division was federalized, then was drafted into active duty and sent to France with thirty-two other American divisions to fight in World War I.

When the National Guard's 41st Division was federalized on 25 March 1917 as tensions between the United States and the Central Powers of Germany and the Austro-Hungarian Empire dramatically increased, it included Washington State's 1st and 2nd Infantry Regiments, which traced their unit histories to 1886 and 1887, respectively. On 26 March, the

2nd Infantry Regiment, in which Roy Keene had not yet enlisted, was ordered to guard communications, public utilities, bridges, and railroads in Washington State. On 6 April, after President Woodrow Wilson's 4 April speech to a joint session of Congress, the Congress voted the Declaration of War and President Wilson signed it.

It was after the division was federalized that Roy Keene enlisted in the 41st, on 17 July 1917. In the meantime, the 41st Division's sentry duties in Washington State were continuing and lasted until 5 August, when the regiment was drafted into federal service as part of the Army of the United States in World War I.

The 2nd Infantry Regiment, after marshaling and beginning more intense organization and training in Washington State, entrained on 25 October, bound for Camp Mills, New York. Roy Keene was on his way to war. At Camp Mills they were joined by members of the District of Columbia Guard and were redesignated the 161st Infantry of the 81st Infantry Brigade assigned to the 41st Division. The regiment left Camp Mills on 12 December for the port of embarkation and arrived in France on 27 December 1917. Roy Keene's 1917 Christmas was on board a troopship bound for war—at least they believed they were going to war—and would later proudly learn that their National Guard division was the fourth of thirty-three American divisions to arrive in France. Now, they must have thought, the division was going to be among the first into battle.

After they arrived in the port of Brest, however, the men of the 161st learned to their dismay and anguish that the 41st was to be assigned as a replacement training unit. As such, many men were assigned to the 1st, 2nd, 26th, and 42nd Divisions.

As the Guard historian goes on to say, the 161st Regiment assembled at St. Aignan in the Pays de la Loire region of France during a relatively lengthy period of the regiment's operations. Much of the 161st's effort was to assist the 16th Engineers Construction Battalion in building an advance camp and regulating station at Is-sur-Tille. While doing the construction work, it was detached from the 41st Division and operated separately. On 31 August 1918, it rejoined the 41st Division and remained with that division through the 11 November Armistice signing. In January and February, the regiment assembled in Brest, France, for shipment home. They sailed 3–7 February on five different ships: the USS *Georgia*, *Huntington*, *St. Louis*, *Pueblo*, and *Ortega*, arriving in the United States near the end of February 1919. On arrival, the regiment was scattered to fifteen forts and camps for mustering out. Homeward bound for mustering out was a good place to be. Roy Keene was discharged on 12 March 1919, and when he reentered OAC, he was granted eight hours of credit for his military work.

While unquestionably the intensely competitive Sergeant Roy S. Keene, on mustering out, was disappointed he didn't see action in France, at some point in his life he undoubtedly also concluded it was a blessing in disguise. Such thoughts and utterances were reasonable and even comforting at times, especially in light of the terrible casualties Americans suffered in those final months, when the American Expeditionary Forces were almost immediately on the offensive with the Allies, intent on shattering the long-stalemated trench and bunker war, driving the Germans out of France, and bringing World War I to a victorious end.

Though heavily involved in student activities the rest of his years in OAC, and having been nineteen months on active duty in the interim during World War I, athletics remained Roy Keene's major interest in life. Thus it was no small irony that Coach Roy Servais "Spec" Keene, and then Oregon state senator James Douglas McKay, who had enlisted in the 91st Division and trained at the newly opened Camp Lewis, Washington, then embarked in July 1918 to fight in World War I. Both were residing in the state's capital city, Salem, in 1941, both graduates of OAC. Both were on the same ship with two football teams bound for Hawaii and a grand time sightseeing and watching or coaching "their hometown" football team in three scheduled games.

Instead, on Sunday morning, December 7, 1941, following the Saturday afternoon Shrine Bowl football game Coach Keene had dreamed of and planned for years, they both, along with Ben Winkelman, a graduate of the University of Arkansas and head football coach at San Jose State College, suddenly became witnesses and wartime leaders—as the twenty-seven Willamette University Bearcats and twenty-five San Jose State Spartans found themselves quite literally mobilized to defend the island to which they had come to play football.

Following Roy Keene's return to OAC after World War I and his graduation, it didn't take him long to realize he would get nowhere in professional baseball. He had hurt his arm in France when he fell off a troop train, and the arm wouldn't come back. And it was during the period after he graduated from OAC that Corvallis beckoned the first time. He had the opportunity to coach Corvallis high school teams.

He decided to consult with the young woman who would become his future wife, Marie Mendenhall, the daughter of Cary and Anneliza Dunlap Mendenhall, whom he had met at OAC and who was teaching home economics in her hometown of Everett, Washington. Born on March 27, 1896, in Everett, she had moved to Corvallis in 1914 to attend OAC. Marie recommended he remain in Corvallis.

Over the next five years he coached Corvallis high school teams first, including a state championship football team, then went to the Oregon State athletic staff as freshman football coach, later as assistant football coach, freshman baseball coach, and physical education instructor. From there, in 1926, he was hired at Willamette University in his hometown of Salem, Oregon, where he would coach football, basketball, and baseball the first two years, then added to his responsibilities by serving as the university's athletic director and head of the Physical Education Department.

While in Corvallis, he married Marie on August 14, 1923, in the home of his sister in Seattle, Washington, and they settled in Corvallis for the next three years while he continued coaching athletics. They relocated to Salem when he accepted the position at Willamette in 1926 and began coaching football, basketball, and baseball that first year. Their oldest daughter, Madeleine, was born in Salem in 1929, and their youngest daughter, Geri, in 1935.

During Spec Keene's years at Willamette, in which he earned many accolades and came to be known as the "father of Willamette athletics," he established numerous records that have stood the test of time in leadership and individual excellence in athletics while

Roy S. "Spec" Keene, coach and athletic director at Willamette University, 1930. (*Source*: OSULSCA)

coaching three sports: football for seventeen years, baseball for sixteen years, and basketball for thirteen years.

In the period 1926–1942, as head football coach, his teams amassed an overall 84–51–6 record. His teams won nine Northwest Conference titles. In two periods as head basketball coach, 1926–1937 and 1942–1943, his win-loss record was 159–100, with a total of seven Northwest Conference titles, the last in 1943. During the 1929–1930 academic year, each of his three teams was undefeated. In his period of service at Willamette, his teams, combined, won or shared nineteen Northwest Conference championships.

While at Willamette he was selected as an associate member of Blue Key, a senior men's honor fraternity that became active at Oregon State after he graduated. At Willamette he was the faculty representative of Blue Key.

He was commissioned a navy lieutenant commander during World War II and served from 1943 to 1947, entering active duty in 1943 following his war-shortened, eight-game 1942 football season at Willamette, when the Bearcats again won the Northwest Conference championship. He was assigned to the 12th Naval District, headquartered near San Francisco, and was in charge of all physical education and athletics in that district, comprising California, Nevada, Utah, and Colorado.

After leaving the navy in 1947, he returned to Salem and bought into a sporting goods business, once publicly remarking with a chuckle, "Maybe I should have stayed with it. I'd have made more money." Then came the second beckoning of Corvallis, and this time it was from Oregon State, when the college president, A. L. Strand, called and offered him the athletic director position. He jumped at the chance and succeeded far beyond what he might have imagined. In an interview in their Corvallis home years later, Marie remarked to the reporter, "I couldn't imagine him selling the store, which was a good business. But Spec said he thought working with boys was more important than selling sweatshirts."

Keene returned to his alma mater, effective March 1, 1947, as athletic director, remarking that his work in the navy's 12th Naval District was a "great experience for my athletic director duties at Oregon State." In returning to the college, he and his family were leaving some deep roots behind and returning to an old home left behind years earlier.

He had been active in state, civic, and fraternal affairs in Salem, having been appointed to the state parole board when it was organized in 1939, and he was reappointed upon release from the navy. He came to OSC having served as president of the Salem Dad's club in the public school system there, an organization of more than five hundred men. He was director of the Salem Chamber of Commerce, chairman of the county Christmas seal and savings bond campaigns, and district chairman of the American Legion junior baseball organization. He was a Mason, an Elk, and a Legionnaire, having served in both world wars; he had been chairman of the Salem City playground committee, chairman of the American Legion boxing commission, and a member of the NCAA television committee for a half dozen years. Quite a list, and it goes on.

During his service as director of athletics at Oregon State, he oversaw construction of three major sports facilities: Gill Coliseum in 1949, primarily for basketball, and Parker Stadium in 1953—the football stadium, including the Bell Field Track for track-and-field competition—later renamed Reser Stadium. Parker Stadium was built on the south side of the campus and when originally built had a seating capacity of twenty-eight thousand.

Twice during Keene's service as athletic director, in the 1956 and 1964 seasons, the Beavers won Pacific Conference championships in football and played in the Rose Bowl in Pasadena, California, the following New Year's Day. Their second championship and trip to Pasadena had come following Keene's retirement as athletic director the summer prior to the 1964 football season. While the Beavers lost to the Iowa Hawkeyes 35–19 in 1957, and the Michigan Wolverines 34–7 in 1965, the Beavers' national athletic stature had been considerably elevated under his leadership. An additional later effect was the increase in Parker Stadium's seating capacity to thirty-three thousand following the 1965 Rose Bowl.

Only in one prior season, 1941, had the Beavers been Pacific Coast Conference champions since the conference was formed in 1915. They were to play the Duke University Blue Devils in the Rose Bowl. Ironically, it was the same season that Coach Spec Keene took the Willamette Bearcats to Hawaii for the Shrine Bowl, where they witnessed the attack that plunged the nation into war. As a result of the attack and subsequent national defense concerns for the West Coast, the 1942 Rose Bowl game was relocated to Duke's home stadium in Durham, North Carolina, where the Beavers won 20–16.

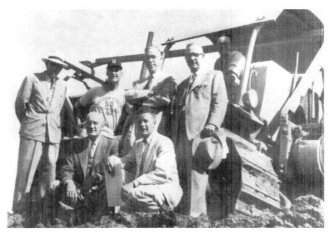

Athletic Director Roy S. Keene, front left, at Parker Stadium construction site groundbreaking. The stadium, completed in 1953, originally seated twenty-eight thousand and was expanded to thirty-three thousand following Oregon State's participation in the 1965 Rose Bowl. (*Source*: OSULSCA)

The construction of Gill Coliseum, built primarily to house collegiate basketball, was completed in late 1949, and the first Oregon State basketball game was held there against the University of Utah on December 16, 1949. At that time, Gill Coliseum was touted as the second-largest suspended-arch type of structure in the nation, as well as the "finest basketball plant west of the Rockies." When plans were being drawn up for the coliseum, Roy Keene had been adamant in demanding that no columns be used in its construction, since they were always irritating obstructions to fans' view of court action. The first commencement in Gill Coliseum was held the following year, with about two thousand members of the class of 1950 receiving degrees and approximately ten thousand relatives and friends

Gill Coliseum, completed in 1949, was ready for its first basketball game, against the University of Utah, on December 16, 1949. The first commencement in the coliseum seated approximately two thousand members of the class of 1950 on the floor of the coliseum, and approximately ten thousand relatives and friends in the stadium witnessing the exercises. (*Source*: OSULSCA)

witnessing the exercises. From 1914 until 1949, commencement ceremonies had been held in the crowded men's gymnasium (Langston Hall).

In 1954, Spec Keene had the opportunity to return to Hawaii, this time flying to Oahu and back with the Oregon State College basketball team on Pan American Airways, when the team went to play the University of Hawaii.

During his seventeen-year service as Oregon State athletic director, Keene also served a term as president of the Pacific Coast Conference Athletic Director's Association and served on the executive committee of the National Collegiate Athletic Association. It was during his service in the Pacific Coast Conference Athletics Director's Association that the conference broke up in 1959, precipitated primarily by "play for pay" scandals at other conference schools. When he retired, he expressed his disappointment at the conference's dissolution and the necessity for Oregon State to play as an independent, but he felt Oregon State and Oregon University would represent their state well and survive as independents in athletic competition.

He retired from the post of athletic director at Oregon State on July 1, 1964, at the end of a stable period in which he had to hire only two football coaches, Kip Taylor and Tommy Prothro, and two track coaches, Hal Moe and Sam Bell. He maintained his active interest in the work of the university. On February 5, 1968, he was appointed head of the Deferred Giving Committee of the Oregon State University Foundation, which seeks, receives, and manages private gifts to the university. At the time of his appointment, the deferred giving program was, and remains, concerned with fund-raising through bequests, trusts, life insurance, and reserved-income agreements.

Prior to Monday, June 27, 1977, *Corvallis Gazette-Times* newspaper reporter, Kevin Miller entered Roy "Spec" Keene's home on the western edge of Corvallis to conduct an interview for a "Monday profile," titled "'Spec' Keene: Living the Sporting Life." It was a memorable conversation with a remarkable man reminiscing about his life, "which has been dedicated to working with young men through athletics." When Kevin later sat down to write the day's story, he began,

> *His hands tremble slightly as he picks up a scarred old baseball. He turns it over and over, looking for just the right spot to grasp it. Satisfied, he grips the ball with the two inside fingers on his right hand. The trembling stops. Roy S. "Spec" Keene is ready to pitch. But there is no baseball diamond. No crowd. At 83, confined to a wheelchair by leukemia, Spec is just remembering.*

As the conversation continued, Spec divulged some little-known facts about his life. After graduating from OAC, he tried out with the Portland baseball team of the Pacific Coast League. The venture didn't work out, and he ended up as player-coach for a semi-pro team in Bandon, Oregon. "I was getting $100 a game," he remembered. "Which was more than I would've made in Portland."

Oregon State Athletic Director Keene and wife, Marie, circa 1960. (*Source*: OSULSCA)

The baseball he was holding when the interview began? About two years prior, a Los Angeles dentist who served with Spec in France brought the ball to him. "'I was flabbergasted,' he says." The baseball he held during the interview was one he hit over a fence in France while playing baseball.

After his death in 1977, Keene was inducted into the Oregon Sports Hall of Fame in 1982 for his coaching. In 1989, Willamette University built a new baseball stadium, which they named Roy S. "Spec" Keene Stadium. In addition to inducting him into the Willamette University inaugural class Athletic Hall of Fame in 1991 during the university's sesquicentennial year, Oregon State University honored him in its Sports Hall of Fame in 1991 for his service as athletic director.

He died in Corvallis, Oregon, on August 24, 1977. Marie died at Heart of the Valley Center in Corvallis on August 27, 1987.

The State Senator of Humble Beginnings Who Served and Was Seriously Wounded in World War I, Went to the Island of Oahu with the Bearcats, Served in World War II, and Served as Governor of Oregon and Secretary of the Interior under President Dwight D. Eisenhower

The life of Oregon state senator James Douglas McKay, who, with his eighteen-year-old daughter, Shirley, sailed on the SS *Lurline* to the Territory of Hawaii, is a marvelous story. He went on the trip with the Willamette Bearcats in part to chaperone Shirley, whose boyfriend, Wayne E. Hadley, was also on board. Senator McKay proved to be a steadying hand and natural leader alongside his friend and Oregon State alumnus, Coach Keene, on the voyage to the islands, then through the shock and turmoil surrounding the team's stay on the island, and finally during the tense and stunning voyage back to San Francisco, as well as on the tension-relieving train ride to Salem. Probably none among the travelers with him, including his daughter, grasped the wealth of experience and wisdom he carried in his forty-eight years of life.

Of Scottish descent, he was born in Portland, Oregon, in 1893. His father, E. D. McKay, was a farmer, and his mother, Minnie Musgrove McKay, was from a pioneer family who came across the plains to settle in Oregon. As a boy, Douglas worked for his grandfather, Malcolm McKay, on Sauvie Island, Oregon. Malcolm, an 1842 immigrant from Glasgow, Scotland, had come to America to be Hudson's Bay Company storekeeper at Fort Vancouver.

After his father's death in 1911, Douglas, age eighteen, decided he must leave high school before receiving his diploma and work to help support his mother. At age thirteen in 1906, he had taken his first job off the farm to help support himself and his parents. Like many children of that era, he later took a succession of jobs as he grew up, including selling candy in Portland theaters, delivering newspapers, and driving a meat wagon. When he quit high school to work, he took a job at a railroad office and attended Oregon Agricultural College (now Oregon State University) in Corvallis. He drove a laundry wagon to help pay his way through school. While at OAC, he entered the college's cadet corps in 1913, became a cadet captain before he graduated, and got his first hint of what was to come later in life, winning an election, his first, to the office of president of his freshman class, then in his senior year to student body president in 1916.

As a cadet, Doug was praised by a classmate and fraternity brother, "Ade" Sieberts of Portland, who said, "We were made captains of companies the same year. He was the outstanding captain in my opinion. He drilled that company with precision and finesse. It was this military training and love for it that made Doug an outstanding soldier."

While at OAC, he was known to seldom go out socially with college girls, though he attended fraternity dances. He was considered serious, was always interested in college politics, and was the personification of honesty and always a true gentleman. He once told the sister of a classmate and fraternity brother who had worked his way through OAC, as Doug did, "I left my girl at home in Portland." Mabel Christine Hill occasionally came to visit him

1917 photograph of Cadet Captain Douglas McKay. (*Source*: OSULSCA)

at the college, and she came to be known as "Doug's one true love." They married on March 31, 1917, in St. Helens, Oregon.

He earned a bachelor of science degree in agriculture in May 1917 and on June 8 was commissioned a second lieutenant, infantry, in the Officers' Reserve Corps. One week later he departed for the Presidio in San Francisco to undergo three months of officer training.

From the Presidio, he reported to Camp Lewis, Washington, near Tacoma in September where regular and reserve officers had also been coming from their training camps, along with small numbers of recruits from Oregon and Washington. They had begun forming the nucleus and skeletal organizations of an army division in the American National Army, the 91st Division, which would be officially activated at Camp Lewis in October 1917. There, Second Lieutenant McKay joined in preparing to receive and begin training a surging influx of new recruits from eight great western states who would be coming by trains, arriving by noon, on 5 September 1917. As the division historian wrote, the arriving soldiers-to-be at Camp Lewis were "the young men of military age, chosen to represent their respective communities in the first five percent of the selective draft," and they were arriving as construction at Camp Lewis was coming to an end.

The 91st Division, known as the "Wild West Division" during World War I, included men from the great western states of California, Washington, Oregon, Nevada, Utah, Idaho, Montana, and Wyoming, plus the Territory of Alaska, and eventually was fully organized, manned, and trained under experienced leadership. Incoming recruits worked hard under the intense demands of tough drill sergeants, sweated, and prepared to go overseas at the army's full, authorized, World War I division strength of twenty-eight thousand men. Throughout September and on into 1918, the original skeletal organization of the 91st remained in place in Camp Lewis, providing leadership and training as the division's ranks filled, except for turnover in senior officer leadership positions.

By the time the division was ready to deploy to Europe, it comprised four infantry regiments, three artillery regiments, land transportation for an organized division (vehicles and equipment called trains), three machine-gun battalions, an engineer regiment, and a signal corps battalion, all with a supporting medical department and ambulance companies. There were two infantry regiments and one machine-gun battalion in each of two infantry brigades, the 181st and 182nd, with the 181st Infantry Brigade comprised of the 361st and 362nd Infantry Regiments and the 347th Machine Gun Battalion. Lieutenant McKay's assigned unit was the 361st Infantry Regiment, where he would eventually join the 3rd Battalion's Company K.

The three artillery regiments, 346th, 347th, and 348th, with the 316th Trench Mortar Battery, constituted the 166th Field Artillery Brigade. As the 91st Division gained strength at Camp Lewis, filling out, organizing, and training its units the remainder of the year, the War Department made several levies upon the division for thousands of troops to be sent east for replacements and for filling other units, the largest levy coming in December 1917. The levies continued into 1918; nevertheless, the division's goal remained fixed—readiness to move across the United States to the port of embarkation, ship overseas, and once in France continue training in preparation to join the Allies in the frontline battles against the Germans.

Finally, after all the toil, building, and training to fill other units going where the men of the 91st most wanted to go, from the War Department and the army staff came movement orders. When the orders came, the original foundation of the division, the officers and men who had built it at the skeletal troop level, were still there, and they would be there when the division entered its first battle in France. They were the same ones who were in the 91st during the days of September, October, and November 1917.

The 361st Regiment was composed largely of Oregon and Washington men. As the historian wrote, "the spirit of Montana dominated in the 362nd." California laid claim to the 363rd and 364th Regiments because of the large number of sons of the Golden State in those two organizations.

On 24 November 1917, Major General H. A. Greene, who had been given the task of forming the 91st Division, left Camp Lewis for France with his chief of staff to survey and study the conditions in which the division would be called upon to cope while performing their missions. He returned in March 1918, having in the interim continued to organize his staff and subordinate commands for intended permanency.

In the meantime, while command changes were in progress and the division was still in training at Camp Lewis, Douglas McKay received, and on 19 March 1918 accepted, his promotion to first lieutenant, with a date of rank of 21 January 1918.

On 6 May 1918, Brigadier General J. B. MacDonald succeeded Brigadier General Wilhem D. Styer as commander of the 181st Brigade, the brigade to which Douglas McKay was assigned, followed by the relief of Major General Greene just prior to the division's move toward the east coast and overseas. Greene had been ordered to the Philippines, leaving Brigadier General Frederick L. Foltz in command for the overseas move.

The end of ten months of intense training found the 91st preparing for the long-anticipated move overseas. Orders came almost daily, covering the countless details of the division and the huge quantities of materials to be transported across the continent to the port of embarkation, then across the Atlantic to the shores of France. The move was but one relatively small part of an unprecedented, growing flow of American military force into a European and world war, with all necessary logistical support, crossing the Atlantic in heavily loaded convoys, with the flow of the 91st and the entire American Expeditionary Force beginning to reverse toward home less than five months in the future.

Late in June 1918 the troops began loading on trains. On 19 June, the advance party left Camp Lewis. And in a little-noticed wedding ceremony on 20 June, a day or two before he boarded a train for the East Coast, Private Howard Marshall Wight, Company I, also 3rd Battalion, 361st Regiment, married Charlotte N. Hurd, then assistant professor of psychology at OAC. Private Wight, a graduate and zoology major at Bates College in Maine, four years senior to Douglas McKay, and a former teaching fellow and zoology instructor at OAC who had taught McKay in the classrooms at OAC, had just been awarded a master's degree at the college. One day later, on 21 June, Brigadier General Foltz, the division's commander in the absence of Major General Greene, and Foltz's staff, the Headquarters Troop and Detachment, entrained, with the remainder of the division following as rapidly as possible.

On their six-day trip across the continent, the men from the far west had an excellent opportunity to witness the swelling patriotic unity that would ultimately bring the defeat of Germany. After seeing and hearing demonstrations and cheers of encouragement from coast to coast, the men felt assured they were backed by an undivided nation. The trip also gave the citizens, especially in the East, a better conception of the high quality of manhood the West was contributing to the army. Virtually all of the division arrived in Camp Merritt, New Jersey, between 24 June and 30 June. The train carrying the staff and Headquarters Troop and Detachment arrived at midnight on the 26th, and the morning of the 27th the commanding general embarked on a transport for France.

The division remained at Camp Merritt until 5 July, where they received complete new uniforms, including steel helmets and two new pairs of hobnailed trench shoes, and all officers and men were given final physical examinations. Any man determined to be unfit had to remain behind.

The morning of 6 July, the men were wakened earlier than normal to load onto ferries to transport them to docks where they loaded aboard their two assigned giant liners, vessels that would leave port later that day and depend on speed instead of destroyers to protect them against submarine attacks. The heavily protected, escorted convoy required twelve days to make the crossing and arrive in the port of Liverpool. The *Pennsylvania*-class armored cruiser *San Diego* (ACR-6) escorted the transports and turned back on 15 July before twelve British destroyers met the transports on 16 July. The destroyers convoyed them into Liverpool and Glasgow. Entering the Irish Sea, the convoy received additional escorts by dirigibles, hydroplanes, and submarine chasers. The convoy had safely passed through dangerous waters.

The convoy guide dropped anchor off the Liverpool docks at six o'clock in the evening of 17 July. While several of the division's military bands played popular airs, thousands of civilians cheered as each ship proceeded to its berth. Some of the original convoy put in at Glasgow, Scotland; one to Southampton; and others to La Havre, France.

The Americans were warmly received in both Scotland and England. The men who landed in British ports went to so-called English rest camps, which were not what men of the 91st anticipated after their long voyage, because the foodstuffs at the camps clearly illustrated the effectiveness of the Germans' relentless submarine warfare. Their stays at the camps were not long, however, because the men in England and Scotland had to travel by train across the two countries to ports of embarkation and cross the submarine-infested English Channel to France. That last leg of the long journey was a slow-going ten hours and hazardous, but it went off without a hitch. The preponderance of the American contingent coming from England and Scotland, though not the majority of the division, set foot on French soil on the morning of 23 July at the port of La Havre, where other ships from the convoy had previously arrived.

In the meantime, at 1105 the morning of 19 July, the armored cruiser San Diego, which left the division's convoy on 15 July to return to the States, met a stunningly different fate. That morning she was steaming northeast of the Fire Island Lightship, not far from Long Island, New York, en route to take up her next assigned convoy escort duty, when a heavy explosion occurred on her port side (left side), adjacent to her port engine room and well below her waterline. In a board of inquiry after the sinking, her captain, Harley H. Christy, stated that he had ordered a zigzag course at a speed of fifteen knots (seventeen miles per hour) to avoid submarine attack; that all lookouts, gun watches, and fire-control parties were at their appointed stations on full alert; and that all necessary orders to safeguard the watertight integrity of the ship in dangerous waters were being carried out.

The explosion was fatal for the ship, warping the bulkhead at the site of the powerful explosive force and preventing the closing of the watertight hatch between the engine room and no. 8 fire room. Both compartments immediately flooded. Captain Christy assumed the ship had been struck by a torpedo, sounded the submarine defense quarters, and ordered all guns to open fire on anything resembling a periscope. He called for full speed ahead on both engines and hard right rudder, but he was told that the engines were out of commission and the machinery compartments were rapidly flooding. The ship had taken on a nine-degree list, and water began pouring in through one of the six-inch (150 mm) gun ports, flooding the gun deck.

Informed that the ship's radio had failed, Christy ordered the gunnery officer to take a boat crew to shore to summon rescue vessels.

Within ten minutes after the explosion, the cruiser had begun to sink. Orders were given to lower the life rafts and boats, with Captain Christy holding off the order to abandon ship until he was certain *San Diego* was going to capsize. The crew abandoned the vessel in a disciplined and orderly manner, and Christy was the last man to leave the ship. She was gone in twenty-eight minutes with the loss of six lives, the only major combatant lost by the United States in World War I. Two men were killed instantly when the explosion occurred. One crewman who had been oiling the port propeller shaft was never seen again. Another man was killed by one of the smokestacks breaking loose when the ship capsized. One more was killed when a life raft fell on his head, and the sixth was trapped inside the crow's nest by the ship's rapid list and drowned.

Meanwhile, the gunnery officer reached shore at Point o' Woods, New York, two hours later, and vessels were at once sent to pick up survivors.

The Naval Court of Inquiry concluded in August that *San Diego*'s loss was caused by a contact mine, since six other contact mines had been located in the general vicinity by naval forces, a conclusion augmented by no torpedo wakes having been observed by the ship's crew, no evidence of German submarines present in the area at the time, and the fact that German submarine U-158 had earlier laid a number of mines along the south shore of Long Island. The loss was attributed to the activities of U-158.

The 91st Division's stop at La Havre in the midst of good weather, and plenty of good food, made the unit's several days' stay a well-earned and appreciated recuperation from their monthlong travel from the northwestern United States. Now circumstances were about to change. In the last days of July, the final leg of their journey began with another train ride, this time in the small "side-door Pullmans" known to every Allied soldier who served in France in World War I. They were called 8:40 trains, and the boxcars were stenciled "40 Hommes—8 Chevaux." The division historian injected some humor in the narrative at this point, writing,

It was never anticipated the military authorities would have to crowd forty huskies of the 91st into them. By reducing the number assigned to each car to about thirty-five it was possible to pack them in. Two nights and a day gave the men all the "chevauxing" they desired for a long time to come.

By 1 August, the division settled into its training area in the French department of Haute Marne. The town of Montiguy-le-Roi, where divisional headquarters was established, was near surrounding villages where the troops were billeted, and the surrounding terrain could not have been more perfect to train for conducting open warfare, in which they would be participating later. What's more, the weather cooperated, providing the right conditions to whip the men into the best possible physical condition. The training schedule for the balance of the month of August was filled with incessant drilling, long marches, and frequent military exercises for the entire division.

On 29 August, Brigadier General Foltz returned to command of the 182nd Brigade when Major General William H. Johnston came to the division as its commanding general. The division left the training area for "the front" on 7 September, moving to the vicinity of Gondrecourt where they were placed under what was called an army post of command— a PC, a higher-headquarters command, in this instance, the 1st American Army, in which the division was part of the reserve in the planned reduction of the St.-Mihiel salient. The Allied counteroffensive to reduce the salient began five days later.

The next PC was reached by marching the division from Gondrecourt to the vicinity of Void, Pagny-sur-Meuse, and Sorcy-St.-Martin, where it was established in Sorcy on September 11 and remained through the 13th. While there, they were prepared to support the 4th American Corps or the 2nd French Colonial Corps. When the drive from the south to reduce the salient was determined successful, the division moved at night, by truck train, to the Vavincourt area, west of St.-Mihiel, passing to command of Major General Hirschauer, 2nd French Army. In just three days, the St.-Mihiel salient had been reduced, and there was no further reason to hold the 91st in reserve. The division's headquarters moved from Vavincourt on 17 September to Autrecourt under orders from the new PC, the 2nd French Army, placing it under Major General Garvier Duplessix, 9th French Corps.

In Autrecourt, the division staff became acquainted with the big task ahead, the Allied offensive that would include the 91st's role in Meuse-Argonne, where they would go over the top in the coming drive. On 19 September, PC went from Autrecourt to Vraincourt, 5th Army Corps, and Major General George H. Cameron, U.S. Army, then just six miles from the front line held by the French. The Wild West Division's troops moved by night marches with great secrecy until all were safely bivouacked in the woods of Foret de Hesse surrounding Cote 290, Bertrame Farm. The new PC was now Cote 290, as of 20 September, while the administrative staff remained at Vraincourt.

To assist in ensuring surprise, troops necessarily had to move as guardedly as possible. When aircraft approached overhead, bugles sounded the alarm, and troops took cover. The staff were located in dugouts on the southern slope of the hill.

The Americans would initiate the coming assault, but General Cameron directed that the French continue holding the line in the 91st's sector until the night immediately preceding the attack. In the interim, men in the division who had to go into the line to acquaint themselves with the terrain over which they and the men in their units were shortly to battle were to wear helmets and overcoats of the French. Among those required by General Johnston to make such reconnaissance were all brigade and regimental commanders.

Hostile action was limited to harassing artillery fire and some intelligence-gathering raids by strong German patrols in the sectors of the 35th and 79th Divisions. In both instances the Germans threw artillery barrages over the two divisions to cover the raids, and in the raid against the 35th several men of the 91st were wounded. Despite the intense efforts to conceal the movement of the Americans into the sector, the Germans became aware of the unusually heavy traffic involved in moving up artillery, munitions, and supplies and sent patrols to gather intelligence. On 24 September, the division issued orders for the last preparations for going into the line—and preparations continued. The historian took note of the fact that despite occasional rain showers in their wooded bivouac area, the men's ardor had not been dampened. On the 25th, the last orders were issued, with 26 September designated as "D" day and 0530 as "H" hour the next morning.

General John J. Pershing, commander in chief of the American Expeditionary Forces and personally commanding the 1st American Army, visited the PC at Cote 290 that afternoon. He asked Major General Johnston to express his confidence that officers and men of the 91st would do their duty. Later in the day General Johnston issued a memorandum read to all troops before they marched to their attack positions. Officers and men were pleased that the commander in chief was with them at the front and not dictating orders from some headquarters far in the rear.

The 166th Field Artillery Brigade that sailed to France as a unit of the 91st would not be participating in the assault, as they were detached in a training area in France and did not join with the division. Instead, attached to the 91st were the following: the 58th Field Artillery Brigade; one regiment of the 58th Field Artillery Brigade; one battalion of the 65th Regiment Coast Artillery Corps; one battery of French artillery; Company B, 1st Gas Regiment, less one platoon; the 104th Squadron, Air Service Corps, less one flight.

At 2330 hours that night, the heavy long-range guns of the army artillery opened fire on selected enemy targets. As the hours passed into the morning of the 26th, the power and intensity of the heavy's bombardment grew. At 0230 hours, after remaining silent during the long-range bombardment, corps and divisional artillery joined in the increasingly deafening thunder of a night no one present could ever forget. Men who were keyed up and sleepless considering the unknowns of going "over the top" would have found it impossible to sleep any single moment of the night under the force of the endless overhead barrage. Observers peering through binoculars and telescopes could see German trenches marked in the darkness by a line of leaping fire, which was occasionally punctuated by the higher bursts of particularly heavy shells.

German retaliatory fire passed over the division's lead regiments, but the 363rd, in the rear behind the lead regiments, found no trenches adequate to protect them and instead, since the weather was relatively warm that night, preferred lying on the ground on a hill. All outgoing artillery passed over regiments awaiting the move forward.

When 0530 hours arrived, the infantry moved forward out of their trenches, the American 1st Army driving north with the 91st Division, as one of three divisions in the 5th Corps, left to right with the 37th and 79th Divisions to the right of the 91st. The 32nd Division, just arrived from the Paris group of armies, was the 5th Corps reserve. To the left of the 91st were three divisions of the 1st Corps, the 35th, 28th, and 77th, with the five-division 3rd Corps to the right of the 5th Corps, with 3rd's right flank anchored on the generally north–south flowing Meuse River. To the right and left of the American 1st Army were divisions of the French army. On the right, along the Meuse River, was the 2nd Army, composed of American and French divisions and corps, protecting the right flank of the 1st Army as it struck north.

The division historian paused at this juncture and laid out his narrative view of the terrain the 1st Army and the 91st Division would fight their way through in the coming days.

The front assigned for the American advance extended from the Argonne on the west to the Meuse on the east, a stretch of some eighteen miles. The country between these limits is hilly and broken, with a large part of it heavily wooded. It may roughly be divided into three parts: on the west is the great Argonne Forest; then the open valley of the Aire, a tributary of the Aisne, which, at this point, runs nearly parallel to it; and lastly the strip of country between the Aisne and the Meuse, approximately equal in width to the other two. This section contains many large and thick woods, interspersed with small open valleys and rolling uplands. The Hill of Montfaucon, topped by the town of the same name, is the highest point in the region and commands views over the entire district.

The two regiments of the 181st Brigade went over the top together with the 361st on the left and the 362nd on the right. To the right of them the 182nd Brigade's two regiments, the 363rd and 364th, moved forward, the 364th behind the 363rd by five hundred yards. The Germans, having anticipated a major effort but uncertain as to when and where, had pulled back from the first of three lines of defense and were actually in the midst of the pullback when the Allies struck. Thus the two regiments of the 181st were able to cross "no-man's land" on the 26th, unopposed and with no casualties, as did all the waves of the 363rd to their right.

Later in the morning, the 364th, delayed in their "jump-off" by mist and smoke and having trouble finding their way through prepared lanes in the old French wire in no-man's land, fell behind schedule, and when the mist and smoke lifted, their 2nd Battalion encountered German machine-gun fire, then artillery, and took many casualties.

By nightfall of the first day, the 91st had pushed north approximately five miles. The 91st regiments had crossed the Germans' first line of trenches, which showed evidence of only a few defenders and hasty withdrawal, probably the previous night. However, as the day wore on, resistance stiffened considerably. Late in the afternoon, the 181st Brigade had fought its way to open ground and could see German positions two thousand yards to the north, near Epinonville. The brigade commander ordered an attack. From a position near the Very road, the division commander observed their lines advancing bravely over open ground under heavy fire until halted at the ridge that was Epinonville. Some men fought their way into the town, but the brigade had to pull back into the ravine south of the town for the night to consolidate their positions and prepare for the next day's operations.

The next day, after a night of establishing the locations of the division's units and determining the objectives and lines of attack on the 27th, the assault on Epinonville resumed. During the night the Germans had strengthened their positions, reinforcing them with numerous machine-gun nests supported by intense and accurate artillery fire. The 181st, with the 361st on the left and the 362nd on the right, drove through Epinonville, clearing out groups of the enemy as they passed, but when the 361st attempted to move west on the road out of town, they met hails of machine-gun fire from the woods and orchards, stopping their progress. Time and again the assaults were stymied. Hostile shelling became severe, hitting assaulting troops and supporting units dug in on the south slopes of the town. The fire was persistent and accurate, and it was almost constantly observed and adjusted by enemy planes overhead. Three separate assaults on the town on the 27th forced the 181st back into the ravine south of town.

That night, after enemy artillery had brutalized the 181st and supporting units nearly all day, friendly artillery struck hard, unleashing army artillery in front of the 182nd Brigade, to the left of the 181st, and on Epinonville.

On the 28th the advance was renewed, the 181st Brigade attacking with the 361st in front with two battalions, followed by the 362nd, with the remainder of the 361st in support and the 362nd formed as the brigade reserve. The brigade passed through Epinonville and took Les Epinettes Bois and Bois de Cierges. During the day's advance, Major Oscar F. Miller, commanding the 361st's lead battalion, encountered the enemy in a prepared position south of Gesnes. Though almost exhausted after two days of intense pressure and nonstop effort, he energetically reorganized the battalion and ordered an attack. Upon reaching open ground, the advancing line began to waiver in the face of machine-gun fire from the front and flanks, as well as direct artillery fire. Personally leading his command group forward between his frontline companies, Major Miller inspired his men by his personal courage, and they again pressed on toward the hostile position. As he led the renewed attack, he was shot in the right leg but nevertheless staggered forward toward the head of the command. Soon afterward he was again shot in the right arm but continued the charge, personally cheering his troops on through the heavy machine-gun fire. Just before the objective was reached, he received a wound to the abdomen, forcing him to the ground. He continued to urge his men on, telling them to push on to the next ridge and leave him where he lay. Mortally wounded, he died the next day. He posthumously received the nation's highest decoration for valor, the Medal of Honor, later presented to his widow.

To the left of the 181st Brigade, the two regiments of the 182nd Brigade were being drawn toward a more northwesterly course into the area of the adjoining 1st Corps' 35th Division to establish contact with the 35th and avoid leaving the 91st's left flank exposed. As they moved, they had to fight through two heavily defended farms, both strong centers of resistance. A similar circumstance existed to the right of the 181st Brigade, with the division's right flank "in the air." There was no direct contact with the 37th Division when nightfall came, but the 181st Brigade deployed the 362nd Regiment so that it lay behind the 361st, arranged in a position to repel any attempt to encircle the two advanced units. In the early afternoon the division headquarters had moved into Epinonville, and the division reserve dug in at an orchard southwest of the town. Artillery fire had become much more severe from the morning on, and it continued throughout the night.

A heavy rain began to fall as darkness closed in, making the night more difficult. Assigned to Company K, 3rd Battalion, 361st Regiment, Doug McKay, along with all the men in the 361st, had been fighting steadily for three days. They had had no blankets to protect them against the cold September nights. Their rapid advance had made it impossible to serve them any hot food since before the jump-off. The first ambulances reached Epinonville and the division PC on the 29th. Until that time, trucks and wagons were the only transportation for the wounded, and they had been caught in the jammed Avocourt–Very road behind traffic such as artillery and trucks. There would be insufficient ambulances to evacuate the wounded until 30 September.

The 91st Division's relentless drive forward, though painful and increasingly costly the first three days, didn't seem to dampen the unit's ardor in spite of the cold, rainy weather and the lack of blankets, hot food, and medical transportation since the 25th. The next day, Sunday the 29th, continued with heavy fighting and ended similarly to the first three days, with the division moving ahead to a position where once again its flanks were possibly overexposed, requiring pullback at the end of the day to avoid potential encirclement by the Germans.

At 2300 hours on the night of the 28th, the 5th Corps commander ordered renewal of the attack at 0700 hours the next day, adding, "Divisions will advance independently of each other, pushing the attack with utmost vigor and regardless of cost." As the division historian further explained,

> *The 91st Division obeyed this order on that memorable Sunday with renewed energy and inspiration, believing each division would be prompted by the same impulse to "do or die" for the Fifth Corps which inspired the 91st when assigned the important task of "carrying the ball through the center of the First American Army." Division orders at 2330 hours directed heavy artillery fire on Gesnes, support of each brigade by a light regiment (75's), and advance by each brigade in its proper zone toward the American Army objective (line of hills north of the Gesnes–Exermont road).*

Through a day of bitter fighting, which further bloodied the division's 181st and 182nd Infantry Brigades, brigades in the divisions to the right and left of the 91st advanced and then pulled back due to heavy casualties, creating a potentially dangerous situation for the 91st Division by mid-afternoon.

The renewed drive began at 0700 hours the morning of the 29th when the 181st Brigade's 362nd Infantry passed through the 361st, as the 362nd moved north through Bois de Cierges toward Gesnes. When they reached a line abreast of Grange aux Bois Farm—which was in the zone of the 37th Division—the 362nd received artillery and machine-gun fire from the farm and from the hills (part of the 1st Army's objective) northeast and northwest of Gesnes. The heavy fire forced the 362nd back to positions held all night by the 361st. At 1000 hours the advance was renewed but ran into the hail of fire that previously checked them and had to pull back once more. At the same time that the 181st was attempting to drive toward Gesnes, the 182nd's 363rd Regiment, with two companies of 316th Engineers, was directed to pass through the 364th Regiment and cross the open ground north of Bois de Baulny. It too was checked at the road from Tronsol Farm to Grange aux Bois Farm, from the latter place.

The 181st Brigade was then ordered by the division commander to take Grange aux Bois Farm to cover the right flank of the division. This time with the firepower of the supporting 122nd Field Artillery, machine guns, and other powerful weapons, a battalion of the 361st Infantry occupied the farm. Another battalion covered the right flank, facing Bois Emont. During this series of assaults, Major George W. Farwell, 361st Infantry, was fatally wounded, and his widow later received his posthumous award of the Distinguished Service Cross, the nation's second-highest decoration for valor. He was the second 361st field-grade officer lost in two days, a growing measure of the fierce nature of the fighting.

Holding the Tronsol Farm, just inside the 35th Division zone on the left, and Grange Farm, just inside the 37th Division zone on the right, at 1430 hours the 91st Division was ready to advance farther. The 181st Brigade was directed to advance toward Gesnes. The 182nd Brigade, as soon as its right was covered by the 181st, was to advance across the Exermont–Gesnes road toward the American Army objective, the line of hills overlooking the road.

An early indication of trouble ahead came at 1530 hours when the commanding general of the 181st Brigade reported that the 74th Brigade (37th Division) had pulled back to the south and east of Bois Emont at 1410 hours. Nevertheless, he directed his brigade, less two battalions of the 361st protecting his right, to take Gesnes. In three lines, the 362nd Infantry, with two companies of the 347th Machine Gun Battalion, advanced. Colonel J. H. Parker led the advance battalion, with the 2nd Battalion, 361st, following. Preparation for the attack began with an artillery barrage, and a rolling barrage preceded the lead battalion.

The Germans countered the assault right from the jump-off by a terrific barrage, accompanied by deadly machine-gun fire from the front and right flank. The assault went forward grimly, passed across the open field, and, in spite of numerous casualties, reached Gesnes and drove out the enemy, one battalion of the 362nd reaching Hill 255, from which enemy observers had commanded sweeping views of American forces' dispositions and movements. The 2nd Battalion, 361st Infantry, passed beyond the town and up the slopes to the northwest, reaching the army objective behind the battalion of the 362nd. At nightfall the advanced units of both brigades were consolidating their positions, and the 361st, less one battalion, was covering the division's exposed right flank where it was subjected to a severe pounding by artillery from the northeast.

Just prior to the 91st commander's receipt of this good news, information had come to him via a liaison officer and a runner that brigades adjoining his division on both flanks were stalled and beginning to pull back to hold more defensible positions in the face of heavy casualties. Both commanders, of the 35th Division to his left and the 37th Division to his right, had been asking for help or said they were unable to push forward due to heavy losses. Thus the 91st Division commander and his two regimental commanders faced agonizing decisions.

As the 5th Corps commander had asked, the Wild West Division, at great cost, had tried and tried again to reach the 1st Army objective and had succeeded, while divisions on either flank hadn't moved as fast and as far, and not only were they both pulling back, but one of the two was also asking for help. Then came the realizations that the 361st, 362nd, and 364th were now in a broad, extended front, four times the length of front they should be covering. If the remainder of the division moved forward to join the advance units on the army objective, insufficient infantry support would be available for the 58th Field Artillery Brigade, still in the ravine south of Epinonville. The enemy had appeared in force on both flanks, while units of the two 91st brigades were three miles ahead of the 74th Brigade, 37th Division, on their right, and four miles ahead of the 70th Brigade, 35th Division, on their left. Later, the commanding general, 37th Division, sent a message that his division could not move up to support the 91st Division or cover its right flank.

Orders were sent to prevent the 361st and 364th from advancing, and to units farther ahead to hold their positions. The most difficult decision came shortly thereafter when the advance units of the 362nd and 363rd were ordered to pull back during the night, withdrawing advance elements of each brigade to the line along the border of the Bois de Baulny and Bois de Cierges, holding the two farms they had taken earlier, which were to be held as centers of resistance. Patrols guarded Gesnes, and the Germans never again entered that town in force. The 5th Corps and its divisions made other force adjustments with reserves and various other units to ensure a defensible line with adequate mutual support, ready for the next day's action, while throughout the night of 29–30 September, wounded were carried back to Bois de Cierges.

The day's attack had been particularly costly to the 362nd Regiment, 181st Brigade, with losses totaling at least five hundred killed and wounded, including a number of valuable officers from among the regiment's leadership.

On the night of 29 September, a few rolling kitchens per regiment were drawn up into the woods and remained until withdrawal on the morning of 4 October. As the division historian pointed out,

> the men were able, in turn, to go back to the kitchens and get the first warm food they had had since 25 September. It was impossible to use the kitchens in the daytime without exposing the vicinity to heavy shellfire. Some of the men serving the kitchens were killed and wounded, and some men going to the kitchens for hot coffee were wounded.

In four days the division had lost 8 field- and 125 company-grade officers and three thousand men.

At 0300 hours on the morning of the fifth day, 30 September, while wounded were being evacuated from Gesnes, the division received orders that the attack of the 5th Corps would not be continued that day, but efforts would be made to resume the offensive on 1 October. The line of resistance ordered by the 5th Corps for possible defense would soon be in place, intended to hold against a strong enemy force reported arriving in Exermont. The 91st Division commander ordered a line of surveillance set up in front of each brigade, the 361st Regiment to cover in front of their 181st Brigade and the 363rd in front of the 182nd. The division reserve was located near Eclisfontaine, and the battalion of engineers that had been with the 182nd Brigade rejoined the reserve, which then consisted of the 346th Machine Gun Battalion and 316th Engineers, less one company remaining engaged in repairing the road between Epinonville and Very.

The 362nd Regiment assembled in a stone quarry north of Exmorieux Farm between the Bois de Cierges and the Bois de Baulny, and later, at 0900 hours, the division commander found only five hundred men of the 362nd present. Others rejoined from Bois de Cierges during the day, and that night more wounded were evacuated from Gesnes, having concealed themselves in dugouts and cellars throughout the 30th.

Beginning at 1000 hours on 30 September until 0800 hours the next morning, enemy artillery shelled the entire division area. To prevent enemy traffic at intervals during the same period, the 58th Field Artillery Brigade shelled Gesnes and the Gesnes–Exermont road.

Colonel W. D. Davis, 361st Infantry, wounded on 28 September, insisted on retaining command of his regiment and was coolly stationing his units on the line of surveillance with his arm in a sling. One battalion of the 363rd Infantry found Bois de Cierges full of gas, moved forward to the ridge north of Bois de Cierges, and occupied shell holes made by the German counterbarrage on the 29th but had no overhead shelter.

On 1 October, after its wounded had been evacuated and able-bodied men rested and fed, the 91st was ready to advance again and orders were issued, but the 5th Corps required the division to wait while the 37th Division was relieved by the 32nd on its right and 35th division by the 1st Division on its left. Both relieving divisions could be clearly seen moving forward toward their positions during the day, the 32nd moving up to Bois Emont and further east, and the 1st Division near Seneux Farm. A 182nd Brigade combat liaison group moving with a battalion of the 1st Division suffered heavy losses as it advanced.

Again commenting on the overall status and welfare of the men, the division historian wrote,

> Many men were suffering from diarrhea due to exposure for five days without warm food, or overcoats and blankets. Most officers and men had raincoats, and some had found German blankets in dugouts. The men built shelter from small-arms fire by excavating the northern edges of shell holes. But they were observed by hostile planes and subjected to heavy fire (shrapnel and shell) from German artillery in the Argonne and northeast of Gesnes. Although many casualties resulted the morale was high.

On 2 October, troops were still under orders to hold positions awaiting corps orders for attack, a continued welcome respite from the fierce fighting of the first four days. An Allied plane brought down a hostile airplane in front of the 364th Infantry. A machine-gun company of the 364th in a position west of Tronsol Farm fired on the enemy in front of the 1st Division as it was marching up on the left of the 91st. On the right the advance of the 32nd Division through the Bois Emont protected the 91st from machine-gun and sniper fire onto the line, but all parts of the area were subjected to artillery fire nearly all day.

At this time, 2 colonels, 2 lieutenant colonels, 8 majors, and 123 company-grade infantry officers were killed or wounded during the six days of advance. The total casualties amounted to nearly 150 officers and 4,000 men.

Then came 1800 hours, when twenty-eight German bombing planes raided the division headquarters in Epinonville, the 58th Artillery Brigade, and engineers in the ravine between Epinonville and Very. The first bomb fell in front of the small brick cottage on the hill occupied by the division commander. The bomb killed one orderly and wounded First Lieutenant A. S. MacDonnel, an aide, and one enlisted man. Almost immediately afterward, enemy artillery shelled division headquarters and the ravine occupied by the artillery and engineers. In one hour the division's losses were 35 killed and 115 wounded. Though antiaircraft guns and machine guns in the reserve areas fired on the bombers, none of them fell in the division's zone. Ironically, the raid came a half hour after a squadron of Allied planes had passed over division headquarters flying toward the Argonne Forest. The division historian went on to point out, "It is no reflection on our air service that such a raid was possible. It was realized by Division Headquarters that it was impracticable to have Allied airplanes over the Division constantly."

At 2000 hours, troops were warned to be ready for the advance to resume on 3 October; however, the other divisions weren't ready, and the order never came. An hour later, the division PC, located in a splinter-proof on the north slope of a depression where it was protected from artillery fire from the south but not from the north, was struck by a high-explosive shell entering the room occupied as a "message center," killing two men (both liaison runners) and wounding two officers and one enlisted man. This man later died. One of the officers wounded was a liaison officer from the 1st Division, and the other officer was in charge of the message center for the night. Then came another artillery round that hit the stone ruins in which members of the headquarters troop and horses were sheltered, killing seven horses. The division PC with telephone switchboard was then moved to a cellar under a ruined building in Epinonville, which had, since the 29th, been used as headquarters for the 58th Artillery Brigade.

On 3 October, the eighth day, there was little enemy activity until 1040 hours. From that time until 2000 hours, hostile artillery fire was more violent than at any time during the previous engagement. The Germans had observed the two relieving divisions and were covering the entire 5th Corps front and the breakup formation of the relieving divisions, undoubtedly also intending to blunt any coming renewal of the 1st Army offensive in the Meuse-Argonne.

It was during the relentless enemy artillery fire of that day that First Lieutenant Douglas McKay's war ended. Assigned to Company K, 3rd Battalion, 361st Infantry Regiment, holding the assigned surveillance line in front of the 181st Brigade, he suffered severe wounds from an exploding enemy shell that fell two hundred yards behind the 361st's line while he was preparing a detail for a dangerous scout raid. He nearly died. Fragments from the exploding shell killed two of his men standing next to him and struck him in six places. In addition to clipping a bit of his left ear, fragments badly shattered his right arm and hit him in the chest, shoulder, and legs. His wounds earned him the Purple Heart, though he would

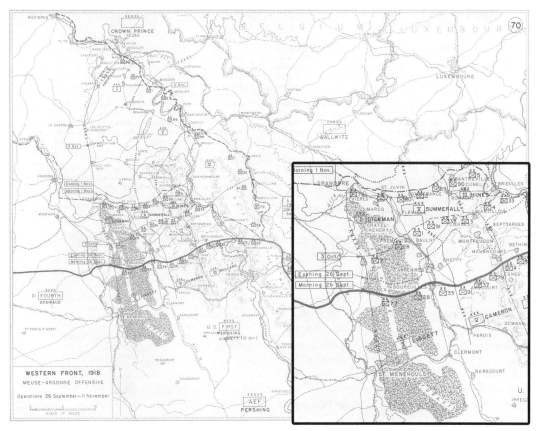

Map, Meuse-Argonne Offensive, 26 September–11 November 1918. Note the 91st Division symbol is at Cameron's V Corps left flank boundary, against the I Corps' boundary, where its line of advance can be traced northward to the 3 October gray dotted line, the area where First Lieutenant McKay was seriously wounded on that date. The inset blowup of the area provides an expanded, clearer view of the total advance in one week of fierce fighting before he was wounded. (*Source*: WPA, page 70)

be counted on this eighth day of the Meuse-Argonne Offensive as one among 36 officers and 793 men lost from the 361st Infantry Regiment.

Fortunately, his former zoology instructor, an OAC teaching fellow, Private Howard Marshall Wight, who was a runner (message carrier) assigned to Company I, a sister company in the 3rd Battalion, 361st Regiment, and from whom Lieutenant McKay had received classroom instruction at OAC, gave him first aid and carried his severely wounded former student to safety while the German artillery barrage continued. It was one act among a considerably larger number of similar instances when Wight aided wounded soldiers, acts for which he was later awarded America's second-highest decoration for valor, the Distinguished Service Cross, and from France their nation's Croix de guerre (Cross of War) for acts of heroism in war against an enemy.

In McKay's case, the young officer credited Howard Wight with saving his life. Later, after McKay learned of his former instructor's remarkable care and courage in saving many other wounded men on the battlefield, and of his well-earned Distinguished Service Cross and Croix de guerre decorations, he was heard to remark, "The old boy sure covered himself with glory."

The *Portland Oregonian* unfortunately—and erroneously—was notified of Douglas McKay's death and printed the notice, but the family had already received a cable assuring them that he was receiving care in Field Hospital 46 in Paris—a cable to which Douglas's wife, Mabel, had promptly replied by a cable date-stamped 27 October 1918 to a nurse Mabel knew personally, her sister-in-law, and had cabled the family in advance of the death report published in the Portland newspaper. Mabel's cable was stamped COMMERCIAL and addressed to EFM EVELYN HILL BASE HOSPITAL 46 AMCN ARMY FRANCE:

CABLE RECEIVED NATURALLY SHOCKED AND ANXIOUS BUT ALWAYS BRAVE SO GLAD YOU ARE WITH HIM WILL MAIL SENT NOW YOUR HOSPITAL REACH HIM KEEP ME FULL ADVISED OFTEN ALL WELL MY LOVE TO HIM AND YOU MABEL MCKAY

Mabel and Douglas's family would eventually learn that his former OAC instructor in the Zoology Department was the man who saved Douglas's life while under heavy bombardment on the battlefield.

Many Oregon Agricultural College men contributed to the American Expeditionary Forces' victory in the Meuse-Argonne Offensive, part of the final Allied offensive of the war, later called the Grand Offensive (also known as the Hundred Days' Offensive), and the longest battle in American military history. The offensive had begun on 26 September 1918, involved 1.2 million American soldiers, and lasted for forty-seven days, until the Armistice was signed on 11 November. The Americans suffered 26,277 killed and 95,786 wounded, while the French suffered approximately 70,000 killed and wounded and the Germans an estimated 90,000–120,000. While the Meuse-Argonne Offensive involved American and French forces, the rest of the Allies, including France, Britain and its dominion and imperial armies (mainly Canada, Australia, and New Zealand), and Belgium, fought major battles in other sectors across the whole front.

Though his wounds took him out of the fighting, Douglas McKay probably learned that the 181st Brigade, including the 361st Infantry and the 91st Division, were relieved and replaced on the line beginning at midnight the day he was wounded and hospitalized. All units were given a brief rest, were reequipped and refilled with replacements, and reentered the final days of fighting in World War I in both France and Belgium.

The 91st Division was placed in the V Corps reserve on 4 October 1918 and in mid-month transferred north to participate in the Ypres-Lys campaign, while the Meuse-Argonne Offensive continued. The division excelled in the campaign, liberating the town of Audenarde, Belgium.

Before and after the Armistice was signed, glowing letters of praise started pouring into the 91st Division, and numerous ceremonies were held in which officers and enlisted men received decorations for their heroism, valor, and discipline in battle.

The division had entered the Meuse-Argonne Offensive with a strength of a little less than twenty thousand, including noncombatant arms, and after continuing in the war until the Armistice was signed had suffered a total of 6,108 casualties, 1,134 killed in action, and 4,974 wounded. Major General William H. Johnston had commanded and led the division all the way through the fighting in Europe, in the Meuse-Argonne and Ypres-Lys Offensives, until its return home in April 1919 and subsequent deactivation the following month.

Lieutenant McKay left Brest, France, on the French transport *La France* on 13 December 1918, the same day President Woodrow Wilson arrived in Brest to begin his efforts to negotiate a lasting peace treaty based on his historic "Fourteen Points." Douglas McKay had the good fortune of witnessing President Wilson's arrival before the *La France* left for its voyage to New York. He sailed past the Statue of Liberty on Christmas Eve, shortly before he disembarked in the port of New York for the train ride home. Douglas McKay returned home to Portland bearing the still-serious but healing wounds that earned him the Purple Heart.

As soon as he arrived in Portland, he began additional surgeries to attempt to avoid amputation of his right arm. The attempts were successful, and he credited and praised Major Tom Joyce of the Portland Hospital unit for the surgical attention that saved his arm from amputation.

Despite Douglas's successful recuperation, the recovery was lengthy, and the wound's lingering effects prevented his hoped-for life in agriculture, causing him to take a different path for a time.

After the war, he began his business career selling insurance, but the growing popularity of automobiles caught his attention and imagination, and he began selling cars for Francis Ford in Portland, becoming sales manager. All of his children, Douglas, Shirley, and Mary-lou, were later born in Portland. He was offered an automobile sales organization in Salem, then located at Center and Commercial Streets. He purchased the agency, which became Douglas McKay Chevrolet—and later Capitol Chevrolet.

He and his family moved into their home in Salem by 1929, at 395 Jerris Street, which would be their only home in Salem. It was there, while his automobile business continued to prosper and support his family, that he added a Cadillac dealership while his natural and growing inclination to enter politics resurfaced. He later served as the president of the Oregon Automobile Dealer's Association and was elected mayor of Salem, serving in 1933–1934, when he guided his city through fiscal troubles in the wake of the Great Depression. Steering the city into recovery earned him a reputation as a firm advocate of government as well as business, preserving and guarding the financial foundation. He then won races for state senator from 1935 to 1949, the elected office he held when he, his daughter, and her husband-to-be took their fateful 1941 voyage to Hawaii and back.

It's interesting to note that his wife, Mabel, and the landscape gardening firm of Lord and Schryver created a garden at their home, his political positions in Salem were unpaid jobs, and the state's legislators met only two months each year. And sadly, in 1939, a family tragedy occurred when his son died in an automobile accident while a student at Oregon State.

While on Oahu with the 1941 Bearcat team, Senator McKay's World War I service and leadership proved valuable. Though he immediately volunteered to reenter active duty in the army during the thirteen days he was on the island after the Japanese attack, an offer that was politely declined, he helped the young Bearcats, nearly all of whom had never worn the uniform, and the great majority had never held or fired a 1903 Garand bolt-action rifle and certainly had never carried one with a fixed bayonet, dug trenches, or laid barbed wire preparing for battle. He helped give them instructions on donning gas masks; loading, carrying, and firing a rifle; and fixing and using bayonets, preparing themselves to absorb the basics of performing sentry duties at Punahou School, all in the days they served after the team was mobilized on 7 December.

And when they returned to Salem as "war heroes," he helped immensely in telling the story of their journey. He was also anxious to return to Salem to pursue his responsibilities as defense chairman for Marion County. But his anxiousness to serve again didn't end there. His World War I wounds had taken years to heal, and he could have relied on his previously being awarded 60 percent disability to avoid duty in World War II. Instead, at the age of forty-eight, he volunteered to return to active duty in the army on 31 October 1942, accepting a commission as a captain serving in the Army of the United States and returning from the retired list on which he had been placed as a first lieutenant on 12 June 1928. His brief first duty assignment was at Camp Murray, adjacent to Fort Lewis, Washington, and then to Camp Adair, north of Corvallis—the city thirty miles south of Salem—both training facilities for army divisions preparing to deploy to the European and Pacific theaters.

His World War II stint in the army added to his storytelling inventory. He enjoyed telling how he was sent to Baker's School and returned to the post to be made range officer. In spite of his good-humored poke at himself, as always, he took his responsibilities seriously, and while at Camp Adair after World War II, he held important positions in the camp's organizations.

For three months he was the headquarters company commander, and while holding that position he was the range maintenance officer for the rifle and artillery ranges, a duty that lasted an additional month and a half. As director of training for ten months, he directed military training for all members of the Service Command Unit at the camp while supervising the small-arms and artillery ranges for the army ground forces at the same post. It's important to note that while he was on duty at Adair, four army infantry divisions cycled through Camp Adair to conduct field training prior to deployment overseas: the 96th, 104th, 70th, and, ironically, the final one, the 91st Infantry Division, the Wild West Division in which he had served during World War I.

In World War II, the 91st carried the nickname "Powder River Division" and the slogan "Always Ready" while wearing the same shoulder patch as in World War I, the distinctive green fir tree. Organic to the reactivated 91st were three of the original four infantry regiments, the 361st, in which Captain McKay had served as a first lieutenant in the Meuse-Argonne Offensive, the 362nd, and 363rd, plus many of the same-numbered World War I units but of slightly different designations because of changes in weapons or functions.

Perhaps most notably for Douglas McKay was the updated history of the 91st, which came after the division arrived in Camp Adair from Camp White in Oregon in November 1943.

The division's commander when it arrived at Camp Adair was Major General William G. Livesay, and he took the division overseas to the Italian theater of operations in April 1944 and remained in command to the end of World War II as they fought their way through the bitter, bloody, and cold Italian campaigns, then after war's end he marched the division into the city of Trieste, a coastal city in northeast Italy on the Baltic Sea. The division carried with it a war whoop throughout World War II, "Powder River! Let 'er Buck!" which came from a World War I incident.

In France, when asked where the men of the Wild West Division were from, a detachment—undoubtedly a detachment of Montana boys of the 362nd Regiment—was said to have yelled, "Powder River! Let 'er Buck!" The wife of the World War II Powder River Division commander, Mrs. Olga L. Livesay, wrote the division's World War II song, "Doughboy," a direct reference and tribute to the division's marvelous World War I history.

Captain McKay's final position at Camp Adair was as director of personnel, in which he supervised the military and civilian personnel and the prisoners of war assigned to the station complement. On 20 December 1945, he received a promotion to major in the Army of the United States and served until relieved from active duty on 18 March 1946, at Madigan General Hospital in Fort Lewis, Washington. His military service ended when America's postwar demobilization was well under way. He returned to Mabel and his home in Salem, where he continued managing his business while rekindling his keen interest and participation in politics.

Following an October 28, 1947, plane crash that killed Oregon's governor, Earl W. Snell, along with the secretary of state and the president of the state senate, John Hubert Hall, as Speaker in the State House of Representatives and fourth in line of succession, became acting governor for a little more than a year until Douglas McKay was elected governor in 1948. Because Governor Snell had been elected for a second term the fall of 1946 before his tragic and untimely death, Douglas McKay had to stand for reelection in 1950 and won with the biggest majority ever given any man seeking the office.

At the 1952 Republican National Convention, Governor McKay met General Eisenhower and later campaigned for his presidential candidacy in Oregon. After Eisenhower's election victory, he appointed Governor McKay secretary of interior, and the McKays moved to Washington to live in the capital city for the next four years. Always eager to return to their home in Salem whenever possible, he would enjoy riding his horse in the nation's busy, urban capital city. And whenever he and his family could make the trip home and he could transport his horse, the animal went to Salem by auto van, where the secretary enjoyed riding in the woodlands of Rock Creek Park.

Secretary McKay's political supporters convinced him to run for the United States Senate against Wayne Morse in 1956, but the election proved to be his only loss in a lifetime of service. After his defeat, he chose to continue serving President Eisenhower on the International Waterways Commission.

His health began to decline, and in the spring of 1959 he entered Walter Reed Army Hospital for a period of two weeks after suffering a heart setback. He attended the dedication of the St. Lawrence Seaway and then returned to Salem to see his doctor. After medical tests, the McKays went to their cabin on the coast, at Neskowin, where they stayed only thirty-four hours because he became seriously ill. He entered the Salem general hospital on June 12 for treatment of a recurring heart ailment. He remained in the hospital, and later under an oxygen tent, until he died at the age of sixty-six, with his wife Mabel at his side, on July 22, 1959.

His funeral was a state service inside the House of Representatives in the capitol. Among his six pallbearers were four Oregon State alumni. They were Roy S. Keene, class of 1921, at that time the director of athletics at his and Douglas's alma mater; Charles Reynolds, 1913; Colonel Everett May, 1914; and G. F. Chambers, 1916. He was buried on July 25, beside his son, Douglas Jr., in Belcrest Memorial Park in Salem. The city's Douglas McKay High School, built in 1979, bears his name.

Mrs. Mabel Christine McKay survived Douglas McKay for more than eleven years, continuing his legacy of service to the city of Salem and the state of Oregon. While he served in World War II, she was director of home services for the Red Cross and had been chairman of the women's division of Community Chest and United Good Neighbors several times. Later she was active in Salem's Woman's Club drive to purchase a special lamp for an eye bank in Portland, having become interested in the eye bank because her husband bequeathed his eyes for its purposes.

She also served as an elder in the First Presbyterian Church, on the YWCA board, on the Salvation Army Board, on the Easter Seal campaign, and for five years on the state board of the Oregon Federation of Republican Women.

In 1968, she received the distinguished service award from the Salem Area Chamber of Commerce.

She died of cancer in a Salem hospital on Sunday, November 1, 1970. Memorial services were held the following Wednesday at the First Presbyterian Church, and afterward she was interred in a private service at Belcrest Memorial Park.

CHAPTER SIXTEEN

Life before and after Pearl Harbor for 1940
High School Classmates from Portland, Oregon

WARTIME SACRIFICE AND MANY MORE VICTORIES
COACHING WILLAMETTE'S BEARCATS

TILLMAN THEODORE OGDAHL WAS BORN ON OCTOBER 1, 1921, IN GLENWOOD, MINNE-sota, and moved with his family to Portland, Oregon, where they were residing when he entered Willamette University in August 1940 with the aim of playing football under Coach Keene. Like others on the team that year, he had been caught up in his coach's dream of a Shrine Bowl trip to Hawaii. His Franklin High School classmate and football teammate Marshall Hall Barbour entered Willamette the same year.

Ted Ogdahl was imminently successful in the game of football, starring as a speedy, elusive halfback and scoring Willamette's only touchdown in the December 6, 1941, game. He enlisted in the Marine Corps Reserve on April 6, 1942, but remained in inactive reserve status while he continued his education. He had been elected captain for the 1942 season and fortunately was able remain in school for the 1942–1943 academic year and played through the Bearcats' entire war-shortened, six-game conference schedule plus a powerful Portland University team—their only loss in another year as the Pacific Northwest Conference champions. He was named a Little All-American halfback as a junior that year.

Following the 1942–1943 academic year, he was called to active duty on 1 July 1943, proceeded through boot camp, and on completion of officer candidate school was commissioned a second lieutenant in the Marine Corps Reserve on 12 April 1944. He was assigned to Camp Pendleton, California, near San Diego in July 1944, where he served as physical training instructor until November 1944, when he was assigned to the newly formed 6th Marine Division, which had been activated in the Solomon Islands. On 12 May 1945, he nearly lost his life in the bloody battle for the island of Okinawa—the second time he had been wounded. The final incident of his wounding was related in part to journalist Frank Marqua of the *Santa Rosa Press Democrat* in 2011 by one of Ted's sons. He was shot in the chest as he and his fellow marines attempted to take a beach, fell, and was "bayoneted by Japanese," said his son, Wally. The marines retook the beach, and Ted Ogdahl survived. "He pretended he was dead, which wasn't very hard, because he was close," said Wally, a lawyer in Salem, Oregon. However, there was much more to his father's story.

Ted Ogdahl was a platoon leader in E Company, 2nd Battalion, 22nd Marines, 6th Marine Division, Fleet Marine Force. The 6th Marine Division was the only marine division formed overseas during World War II, then deactivated overseas after the war ended. The division formed in the Solomon Islands on 7 September 1944 from three infantry regiments—the 4th, 22nd, and 29th—and other units such as engineer, medical, pioneer, motor transport, tank, headquarters, and service battalions. They trained on Guadalcanal specifically to participate in the final, major island-hopping campaign toward the planned invasion of the Japanese home islands, the invasion and capture of Okinawa. When training was complete, the division embarked to accompany a huge and growing assault force moving toward the main landing on Okinawa's Hagushi beaches. The main landing on 1 April 1945, coincidentally Easter Sunday and April Fool's Day, began on the west coast of the island, south of the midpoint of its northeast-to-southwest length, coming ashore from Task Force 56 onto Green Beach.

Task Force 56, the Expeditionary Troops under Army Lieutenant General Simon Bolivar Buckner Jr., 10th Army, was to secure the left flank of the landing force and was built around the 10th Army. The 10th had two corps under its command, III Amphibious Corps, consisting of 1st and 6th Marine Divisions, and XXIV Corps, consisting of the Army's 7th and 96th Infantry Divisions. The 6th Division anchored the entire landing force's left flank—with the 22nd Marine Regiment, to which Ted was assigned, on the division's far left flank. To the right of the 6th Division when the 10th Army came ashore on 1 April, in sequence, north to south, was the 1st Marine Division and the army's 96th and 7th Divisions.

By World War II standards, the 10th Army moved more than rapidly across the south-central part of the island, capturing the Kadena and Yomitan air bases within hours of the landing. General Buckner, observing the weak opposition, decided to proceed immediately with phase 2 of his plan, the seizure of northern Okinawa. The 6th Marine Division, assigned that mission, moved speedily up the Ishikawa Isthmus and by 7 April had sealed off the Motobu Peninsula on the west side of the island. Six days later, on 13 April, the 2nd Battalion, 22nd Regiment, Ted Ogdahl's battalion, reached Hedo-misaki at the northernmost tip of the island.

At this point in the campaign the bulk of the Japanese forces in the north—code-named the Udo Force—was cornered on the Motobu Peninsula, which the 6th had bypassed and sealed off as they drove north. The peninsula's terrain was mountainous and wooded, and the Japanese concentrated their defenses on Yae-Take, a twisted mass of rocky ridges and ravines on the center of the peninsula. Fighting was heavy before the marines finally cleared Yae-Take on 18 April.

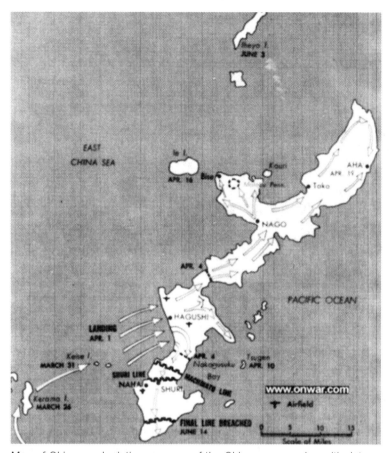

Map of Okinawa, depicting progress of the Okinawa campaign with date-lines. The 6th Marine Division came ashore at the point of the arrowhead to the left (north) of Hagushi and drove northeast up the island to its northernmost point before turning back southwest to later participate in the fierce battles to breach the Shuri Line. (*Source*: USMC)

In the meantime, while the 6th Marine Division was clearing northern Okinawa, the army's 7th and 96th Divisions wheeled south where the bulk of the enemy's 32nd Army was located and the XXIV Corps would run into increasingly strong resistance and heavy losses. At the end of April, after the army forces had pushed through the Machinato defense line, the 1st Marine Division relieved the 27th Infantry Division, which had come ashore on the west side of the island on 8 April, and the 77th Infantry Division relieved the 7th, which was on line to the east. When the 6th Marine Division arrived in the south half of the island, III Amphibious Corps took over the right flank, on the west end of the line, which would move south, with its right flank on the island's west coast shores.

On 4 May, the enemy's 32nd Army launched its second counteroffensive and this time attempted amphibious assaults on the coasts behind American lines. To support this offensive,

Marines of the 2nd Battalion, 22d Regiment, land at Green Beach One on Okinawa. The first marine off the amphibious tractor is carrying a submachine gun, and the second is carrying a flamethrower in his left hand with the fuel tank strapped to his back. (*Source*: USMC)

the Japanese artillery moved into the open and was able to fire thirteen thousand rounds in support, but effective U.S. counterbattery fire destroyed dozens of Japanese artillery pieces. The attack failed.

General Buckner launched another American attack immediately thereafter, on 11 May, and ten days of fierce fighting ensued. On the west coast, the 6th Marine Division battled southward toward "Sugar Loaf Hill," a major objective anchoring the western end of the enemy's heavily defended Shuri Line. On 12 May, the second day of those ten days of bitter fighting, on a west coast beach, on the island of Okinawa, Ted Ogdahl received his near-fatal wound, a gunshot wound to his chest and back, the second of two wounds he received on Okinawa. His forty-two consecutive days on Okinawa, in and out of battle, were over, and so was his active participation in World War II, as the Allies relentlessly pushed toward the Japanese homeland. But on that day his actions resulted in far more than most of his friends and associates would ever know, and they told volumes about his courage and leadership in a crisis.

His actions were described in a citation to accompany the award of the Silver Star Medal, awarded to Second Lieutenant Tillman T. Ogdahl, U.S. Marine Corps Reserve, by Lieutenant General Roy S. Geiger, U.S. Marine Corps, in the name of the president of the United States. The following is the narrative in his Silver Star Medal citation as described in the copy awarded for the president by Secretary of the Navy John L. Sullivan:

The President of the United States takes pleasure in presenting the SILVER STAR MEDAL
to
SECOND LIEUTENANT TILLMAN T. OGDAHL,
UNITED STATES MARINE CORPS RESERVE,
for service set forth in the following
CITATION:

For conspicuous gallantry and intrepidity in action against the enemy while serving as Leader of a Marine Rifle Platoon of Company E, Second Battalion, Twenty-Second Marines, Sixth Marine Division, in action against enemy Japanese forces on Okinawa Shima, Ryukyu Islands on 12 May 1945. When his platoon was taken under heavy machine-gun fire from well-concealed hostile emplacements, while deploying for an assault on strongly-defended enemy positions, Second Lieutenant Ogdahl quickly directed the withdrawal of his platoon to protective cover and, after requesting support by tanks, proceeded alone in the face of continuing hostile fire to a position from which he could observe probable locations of enemy emplacements. When the tanks arrived, he personally led them forward on foot, pointing out hostile emplacements and directing fire of the tanks until these positions were reduced. Although seriously wounded in the course of this action, Second Lieutenant Ogdahl contributed materially to the success of his forces in destroying a Japanese strong point. His able leadership, courage and aggressive spirit were in keeping with the highest traditions of the United States Naval Service.

Ted Ogdahl had unquestionably fought in several intense firefights in his forty-two days in a leadership role as a platoon leader in E Company, 2nd Battalion of the 22nd Marine Regiment, prior to his wounding and evacuation by air from Okinawa to Field Hospital No. 103 on Guam, where he arrived on 17 May. There, due to the assistance of his friend, Lieutenant Arnold Baker, 3rd Marine Division, he would eventually be visited by two of his Willamette Bearcat teammates, army air force P-38 fighter pilot Lieutenant Charles "Chuck" Furno and marine air observer Lieutenant Andrew Rogers, who was Arnold's tent mate in the 3rd Marines' headquarters.

Chuck was passing through Anderson Field on Guam en route by army air transport to his combat assignment in the Philippines, and Andy Rogers was in training in the 3rd Marine Division for the planned invasion of the Japanese homeland. He had arrived on Guam after a brief, harrowing, and nearly disastrous assignment on board the iconic aircraft carrier *Saratoga* (CV-3) off Iwo Jima on 21 February, followed by a return to Iwo Jima in March to fly air observer missions in the OY-1 light observation aircraft during the final days of the bitter Iwo Jima battle.

For Ted Ogdahl, the 22nd Regiment and its rifle battalions, including the 2nd Battalion, were part of an Okinawa campaign that would bring numerous awards, including a Presidential Unit Citation to the Marine Corps' 6th Division. Ted Ogdahl, like millions of others in all the armed services, was authorized to wear numerous ribbons on his marine uniform after World War II. But he could add three more important decorations to the numerous ribbons he could wear: a Silver Star, the third-highest of the nation's decorations for gallantry in action, and two Purple Hearts—including the one for wounds that nearly ended his life. The Purple Heart citation read as follows:

U.S. FLEET HOSPITAL NO. 103
C/O FLEET POST OFFICE
SAN FRANCISCO, CALIFORNIA
23 May 1945
From: The Medical Officer in Command.
To : 2nd Lieutenant Tillman Theodore OGDAHL, 036 875, USMCR.
Subject: Purple Heart—Award of.
Enclosure: (A) Purple Heart Medal.
In the name of the President of the United States, and by direction of the Secretary of the Navy, the Purple Heart is awarded by the Medical Officer in Command, U.S. Fleet Hospital No. 103, in accordance with A1Nav 79-45, to:
TILLMAN THEODORE OGDAHL
SECOND LIEUTENANT
UNITED STATES MARINE CORPS RESERVE
for wounds received in action against an enemy of the United States on
12 May 1945
E. P. KUNKEL

In the lengthy, bloody campaign to take Okinawa, which lasted from 1 April to 22 June, the Allies suffered staggering losses—as did the enemy. The losses were seen as mild foretastes of what was to come in the planned invasion of the Japanese home islands, designated Operation Downfall. The huge, planned Allied undertaking against the Japanese home islands was to be in two phases, the first being Operation Olympic, landings on the southernmost Japanese island of Kyushu, initially planned for approximately 1 October 1945, then slipped to 1 November. The second phase would be in March 1946, landings near Tokyo, code-named Operation Coronet. Each phase of the invasion was to be massive in terms of the naval, air, and ground forces believed necessary to be successful, and each phase would dwarf the 6 June 1944 landings on the beaches of France, particularly with respect to casualties expected on both sides.

The Allies, in seizing Okinawa and approaching the Japanese home islands to within 340 miles, were planning to use the large island as a base for air operations in the invasion of Japan. Codenamed Operation Iceberg, Allied forces included the United States, the United Kingdom, Canada, Australia, and New Zealand units in a battle that has been referred to as the "Typhoon of Steel." The nickname refers to the ferocity of the fighting, the intensity of kamikaze attacks from the Japanese defenders, and the staggering numbers of Allied ships

A 6th Marine Division demolition crew watches explosive charges detonate and destroy a Japanese cave on Okinawa, May 1945. (*Source*: USMC)

and armored vehicles that assaulted the island. The battle pitted 183,000 men from American ground units against 120,000 Japanese and resulted in the highest number of casualties in the Pacific theater during World War II. Japan lost about 95,000 soldiers killed, 7,400–10,755 captured, and the Allies suffered 65,000 casualties of all kinds in the ground war. Simultaneously, tens of thousands of local civilians were killed, wounded, or committed suicide.

The Japanese had used kamikaze tactics since the Philippines' Battle of Leyte Gulf in October 1944, but for the first time their use became a major part of an increasingly fanatical, fight-to-the-death defense. Between the American landing on 1 April and 26 May, seven major kamikaze attacks were attempted, involving more than 1,500 planes. During the period 26 March–30 April, 20 American ships were sunk and 157 were damaged by enemy action, and the Japanese, up to 30 April, had lost more than 1,100 planes in the battle against Allied naval forces alone.

The U.S. Navy's dead exceeded its wounded, with 4,907 killed and 4,874 wounded. American ground forces lost 12,513 killed, 38,916 wounded, while another 33,096 were noncombat losses. Among the ground force casualties, the 6th Marine Division suffered 2,662 marines and navy corpsmen killed in action and 7,470 wounded.

On 21 June 1945, Ted Ogdahl departed from Guam, en route to a naval hospital in the continental United States, arriving first in the naval hospital at Mare Island, near San Francisco, on 26 July, then transferred to the naval hospital in Corvallis, Oregon, arriving on 4 August to continue his recuperation. When V-J Day arrived, he was among a patient census of 1,573 still recuperating from wounds in the naval hospital in Corvallis.

After the war, he completed his physical rehabilitation in the Corvallis hospital not far from his wife, Jean, in Salem and his parental home in Portland. After his physical rehabilitation, he was transferred to headquarters, 13th Marine Corps Reserve District, from which he was released from active duty on 3 March 1946, went into inactive reserve status on 4 March, and remained in the inactive reserves in the redesignated 12th Marine Corps Reserve and Recruitment District until he was discharged honorably on 24 February 1958.

Meanwhile, he elected to enroll in the College of the Pacific in Stockton, California, in May 1946 to complete his education with a bachelor of arts degree and play his senior year of football eligibility under the legendary coach Amos Alonzo Stagg. Afterward, under an assumed name, he played football professionally in 1946 and 1947 for the San Diego Bombers—doing additional duty as a backfield coach for the Bombers while doing some work toward a master's degree in education at San Diego State, and later at Oregon State College.

After his professional football playing days were over, Ogdahl worked as an assistant and backfield coach under Jerry Lillie at Willamette. Offered the head coaching job for the Grant High School Blue and Gray Generals in Portland, Oregon, he doubled as a social studies teacher and head track coach and remained there from 1948 to 1952, winning two Portland city and Oregon state grid championships in 1949 and 1950, a city co-championship in 1951, and playing a tie game in the state championship football tournament on 8 December 1951, all in four years, compiling a record of 37–3–3, including twenty-seven straight wins. Carrying a sense of humor with his talents as a speaker, motivator, and head coach, his 1949 championship team was undefeated in an eleven-game season and held their opponents scoreless in eight games. His four sterling seasons as head football coach were complemented by two Portland City Relay championships in his four years as head track coach.

As a result of his marvelous success with the Blue and Gray of Grant High School, the 1939 graduate and All-City football player at Portland's Franklin High School was hired as head football coach and later was named head track-and-field coach at Willamette. During the period 1952–1972 at Willamette University, former student and halfback on the 1941 Bearcat football team Ted Ogdahl established remarkable records in coaching both sports at the university, resulting in his entry into Willamette's sesquicentennial year, premiere Hall of Fame class of 1991.

In his twenty seasons leading the football team, the Bearcats went 98–64–10, making him the winningest coach in school history, a record that stands to this day. His winning record exceeded that of the gentleman considered the father of Willamette athletics, Roy S. "Spec" Keene. Ted's teams won or shared seven conference titles, and his 1960 and 1968 teams were the last Willamette teams to go undefeated on the gridiron.

During thirteen track seasons, Ted coached Willamette's first two national champions in the sport—hurdler Dean Benson and three-time high-jump champ Ken Ashley. The Oregon Sportswriters and Broadcasters Association named Ogdahl Oregon's Man of the Year in sports in 1960.

In addition to all his other recognition and honors, he gave of his time and energies to the Salem community. He helped coach youth soccer, the Jaycees Relays, and youth track,

Ted Ogdahl, head football and track coach, Willamette University, gives last call for mile relay, 1961. (*Source*: MOHLAWU)

and he was a deacon in the Presbyterian Church and a member of Willamette University's Cardinal Round Table.

Ted and his wife, Jean, who had remained in Salem when he was in the Pacific during World War II, raised two sons, James "Gregory" and W. Wallace Ogdahl, and one daughter, Tracey Jeane Valley.

He died in Salem, Oregon, on July 29, 1988, at the age of sixty-six.

Ted Ogdahl and Marshall Hall Barbour, the classmates and football teammates at Franklin High School in Portland, Oregon, before they entered Willamette and played as teammates under Coach Spec Keene, would come together one final time that summer of 1988. Marshall's eulogy was the first of three given at Ted's funeral; the second by Jerry Long, assistant athletic director at UCLA and assistant football coach under Ted at Willamette, 1955–1961; and the other by Jim Nicholson, a teacher at Sprague High School in Salem who had been a running back at Willamette under Ted's tutelage in the period 1965–1969.

A private graveside service for Ted Ogdahl was held at City View Cemetery in Salem on August 2, 1988.

Twenty-one years later, in 2009, Portland, Oregon's Grant High School established their inaugural Athletic Hall of Fame, and Tillman Theodore Ogdahl, who had begun serving there sixty-one years earlier was among those inducted into Grant High School's first Hall of Fame class.

The purpose of the Grant High School Athletic Hall of Fame, stated in the school's October 19, 2009, ceremony program, is to recognize outstanding athletic accomplishments and honors of Grant athletes and coaches. The stated nominating criteria are as follows:

Inductions will be predicated on accomplishments while representing Grant as a student or coach. However, an individual's sports accomplishments after graduation may also be taken into consideration. An athlete will be eligible for induction no sooner than five years after graduation.

Ted Ogdahl's citation for his 2009 induction read as follows:

Ted Ogdahl 1948–1951 Head football coach of some of Grant's greatest football teams. The 1949 and 1950 Public Interscholastic League and State championship teams went undefeated for 22 straight games (11–0 each season, including victories in the state play-offs). Unbeaten string extended 4 more games to 26 before loss to Roosevelt in the fall of '51.

A marvelous final mark of leadership, motivation, and inspired results from a man who was an unquestionably strong leader and hero for his country, on the battlefield and on and off the athletic fields where he served the remainder of his life.

MARSHALL HALL BARBOUR, BOMBER PILOT IN WORLD WAR II, TEACHER, AND COACH

Marshall Barbour was born in Victoria, British Columbia, Canada, on June 9, 1921, and the family moved to Portland in 1923. He attended Woodstock Grammar School in Portland and graduated from Franklin High School in 1940, where he was the classmate and football teammate of Ted Ogdahl. He and Ted entered Willamette University in 1940 with Spec Keene Scholarships and gained a year's experience as an end under Coach Keene before going to Honolulu with the 1941 Bearcats to play in the Shrine Bowl game.

When the Bearcats returned home from Hawaii, he and many of his teammates faced being drafted soon after the next semester began. He, like Ken Jacobson and Chuck Furno, individually decided he wanted to join the air force reserves and went to his hometown of Portland and took a battery of tests to determine whether he was qualified to enter officer candidate school. Like his two teammates, he was told that he was successful and he should return to Willamette and continue in school until he was called to active duty.

According to a one-page military record provided by the National Archives in St. Louis, Missouri, plus, far more important, extensive additional records provided by his son, John, a 1977 Willamette graduate, he entered active duty and training on 8 May 1942. He began his training as an enlisted man in the army air force's aviation cadet program, 883rd Pilot Training Squadron (P)—meaning "Primary"—at Brooks Field's San Antonio Aviation Cadet Center in San Antonio, Texas. He remained at Brooks Field through primary pilot training, then entered the 57th Basic Flying Training Group at Eagle Pass Army Airfield nearly eleven miles north of Eagle Pass, Texas, where he accumulated one hundred hours of basic flying training in the AT-6 "Texan" trainer. On graduating from basic training on 29 August 1943, he received his pilot's wings and on 30 August was given a letter with an attached oath of office form, requesting him to complete and return it. Completing the oath

Lieutenant Marshall Barbour in flight training beside his primary trainer, a PT-22 at Brooks Field, Texas. (*Source*: JBC)

and returning it constituted an acceptance of his appointment as an active-duty commissioned officer, a second lieutenant in the army air force reserves, effective 30 August 1943.

At Eagle Pass, he was handed orders dated 31 August from the 3rd Air Force's 335th Bombardment Group at Barksdale Field, Louisiana, granting him ten days' leave beginning 31 August before entering advanced and combat crew training, to qualify first as a B-26 bomber copilot, bound for the European theater of operations (ETO). On completing his 170 hours of two-engine combat crew training in the B-26 at Barksdale, he was reassigned to the ETO where he trained into the B-25 as a copilot, in the 12th Air Force's (or Mediterranean Allied Tactical Air Force's) 57th Bombardment Wing, 321st Bombardment Group (M)—meaning "Medium"—and the group's 448th Bombardment Squadron. The 321st was composed of four squadrons, the 445th, 446th, 447th, and Marshall's 448th.

Before Marshall Barbour arrived in Italy, the Italian dictator Benito Mussolini had been ousted in July 1943 during the Sicilian campaign, three days after the Allies occupied the island's city of Salerno. His ouster caught Adolph Hitler by surprise, but he reacted strongly, resulting in his more massive insertion of German forces into Italy while ordering German forces to withdraw from Sicily, Sardinia, and Corsica to Italy to establish and tighten control of the entire nation. Early the morning of 3 September, the new Italian government signed a secret armistice agreement with the Allies, the same day the Allies invaded Italy, with the British 8th Army striking across the Strait of Messina to land on the toe of Italy, near Reggio Calabria. Six days later a combined force of British and Americans landed near Salerno to begin the long, bloody Italian mainland campaign.

The Allies had landed to begin occupying the island of Corsica in the period 13–30 September 1943, while the Axis forces evacuated the island in the period 18 September–3 October and departed Sardinia on 18 September.

By the time Marshall Barbour arrived in Italy to begin flying combat missions the following February in 1944, Allied ground forces had driven north up the Italian boot to the "Winter Line," a short distance south of what the German commanders called the Gustav Line. The Gustav Line's left end was on the coast approximately thirty-five miles north of Naples and extended northwest to the opposite coast about five miles south of Pescara.

The first base to which he was assigned was Vincenzo Airfield, Italy, within the Foggia complex of Allied airfields not far north of the port of Bari, Italy, on the country's southeast (Adriatic) coast. He arrived at Vincenzo just as the 321st was preparing to move southwest, directly across Italy to Gaudo Airfield, ten miles south of Battipaglia, two miles inland on the west coast, with one runway ending near the waters of the Tyrrhenian Sea, about forty-three miles southeast of Naples. There they would remain until the third week of April of that year. By road it was a ninety-mile trip by truck for those who didn't fly from the Foggia area. Some were moved by aircraft in ferry flights. Most aircraft that were assigned to Vincenzo and flew missions on the 18th landed at Gaudo after their missions were complete.

Though the new airfield was essentially a "bare-base operation," construction was coming along, with a mess hut completed and tents going up. The 445th reported that the Statistical tent was erected and the framework and flooring for the Operations and S-2 (Intelligence) tent was set up. The squadrons of the 321st were units that had already moved frequently as the Allies fought their way across the Mediterranean from Africa, through Sicily and Corsica, and now were pushing up the peninsula that was Italy, the peninsula shaped like a boot.

Second Lieutenant Marshall Hall Barbour's first combat mission as a new B-25 copilot in the 448th was flown from Gaudo, Saturday morning, 19 February 1944, when the 321st Group launched two missions of twenty-four aircraft each that day, both against troop concentrations in an area a short distance inland from the west coast, to the north of the bitterly contested Anzio beachhead, where fierce fighting was in progress on the ground. He logged 2:40 flying time on a mission that was more than eventful for all four squadrons involved in the strike.

Preparations for missions constituted a deeply engrained routine. Pre-mission briefings for crews normally began approximately two hours prior to takeoff, with briefings given by operations officers and commanders on the overall mission plan, targets, routes into and out of the target area; intelligence officers on what to expect from enemy fighters and antiaircraft weapons en route and on return, with photographs of the target area; and communication procedures for combat, emergency escape, bailout, evasion, ditching, and rescue.

The Allies had landed forces at Anzio on 22 January, northeast up the coast from Gaudo, and, operating within a natural basin, had advanced inland toward the Alban Hills, which were in an arc ringing the basin. The German commander in the Italian theater, Field Marshall Albert Kesselring, with forces arrayed across their Gustav Line, south of Anzio, reacted immediately when notified of the landings at 0300 the morning of the

22nd, rushing forces to counterattack and halt the Allied forces threatening the Hills and a possible breakout toward Rome to the north. The B-25s of the 321st Bombardment Group were part of a heavy commitment of 12th Air Force fighters and bombers attacking enemy targets in the Anzio area.

Marshall was in the first of two group missions that day, Mission No. 216 consisting of twenty-four aircraft total, with each squadron in the group contributing approximately the same number of aircraft, launched at 0820 hours. The ingress to the target included fighter escorts, northeast up the west coast and across the Gustav Line until the bombers entered the target area, where they would break off on separate missions supporting the beachhead. The bombers continued to their target, and once their bombs were released, they were to similarly break left toward the Tyrrhenian Sea, then turn back southeast toward Gaudo at a designated point on their maps. They were one hour and twenty-five minutes en route to the target and dropped 1,162 fragmentation bombs weighing twenty pounds each from 10,500 feet of altitude, flying through flak described as "heavy, intense and accurate from bomb line to target and out to coast, barrage type, with weather clear and visibility unlimited at target."

To compound the fierce defense of the target against the morning mission, the B-25s encountered groups of six to eight and from fifteen to twenty enemy fighters—Me 109s, FW 190s, one Me 210, a German twin-engine fighter, and an MA-282 were reported over the target and, afterward, as attacking the formation in pairs. Most attacks were from the rear, and one tactic was for one fighter to come from six o'clock level, hanging back while another dove from above at seven o'clock. Some Messerschmidts attacked after diving. Fourteen aircraft were holed, meaning fourteen of the returning aircraft had at least one or more flak or machine-gun holes in them—a clear measure of the fierce antiaircraft and fighter defenses the bombers encountered.

Two B-25s were shot down, one by flak and one by flak and enemy aircraft, and one was missing, reported down in the water. Four persons were seen in the water, and a dingy was dropped by another plane. Another report came in of a plane shot down, with three chutes observed. The 446th had a disastrous time of it on their first day of operation at the new base, losing one of the two aircraft shot down, and two others damaged beyond repair.

The normal crew of six on the B-25 missing was augmented this day with a photographer. The 446th crew lost on the missing aircraft were as follows: Lieutenant Harold R. Brellenthin, pilot; Lieutenant Robert P. Burgess, pilot; Staff Sergeant Joy L. Bedwell, gunner; Staff Sergeant Charles H. Blake, photographer; Technical Sergeant Charles C. "Spike" Kendall, radio/gunner; and Staff Sergeant William W. Parrish, gunner. A report from a British hospital ship anchored off the coast stated that the plane that had crashed into the water was so low it crashed on one wing, while turning to avoid hitting the vessel of mercy. A lifeboat was lowered, but only one survivor was picked up: Staff Sergeant Parrish, who was unconscious and despite artificial respiration never regained consciousness. Another 446th aircraft flown by pilot Lieutenant John R. Hurley of Houston, Texas, with pilot James E. Chudars, was "tail-end Charlie" in their formation and crash-landed on return to Gaudo with the hydraulic system shot out and one rudder shot away. On debriefing, Hurley described what happened:

Immediately after "bombs away" he felt his plane lurch badly and knew that it had been hit. Fighters closed in afterward, attacking from the rear and sides. In the ensuing action a 20 mm shell burst in the pilot's compartment, causing plexiglass to scatter throughout the compartment. Fragments struck both Hurley and his co-pilot, Lt. Chudars, in the face. The two experienced extreme difficulty in flying the aircraft after the hit and fighters kept coming in. S/Sgt. Michael L. Mowry, gunner poured several hundred rounds of .50-caliber ammunition into an attacking fighter and swore he hit it, but couldn't verify his claim because of another fighter's nearness.

Upon circling the home field, Hurley discovered that his hydraulics were out and that the landing gear would not come down. He crash-landed the plane with wheels partly lowered and bomb-bay doors slightly open. The after-landing inspection revealed that the aircraft had sustained approximately four hundred hits, the rudder cable was cut, and there was a large hole in the elevator. Staff Sergeant E. F. Martin was hit in the leg by 20 mm shell fire and was hospitalized. His wound was later reported to have been in the stomach, and he remained in the hospital through the end of the month.

The 447th reported that Lieutenant Gordon G. Baker's aircraft 493 was shot down over the target by flak, and all aboard were apparently lost. The copilot was Second Lieutenant Harvey A. Dean, with Staff Sergeant Allen Evans, bombardier; Staff Sergeant Paul S. Baringer, engineer/gunner; Staff Sergeant James M. Crowell, radio/gunner; and Technical Sergeant Otis W. Moomaw, gunner.

Mission results observed on the first attack indicated the target area well covered with one string of bombs crossing the bend in the river just north of the aim point and south of the railroad. Bombs were also seen along the railroad tracks just west of the target.

The group claimed seven Me 109s destroyed, two FW 190s destroyed, and two Me 109s damaged. In the 448th, Sergeant Charles J. Mauder, gunner, claimed two Me 109s; Sergeant Warren H. Coleman, gunner, one; Sergeant Edward W. Van Cura, gunner, one; and Sergeant Louis Chosta, gunner, one FW 190.

As for the 448th, they lost one aircraft in what proved to be a rough morning mission for the entire 321st Group. The complete description of its loss wouldn't be fully known until near the end of February, and as facts were disclosed, the mission debrief by aircrews in which three chutes were seen descending into the water offshore was the 448th aircraft. Over the target, the ship was hit in the navigator's compartment by flak, its wheels dropped, and one engine began to smoke. Lieutenant Annear, the pilot, was knocked out for a short time when a machine gun bullet creased his forehead. Lieutenant Kuykendall, copilot, took charge of the ship while Annear was out. When the pilot regained consciousness, he immediately instructed the crew to bail out as he was going to attempt a water landing. The three enlisted men in the rear of the ship, Sergeants Morris, Tudor, and Nesbit, bailed out.

The ship was skillfully handled and made an excellent landing in the water due to the wheels being down. The aircraft momentarily went beneath the surface and then reappeared. The three officers hurriedly made their exit, but repeated calls to the rear of the ship brought no answer. A Lieutenant Stokes (there were two with the same last name) in another plane dropped a second life raft. Thus, Lieutenants Annear, Zinkand, and Kuykendall found themselves afloat in two small rubber boats just off the Anzio beachhead.

Two boats immediately put out to rescue them. One was sunk by a submarine, and the rescue was finally accomplished by an English crash boat no. 182. After a short stay in the hospital in Anzio, the officers were returned to the squadron. Of the three enlisted men, word was received that Sergeant Tudor was in the hospital. By the end of February, nothing had been heard from the others.

Crew members on the aircraft were Second Lieutenant Warren R. Annear, pilot; Second Lieutenant James W. Kuykendall, pilot; Sergeant Andrew I. Nesbit, gunner; Sergeant Goldburn H. Tudor, gunner; Lieutenant Willard T. Zinkand, bombardier; Sergeant Raymond A. Morris, gunner, or Sergeant Raymond J. Morris, gunner. (When the war diary summary was drafted at the end of February 1944 operations, the facts as to which Morris was on the downed aircraft had not been determined.)

The second mission to the Anzio beachhead, Mission No. 217, was airborne at 1500 hours, with a planned time on target (TOT) of 1615 hours, with six aircraft from the 445th, six from the 446th, five from the 447th, and seven from the 448th. They dropped 1,542 fragmentation bombs from 11,000–11,500 feet at 1650 hours, with an axis of attack of 358 degrees, almost due north. Twenty-three of the mission aircraft returned at 1707 hours, and one crash-landed at an alternate airfield and burned, the crew safe, with seventeen planes holed. Six enemy Me 109 fighters were seen heading south but didn't attack.

This final, crash-landing emergency recovery late the afternoon of 19 February was at Pompeii, near Mt. Vesuvius, flown by another 446th pilot, Lieutenant John J. Herbert of West Orange, New Jersey. Flak had knocked out one engine. Herbert fought to keep the aircraft in the air long enough to reach the emergency recovery field, then successfully maneuvered onto the final approach—and at what he believed to be the right time, directed his copilot, Lieutenant Frank Paul Vivas of Honolulu, Hawaii, to lower the landing gear. Vivas promptly discovered that the hydraulic system was "out." The engineer, Sergeant Donald W. Clay, said, "Circle the field while I hand-crank the gear down." Just at that moment, the second engine "coughed," starting to fail, and the oil pressure dropped sharply. Lieutenant Hebert quickly feathered the prop while lining up with the runway. Everyone held their breath and waited for the crash. The landing was a beautiful one until one prop dug into the earth, ripping the engine from the nacelle. Gasoline was sprayed all over the fuselage, and friction quickly ignited the gas as the aircraft came to a sudden halt. Crew members hurriedly exited through the pilot's escape hatch and watched the ship completely burn.

Though Marshall Barbour probably witnessed little of all the events of that first day, over the next eight days there would be plenty of time to talk with other crew members and others who participated in his first mission. His next mission was 28 February, and afterward he didn't fly another mission until 7 March.

The month-end 448th war diary summary written in part by Major Albert R. Bell and squadron adjutant Captain Martin K. Marrich illustrated that somewhat more pleasant circumstances had been realized and accepted by the entire squadron when they completed the unit's move from Vincenzo.

Upon their arrival at the new base, the men were surprised and delighted to discover that the 448th had a large "mansion" at their disposal. The baron, a gracious and obliging "ex-Fascist," opened wide the portals of his domain and began immediately to take in washings for his many women vassals. The "Baron's Mansion" was a huge stone building consisting of three floors, parts of which dated back to 1810. After much discussion, it was decided to have the kitchen and orderly room on the ground floor and officer's quarters on the second floor. Eventually the S-2 (Intelligence) and Operations section moved to the third floor. In the area to the rear of the house the tents were erected, and by February 20 everyone was snugly domiciled in their quarters.

Marshall's next eight missions as a copilot were on 7, 9, 13, 14, 16, 17, 28, and 30 March, against targets in or near Littorio, San Stefano, Spoleto, Orte, Piedmonte, Castroceilo, Perugia, Orvieto, and Orte again, all in Italy. Weapons loads varied according to targets: one-thousand-pound bombs, five-hundred-pound bombs, and fragmentation bombs. Fighter escorts variously included P-40s, P-47s, and British Spitfires. The amount of antiaircraft fire varied widely, but no mission was easy or without risk. Particularly noteworthy was the Mediterranean theater of operations, 12th Air Force Tactical Operations, that began in Italy on 15 March 1944. From the USAAF chronology comes the following:

> *MTO Tactical Operations (12th AF): In Italy, medium and fighter-bombers, together with Mediterranean Allied Strategic Air Force (MASAF) heavy bombers and other aircraft of the Mediterranean Allied Tactical Air Force (MATAF) in the greatest air effort yet made in the MTO, rain bombs upon enemy concentrations in Cassino and surrounding areas as the New Zealand Corps begins the third battle of Cassino; light and medium bombers also hit a command post east of Ceprano and the town of San Benedetto de Marsi; fighters on patrol and a sweep over Anzio, Cassino and Rome meet no air opposition.*

On 16 March, Marshall Barbour flew his fifth mission that month, while fighting continued to rage below in the Cassino-Piedmonte area. The 321st Bombardment Group put up twenty-four aircraft at 1345 hours: six each from the four squadrons. All but one—which had to return early due to partial power loss—returned safely at 1535 hours. No airplanes were lost, and only one aircraft was holed. Weather at intermediate altitudes hampered the mission, causing lower bomb-release altitudes than normal, as low as 6,500 feet. The weapons released were fragmentation bombs.

On the 17th, he flew again, in one of twenty-four aircraft from the group carrying five-hundred-pound bombs, for a total of 188 bombs released at eleven thousand feet at 1110 hours, and all returned safely at 1155—with only one airplane holed. Antiaircraft fire was described as slight to moderate, with inaccurate to heavy flak on the bomb run and scattered heavy of the tracking type, mainly inaccurate, on breakaway, experienced from Rocca Secca to Atina. The weather was clear and visibility unlimited (CAVU).

On the 19th, the Mediterranean Allied Tactical Air Force (MATAF) issued a directive for Operation Strangle, to interdict supply movements in Italy by destroying marshaling yards and attacking rail lines and ports in a concentrated campaign. At Gaudo, not far from Pompeii and Mt. Vesuvius, the men of the 321st had a ringside seat—for the moment—to the eruption of the Mt. Vesuvius volcano. Four transition flights from the 445th Squadron went to the mountain to see the sights and take some pictures while the war continued unabated.

Marshall Barbour's flight as a copilot on 28 March was another difficult mission. At 1436 hours, twenty planes from the group were airborne to bomb the railroad bridge at Perugia and dropped seventy-two bombs, one thousand pounds each, from eleven thousand feet at 1635 hours. Eighteen airplanes returned, seventeen were holed, and two were lost. They were escorted by twenty P-40s. Plane 498, named "Dumbo" and flown by First Lieutenant Lyle L. Edwards of the 447th, took an apparent direct hit by flak just after bomb release and was seen to go down in flames. Three parachutes were seen, and two opened. Lieutenant Edward's crew members were Second Lieutenant Fred E. Abbott, copilot (nineteenth mission); Second Lieutenant John D. Snyder, bombardier (twenty-second mission); Sergeant Albert Wise, engineer-gunner (eleventh mission); Staff Sergeant Robert S. Champlain, radio-gunner (seventh mission); and Staff Sergeant Harry B. Harmer, armor gunner (forty-seventh mission). The 447th lost their tenth airplane in combat that day on the squadron's 211th mission.

An eyewitness account was provided by Captain K. L. McFadden, pilot of 695, lead ship of the first element:

About 35 seconds after bombs away, I felt a heavy concussion, and a wave of heat in my face. I looked right and saw my right wing ship in flames from what appeared to be a direct hit in the Bombardier's compartment. I veered left as the flaming ship went into a steep climb but still staying close to our formation. I saw the bomb bay doors fly open and the wheels drop down. Col. Smith, flying as co-pilot [with me], motioned me down and as we lost altitude, Lt. Edward's ship rolled over our formation flaming all over.

Other comments during debriefing brought little comfort to mission crews.

The crew of ship 667 of the 445th Squadron: "Flak picked us up at the IP [initial point, the point from which the bomb run begins], but all hell broke loose after bombs-away: At about 12,500 feet altitude, no. 2 of the first element seemed to be hit by a 4-gun battery simultaneously, wrapping it in flames from nose to tail. It pulled up in a sharp loop, then fell over and down into a steep dive, burning fiercely amidships and around the left engine. As it spun in, the tail broke off, and the plane seemed to hit in the smoke of the target area. We saw one chute open at 8/9000 feet."

From ship 509 of the 446th Squadron: "Saw a flaming B-25 hit the ground, three chutes came out."

From ship 005 of the 448th Squadron, Second Lieutenant Donald R. Armstrong, pilot: "Three chutes were seen to come out; only two opened."

From ship 655 of the 448th Squadron: "Lt. Edwards ship blew up in a ball of fire, climbed about 200 feet, then fell down 2000 feet and seemed to explode again. Two chutes came out O.K., possibly one scorched. Another came out on fire."

The 448th Squadron also lost a ship that was last seen apparently trying a controlled landing in Lake Trasimeno. The fact that the target results were only fair, and that the 340th Group also lost a ship when they flew over the target, made the day unprofitable as well as tragic. There was very little conversation at the evening meal, but an unspoken prayer in everyone's heart that by some miracle all our friends had gotten out of the ship alive and safe.

Second Lieutenant Truman R. Jones's crew, 448th Squadron, in 552, reported their air-plane hit just after leaving the target, and other mission crews reported observing the plane in a controlled landing near a small island in Lake Trasimeno. Crew members on board were Second Lieutenant Stewart B. Gilbert, copilot; Second Lieutenant Robert C. Bell, bombardier; Staff Sergeant James L. Currie, engineer/gunner; Sergeant Paul (NMI) Anglin, radio-gunner; Staff Sergeant Joseph A. Gately, gunner; and Private First Class Kenneth J. Feagans, photographer.

The mission results that day, provided by the flight leader, First Lieutenant Weymouth (NMI) Crowell, seemed only to deepen the losses. Bombs were reported scattered, with hits on both east and west approaches to the bridge, with others short and east near the road-bridge to south. One report had that the west span of the bridge was hit. Flak was heavy, intense, and accurate, with four gun salvos southwest of the bridge along the river and from batteries on the west side of the air defenses and from northeast of the town. Also, from just east of Baschi and Orvieto, flak was heavy, meager, and accurate. The weather was CAVU at target.

The lengthy 448th month-end report was comprehensive and remarkable, perhaps the most startling part being the impact of the Mt. Vesuvius eruptions:

On March 21, after smoking and burping for several days previously, Mt. Vesuvius burst forth in a lavish display of power and might. All that night and the following week the volcano belched forth tons of molten lava on the surrounding countryside. It was regarded as a marvelous display of a great natural phenomenon by the members of the squadron until the night of March 22. [It was instead a staggering disaster that added torment to Italians in the surrounding towns and cities, and hampered military ground and air oper-ations. The Italians had endured first the dictator Benito Mussolini, followed by a brutal Nazi occupation when his government fell, and a grinding, bitter, bloody war as the Allies fought their way north toward Rome.]

Then on the 23rd came rumors that the 340th Bomb Group's field at Pompeii had been destroyed; 150 men of that group came straggling into the squadron mess hall with tales of the destruction of their airplanes and equipment by the falling rocks. The upheaval was no longer regarded as a mere fireworks display. (The eruption destroyed an estimated seventy-eight to eighty-eight B-25 aircraft in the 340th Bombardment Group.) The next day dust began settling down on the 448th squadron area and effectually kept everyone closely confined either to the Baron's Mansion or to their tents.

The group stood by awaiting orders to abandon the field but discovered a few days later that it would not be necessary. Only dust traveled the distance from Pompeii to Paestum. Within a few days after the destruction of their field, the 340th Bomb Group moved onto the field occupied by the 321st, causing the 448th to move their planes toward the center of the field, further away from the squadron area and the transfer of four planes to the new group. By 27 March, the two groups were well set up in their own areas and were not interfering as much with each other as was first expected. It was now possible to see two movies at group if anyone so desired.

On 26 March, Colonel Richard H. "Red" Smith, the new commanding officer of the group (the copilot who flew with Captain K. L. McFadden in the 447th on the tragic 28 March mission), made his appearance and put down very stringent rules as to the use of vehicles to eliminate much wasteful driving. A very heavy training schedule was inaugurated that kept all flying personnel very busy. New crews continued to pour into the squadron, and seasoned veterans immediately filled the ears of the newcomers with harrowing tales of their experiences in the Italian campaign.

In April, Marshall Barbour flew thirteen more missions as copilot. On 15 April, on their radios, men in the 321st Group heard "Axis Sally"—whom they called the "Berlin Bitch"—inform them that they would soon be moving to Corsica, where they would receive a "warm welcome." On the 16th, the 448th received word the squadron was to prepare to move, and immediately all sections began to pack and crate their equipment for an overseas move. On the 17th they continued packing to move, with some in other squadrons remarking sarcastically that the "Berlin Bitch" was right.

On the 18th, after their attempted mission had been frustrated by weather, seven crews and crew chiefs out of the 445th flew to Corsica to operate temporarily with the 310th Bombardment Group while packing was still in progress at Gaudo. By Wednesday the 19th, preparations to move were nearing completion, but there were no orders yet as to the exact time. On the 19th, the 340th Bombardment Group (M), which had moved from Pompeii to Gaudo in March following the Vesuvius eruption, moved from Gaudo Airfield to Alesan, Corsica, with their B-25s.

At Gaudo on the same day, the 448th's Marshall Barbour flew his nineteenth mission as a copilot, while preparations were under way to follow the advance air echelon to Solenzara Airfield, Corsica. At 1210 hours, twenty-five 321st planes were airborne, planning to bomb a railroad south of Ficulle, but they were diverted to an alternate target at Piombino Harbor. Escorted to the target area by twelve British Spitfires, they released ninety-eight bombs of one thousand pounds each from 11,500 feet at 1340 hours, and all planes recovered safely at 1440 hours. Debriefings revealed that the target area was well hit, with the longest concentration of hits observed starting short and northeast of the junction of the north jetty and dockside and carrying through into the railroad yards, causing large explosions and fires in fuel storage tanks. Other hits were observed on a large factory building and in the powerhouse area.

Two boats on the north side of the north jetty were reported hit, as well as scattered bombs just south and over the boatyard near the south jetty. The flak was heavy, intense, and accurate from the target area and from the island of Elba. Crews reported observing five to eight small military vehicles and three two-hundred-foot ships in Piombino Harbor, seven "F" boats in Talamone Harbor, and a large moving vessel off the coast of San Vincenzo. The weather was clear with visibility unlimited.

On 21 April, the 445th diary noted that theirs and some of the ground echelon of the 321st Group left Salerno, Italy, in a British LST (landing ship, tank) bound for Porto-Vecchio, Corsica, from where they would proceed by navy and British-provided trucks to the group's new base, Solenzara Airfield. The ship provided no meals for the enlisted men, who were compelled to eat C rations. They slept in the hold and on deck. They were accompanied by a sister ship carrying other squadrons and were escorted by a destroyer. The move stretched out to the end of the month and beyond due to one LST's turbine malfunction that required it to be towed back to Naples, which led to offloading men and equipment from the 447th and temporary housing and bivouacking in and near the city to await further orders to reload and proceed to Corsica.

The same day, the 448th diary indicated that circumstances, including an air-raid alert and heavy rain, kept altering and delaying the time of loading and departure of the squadron's ground echelon on two British LSTs—the HMS *Bruiser* and *Thruster*—until 22 April. But that wasn't the end—not yet. When the ships attempted to back off the beach where they had loaded, they couldn't. Two tugs couldn't provide sufficient power, and finally the escorting destroyer succeeded in attaching towing lines and pulled while the ships' crews provided backing power. Finally, at about 1600 hours, they were off the sandy beach and, with the destroyer leading, steamed up the Italian coast, past the Isle of Capri, and then turned westward toward the port of Vecchio, Corsica. From there, they unloaded and traveled by truck in a convoy of 448th vehicles to their new base.

On the same day, 23 April, the army air force chronology indicated that the headquarters of the 321st Bombardment Group (M) and the 445th and 448th Bombardment Squadrons (M) moved from Gaudo Airfield, Italy, to Solenzara, Corsica, with B-25s. In the meantime, the ground echelon, after some back-and-forth and uncertainty, began setting up a camp and digging foxholes in a small meadow with few trees and surrounded by dense desert a mile and a half from the air base.

The next day, Marshall flew his first mission from Corsica in one of twenty-six planes against a bridge south of Orvieto, Italy. Airborne at 1445 hours, the formation dropped 201 bombs of five hundred pounds each from 8,500 feet at 1615. They were escorted by twelve British Spitfires, and all returned safely at 1725 with no planes holed. The target was observed "well hit," with several descriptions of specific hits seen by crews. Barbour flew four more missions on 25, 28, 29, and 30 April. He flew missions again on 1 and 12 May, while on the 5th the 445th diary reported that an "old" 445th pilot in the Ferry Command flew

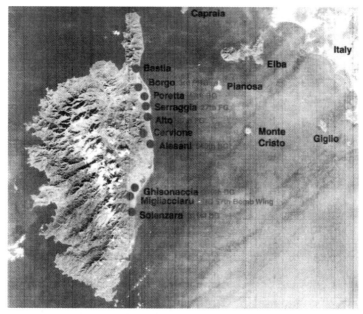

Map depicting airfield locations and army air force units on Corsica during 321st Bombardment Group operations, 1944. The 310th, 321st, and 340th Bombardment Groups (M) on Corsica's east coast were under the command of the 57th Bombardment Wing, based at Migliacciaru. (*Source*: USAAF)

a new, shining-silver B-25J to the squadron, the beginning of reequipping the entire group with a more powerful, more heavily armed aircraft.

On 3 May, a 447th aircraft crashed into the sea just after liftoff, one of twenty-seven that departed for a mission against a railroad bridge at Ficulle, Italy. The entire crew was picked up by an army Air Sea Rescue launch, and fortunately no one was seriously injured. The plane was a total loss and sank in five minutes.

On 12 May, Marshall was in one of nineteen planes airborne at 0700 hours to bomb Vallecorsa, Italy. On reaching the Italian coast, weather caused the formation to return to base. His early-morning mission was his twenty-sixth mission, and his last as copilot. During the afternoon mission, which he didn't fly, his squadron lost an aircraft in a raid on a command post at Pico, Italy, but fortunately all crew members survived following the pilot's skillful handling of the emergency of a direct hit by flak over the target and the ditching of the heavily damaged plane twelve miles short of Corsica.

On Saturday, 13 May, Marshall Barbour flew his first mission as a B-25 pilot and aircraft commander, then added eleven more in May. As reported in the 445th and 446th war diaries, the morning began with a jolt, a 0400 air alert and the sight of many fireworks north of the 321st home base at Solenzara Airfield. The 340th Group's new home field at Alesan was bombed by German aircraft. The 445th war diary went on to point out,

The effect upon our squadron, through the seriousness, had an aspect of humor. For the first time overseas, Officers and E.M. griped about the shortage of picks and shovels. The

Engineering and Armament Sections have been directed to move their tents from the line to the area as a precautionary measure. The 445th silver colored planes are being covered with camouflage nets and are being dispersed as much as possible.

There were two missions on the 13th, one with nineteen planes airborne at 1545, the other with twenty-five planes airborne at 1615, both against targets in or near the same town, Itri, Italy, which had the not-so-affectionate nickname of "Hitler Town." Flying time en route was the same for both missions, and records were insufficient to determine which mission Marshall Barbour flew—although it was probably the second mission, because a 448th pilot led the 321st formation. All aircraft returned safely, with three planes holed on the first mission. That mission, aimed directly at "Hitler Town North," released 149 five-hundred-pound bombs from ten thousand feet, with the entire north section of the town reported well covered.

The second mission, to "Hitler Town South," led by First Lieutenant Tony K. Sowder of the 448th, dropped 104 five-hundred-pound bombs from ten thousand feet against a tunnel mouth, with several direct hits on the mouth of the tunnel, with a pattern across the railroad tracks and rail junction southeast of the tunnel. Flak was described as heavy, scant, and inaccurate on both missions. Aircrews observed six Me 109s under their formation at breakaway from the target, but they didn't attack. All recovered safely with three planes holed.

On Sunday, 14 May, Barbour was airborne with his airplane and crew and nineteen other aircraft at 1522 to bomb the Castiglione Del Lago railroad bridge, and the twenty aircraft dropped seventy-eight one-thousand-pound bombs at 1655 hours from ten thousand feet. All returned safely at 1805 hours. Results reported were a concentration of bursts in the target area, with probable hits on the bridge. Several bombs fell west among buildings causing several explosions. There was no flak, and weather included a slight haze.

On the 15th, Barbour's plane was one of ten aircraft to be airborne at 0840 to bomb the Orvieto south railroad bridge, dropping forty one-thousand-pound bombs on the primary target at 1040 from ten thousand feet. Clouds covered 90 percent of the primary target area. Nine planes (one returned home with an oil leak in the right engine) proceeded to the alternate target of Porto Ferraio and dropped thirty-two more one-thousand-pound bombs. The mission proved to be disastrous for the 446th Squadron.

Escorted by twelve Spitfires, the mission encountered no fighter attacks, but flak hit a 446th aircraft over the alternate target; the entire crew suffered wounds, but fortunately the pilot, First Lieutenant Allan T. Sampson, headed for the open sea and ordered his crew to bail out over the water. Sampson was the last to bail out, and shortly after he left the aircraft it exploded in flight. Every member of the crew was successfully picked up by Air Sea Rescue.

Another 446th aircraft crash-landed on Pianosa Island, an island held by the Germans, and presumably all crew members were taken prisoner by the enemy. A third aircraft from the 446th, piloted by First Lieutenant George F. Walsh, crash-landed at home base, caught fire, and exploded, and the entire crew was lost. Upon hitting the runway, the plane exploded and burned due to the fact that it was saturated by gasoline from leaking fuel lines.

Lieutenant Walsh was thrown clear of the plane, but he died in the hospital of burns he received. The other crew members could not be rescued, and all perished in the burning bomber. A fourth 446th plane also made an emergency landing at the home base, but the crew was safe. While on landing rollout Second Lieutenant Richard E. Hodges's emergency brakes failed, and the plane went into a ditch, collapsing the landing gear. Tragically, three aircraft in the ten-plane mission were lost, and one was heavily damaged, all from the 446th. That same day, the 446th sent two airplanes on a "nickeling mission" (leaflet drop) over Velletri, Italy, ten miles southwest of Rome. Flak was reported light, medium, to intense from air defenses, but all returned safely.

On the 16th, Barbour's plane and crew were in a twenty-seven-plane mission airborne at 1255 to bomb Foligno railroad bridge and dropped ninety-eight one-thousand-pound bombs from ten thousand feet. Escorted again by twelve Spitfires and encountering no flak, all returned safely, with observers reporting a good concentration of bombs across the bridge, with hits on both approaches. The bridge was reported completely demolished. Other strings hit the center of town. On the 17th, though he didn't fly another mission, there was considerable excitement when an apparently damaged B-24 Liberator heavy bomber flew over the home field and six crew members bailed out. One landed about four hundred yards from the 445th Squadron area and was treated for a broken leg by the flight surgeon, Captain William C. Smith.

Marshall Barbour flew eight more missions the rest of the month, on 18, 24, 25, 26, 27, 28, 29, and 30 May, in sequence against targets at Foligno, Aulla, Pontassieve, Todi, Cecina, Massa, Zoagli, Viareggio, and Tarquinia, Italy. His squadron flew in thirty-four of the fifty missions flown by the group in the month of May. Several of its bombings were effective in preventing German counterattacks as the 5th (U.S.) and 8th (British) Armies began a new offensive to capture Rome.

The 448th war diary also noted that they had not lost one airplane in May, until the last day, when one plane was hit just prior to the target. The pilot, Lieutenant Mathews, through heroic, skillful handling of the aircraft and devoted attention to a seriously wounded crew member, Sergeant Anderson—accompanied by another volunteer crew member, Sergeant Bell—ordered the remaining crew to bail out. And in spite of four thousand pounds of bombs that Lieutenant Mathews couldn't release or salvo, one engine out, and leaking fuel, he elected to land on a short fighter strip, and did so successfully. The three men who bailed out, Lieutenant Apple, Lieutenant Norris, and Sergeant Carrick, were picked up by Italian fishermen and returned to the field where the plane landed. Another 448th pilot, Lieutenant Dossey, skillfully landed at the fighter strip and picked up the five remaining crew members and returned them to Solenzara, while Sergeant Anderson was taken to a hospital.

Another piece of good news in the end-of-month 448th war diary entry was the return early in the month of Lieutenant Truman R. Jones, the 448th pilot whose aircraft 552 was hit during the difficult mission of 28 March, and his aircraft was observed making a "controlled landing in Lake Trasimeno," which was in German-held territory. The war diary entry explained:

Early in the month [of May] Lieutenant Jones returned after successfully escaping from German held Italy. His story of his terror raising experience during his six weeks stay in enemy territory sounded like an excerpt from a thrilling adventure magazine. His information on escape and traveling across Italy was greatly appreciated by all combat members of the squadron. His graphic description of the German difficulties in supplying their front line troops gave ample proof of the effectiveness of the 321st Bomb Group prowess.

In the less pleasant part of the 448th's war diary summary for May, writers summarized the deadly effects of the Axis bombing of the 340th Group's base to the north the night of 13 May, which had filtered through the rumor system the next morning.

About 20 men were fatally injured, several more seriously injured and many planes were put out of commission. Little satisfaction was felt when Axis Sally announced that the 310th was next and then would come the 321st's turn. Dirt flew as picks and shovels dug deeper and deeper into the concrete-like soil of Corsica. Fox holes ranged from deep holes to log-covered, dirt-packed air-raid shelters. All personnel who slept on the Line were immediately withdrawn to the area. The tents however still remained in straight company streets. This condition continued until all foxholes were completed then the order came to disperse the tents back into the brush. This order was complied with in a short time.

Holding to an intensive pace in combat missions, Marshall Barbour flew eleven more in June, completing his forty-ninth mission on 22 June. On 1 June, he and his crew were among nineteen planes that were airborne at 0925 to bomb Narni, Italy's south road bridge, releasing 152 bombs, five hundred pounds each, from eleven thousand feet at 1110 hours. They were escorted by twelve Spitfires. The north end of the north approach to the bridge was believed hit. Other bombs fell across the adjacent road, while another element bombed a smaller road bridge one thousand feet east of the target. Six unidentified aircraft flew parallel to the formation but didn't attack. There was no flak, and all returned safely at 1225. Weather was clear, and visibility was unlimited.

The next day, Barbour's plane was among twenty that took off at 0917 hours to bomb a Subiaco town road block, and nineteen again dropped 152 five-hundred-pound bombs from eleven thousand feet at 1105. All were home at 1250, there were no enemy aircraft, and no planes were holed, in spite of flak that varied between heavy and scant but inaccurate. Weather was clear and visibility unlimited, and the target area was covered well with bombs. The greatest concentration of bombs fell across the southeast intersection and through the center of town.

One day prior to 5 June 1944, the date Marshall Barbour flew his forty-third mission, the Allies had captured Rome. News of Rome's fall to the Allies spread around the world like wildfire. The Allies were continuing to drive northward to eject the German army from Italian soil. On the day of his forty-third mission, President Franklin D. Roosevelt spoke to the nation in an inspirational radio address, telling of the United Nations' victory. A partial quote from his address illustrates the power of his words and the meaning of the fall of Rome:

In addition to the monuments of the older times, we also see in Rome the great symbol of Christianity, which has reached into almost every part of the world. There are other shrines and other churches in many places, but the churches and shrines of Rome are visible symbols of the faith and determination of the early saints and martyrs that Christianity should live and become universal. And tonight it will be a source of deep satisfaction that the freedom of the Pope and the Vatican City is assured by the armies of the United Nations. It is also significant that Rome has been liberated by the armed forces of many nations. The American and British armies—who bore the chief burdens of battle—found at their sides our own North American neighbors, the gallant Canadians. The fighting New Zealanders from the far South Pacific, the courageous French and the French Moroccans, the South Africans, the Poles and the East Indians—all of them fought with us on the bloody approaches to the city of Rome.

The Allied invasion of Normandy came two days after the fall of Rome, beginning the eleven-month-long series of campaigns through France into Germany to finally crush the Nazis—as the Soviet army battled relentlessly westward, closing the vice on Hitler's dream of a Thousand-Year Reich. On the day of the Normandy landings, 6 June 1944, President Roosevelt again broadcast to the nation on radio, leading America's people in an emotional and unprecedented prayer for the invasion's success.

At Solenzara there was much excitement generated by the cluster of major events that came in early June, and on D-day, the 6th, particularly, men gathered around all available radios to listen attentively to news reports.

On 6 June, Brigadier General Knapp, the commander of the 57th Bombardment Wing, sent the following message to all units under his command, including the 310th, 321st, and 340th Bombardment Groups, quoting a message from the commanding general, Mediterranean Allied Tactical Air Force:

QUOTE: GENERAL EISENHOWER HAS CABLED ME AS FOLLOWS FOR COMPLIANCE. QUOTE: THE BATTLE WHICH COMMENCED ON TWELVE MAY IN ITALY HAS ADVANCED TO THE POINT IT IS, BY ITSELF, A FIRST CLASS MAJOR ALLIED VICTORY ALL OFFICERS AND ENLISTED PERSONNEL OF EACH NATIONALITY PARTICIPATING MAY FEEL PROUD OF THE SERVICE RENDERED THE COMMON CAUSE BY THEM. THIS ENTIRE COMMAND IS ASSUREDLY PROUD OF THESE ACCOMPLISHMENTS. EXTEND PLEASE TO ALL COMMANDERS CONCERNED MY PERSONAL CONGRATULATIONS. UNQUOTE. I REPEAT I TAKE PLEASURE IN ADDING MY PERSONAL COMMENDATION AND THANKS FOR SUCCESSFUL EFFORTS OF ALL PERSONNEL IN MY COMMAND IN WINNING SUCH HIGH PRAISE. UNQUOTE.

In rapid succession congratulatory messages came in from General George C. Marshall; Major General John K. Cannon, 12th Air Force commander; and numerous other senior officers, American and Allied.

Missions in quick succession came on 7, 8, 10, 13, 21, and 22 June. Promoted to first lieutenant on 11 June, he participated in his next mission against the railroad viaduct at

Sassoferrato on 13 June. The mission, which proved to be more difficult than most, consisted of nineteen planes airborne at 1018 hours, with seventy-two one-thousand-pound bombs dropped at 1133 from ten thousand feet. Crews reported a good concentration, especially heavy on the north end and approach, and the north span was believed knocked out. Heavy to moderate and accurate flak from southeast of Lake Trasimeno holed five planes, and one plane, piloted by First Lieutenant William A. Greene, was lost due to a direct hit in the aircraft's nose, killing the bombardier, First Lieutenant Rene P. Petite, and the navigator, Second Lieutenant Henry (NMI) Olszewski, and causing the rest of the crew to bail out over the home base to safety. Other crew members who bailed out were copilot Second Lieutenant Harvey S. Tilton, engineer-gunner Sergeant Jimmie L. Davis, radio-gunner Sergeant Clifford R. Everhart, and gunner Sergeant James E. Parham.

Marshall Barbour's 21 June mission was late in the day, with nineteen planes airborne at 1720 hours to bomb a block ship—a ship filled with concrete—in Leghorn Harbor and dropped thirty-six one-thousand-pound bombs from ten thousand feet at 1818 hours. Heavy, inaccurate, intense flak holed one aircraft. Window, strips of aluminum intended to confuse and adversely affect radar detection and tracking, was dropped for the first time by the 321st and was believed by crew members to cause antiaircraft guns to be inaccurate. Crews reported fine concentrations across the north entrance to the outer harbor. There were several direct hits on the block ship that was oriented in an east–west position to block the north end of the harbor. Hits were also registered on the north end of the quay. Mission photos showed 100 percent accuracy. The same day, the 448th sent three planes on a nickeling mission over Volterra, Gimiginano, Corigliano, and Siena, with no flak observed.

Barbour's final mission in June was on the 22nd, his total now at forty-nine. Again, late in the day, seventeen aircraft lifted off at 1820 hours with their primary target a railroad bridge north of Marradi, Italy, but they found the target obscured by clouds and diverted to the alternate target, the railroad bridge at Pisa Albavola. Sixteen of the seventeen planes were able to release their bombs at 1947 hours from eleven thousand feet, and all returned at 2050 hours. Crews reported probable hits on the bridge and both approaches from a good concentration, and tracks southeast of the bridge were cut. Weather was clear with unlimited visibility at the alternate target, and flak was heavy to moderate and fairly accurate.

At the end of June, the 448th's summary noted that a significant number of officers and enlisted men took a week off to rest on the island of Capri. Though names weren't listed, it's probable that Lieutenant Marshall Barbour was among the officers ready for a rest in late June, an event years later called R & R (rest and recuperation). The daily, hard push in training, preparing for, and flying combat missions, sometimes in brief hectic periods, one day after another, or on average nearly one every other day, is physically and emotionally wearing. The constant roar of B-25 engines on takeoff with heavy bomb loads, throughout the flight, sometimes in weather, sights and sounds of radio and intercom chatter among flak bursts approaching and over targets—interspersed with fighter attacks flying against heavily defended targets, while seeing an aircraft and crew take a direct hit by flak, and even learning of such events on the ground, takes its toll, without question. Marshall Barbour was deserving and ready for a rest after nearly five months. Also summarized in June were the names of twenty-two officers and seventeen enlisted men who were awarded Purple Hearts for wounds received in action in the period following Marshall Barbour's arrival in the squadron and his first combat mission on 19 February from Gaudo Airfield on the mainland. Two of the twenty-two officers had been killed in action: First Lieutenant Rene P. Petite, bombardier, and Second Lieutenant Henry (NMI) Olszewski, navigator.

While he was on Capri on 30 June, the 321st conducted a formation flyover in honor of the commander of the Mexican air force.

Following his week on Capri, and becoming retrained to the current operating environment and missions, he flew his first mission on 12 July to bomb the railroad and railroad bridge at Ostiglia, Italy. The thirty-eight planes were airborne at 0840 hours and released 136 one-thousand-pound bombs at 1027 hours from ten thousand feet. Four planes didn't drop due to bombardier error. All planes returned at 1127, and none were holed. Crews reported strings of bombs across the southwest portion of the bridge. Photographs showed a direct hit on the north end of the bridge and a good concentration on the south end with probable hits. The enemy had used smoke pots to obscure the target.

The next day, Barbour and his crew returned in a twenty-five-plane mission to Ostiglia to attack the bridge again. Airborne at 1700 hours, the formation dropped 140 more one-thousand-pound bombs at 1837 from ten thousand feet, in spite of heavy though scant and inaccurate flak, and through ineffective smoke screens. Crews reported a good concentration on the center of the bridge with two or three direct hits observed, plus a cut in the southwest approach to the bridge. No planes were holed, and all returned at 1948 hours. The following day they flew another mission, and the next would be on 24 July, with twenty planes against the railroad bridge at Peschiera, Italy.

At this point in his combat tour in the Mediterranean theater, where and under what conditions he would fly additional missions would dramatically change in the coming eleven days. The Allies were about to break through German lines holding the southern flank of the Normandy beachhead, which was swelling with planned landings of additional powerful ground forces into the now well-established beachhead.

Known as the "breakout at St. Lo," the breakthrough that began on 25 July was preceded by a devastating "carpet bombing" of German lines in a 2,500 × 6,000 yard area southeast of, and well away from, the city. There were thousands of rounds of artillery and more than 4,200 tons of bombs dropped by more than three thousand heavy, medium, and fighter-bombers that saturated the area with devastating effects, while, unfortunately, bombs that were dropped short of the German line "walked through" some American units, causing 558 American casualties. It was a vivid illustration of concentrated World War II airpower that also tragically illustrated the hazards of bombing enemy ground forces in an approach perpendicular to enemy lines. As for German units caught in the devastating bombardment, they were shattered, dazed, and confused, allowing immediate exploitation of its effects.

On 1 August, General George S. Patton, who had been part of a months-long, well-planned and executed hoax suggesting that the 6 June invasion of France would be well north of the actual landings on the Normandy beaches, suddenly appeared in command of his 3rd Army, which with many other American units tore through the breached German lines as Allied armies in Italy appeared to be on the verge of decisive results. In the meantime, another Allied plan was already well along and would begin another major operation on 15 August—the landing of Allied forces in southern France, known as Operation Anvil.

The invasion of southern France was to accomplish two major objectives: (1) secure the southern flank of Allied forces, which had breached the German line near St. Lo, broken out of the Normandy beachhead, and were extending deep toward the southeast to swing wide around the Germans' left flank, and (2) provide a second, critically needed supply port in France—namely, Marseilles. Anvil's air support was to be provided by the Americans' 12th Tactical Air Force and included other Mediterranean Allied Tactical Air Forces also based in Corsica and 15th Air Force heavy bombers in Italy. The 321st Group began participating in pre-invasion attacks on selected targets the first days of August.

The detailed, secretive planning in support of Anvil began well before 15 August, and while the hard work in planning and preparations were in progress on Corsica, on 1 August the group was celebrating the second anniversary of its activation at Columbia, Mississippi, while receiving word that they had been awarded a Presidential Unit Citation for their work in bombing the Balkans—which had occurred prior to Marshall Barbour's arrival in Italy.

The entire group stood down from missions, and the day on into the evening was filled with formations, awards, and decorations. Awards included distinguished flying crosses and legions of merit to officers and enlisted men, and during the formations of combat officers and enlisted men that began at 1000 hours, there were talks to the assembled officers and men by senior air officers, from colonels to senior generals. Speakers included Brigadier General Robert D. Knapp, commander, 57th Bombardment Wing, and Colonel Richard H. "Red" Smith, pilot and commander, 321st Group. In the evening there were celebrations at newly built and opened officer and enlisted clubs, built in part by officer and troop labor—and the evening's festivities included an African American band from the 41st Engineers. Bars at both clubs opened at 1400, there was a stage show at the "Hilltop Theater" that night, and the day grew happier as it passed into night.

But the next day, while training for what was to come, the war and a few combat missions over Italy promptly began anew for the 321st. The 448th, however, began with a glimpse into the future, sending nineteen planes to bomb the Var River Road Bridge, near Nice, France. Airborne at 0822 hours, fourteen planes dropped fifty-six one-thousand-pound bombs from eleven thousand feet with a heavy concentration of bombs on the west approach, probable hits on the approach, and possible hits on the bridge. This time the squadron became reacquainted with heavy, moderately intense, and accurate to inaccurate flak, all the way from the initial point, to and across the target, and along the breakaway, with sixteen of the nineteen planes holed.

Marshall Barbour and his crew didn't fly on this mission. His welcome to France would come two days later, a nineteen-plane mission against the same bridge, in which all bombs were returned to base due to complete cloud cover over the target—followed by a strike on the bridge on 8 August.

On that day, a Tuesday, a large number of men from the 447th attended heavyweight boxing champion Joe Louis's exhibition bout at the 41st Engineers' recreation field, but mission preparations and the mission briefing kept Marshall and his crew away from recreational pursuits. The mission of twenty planes, ten from the 448th and ten from the 447th, was airborne at 1550 hours, intending to bomb the primary target of the railroad bridge at Pont St. Esprit North, but heavy cumulonimbus (potential thunderstorm) clouds, with cloud bases at eight thousand feet, made bombing too hazardous and virtually impossible, and the entire formation diverted to the alternate target—Var River Bridge No. 1, which was hit hard with the release of eighty one-thousand-pound bombs. The results were a good concentration of bombs in the target area, with both approaches believed hit, with clear weather, and in spite of heavy, intense, and accurate flak from known positions in the target area—which holed half of the aircraft flying the mission. It was a seemingly routine, yet flak-shrouded mission that Marshall Barbour would remember the rest of his life.

On the 11th came a 1705 hours takeoff for Marshall and his crew on a twelve-plane bomb attack on gun positions at Frejus, France, with ninety-six five-hundred-pound bombs dropped from eleven thousand feet—with excellent coverage in the target area, no flak, and no enemy aircraft.

The next day, the 445th war diary reported, "the mail situation is falling off and the men believe that is indicative of another invasion. Rumors have it that southern France is next what with our group hammering at gun positions there." Indeed, that day all four squadrons reported attacks on gun positions in southern France. And again on the 13th, Marshall Barbour, with his crew and eleven more planes, airborne at 0905 hours, bombed gun positions at La Ciotat, France, dropping seventy-two one-thousand-pound SAP (semi–armor piercing) bombs, with direct hits, all on the target, with 100 percent accuracy.

On 15 August, the 321st operated in direct support of the invasion of southern France, Operation Anvil, which was later renamed Operation Dragoon, begun at 0800 hours with the landing of troops at various areas on a broad front, and including predawn air strikes against beaches. The invasion is described briefly in three paragraphs of volume 2 of a U.S. Military Academy textbook titled *The West Point Atlas of American Wars*:

The inset sketch (this map) shows, generally, the origin, composition and movements of the ANVIL assault and follow-up forces. All units, except some of the French, were veterans of the fighting in Italy. Besides the American VI and French II Corps, the force (designated United States Seventh Army, under Lt. Gen. Alexander Patch) included two special units: the 1st Airborne Task Force (1 TF), a composite, predominantly American force of parachute and glider infantry and artillery units numbering 8,000; and the 1st Special Service Force (1 SSF), an American–Canadian unit originally created for specialized operations in the Aleutians. Air support was to be provided by the XII Tactical Air Command in

Corsica, and to some extent, by strategic bombers of the Fifteenth Air Force in Italy. Naval support would come from Vice Adm. Henry K. Hewitt's Western Task Force.

Opposing this formidable force was the German Nineteenth Army—seven second-line infantry divisions and the 11th Panzer Division. Coastal defenses were similar to those in Normandy, but neither as extensive nor as well manned.

On the night of 14 August, naval and airborne demonstrations (the latter consisting of the dropping of dummies equipped with noise devices and demolition packages) were made as shown (main sketch) on the flanks of the landing area. Also, French commandos were landed to block the coastal highway, and the 1 SSF seized Port Cros and Levant in order to destroy suspected gun emplacements (found to be dummies). At 0800 the next morning the assault force (Maj. Gen. Lucian C. Truscott's VI Corps) began landing. The landing was preceded by intensive aerial and naval bombardments and one of the most effective and best-executed airborne operations (1 TF at Le Muy) of the war. Only Camel Force met much resistance. The follow-up force (French II Corps) landed in the wake of the VI Corps. By noon, 17 August, all units had crossed the beachhead line (solid blue line). The French II Corps began their task of capturing Toulon and Marseille, while the American VI Corps set off in pursuit of the retreating Germans.

Vice Admiral Hewitt's naval support included the battleships *Nevada, Texas,* and *Arkansas,* HMS *Ramillies,* and the French battleship *Lorraine;* with twenty cruisers for gunfire support and naval aircraft from nine escort carriers assembled as Task Force 88.

Flying in support of the invasion, Marshall and his crew were on one of two 448th planes that were spares with the 446th in a total of twelve planes attacking Antheor Beach, near San Raphael, in direct support of the landings. (Antheor Beach is in the area where Camel Force, composed primarily of the American 36th Infantry Division and supporting units, came ashore, the same area in which Operation Dragoon encountered the strongest resistance.) The twelve aircraft from the 321st were among 1,300 Allied bombers from Italy, Sardinia, and Corsica that began aerial bombardment before 0600 and continued until 0730, when battleships and cruisers launched spotting aircraft to begin firing on specific targets in advance of the landings. Led by Lieutenant Robert P. Moss, from another group, in a two-hour-and-ten-minute mission, they "walked" a double load of one-hundred-pound demolition bombs, starting in the water and up through the beach, over a road and railroad viaduct, and on both sides of the cove. Flak was heavy to moderate, inaccurate, and out of range. Above them they observed two Me 109s make a pass on B-24 heavy bombers.

Then on Friday, 18 August, in a mission Marshall and his crew didn't fly, the 321st completed a hazardous, difficult, but stunningly effective strike on ships in Toulon Harbor, in which, fortunately, there was no loss of life. Thirty-six planes total from all four squadrons participated and launched at 1053 hours, dropping 151 one-thousand-pound SAP bombs from thirteen thousand feet. Another twenty-eight one-thousand-pound GP (general purpose) bombs were returned and salvoed due to a mechanical failure in the lead aircraft in one flight. Flak was heavy and intense, of the barrage and tracking type, and holed twenty-seven planes, wounding twelve crew members, eight from the 448th, two from the 447th, one from the 445th, and the group commander, who was copilot in the lead aircraft, a 448th aircraft number 43-27720—a B-25J. The raid at Toulon has been called the most successful single mission ever carried out by medium bombers. The large Axis battleship *Strasbourg* was severely damaged and listing heavily. The light cruiser *La Gallissoniere*, which had been shelling Allied troops near Toulon on D-day in southern France, lay capsized, and a submarine was sunk. All damage to surface vessels was verified by aerial photography.

The following personnel of the 321st Bombardment Group (M) were wounded in action during the attack on Toulon on 18 August 1944 and awarded the Purple Heart or their first Oak Leaf Cluster (OLC), as circumstances required. Additionally, the lead bombardier, First Lieutenant Robert "Dead-Eye" Joyce, was awarded the Silver Star for initiating a nearly perfect bomb pattern:

Colonel Richard H. "Red" Smith, 0-108850 Purple Heart, copilot, 321st BG commanding officer

First Lieutenant Frank M. Furey, 0-748954 1st OLC to PH, pilot, 448th BS

First Lieutenant Robert "Dead-Eye" Joyce, 0-744314 Purple Heart, bombardier, 448th BS

First Lieutenant William O. Hickey, 0-805278 1st OLC to PH, navigator, 448th BS

First Lieutenant Louis P. Greene, 0-739246 1st OLC to PH, bombardier, 448th BS

First Lieutenant Henry O. Schlenk, 0-749861 Purple Heart, bombardier, 448th BS

Staff Sergeant Nico M. Pineda, 39691629 Purple Heart, engineer/gunner, 448th BS

Staff Sergeant Charles M. Richards, 13093897 Purple Heart, turret/gunner, 447th BS

Staff Sergeant Milton M. Slafkes, 12185949 1st OLC to PH, gunner, 448th BS

Staff Sergeant Rufus (NMI) York, 6937037 Purple Heart, engineer/gunner, 445th BS

Sergeant Edward B. Markiewicz, 13089779 Purple Heart, gunner, 448th BS

Sergeant James R. O'Neil, 20912657 Purple Heart, engineer/gunner, 447th BS

Four of those wounded were in the lead plane, a 448th aircraft, number 43-27720: Colonel Smith, copilot; Lieutenant Furey, pilot; Lieutenant Joyce, bombardier; and Lieutenant Hickey, navigator/gunner.

On 20 August, in a three-hour-and-twenty-five-minute mission, the 448th, with Marshall Barbour's plane as one of eighteen aircraft sent to bomb the railroad bridge at Longeavous, France, with fifteen planes dropping sixty one-thousand-pound bombs at eleven thousand feet. Bombs were returned by three planes due to bombsight malfunction in the lead plane. The south approach was hit and tracks cut two hundred feet south of the bridge. There were damaging near misses at the foundation of the center pier. No flak or enemy aircraft were observed, while fighters provided area coverage and escort.

On 24 August, the 448th turned its attention back to Italy, where at 0853 eighteen planes, including Marshall Barbour and his crew, attacked a railroad bridge at Taro Solignano, with sixty-eight one-thousand-pound bombs from ten thousand feet—with results of a heavy concentration of bombs on the center in the west end, with very probable hits on the bridge and adjacent tunnel entrance. There was no flak or enemy aircraft.

On 25 August, in a three-hour-and-forty-five-minute mission, the second longest of all he flew, with takeoff at 0821 hours, sixteen of the eighteen planes dropped sixty-two one-thousand-pound bombs from twelve thousand feet, the target a railroad bridge at Pont-d'Ain, France. An excellent concentration of bombs in the target area resulted in several direct hits, and the bridge was observed down. No flak and no enemy aircraft were observed.

On 28 August, in the longest of all of Marshall Barbour's missions (4:15), eighteen planes from the 448th struck a railroad bridge at Dois Dieu, France, dropping seventy one-thousand-pound bombs from ten thousand feet. The bridge and both approaches were hit, but weather necessitated a change in bombing altitude, and most bombs were scattered to the north and northwest. Flak, though heavy at times and also scant, was inaccurate, from three miles south of Cueo. No enemy aircraft were observed.

The 448th began the month with 93 officers and 321 enlisted men assigned. The end-of-month summary included this paragraph:

Many new faces were seen in the squadron as replacements for combat and ground men continued to pour in and it was a common expression among the veterans of the squadron to remark "I just don't know anyone, the outfit has sure changed." The combat men and ground men who were fortunate enough to be rotated to the good old U.S.A. departed with broad smiles on their faces anxious for their return home.

Among those departing for home with broad smiles on their faces was First Lieutenant Marshall Hall Barbour, a sixty-two-mission veteran, who completed 168:35 hours of combat flying time before returning and later would receive a Distinguished Flying Cross for his 8 August mission against the railroad bridge over the Var River near Nice, France. The citation accompanying the DFC award, signed by the 12th Air Force chief of staff, Colonel John W. Monahan, on behalf of the 12th Air Force commander, Major General John K. Cannon, and dated 18 September 1944, a week after Barbour left for the United States, reads:

MARSHALL H. BARBOUR, 0-688784, First Lieutenant, 448th Bomb Sq, 321st Bomb Gp. For extraordinary achievement while participating in aerial flight as a pilot of a B-25 type aircraft. On 8 August 1944, Lt. Barbour flew an attack upon a road bridge over the Var River in southern France. Upon approach to the target, intense anti-aircraft fire enveloped his formation, damaging ten airplanes. Displaying great courage and flying ability in the face of this continued barrage, Lt Barbour maintained perfect formation, thereby enabling his bombardier to release his bombs with devastating effect upon this vital objective. On more than sixty combat missions his outstanding proficiency and steadfast devotion to duty have reflected great credit upon himself and the Armed Forces of the United States. Portland, Oregon.

* * *

By command of Major General CANNON

On 28 July 1944, a month prior to his last mission, General Order No. 111, headquarters, 12th Air Force, directed that he receive his first Air Medal and first Bronze Oak Leaf Cluster for the Air Medal, each Air Medal symbolizing his completing ten combat missions. He was awarded the first two decorations on 27 August, at Solenzara Airfield, one day prior to his final mission. In October, after he returned to the States, he would receive four more Bronze Oak Leaf Clusters, for a total of six, and be authorized to wear one Silver Oak Leaf cluster in lieu of five Bronze Oak Leaf Clusters.

As was common practice in the army air force, Marshall Barbour, after being ordered back to the United States by the 321st Group's flight surgeon, "Doc" Smith, returned home and retrained to become an instructor in the same type of aircraft he had flown in combat, in his case, the TB-25. He attended two additional schools at Brooks Field in San Antonio in January and February 1945, then began training crews at Douglas Army Airfield and Luke Field Army Air Base, March 1945 to May 1945. But in his mind, he wasn't through with combat, not yet.

The war in the Pacific hadn't ended, and though the American armed forces were being partially demobilized, men returning from Europe and remaining on active duty were aware of the Allies' fierce Okinawa campaign against the suicidal enemy in the Far East, the Japanese Empire, and the huge buildup of Allied forces in the Pacific. There was growing certainty that the Japanese home islands would have to be invaded to destroy the rule of the Japanese militarists and finally bring the war to a successful conclusion.

On 10 May 1945, at the age of twenty-three, Marshall Barbour submitted a letter addressed to "Commanding General A.A.F. Western Flying Training Command, 1104 W. 8th Street, Santa Ana, California. THRU: Commanding Officer, Luke Field, Phoenix, Arizona." The subject of the letter was "Request for a second tour of duty overseas," and paragraph 1 read, "Request is hereby made by the undersigned for a second tour of duty overseas in a B-25 or A-26 type aircraft." He carefully laid out his qualifications and rationale, including a total flying time of 870 hours. The hours listed were 100 in the AT-6 trainer, 7 in the P-38, 170 in the B-26, and 450 in the B-25. He clearly was determined to reenter the war as a combat pilot against Japan.

His letter was dated three days after the German surrender in Europe. And, unknown to Marshall Barbour, on Okinawa, two days after his letter was submitted, his Franklin High School classmate and football teammate, as well as his Willamette Bearcat teammate on Oahu in December 1941, Ted Ogdahl, was seriously wounded in the battle for Okinawa.

To the good fortune of Marshall H. Barbour, Ted Ogdahl, and all the Willamette University Bearcats of 1941, the dropping of the atomic bombs on Hiroshima and Nagasaki ended the war, avoiding Operation Downfall and what clearly would have been an even more horrible, protracted bloodbath for both sides in a ground, air, and war at sea on the Japanese home islands.

In addition to his Distinguished Flying Cross and Air Medal with a Silver Oak Leaf Cluster and one Bronze Oak Leaf Cluster, he returned home with decorations including the European-African Middle Eastern Campaign Medal with the Bronze Service Stars for the Rome-Arno and Southern France Campaigns, the American Campaign Medal, the World War II Service Lapel Button, and the World War II Victory Medal. He was relieved from active duty on 17 September 1945 and returned to Oregon, where he undoubtedly learned Ted Ogdahl was in a naval hospital in Corvallis, Oregon, recuperating from the serious wounds he received on Okinawa.

He reentered Willamette University, apparently receiving partial credit for his officer training, obtained his AB degree on May 19, 1947, and, while in school, married Jean McLaughlin in Grants Pass, Oregon, on July 16, 1946.

They moved to Woodburn, Oregon, in 1948, where he served as a teacher, coach, athletic director, and counselor, retiring after thirty-five years. In those thirty-five years, he variously coached football, basketball, track, and baseball. During the 1949 football season, he was the Bulldogs' assistant or co-coach when they played their next-to-last game of the season and defeated Ken Jacobson's Dallas High School team 30–12, when Ken was the new head coach in Dallas. By 1953, Woodburn's student population had gradually decreased, causing the school to compete in seven-man football, in a season when a polio outbreak caused the cancellation of two games of an eight-game schedule.

Over his period of service at Woodburn High School, "Mush," as he was known to his Willamette teammates, friends, and professional associates, taught such diverse subjects as biology, physics, science, chemistry, driver training, agriculture, and auto mechanics.

Marshall's close and continuing association with his former 1941 Bearcat teammates was expressed in the eulogy he gave at the funeral of Ted Ogdahl after Ted's 29 July 1988 death in Salem. He and Ted had been classmates and football teammates at Franklin High School in Portland, Oregon, before they both entered Willamette and played as teammates under Coach Spec Keene at Willamette. Marshall's eulogy was the first of three given at Ted Ogdahl's funeral.

Marshall and Jean raised six children, five daughters and one son, all of whom survived him when he died in a Salem hospital on January 21, 1992—six weeks after he and Jean returned from the 1941 Willamette Bearcats' fifty-year reunion at the Moana Hotel in Honolulu. At the time of his death, daughters Marsha Brittan, Susan Packer, and Sarah Barbour were living in Woodburn; Molly Faria in Wasco; and Joan Barbour in Washington, DC. Son John M. Barbour, a 1977 graduate of Willamette, was and remains in Beaverton, Oregon.

The measure of this man's stature as a World War II veteran, and in all he did at Woodburn High School over the thirty-five years of his service there, is seen in his name on a key athletic facility at the school: Marshall Barbour Gymnasium.

Chapter Seventeen

Two Teammates Who Served as Marines in the Pacific Theater

A Sophomore and a Marine in the 4th Air Base Defense Wing

Gilbert Cecil Conner, a Native American from the Umatilla Indian tribe and believed to be a direct descendant of Chief Joseph of the Nez Perce Indians, is second from the left in the front row of the Bearcats' team photograph. Born August 13, 1923, in Tutuilla, Oregon, he was eighteen years old and listed on the team roster just prior to the December 6, 1941, game as a freshman halfback. He had graduated in the spring of 1941 from Pendleton High School in Pendleton, Oregon, where he starred playing quarterback on the football team.

He loved the game of football and, like many others on the Willamette team, such as Ted Ogdahl and Ken Jacobson, elected to continue in school and play football in the 1942 season. It was one more year in which Coach Keene brought a fourth consecutive conference championship to the Bearcats, with one loss in an eight-game schedule, ending with a 17–0 win over Whitman on Thanksgiving Day.

After completing the first semester of the 1942–1943 academic year, he must have known his draft number was near, as he chose to enlist in the Marine Corps and was inducted in the 13th Naval District in Spokane, Washington, on February 19, 1943. On his application form he identified himself as a Nez Perce Indian and listed his main occupation as "student," noting that for four summers he had worked as a truck driver in a farming business in which his employer was Mr. Irving Mann, who lived in Adams, Oregon. He drove trucks having five forward speeds and a capacity of two tons, hauling peas and wheat.

The last day of his summer employment was August 30, 1942, just prior to the beginning of the Bearcats' football practices. He listed his major in Pendleton High School as math, having taken algebra, plain geometry, solid geometry, physics, and chemistry. An all-around athlete in high school, in addition to football, in his year and a half at Willamette, he listed his desired major as physical education, and in addition to football, he participated in

Gilbert Cecil Conner as pictured on the 1941 Willa-mette Bearcats football team. (*Source*: MOHLAWU)

Gilbert Conner, star quarterback at Pendleton High School. (*Source*: LCC)

basketball, softball, and tennis, also noting that he took one semester of trigonometry. From Spokane, where he was given the serial number 830340, he traveled as a member of the 2nd Recruit Battalion to the recruit depot in San Diego.

Cece, as he was known to his Willamette teammates, carried the same name as his father, who had been an actor with speaking parts in at least two western films in which Jeff Chandler starred: *The Great Sioux Uprising* (1953) and *Pillars in the Sky* (1956)—facts given by Leah Conner, Cece's younger sister, to author Joan Burbick for her 2002 book *Rodeo Queens and the American Dream*. Leah, herself, was a rodeo queen at the time she provided the information about her brother to the book's author.

He arrived in San Diego on 23 February, and on 25 February, following his first interview after being inducted, he entered basic training at Camp Kearny, on the east side of the city, a military base that had been in operation since 1917, with a small airfield, Gibbs Airfield, added in 1937. He completed the tough marine basic training, in which he expressed infantry as his first choice for service and aviation as second. His education background, test scores, and the Marine Corps' needs probably resulted in his being selected for his second choice, marine aviation. He took his basic training in Training Squadron 131 at Marine Aviation Base (formerly Gibbs Field), Kearny Mesa, completing basic on 14 April.

On 20 April he reported to the Marine Aviation Detachment at Texas A & M College, in College Station, Texas, and on the 26th began nearly five months of technical training to become a radio operator, with a secondary capability as a teletype operator. His final grade in the 582-hour course was 83.0, qualifying him for the SSN 776 specialty (Service Specialty Number). The intense schooling required him to successfully complete courses in code copying, code sending, typing, procedures, lectures, theory, and operations procedures. When he completed what was considered a "Class A" service school on 7 September 1943, simultaneous with his promotion to private first class, he probably was unaware that he was preparing to become part of the U.S. Marine Corps' painfully earned but steady buildup of what was to be the powerful marine and navy air-ground teams that developed during the World War II Pacific campaigns. On 9 September, he was assigned to Aviation Regulating Squadron 1, but he would soon join the Headquarters Squadron of the 4th Marine Air Base Defense Wing and be involved in supporting three major Pacific campaigns following the Guadalcanal campaign, which was the defining period in the growth of marine aviation and its air-ground teams.

His next set of orders sent him to San Diego to board the Liberty ship U.S. Army transport *Puebla* in San Diego on 29 September. The next day he was bound for the island of Tutuila, American Samoa; crossed the equator on 12 October; arrived the 14th; and debarked the next day at the expanding navy port in Tutuila's largest town, Pago Pago. He remained on the island, training and preparing to participate in the buildup of the 4th Marine Air Base Defense Wing while at the Naval Air Station at Fafuna. Marine Air Group (MAG) 13, with Marine Fighting Squadron VMF-224, was operating out of Tutuila, and pilots in the squadron, having transitioned into the new F4U Corsair fighters, described their lives as "constant patrol and alert, chasing bogeys that always turned out to be friendly."

Certainly there were enough alarms, and undoubtedly Cece Conner was gaining experience to prepare him for future aviation base defense operations with duties in communications.

What type of communications work might he have done at Fafuna? Marine Air Group 13 had ground-to-air and air-to-ground communications. Coded messages from and to higher headquarters cycled in and out of the group through a command-and-control element, transmitted by teletype and in some instances by radio. There were communications contacts with radar sites, antiaircraft defense and other ground-based units, as well as other air-raid warning systems developing in the island's civilian populace. There were fire, air, sea, and rescue organizations, as well as naval units operating in and out of the anchorages on the island.

He remained on Tutuila until 2 January 1944, when he embarked on the Liberty ship SS *Horace Greeley*, which sailed the next day in convoy to Funafuti Atoll in the Ellice Islands, where he arrived and disembarked on 6 January 1944, four days after the rear echelon of the 4th Marine Base Air Defense Wing arrived on Funafuti from Tutuila. While on Funafuti, on 8 March 1944, Cece received his promotion to temporary corporal.

On 2 October 1942, the 5th Marine Defense Battalion, Reinforced, had come from Tutuila Island in American Samoa and made an unopposed amphibious landing on Funafuti Atoll, part of the British-owned Ellice Islands. "Funafuti is largely forgotten today," said William Bartsch, a historian and author from Reston, Virginia. "It [the little-known battle there] marked the beginning of the great U.S. advance in the central Pacific, but not everyone remembers that today."

An article written by air force veteran Robert F. Dorr for the *Marine Corps Times* issue of 21 June 2004, posted online in Leatherneck.com, lays out the reasons for U.S. interest in Funafuti Atoll and the Ellice Islands:

> *An article in Leatherneck magazine during the war expressed wonderment that the Japanese never occupied Funafuti, but left it open to occupation. Funafuti gave the Allies a protected rear area as they prepared for Operation Galvanic, the invasion of Tarawa in the Gilbert Islands in November 1943.*

A document retrieved from government archives explains why the marines went there:

> *The sudden decision to occupy Funafuti appears to have been based upon an estimation of the enemy's intentions. Headquarters believed that the Japanese on Tarawa would soon move into the Ellice Group. It was known that the enemy made extensive aerial reconnaissance of Funafuti in late September [1942]. Evidently, our bold move forced the Japanese to change their plans.*

The initial marine contingent that came ashore in the lagoon at crescent-shaped Funafuti consisted of the antiaircraft battalion, two infantry companies from 3rd Marines, a group of navy Seabees, and a detachment of navy Scouting Squadron 65 with four OS2U

Kingfisher observation planes. Initially, there were fewer than one thousand Americans on Funafuti, including 853 Marines.

In early 1943, while Cece Conner was still in basic training in San Diego, the Japanese began air attacks on Funafuti. The first marine casualty was antiaircraft gunner Private William Sleider, who was killed during an attack by twelve Japanese bombers striking from nearby Nauru.

In a letter written in 1976, the late Major General Ralph H. "Smoke" Spanger, who was a first lieutenant in 1943, remembered friendly fighters being brought in:

We were flying the older F4F-4 Wildcats while the remainder of the [marine] fighter squadrons in the Pacific were transitioning into the F4U Corsair. At the urgent request of the Seabees on Funafuti, I was part of a four-plane advanced echelon to fly north from American Samoa to the Ellice Islands. With external tanks we flew 700 miles with only one stop at the French island of Wallis and arrived over Funafuti, the largest island in the Ellice group. To our dismay, the Navy Seabees' desire to be protected by us exceeded their constructive efforts and we were forced to land on barely 1,500 feet of unprepared coral surface.

The next day [22 March 1943], we were alerted for our first business and did, in fact, chase a Japanese Emily flying boat but lost it in some rather severe weather.

On March 27, Capt. [William P.] Boland and I launched against a possible radar target and ended up in hot pursuit of four twin-engine Japanese "Betty" bombers. Our tired F4Fs had to strain to get into position for the attack.

On the first attack, Boland shot down the lead bomber, which exploded under fire of his six 50-caliber machine guns. Contrary to [an official marine] history, my guns did not jam and I was able to do some damage to the number four bomber.

Boland shot down a second Mitsubishi G4M bomber several weeks later. Boland's two aerial victories were the only two air-to-air kills of the Funafuti campaign.

During the thirteen months ending in November 1943, Japanese bombers struck Funafuti nine times. The 90 mm antiaircraft guns manned by marines were credited with shooting down four enemy aircraft.

In November 1943, on Armistice Day, a month before Cece left Tutuila Island for Funafuti in the Ellice Islands, Major General Lewie Griffith Merritt set up 4th Wing headquarters at Funafuti in final preparation for the central Pacific thrust into the Gilbert and Marshall Islands, Operation Galvanic. The 4th Wing then comprised two air groups: Marine Air Group 13, with VMF-111 and 441 and VMSB-151 and 241; MAG 31, with VMF-224, 311, and 321; scout bomber squadrons 331 and 341; and transport unit VMJ-353. The wing's complement of aircraft at that time was forty F4F Wildcat fighters, sixty F4U Corsairs, seventy-two Douglas Dauntless SBD scout and dive-bombers, eleven R4D transports (equivalent aircraft is the army air force C-47 "Gooney Bird"), and three PBYs scattered from Samoa to Nanumea. Once again, Cece Conner had more than enough to do in 4th Wing headquarters because planning and preparations were under way to move northwest toward the targeted Gilbert and Marshall Islands.

Operation Galvanic's target date was 20 November 1943, before Cece arrived on Funafuti in January. On that date the battle for Tarawa Atoll in the Gilbert Islands—located in what is now the nation of Kiribati—began with amphibious landings on the small island of Betio in the atoll. The 2nd Marine Division, part of the Army's 27th Infantry Division and supporting forces, totaling thirty-five thousand, were in for a rude and costly lesson. The Battle of Tarawa was the first American offensive in the critical central Pacific region, and also the first time the United States faced serious opposition in an amphibious landing.

In eighteen months of preparations, the garrison of 2,619 Japanese troops, augmented by 2,200 laborers (1,000 Japanese and 1,200 Koreans), were well supplied, well prepared, and had constructed defenses that made the island a veritable fortress. The battle the enemy was preparing for would be fought on the largest island in the atoll, though it was only two and a half miles long and at its widest point only eight hundred yards across, with an east–west airfield runway right down the middle of the island. On the heavily fortified island, the airfield gave the island additional significance as a prickly threat to the northwestern advance of the Allies through the Marshall and Mariana Islands toward the Japanese home islands.

Americans had suffered similar losses in the Solomon Island campaigns of 1942 as they would in this battle, but amphibious landings in the Solomons had nearly always been unopposed and had stretched over a period of six months. This Japanese defense network on a virtually flat island surface included more than five hundred pillboxes, or "stockades" built from logs and sand, with some reinforced by concrete; forty artillery pieces scattered about various reinforced firing pits on the island; and a series of fourteen coastal defense guns, including four large Vickers eight-inch guns purchased from the British during the Russo-Japanese War. In a seventy-six-hour battle to secure Betio Island, the fierce, to-the-last-man enemy resistance cost the Marine Corps 1,696 killed and 2,101 wounded, many of the casualties precipitated by the occurrence of unusual but predictable tidal activity called neap tides that planners had failed to take into account. The north side of the island was on the lagoon side of the atoll, the deep ocean was on the south and west sides, and the Japanese defenders believed the Americans would land on the south side. On the north side the Japanese had constructed a long pier extending beyond the coral reef so that vessels could moor in the better-protected lagoon and unload cargo at low tide to move on the pier to the island.

Contrary to what the Japanese believed, the Americans' landings were on the lagoon side, on Red Beaches 1 and 2, to the west of the pier, and Red 3, to the east of the pier. Green Beach on the western shoreline was a contingency beach and was used on D+1. Black beaches 1 and 2, on the south side of the island, weren't used. When the three-hour naval bombardment lifted for the first wave to move onto the beach, allowing defenders to emerge from protected shelter and enter their firing pits, the assault waves discovered that their troop-loaded, four-foot-draft Higgins boats couldn't cross the three-foot deep water covering the coral reefs. The only vehicles that could navigate across the reef were the tracked but thin-plated amphibious marine LVT (landing vehicle, tank) Alligators, but many of the Alligators were holed, badly damaged, or destroyed by enemy fire, while hundreds of troops attempted to wade from Higgins boats to the beaches through the shallow water while under fire from pillboxes and firing pits. The slow buildup of force on the three beaches additionally permitted the enemy time to shift troops from the south side to the north side of the island to occupy the numerous pillboxes and firing pits the defenders had built overlooking the beaches—and increase their deadly fire against the assaulting troops. Marines who managed to reach the sandy beaches were increasingly pinned behind log-reinforced sea walls on both sides of the pier, in desperate bids to survive the storm of enemy fire sweeping the shallow water. To complicate matters further, enemy snipers were active, firing from the long pier into the flanks of the landing units.

A number of the LVTs went back onto the coral reef to attempt moving men to the shore who were stranded on the reef, while the senior officer among the landing troops, Colonel David Shoup, took action upon his arrival on shore. Although an exploding shell wounded him soon after his arrival at the pier, the troops cleared the pier of snipers, and he rallied the first wave of marines who had become pinned down behind the limited protection of the sea wall. Working without rest the next two days and under constant withering fire, he pushed forward, directing attacks against strongly held Japanese positions, obstructions, and heavy fire. Throughout the battle, he was exposed to Japanese small-arms and artillery fire, inspiring forces under his command. For his actions on Betio, he was awarded the Medal of Honor.

As the three-day struggle on the island was finally drawing to a close, at sea at 0510 hours the morning of 23 November, the last day of the battle for the atoll, the Japanese submarine I-175, a Pearl Harbor veteran originally designated I-75, torpedoed and sank the escort carrier *Liscome Bay* (CVE-56). So suddenly and violently did the ship explode following the torpedo's strike in the aft starboard quarter into an engine room, triggering the explosion of the ship's stockpile of bombs for her aircraft, that pieces from the ship and body parts landed on the battleship *New Mexico* one mile distant. The shattered *Liscome Bay* listed rapidly to starboard and sank in twenty-three minutes.

From a crew of 916, a total of 687, including 53 officers and 591 enlisted, went down with her. Among the enlisted men lost was another Pearl Harbor veteran and a nationally known hero—the first black American to receive the Navy Cross, the nation's second-highest decoration for valor—Ship's Cook Third Class Doris Miller—who had personally received the decoration from Admiral Nimitz on board the aircraft carrier *Enterprise* (CV-6) at Pearl Harbor as a result of his actions as a crew member on the burning, sinking battleship *West Virginia* during the Japanese attack.

Among those also lost was Rear Admiral Henry M. Mullinix, task group commander for three escort carriers, *Liscome Bay*, *Coral Sea*, and *Corregidor*, and the ship's commander, Captain Irving D. Wiltsie. They were part of what was, to that date, the largest naval force assembled in the Pacific for a single operation, consisting of seventeen aircraft carriers (six CVs, five CVLs, and six CVEs), twelve battleships, eight heavy cruisers, four light cruisers, sixty-six destroyers, and thirty-six transport ships.

Funafuti Airfield, Ellice Islands, late 1943, with aircraft on the ramp. An important starting point for the move forward in the Pacific campaigns. VMF-224, online. (*Source*: USMC)

A month before Cece Conner left Pago Pago for Funafuti, army soldiers had begun replacing marines on the atoll, and an army air force fighter squadron replaced the aging F4F leatherneck aircraft. A small contingent of marines remained on Funafuti until the end of the war was announced on 15 August 1945—making an important contribution on an island that has since become part of the independent constitutional monarchy of Tuvalu.

Coincidentally, fifteen days after marine Private First Class Gilbert Cecil Conner's 6 January 1944 arrival on Funafuti Atoll in the 4th Marine Base Defense Air Wing Headquarters Squadron, marine Lieutenant Marion Edward "Buddy" Reynolds arrived on Funafuti and remained there until May 1944, when he returned to Hawaii to join the 4th Marine Division. No information is available as to whether the two Willamette University teammates encountered one another on Funafuti Atoll, but it's likely they did, as the number of marines on the atoll was decreasing, and "Buddy" Reynolds was performing duties as mess officer in Dining Hall No. 1 and in the battalion police.

While Cece was on Funafuti Island, American forces expanded their Gilbert and Marshall Islands campaign into the Marshalls as part of the Pacific campaign of World War II, employing the hard-learned lessons of the Battle of Tarawa in the Gilberts. The Marshalls campaign began with a successful twin assault on 31 January on the main islands of Kwajalein Atoll, landing on Kwajalein in the south and Roi-Namur in the north. The brief but fierce battles to take control of the atoll lasted until 3 February 1944, with the 4th Marine Division securing Roi-Namur and the army's 7th Infantry Division taking Kwajalein.

Code-named Operation Flintlock, the original plan was to be a cautious series of attacks in the eastern islets of the largest coral atoll in the world, as measured by the area of enclosed water. The ring of ninety-seven islets, comprising a total land area of 1,560 acres, surrounding

324 square miles of water, was one of the largest lagoons in the world, located 2,100 nautical miles southwest of Hawaii.

American plans and preparations for the Marshalls had included decrypted intelligence intercepts that provided extensive knowledge of Japanese troop locations and defensive strength on the islands—permitting the use of army air force airpower (B-24s, B-25s, P-39s, P-40s, and A-24 dive-bombers, after the capture of Tarawa) and a U.S. carrier-based strike on the Japanese airfield on Roi-Namur on 29 January. The carrier strike destroyed 92 of the 110 Japanese planes in the Marshalls.

Japanese defenders on the islands targeted for landings numbered about 8,100 total on the two largest islands, and they were underprepared for the American thrust at the heart of the Marshall Islands. Nevertheless, the two garrisons resisted fiercely, as had become typical of the Japanese soldiers and naval infantry defending against the island-hopping campaigns in the Pacific. Against the two American divisions numbering about 42,000 total, they lost 7,870 killed, with only 105 captured, plus 125 Korean laborers captured, while Americans suffered 372 killed and 1,592 wounded. On the linked islands of Roi-Namur, the Japanese garrison left only 51 survivors of the original 3,500 manning its defenses.

It was necessary to take one other island in the eastern Marshalls on 31 January, Majuro, which could be used as an advanced air and naval base as well as to safeguard supply lines to Kwajalein. Very lightly defended, only the V Amphibious Corps Marine Reconnaissance Company and the 2nd Battalion, 106th Infantry, 7th Infantry Division, were employed to seize the island, without any U.S. casualties.

Seven weeks later, Cece Conner would board LST 20 on 19 March, bound for Tarawa Atoll in the Gilbert Islands. Instead, LST 20 changed destinations en route, and Cece arrived and disembarked on Kwajalein Atoll on 25 March.

When he arrived, after the capture of Kwajalein, the airfield the Japanese had constructed as part of a major port was undergoing repair and expansion, and the army air force was preparing to move the headquarters of 7th Air Force from Nanumea, a move completed in April 1944. The renamed Buchholz Army Airfield began receiving the B-24 Liberator-equipped 11th Bombardment Group from Tarawa, and the 30th Bombardment Group from Abemama to Buchholz in the beginning of April. Along with the heavy bomber groups, the army air force reassigned the F-5 (P-38 Lightning)-equipped 28th Photographic Reconnaissance Squadron to Kwajalein, where they reported directly to 7th Air Force, after flying long-range photographic missions over the Marshalls. The USAAF combat units remained until fall 1944, when they began moving forward again, into the Marianas, and were assigned to airfields on Guam and Saipan.

Cece's change of his 25 March destination to Kwajalein occurred because the 4th Marine Base Defense Aircraft Wing headquarters forward echelon, based on Tarawa after that bitter campaign was over, relocated to Kwajalein in February 1944 and one month later, in mid-March, moved to Majuro Island, approximately 190 nautical miles southeast of Kwajalein. Cece moved to Majuro to rejoin the headquarters soon after he arrived on Kwajalein.

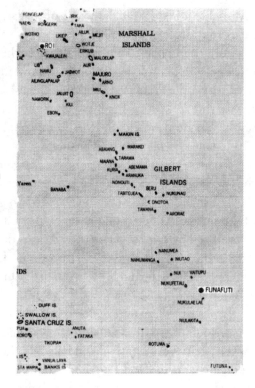

Map depicting relative locations of Funafuti, Tarawa (Betio), Majuro, and Roi-Namur Islands. VMF-224, online. (*Source*: USMC)

First given a defense mission in the Samoan area and designated to support the central Pacific Force (Task Force 51), the 4th Wing had additionally been given the designation Ellice Defense and Utility Group (Task Group 57.4). With the move from Tarawa to Kwajalein came a new mission: conduct offensive operations in the central Pacific against bypassed Japanese islands in the Gilberts, Marshalls, and Marianas with Marine Air Groups 13, 22, and 31. MAG 31 moved to Roi-Namur, north of Kwajalein approximately fifty miles, with 4th Wing headquarters and MAG 13 on Majuro Island.

As soon as the V Amphibious Corps Marine Reconnaissance Company and the army's 2nd Battalion of the 106th Infantry Regiment captured the island on 31 January 1944, during the Battle of Kwajalein, the 100th Naval Construction Battalion began improving the airfield, creating a coral-surfaced 5,800 × 445 foot runway covering most of Delap Island. The field was in limited operation by mid-March, and a month later the airfield, taxiway, aprons, housing, shops, and piers were fully operational. The navy's Seabees added roads and causeways linking Delap to the adjacent islands.

The navy subsequently established the carrier replacement plane pool at Majuro and built a new 4,000 × 175 foot runway on Uliga Island and a two-lane causeway connecting Uliga and Delap. Adjacent to the main runway, an 800 × 150 foot apron was cleared and paved to facilitate transport operations. Following the mid-March move of the 4th Wing headquarters and MAG 13, units stationed on Majuro included VF-39, operating F6F

Douglas Dauntless SBDs of VMSB-231 on Majuro in 1944. (*Source*: WOL)

Hellcats; VMF-155 and VMF-224, operating 4FU Corsairs; and VMSB-231, operating Douglas Dauntless SBDs.

From Bairiki (Mullinix) Airfield, Tarawa, came B-25 Mitchells of the 41st Bombardment Group, staging through Majuro for bombing raids on Maloelap, Wotje, Mili Atoll, and Jaluit during March and April 1944.

Though marine air units were relegated, at first, to conducting air strikes and air operations in areas where Japanese forces had been bypassed, the change of mission, from defensive to offensive, would prove to be significant, as the capabilities, adaptability, performance, and stature of marine air wings continued to increase, albeit slowly—and they would eventually be used more and more in direct support of ground units, beginning first by supporting army troops in the Philippines ground campaigns in October 1944 after fighter pilots like Joe Foss and Pappy Boyington were so successful in flying damaging missions against the heavily defended but bypassed Japanese base at Rabaul on the eastern tip of the island of New Britain—now the eastern province of the country of Papua New Guinea.

On 13 June 1944, the bombardment of Saipan in the Mariana Islands began the campaign to take the islands, which were to provide the air bases and open up the Japanese home islands to increasingly punishing raids by the Americans' newest heavy bomber, the B-29 Superfortress. The assault on Saipan surprised the Japanese. Marine aviation historian Robert Sherrod's opening comments about the Marianas campaign lays out important facts about the progress of marine air support operations in the Pacific as he described the campaign's beginning:

> *By June the Allies were strong enough to stage two amphibious landings half a world apart—Normandy one week, Saipan the next—each of which dwarfed all previous operations in either theater.*
>
> *There was, of course, but little similarity between Eisenhower's Overlord and Nimitz's Forager (as the capture of the Marianas was called). The one eventually involved 2,000,000 troops, the latter only 165,672. Whereas the European landing was only a jump across the English Channel, the Pacific operation was an extension of the front line over 1,000 miles—all the way from Eniwetok to Saipan, Tinian and Guam. No better illustration of the essential differences between the European and Pacific wars can be found.*
>
> *For Forager Admiral Spruance as commander of the 5th Fleet had more than 800 ships—93 of them in Mitscher's Fast Carrier Task Force, 535 in Kelly Turner's Joint Expeditionary Force. Mitscher had 15 fast carriers as the heart of his force which was "prepared for an aggressive, hard-hitting battle if the Japanese did venture eastward," although prevailing opinion had it that the Japanese would not fight for the Marianas. Turner had 11 escort carriers for offshore operations (air support, antisubmarine patrol). Lieut. General Holland M. Smith's Expeditionary Troops included the 2d, 3d, 4th Marine Divisions, 1st Provisional Marine Brigade, the Army's 27th and 77th Infantry Divisions.*
>
> *Amphibious warfare had come a long way since Turner and Vandergrift ventured toward Guadalcanal 22 months earlier with 82 ships.*
>
> *Total shore-based aircraft assigned for the Marianas operation: 879 planes (Marines 352, Army 269, Navy 258). Of the Marines' planes 172 were day fighters, 36 night fighters, 72 dive-bombers, 36 torpedo bombers, and 36 transports.*
>
> *Despite these impressive figures—which included the backstops in the Marshalls and Gilberts—shore-based air played a relatively minor role in the Marianas assault. This was particularly true at Guam, the island most distant from enemy bases, which CinCPac assigned to the Marine flyers.*

The Allied invasion fleet embarking the expeditionary forces left Pearl Harbor on 5 June 1944, the day before Operation Overlord was launched. The Battle of Saipan lasted from 15 June to 9 July 1944, and as relative strengths and casualties indicated, the move northward toward the Japanese homeland was becoming increasingly difficult and more costly. The American forces numbered 71,000, and they suffered 3,426 killed and 10,364 wounded. The Japanese defenders numbered 31,000, and they again fought to the death, with 24,000 killed, 5,000 suicides, and 921 prisoners. Additionally, 22,000 civilians died, mostly suicides.

On 7 July, the Japanese had nowhere to retreat, and their commander, General Yoshitsugu Saito, had laid plans for a final banzai charge. Regarding the fate of the remaining civilians on the island, Saito said, "There is no longer any distinction between civilians and troops. It would be better for them to join in the attack with bamboo spears than be captured." The attack began at dawn, with a group of twelve men carrying a great red flag in the lead, the remaining able-bodied troops—about three thousand men—charging forward in the final attack. Behind them came the wounded, with bandaged heads and crutches, barely armed.

Americans on the front lines found themselves overrun, with the enemy surging through them, battling both army and marine units. The 105th Infantry's 1st and 2nd Battalions were almost destroyed, suffering 650 killed and wounded. Fortunately, the fierce resistance of these two battalions, the Headquarters Company of the 105th Infantry and supply elements of the 3rd Battalion, 10th Marine Artillery Regiment, resulted in more than 4,300 Japanese killed. For their actions during the fifteen-hour battle, three men of the 105th Infantry were awarded the Medal of Honor—posthumously. In this largest Japanese, ground-based suicide attack of the Pacific war, numerous others fought until they were overwhelmed.

At 1615 hours on 9 July, Admiral Turner announced that Saipan was officially secured. Saito and two other Japanese commanders committed suicide in a cave, as separately did Vice Admiral Chuichi Nagumo, the naval commander who led the Japanese carriers at Pearl Harbor and Midway—who was assigned to direct the Japanese naval air force based on the island. As his reward, the Japanese posthumously promoted Nagumo to admiral.

During the battle for the island, between 22 and 24 June, seventy-three P-47s of the army air force's 318th Fighter Group were catapulted from escort carriers (CVEs), a new experience for these particular pilots. During the latter stages of the Saipan battle and during the subsequent Tinian invasion, they helped navy planes furnish close support for the troops.

As for marine aviation during the battle for Saipan, historian Robert Sherrod explained that VMO-2 (marine observation squadron) and VMO-4 flew high-winged "grasshopper" monoplanes as artillery spotters for the 2nd and 4th Marine Divisions. For the first time the grasshoppers flew off carriers (on D+2). They landed on Yellow Beach or on the dirt strip at Charan-Kona and moved to As Lito when that field had been taken by the army's 27th Division. VMO-4 had one pilot killed when he crash-landed after being hit by enemy fire, and an air raid on 26 June killed three enlisted men and wounded three officers and six enlisted men of the squadron (another pilot was killed over Tinian in July). VMO-2 flew 243 missions and VMO-4 400 missions during the Saipan battle.

Air Warning Squadron 5 also operated with the ground troops on Saipan, according to Robert Sherrod, one detachment serving with the corps troops, the other two with the marine divisions. One officer and an enlisted man were killed while serving with the 4th Marine Division. Sherrod went on to say that, although Admiral Nimitz had two squadrons of well-trained marine night fighters available in the Marshalls, he elected to send a flight of army P-61 Black Widows to Saipan. Between 15 June and 7 July, approximately 150 Japanese raiders struck the island, the night fighters shot down eight, and antiaircraft fire brought down seven more. After the battle ended, twelve marine night fighters of VMF (N)-532 flew in from carriers on 12 July to augment the P-61s, but by the time of the intensified Japanese attacks on the B-29s based there, the marines and their F4Us had been withdrawn to Guam and in September returned to the States.

While the battle for Saipan was in progress, a decisive major naval battle began on 19 June, the last of five carrier-versus-carrier battles of World War II—the Battle of the Philippine Sea. In the deadly two-day encounter, the Japanese suffered another disastrous defeat. Admiral Soemu Toyoda, commander in chief of the Japanese navy, saw an opportunity to attack U.S. Navy forces around Saipan. On 15 June, the day Americans landed on Saipan, he gave the order to attack.

Arrayed against one another were, for the Americans, 7 fleet carriers and 8 light fleet carriers, 7 battleships, 8 heavy cruisers, 13 light cruisers, 58 destroyers, 28 submarines, and 956 carrier aircraft, and with the Japanese, 5 fleet carriers, 4 light carriers, 5 battleships, 13 heavy cruisers, 6 light cruisers, 27 destroyers, 24 submarines, 6 oilers, approximately 450 carrier aircraft, and 300 land-based aircraft. The results were clear.

Admiral Marc Mitscher's forces suffered damage to one battleship and the loss of 123 aircraft, while they sunk 3 Japanese fleet carriers and 2 oilers, damaged 6 other ships, and destroyed 550–645 aircraft. American submarines *Cavalla* and *Albacore* sank two of the Japanese carriers, the 30,000-ton *Shokaku*—a Pearl Harbor veteran—and the 31,000-ton *Taiho*.

Among the aircraft the Japanese lost were 366 shot down by American carrier pilots, the biggest single bag in the war. Nicknamed the Great Marianas Turkey Shoot because of the disparity of aircraft losses between the opposing forces, the battle not only eliminated the ability of the Japanese navy to reinforce and sustain the outer ring of what they saw as their new and most important defense perimeter in the Pacific but also laid bare their growing inability to recover from previous losses of experienced aviators in the Coral Sea and Midway battles and the extended Solomon Islands campaign, as well as the surging Allied abilities to overwhelm Japanese forces at sea and in the air. And behind those harsh facts, the outcome foreclosed on the long-held dream that they could engage and defeat the Americans' Pacific Fleet, causing America to weary of the war and let them keep their gains in the south and southwest Pacific.

On 21 July, American forces landed on Guam to begin the second major effort to secure the Mariana Islands. Unknown to Cece Conner, his football teammate, marine Lieutenant Andrew Rogers, who was a platoon leader in the 3rd Marine Division, came ashore on Guam in the mop-up phase of the battle to capture the island, which lasted until 10 August.

On 24 July, the 2nd and 4th Marine Divisions landed on Tinian and, once ashore with a force of thirty thousand, secured the island on 1 August, suffering 328 killed and 1,571 wounded. The Japanese, with a garrison composed of 4,700 soldiers and 4,110 marines, lost 8,010 killed and 313 captured. In this battle, F4U Corsairs dropped napalm for the first time in the war. Again, the Japanese ended the battle for Tinian with a last-ditch suicide charge on 31 July, while the Americans secured the airfield from which the B-29 *Enola Gay* would drop the first atomic bomb on Japan, at Hiroshima, on 6 August 1945—

and the second B-29, *Bockscar*, would unleash the second on Nagasaki three days later, to bring the war to an end.

In spite of the Allied successes in the Gilbert, Marshall, and Mariana Island campaigns, another year of fighting lay ahead in the Pacific. But MAG 21, scheduled to operate off the airfield, faced more troubles and frustration. The much-delayed invasion of Guam, which had created a great deal of waiting aboard ships and boredom for both marine aviation men and the expeditionary force intended to land on Guam, finally began on 21 July, but Orote Peninsula and the airfield had to be reasonably secured before the airfield could be rebuilt. Not until 4 August did marine aviation finally return to Guam after thirteen years' absence.

First in were the F6F night fighters of VMF (N)-534, followed by the flight echelons of VMF 216, 217, and 225, all having flown off the escort carrier (CVE) *Santee*. On 11 August, two squadrons of torpedo bombers, VMTB-131 and 242, departed Espiritu and flew to Funafuti, then to Tarawa, Kwajalein, and Engebi. From the latter base, 131 flew to Guam to rejoin the rest of the squadron, and 242 flew to its new base on Tinian. Both squadrons were assigned to antisubmarine patrol. MAG 21, now an outsized group, had grown to twelve squadrons by mid-November, with a total personnel count of 529 officers and 3,778 enlisted men with 204 aircraft—and had seen extensive action at Pearl Harbor, Midway, and the Solomon Islands, but would see only one more enemy plane the rest of the war.

Yet, finally, on 14 November, the 4th Marine Base Defense Aircraft Wing, still in the central Pacific and flying missions against bypassed Japanese forces, was redesignated the 4th Marine Air Wing. Though marine aviation had been "left in the lukewarm" in the early campaigns, as historian Robert Sherrod put it, CVEs—escort carriers—were being built, to which marine aviation would be assigned in the months ahead and finally fulfill their goal of providing close support of marine troops on the ground. On the island of Iwo Jima, Cece Conner's football teammates Buddy Reynolds and Andrew Rogers would witness firsthand the maturity and effectiveness of what the men of the 4th Marine Air Wing and others had so long worked toward—a fact of history, which a young marine corporal, along with thousands more, had helped build and contributed to during the bloody island-hopping campaigns of the Pacific war.

When Corporal Cece Conner departed from Majuro Island on the SS *Coast Shipper* on 14 December 1944, arriving in San Francisco and debarking on 4 January 1945, the invasion of Iwo Jima was forty-six days in the future, and he was en route to the 9th Marine Aircraft Wing at Marine Corps Air Station (MCAS), Cherry Point, North Carolina. The 9th's mission was to organize, equip, train, and prepare East Coast units for combat. The wing was responsible for all marine auxiliary and outlying air facilities in the Cherry Point area. Cece Conner was assigned to the 9th Headquarters Squadron at Cherry Point on 18 January, and then to the 81st Headquarters Squadron of Marine Operations Training Group 81 on 8 March, where he remained, assisting in training in the mission the corps prescribed.

On 19 December 1945, he was honorably discharged. His records revealed he was authorized to wear the battle stars on the Asiatic-Pacific Ribbon for the Gilbert Islands campaign, 13 November 1943–8 December 1943; the Marshall Islands campaign, 26 November

Cece Conner with his sister, Leah, c. 1945–1946. (*Source:* LCC)

1943–2 March 1944; and the Mariana Islands campaign, 10 June 1944–27 August 1944, for his duty performance in supporting marine air actions. The statement authorizing his wearing of the three battle stars was signed by Major Alan G. Bralower, USMCR.

On returning from World War II and his subsequent discharge, he first returned home, then reentered Willamette University in September 1946 and graduated in May 1951 with a degree in physical education. He obtained employment in the federal civilian workforce in Chemawa, Oregon, serving as an administrative officer in the Bureau of Indian Affairs. He and his wife, Virginia, raised a family of twelve children. He retired with forty-one years of federal service in December 1993 and was living in Pendleton, Oregon, when he died at the age of seventy-four, Saturday night, February 21, 1998. His obituary was carried in the *Salem Statesman-Journal* and the *Portland Oregonian*.

His veterans' gravestone is marked as CPL, US MARINE CORPS WORLD WAR II and is in the Olney Cemetery, 865 Tutuilia Creek Road, Pendleton, Oregon, 97801.

MARION EDWARD "BUD" REYNOLDS AND THE BLOODY BATTLE FOR IWO JIMA

Halfback "Buddy" Reynolds was born on 8 December 1916 in LaGrande, Oregon, and in his senior year at Willamette, he was the oldest and—at five feet, seven inches, and 166

Marion Edward "Buddy" Reynolds, halfback and senior on the 1941 Willamette University football team. (*Source*: MOHLAWU)

pounds—one of the smallest players on the team when he traveled with the Bearcats to play the University of Hawaii in the 6 December 1941 Shrine Bowl.

After graduating with a bachelor of arts degree in 1942, he enlisted in the marines and was called to active duty as an enlisted man in the Marine Corps Reserve in Quantico, Virginia, on 24 July 1942. After completing officer training at the marine barracks in Quantico, he accepted his appointment, executed the oath of office, and was commissioned a second lieutenant on 30 December 1942. On that date he joined the 18th Reserve Officers' Class, Marine Corps Services, remaining at Quantico until 11 March 1943, when he was detached (reassigned) to Marine Barracks, Naval Ammunition Depot, Oahu, Hawaii.

On 8 April 1943, he sailed from San Francisco aboard the troop transport *Kenmore* (AP-62), formerly the American President Lines' *President Garfield*, which was launched in Camden, New Jersey, on 23 February 1921 as the *Blue Hen State*. Following the Japanese attack on Pearl Harbor, the ship was transferred to the War Shipping Administration, was acquired by the navy as a troop carrier on 11 April 1942, and was commissioned on 5 August 1942.

After arriving in Honolulu on 16 April 1943, Lieutenant Reynolds joined the 1st Guard Company as a company officer and platoon leader, serving as a mess officer with duties as a member of the Post Council of Administration and Post Exchange Council. He continued serving in the 1st Guard Company until 11 July, when he was reassigned to the 23rd Provisional Company of the Fleet Marine Force on Midway Island with orders to proceed from Honolulu to Midway on the ship SS *Hualalai*. He arrived on 15 July and joined the 23rd Provisional Company to serve as a company officer and battalion police officer. In December

1943, he was promoted to temporary first lieutenant, acknowledging his promotion on 28 December.

During the period July–December, he was reassigned from Midway to Noumea, New Caledonia, northeast of Australia, where the United States was building up bases to protect the sea-lanes between the United States and Australia, and at the same time to gather strength to move northwest toward the Japanese home islands. In Noumea on 27 December, he embarked on the troopship General John Pope, sailing further east-northeast away from Australia toward Hawaii and the United States, arriving at the base depot in American Samoa on 1 January 1944. In American Samoa he awaited transportation aboard LST 24 and embarked on the LST on 10 January, bound for Funafuti Atoll in the Ellice Islands, located several hundred miles northwest of Samoa and due east of the Solomon Islands about the same distance, arriving 21 January.

Funafuti Atoll was originally named Ellice's Island after Edward Ellice, a British politician and merchant, by Captain Arent de Peyster, who sighted the islands in 1819 sailing on the ship *Rebecca*. Ellice owned the cargo on the *Rebecca*. Today the nine Ellice Islands, which were once part of the Gilbert Islands Colony—a British protectorate—on 1 January 1976 became the independent nation of Tuvalu.

Undoubtedly, while on the atoll, Reynolds was receiving and providing training in amphibious operations and remained there performing battalion police and mess officer duties in No. 1 Mess Hall until he left the atoll in May. Coincidentally, fifteen days prior to his arrival on Funafuti, his former Willamette University football teammate Cece Conner disembarked from the Liberty ship *Horace Greeley* and remained on the atoll until he departed on an LST on 19 March for Tarawa Atoll in the Gilbert Islands. As is described in Gilbert Cecil Conner's story above, there is no information available on whether the two former teammates became aware of the other's presence on Funafuti, but it's likely they did meet due to the nature of their respective duties.

Buddy Reynolds returned to Maui in the Territory of Hawaii in May 1944, and on 12 May he joined the Headquarters Company, Headquarters and Services Battalion, Corps Headquarters Troops, as assistant G-2 (Intelligence). Following on 14 June was a unit designation change from 5th Amphibious Corps, Fleet Marine Force, to Fleet Marine Forces, Pacific (in the field). Later that month he was named assistant G-3 (Operations), which meant he was now learning and partly responsible for and involved in planning and training for combat operations.

Continuing in his G-3 training, and with two more unit assignments, finally, on 26 October 1944, he arrived in the Headquarters Company, 2nd Battalion, 25th Marines, 4th Marine Division, on Maui. The division, which had earlier returned from the Marianas campaign (Saipan and Tinian), possessed a long, illustrious history; was reassembling, absorbing replacements after suffering 6,658 battle casualties in the campaign; and was now training for the next operation. Unknown to Lieutenant Buddy Reynolds, two days earlier the V Amphibious Corps operation plan for the marines' forthcoming campaign was received by the division, but for security reasons, only certain key officers were allowed access to the document. Subordinate units were briefed on most of the details of the plan, but the objective was cloaked under the title of "Island X." Buddy Reynolds was now clearly on a path destined for battle in the Pacific—unless the war came to an abrupt end.

The day for departure drew near while the division was undergoing intense training back and forth between Oahu and Maui. As summarized in the division history, a rehearsal for the "X" landing and ship-to-shore maneuvers, based on the division operation plan, was carried out in the Maalaea Bay area during 14–30 November by the three regimental combat teams. For the last two days of the exercise, all units participated in a divisional CPX—a command post exercise involving primarily the use of communications, the command structure, and simulated unit movements. A full dress rehearsal for the coming operation was held at Maalaea Bay during the period 13–18 January. All units returned to Pearl Harbor and Oahu on January 18, and for the next week, one-fourth of the command was granted liberty each day. Medals for heroism in the Marianas campaign were presented to members of the division during this period, while the days at Pearl Harbor and Honolulu went by quickly. All too soon they were over, and the Tractor Group of LSMs (landing ships, medium) and LSTs sailed on 22 January. On 27 January, the transports with the main body of the division also departed. The division history stated, "Officers and men were in top physical condition and well trained. Morale was at a peak. The Fourth Marine Division was ready!"

Buddy Reynolds was with his company on the attack transport *Pickens* (APA-190), commanded by Commander J. V. McElduff, Naval Academy class of 1920. The ship got under way in a convoy on 27 January, and shortly afterward, word was passed that the objective would be the island of Iwo Jima. From the division history:

> All the details of the operation—so closely guarded in the past—were now revealed to everyone. Iwo Jima was located in the Volcano Islands, 660 miles from Tokyo. It was only 625 miles from Saipan, but 3,330 from Pearl Harbor. In addition to its strategic location in the innermost ring of the Japanese homeland's defenses, it was the enemy's main base for interception of American B-29s.

The convoy would eventually grow into an enormous and powerful amphibious force en route to the one small island among the Volcano Islands. En route as planned, the *Pickens* joined Task Unit 53.2.2., Transport Division 44, an eight-ship division among two divisions in Transport Group Baker (Transport Squadron 15), carrying the 4th Marine Division and its attached units.

Briefings continued steadily during the voyage. The first stop was Eniwetok on 5–7 February. From there the division sailed to the Saipan-Tinian area, arriving on 11 February. One more rehearsal for Iwo Jima was conducted off the western shore of Tinian on 13 February, but rough seas impeded the landings. Final staff conferences were held two days later, and on 16 February, the division left for Iwo Jima.

The 4th and 5th Marine Divisions would go ashore at Iwo Jima as part of the V Amphibious Corps, with the 3rd Division afloat in reserve.

There had been several important objectives in taking Iwo Jima, the first piece of Japanese territory, but the primary goal was to provide a staging area for more and heavier attacks on the empire's home islands.

Prior to the 19 February 1945 invasion, the eight-square-mile island suffered the longest, most intensive shelling of any Pacific island during the war. Initial carrier-borne raids began in June 1944. The 7th Air Force, sending army air force B-24 Liberator heavy bombers out of the Marianas, repeatedly raided the island during the same period. The marines requested ten days of pre-invasion naval bombardment. Due to other operational commitments and the prior prolonged air assault, navy planners limited the bombardment to three days.

In the meantime, in the period 16–17 February, far to the north, heavy, extremely effective American carrier-borne strikes on the Japanese homeland in the Tokyo-Nagoya-Kobe area took place to forestall any Japanese effort to attack American forces at Iwo. They were the first carrier-borne strikes on the homeland since the Doolittle Raid in April 1942. Coincidentally, unknown to either man, Willamette football teammate Andy Rogers was on board the carrier *Saratoga* (CV-3) during those raids, and his ship would a few days later join in supporting the Iwo Jima invasion force.

More than 450 ships, carrying a 4th Division (reinforced) strength of 22,486 men among 83,573 Expeditionary Troops in Task Force 56, massed off Iwo as the H-hour bombardment pounded the island. Though it was a fierce three-day naval air and sea bombardment before landings began, weather affected its success, as did heavily fortified Japanese defenses, with a deep, dense network of bunkers with interconnecting tunnels, caves, hidden light, and heavy machine guns and artillery, many recessed behind retractable concrete doors within caves on Mt. Suribachi. The doors permitted defenders to open them sufficient to fire a limited number of rounds and then close them to avoid return, pinpoint artillery fire or fire from ships offshore.

The Japanese commander Lieutenant General Tadamichi Kuribayashi, had designed a defense that broke with Japanese military doctrine. He hoped to inflict massive casualties on American forces so that the United States and its Australian and British allies would reconsider carrying out Operation Downfall, the invasion of the home islands. His plan allowed the landings to proceed seemingly unopposed at first; yet Kuribayashi was carrying out exactly what he intended. The Japanese enemy would hold their fire until the beaches were crowded, then open fire from Mt. Suribachi to the southwest and the high ground above the cliffs on their right flank to the northeast, unleashing enfilading fire with potentially deadly accuracy and devastating results.

It was also a defense in depth, which allowed Kuribayashi to shift his forces quickly through the labyrinth of tunnels, a defense in which once a bunker appeared to be attacking forces to be destroyed, causing them to move on, they would be surprised again when they suddenly took fire when they later walked past the now reoccupied bunker.

Beginning at 0830 hours on 19 February 1945, the assembled assault waves of the 4th and 5th Divisions, which were to land abreast on beaches Green, Red, Yellow, and Blue, crossed the line of departure inbound to the beaches, with the 4th, under command of Major

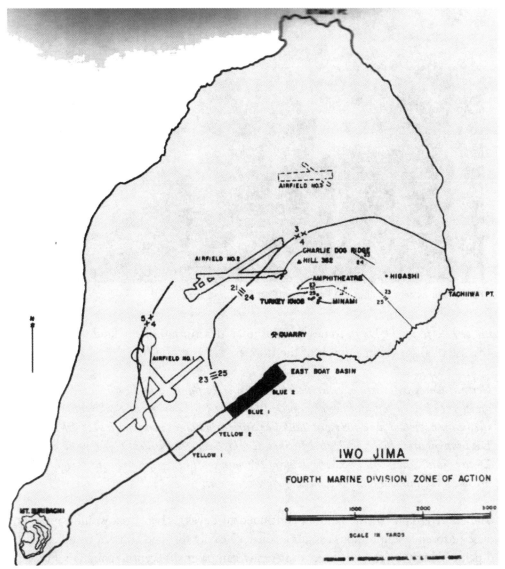

Map of Iwo Jima depicting landing zones of the 4th Marine Division's 23rd and 25th Regiments coming ashore on Yellow and Blue Beaches, respectively. (*Source*: USMC)

General C. B. Cates, moving toward their Yellow and Blue sectors; the 23rd Marines coming ashore on Yellow Beach; and the 25th Marines—Buddy Reynolds's regiment—coming ashore on Blue Beach, with Blue being the far right-flank sector of the four beaches. In Blue 1, adjacent to Yellow, was Battalion Landing Team (BLT) 1, which was the 1st Battalion of the 25rd Regiment, and to their right, BLT 2, the 3rd Battalion of the 25th Regiment, was coming ashore on Blue 2. The first wave arrived on the beach at 0902. The 2nd Battalion, Reynolds's battalion, was in reserve, and with the division's other reserve BLTs, it began arriving at 1233. From yet another history, Joseph H. Alexander's *Closing In: Marines in the*

First landings on Iwo Jima, 19 February 1945. (*Source*: NA)

Seizure of Iwo Jima (D-Day), comes an additional description of the landings on Iwo Jima and the use of airpower in support of the troops:

> *General Cates was already concerned about the right flank. Blue Beach Two lay directly under the observation and fire of suspected Japanese positions in the Rock Quarry, whose steep cliffs overshadowed the right flank like Suribachi dominated the left. The 4th Marine Division figured that the 25th Marines would have the hardest objective to take on D-day. Said Cates, "If I knew the name of the man on the extreme right of the right-hand squad I'd recommend him for a medal before we go in."*

The choreography of the landing continued to develop. Iwo Jima would represent the pinnacle of forcible amphibious assault against a heavily fortified shore, a complex art mastered painstakingly by the 5th Fleet over many campaigns. Seventh Army Air Force B-24 Liberator bombers flew in from the Marianas to strike the smoking island. Rocket ships moved in to saturate near-shore targets. Then it was time for the fighter and attack squadrons from Mitscher's Task Force 58 to contribute. The navy pilots showed their skills at bombing and strafing, but the troops naturally cheered the most at the appearance of F4U Corsairs flown by Marine Fighter Squadrons 124 and 213 led by Lieutenant Colonel William A. Millington from the fleet carrier *Essex*. Colonel Vernon E. Megee, in his shipboard capacity as air officer for General Smith's Expeditionary Troops staff, had urged Millington to put on a special show for the troops in the assault waves. "Drag your bellies on the beach," he told Millington. The marine fighters made an impressive approach parallel to the island, then virtually did Megee's bidding, streaking low over the beaches, strafing furiously. The geography of the Pacific War since Bougainville had kept many of the ground marines separated from their own air support, which had been operating in areas other than where they had been fighting, most notably the central Pacific. "It was the first time a lot of them had ever seen a marine fighter plane," said Megee. The troops were not disappointed.

The assaulting BLTs received moderate enemy fire and on initially coming ashore found little enemy resistance. But coarse volcanic sand hampered movement of men and equipment as they struggled to move up the 40 percent grade in the deep volcanic sand beaches. Then, as naval gunfire's rolling barrage support subsided to allow the marines to advance, the Japanese emerged from their fortified positions to begin a heavy barrage against the invading force, with fire sweeping up and down the beaches and incoming waves from the left, on Suribachi, and from the enemy's elevated positions above the cliffs on the right. In describing the ferocity of enemy fire, the division historian quoted veterans of the Pacific campaigns: it was "the heaviest enemy mortar and artillery fire yet seen in any operation. Boats were hit; they broached and clogged the beaches. Personnel casualties mounted rapidly. Vehicles ashore found sandy volcanic ash nearly impassible."

Nevertheless, as written in the 4th Division history, "supporting arms and personnel kept coming ashore as rapidly as conditions on the beaches would permit." Following the arrival of the reserve BLTs, two artillery battalions were going ashore by 1500 and were firing missions by 1740 hours. Units of the 24th Regiment, the division reserve, were sent in at 1615 to be attached to the assault regiments. The command posts of Regimental Combat Team (RCT) 23 and RCT 25 were set up by 1700. RCT 24 (minus detached elements) was completely ashore at 1945 and then moved to its assembly area. By nightfall on D-day, all three of the division's rifle regiments (less some support group elements), two battalions of artillery, and some heavy shore party equipment were ashore.

Despite heavy enemy opposition and severe losses—the worst being 50 percent casualties in the 3rd Battalion Landing Team from the 25th Regiment—the 4th Marine Division pushed forward on D-day to take the quarry, a Japanese stronghold adjacent to the high ground overlooking the cliffs, and seized part of Airfield No. 1, the southernmost airfield, while linking up with the 5th Division on their left. By pushing that far inland, they had established a line that would ensure they could hold the beachhead and prepare for the next day's operations. The 5th Marine Division's 28th Marines, to the left of the 4th, with the mission of isolating Mt. Suribachi, had made their near-suicidal dash across the narrowest neck of the island, cutting the island defenses in two. Both tasks were accomplished the same day.

When the assault began anew at 0830 the morning of 20 February, it had been preceded by naval gunfire and local preparation by units of the 14th Marines. Through bitter resistance, the 23rd Marines, reinforced with tanks, fought their way across Airfield No. 1 to complete its capture by 1600 hours, but on the other flank the 25th Marines made little headway. Minefields prevented the use of tanks, terrain made advances difficult, resistance was fanatical, and the 25th necessarily had to keep its left flank tied to the 23rd.

The first two days ashore left no doubt that this would be the division's toughest battle. Reported losses were already at 2,011, with the preponderance in the 3rd BLT, on the far right, toward the northeast—under the withering fire from defenders holding the high ground northeast of the quarry and above the cliffs.

But the succeeding five days became increasingly bitter and costly as the 4th slowly wheeled to the right with its right flank anchored on the beach, below the cliffs, and its left tied to 5th Division units. As offensive actions continued and losses mounted, the reserve 2nd BLT, which included Reynolds's Headquarters Company, necessarily became more involved in the fierce fighting.

Those five days spanned the emotional lift of the flag raising on Suribachi, which occurred on D+4, 23 February, a marvelous symbolic gesture of victory which swept through all the units fighting on the island that day, as well as all the forces afloat who witnessed the raising of the national colors. One singular image captured in numerous photographs of six marines raising the flag and published worldwide was to become the model for a sculpted, bronzed Marine Corps Memorial in Washington, DC, an everlasting memory of triumph and glory in Marine Corps history, achieved through courage, heroism, and valor at the incomprehensible expense of the tragic, bloody sacrifice of young men's lives.

One of the six men involved in the flag raising on the volcano's crest was twenty-four-year old Sergeant Mike Strank, considered an "old man" by the men he led and trained, and who would say he knew and trained them not as men but "little boys." While motivating them in training, he didn't use slogans like "Let's go kill some Japs"; instead, he would explain, "You do what I say and I'll get you home to your mothers." James Bradley, the son of John Bradley—one of the flag raisers who was a medic and a battlefield caregiver, and who held probably two hundred of those boys in his arms as they died, crying and screaming in pain—pointed out years later in his best-selling book, *Flags of Our Fathers*, the men who won the Battle of Iwo Jima were seventeen-, eighteen-, and nineteen-year-olds. And those who survived the battle's horrors returned home not wanting to talk with anyone, including their family and friends, of what they had witnessed. They didn't consider themselves heroes. The heroes were those who didn't come home.

And Buddy Reynolds? He undoubtedly felt the same way. The young, married officer and former football player in the 1941 Shrine Bowl in Honolulu, now in Headquarters Company of the 2nd Battalion of the 25th Marines? He was twenty-eight, a "really old man," whose wife, Muriel, had remained in Salem, Oregon, where he had graduated from Willamette when he came ashore on Iwo on 19 February and a few days later volunteered to be an assistant platoon leader and forward observer in a mortar platoon. As a forward observer, he was responsible for moving into positions, often well ahead of frontline assaulting units, where he was often exposed to intense enemy fire and not well supported with protective fire, could observe the platoon's mortar round impacts, and by radio call in corrections in range and azimuth to the weapons' crews.

The following modified excerpt from a 4th Marine Division history, the excerpt beginning seven days later, describes the fierce fighting in the period spanning 1 March, when First Lieutenant Marion Edward "Buddy" Reynolds received a fragment wound to the face and, after treatment from a medic, was immediately returned to duty to continue in the battle. The modification is factual but for the benefit of the reader focuses on Lieutenant Reynolds's 25th Marine's fighting between 26 February and 3 March, when the regiment's 3rd BLT was worn out and depleted by heavy casualties in the fighting.

Starting February 26, the division began working its way into the enemy's main defense line of prepared positions. For the next week it ground slowly forward, suffering bloody losses, and engaged in the most savage type of close combat. The Jap line was based on a series of strong points known as Hill 382, the Amphitheatre, Turkey Knob, and the village of Minami. RCT 23 reached the southwest slopes of the vital Hill 382 on February 26, and was met by a murderous wall of fire. This hill was the key point in the whole Jap defense line, and for days it was the scene of the bitterest kind of fighting, with RCT 23 and then RCT 24 attempting to capture and keep it. Dug-in tanks, deep crevices with long tunnels, and a multitude of camouflaged emplacements took a heavy toll on attacking units.

Often it seemed that the radar station on top would never be taken. "It appeared there were underground passageways leading into the defenses on Hill 382, and when one occupant of a pillbox was killed, another one came up to take his place." Finally, late on March 3, the hill was secured. The anchor of the enemy defense line had been taken by storm, and the success of the division was now assured, but some of the companies which had fought for Hill 382 were nearly wiped out. Over the dead bodies and equipment that littered the battlefield hung the ever-present sulfur fumes.

Left flank elements of the 25th Marines, commanded by Col. John R. Lanigan, and composed primarily of BLT 1/25 units had run into a cliff-line and the Turkey Knob defenses. No amount of shelling, demolitions, flamethrowers, or riflemen seemed to dent the enemy's fanatical resistance in the area. On the right, where the 2nd Battalion was increasingly filling for heavy losses in the 3rd Battalion, the fighting was equally bitter and intense, if not worse.

Time and again advances would be made at the cost of very heavy casualties, only to find that the position reached was untenable at the end of the day, and that a withdrawal was necessary. Every possible solution was tried. A surprise attack was launched without any artillery preparation. Out-flanking and envelopments were attempted. To silence one concrete blockhouse in a commanding position on top of the cliff-line, a 75 mm howitzer was packed up to the front lines, assembled, and put into action. Nothing seemed to succeed.

After days of bloody battering, advances finally were made so that the Jap pocket at Turkey Knob was nearly isolated. RCT 25, however, was worn out, and on 3 March was relieved by the 23rd Marines. The blockhouse on the cliff-top was partially reduced that afternoon. In spite of mined approaches covered by Jap fire, it was attacked by demolition teams and flamethrower tanks. RCT 23 finally succeeded in cutting off Turkey Knob completely, and then mopping up began in the Minami area.

This photograph was taken on 25 February 1945, two days after the iconic flag raising on Mt. Suribachi. Two marines stand next to "Old Glory" and gaze at the rest of the island to the north, where some of the Japanese are still fighting. (*Source*: USMC)

The division had broken the back of the Japanese line, but at a terrible cost. As of 3 March, it had lost 6,591 men killed and wounded. In spite of receiving a draft of replacements, the division's combat efficiency had fallen to 50 percent. By 11 March, the Japanese, fighting to the bitter end, had been reduced to two pockets, one along the northern coastline and the other a small area on the coast near the cliffs. (See the map of the Iwo-Jima landing zones.)

The above summary lays bare the 25th Marines' bitter fighting in a seven-day period on the island of Iwo Jima, one example of one rifle regiment's sacrifices in a seven- to fourteen-day period to participate in taking an eight-square-mile island and bringing a vital base for the air war to within 660 miles of the Japanese homeland. By the time the battle for the island was over, the division had suffered 9,090 casualties, of which 1,731 were killed in action.

Before the division left the island, they were able to witness the 4 March recovery of the first crippled B-29 to land on Iwo, on Airfield No. 1, and others would follow. Also, they witnessed the beginning of the buildup of army air force P-51 squadrons of the 15th Fighter Group on the south airfield, next the 21st Fighter Group on the central field, and finally the 506th Fighter Group on the north field—the 15th's base from which they would provide close support in securing the island in the latter stages of the Iwo campaign and begin long-range escort of massive B-29 formations to their targets in the Japanese home islands.

Lieutenant Buddy Reynolds continued in action against the Japanese until 17 March, when mop-up operations were virtually complete, before he embarked from Iwo with units of the division on 20 March on the attack transport *Lander* (APA-178). When he boarded the ship, where he would resume his duties as battalion mess officer, he was likely unaware that his 1 March actions in attacking the main Japanese line of defense had been noted by senior officers. They would ensure that in the near future he would receive the Purple Heart for the seemingly minor wound to his face, and later the nation's third-highest award for gallantry in action, the Silver Star. The citation for the decoration, signed by Marine Lieutenant General Holland M. Smith, read as follows:

For conspicuous gallantry and intrepidity in action against Japanese forces on IWO JIMA, *VOLCANO ISLANDS, on 1 March, 1945, as assistant platoon leader of a mortar platoon. With the mission of supporting the advance of an infantry battalion, First Lieutenant* REYNOLDS *volunteered to act as forward observer with an assault rifle company and bring mortar fire to bear on an enemy blockhouse in the company's zone of action. He approached the blockhouse under scattered enemy fire to a point well in front of friendly troops and adjusted the fire of the mortars upon the position, his observation post being so close to the position that he was wounded by a fragment from one of the shell bursts. Disregarding his wound he remained at his post adjusting fire until the blockhouse was destroyed, thus materially aiding the advance of the battalion. His courage and conduct throughout were in keeping with the highest traditions of the United States Naval Service.*

The *Lander* sailed on 21 March to return once more to Maui, Hawaii. While en route, news came of the Allies' 1 April invasion of Okinawa, where, unknown to Buddy Reynolds, football teammate Ted Ogdahl had landed with 6th Marine Division's, Company E, 2nd Battalion, 22nd Marines, as the Allies were moving ever closer to the Japanese homeland and Operation Olympic, the planned first phase of the homeland's invasion, Operation Downfall.

Still at sea through 4 April, the transport arrived on the 5th, and Reynolds disembarked for a brief three-day stay at Camp Maui, where he received orders to the San Diego area, through Pearl Harbor to San Francisco. He was going home, ideally to stay. He traveled to Pearl Harbor on 10 April, where he waited for transportation until the 16th, then sailed for San Francisco, arriving on 23 April with thirty days' delay en route in Salem, Oregon, and a joyous reunion with his wife, Muriel, plus four days' travel from Salem to Camp Pendleton, Oceanside, California, arriving on 27 May. At Camp Pendleton, he would participate in training marine riflemen who would unquestionably be involved in the invasion of Japan.

A huge influx of returning air, sea, and ground units to the United States from the European theater had begun prior to V-E Day. Some of the veteran European units were being demobilized, while others, such as Irv Miller's 91st Bomb Group, 322nd Squadron, were reconstituting and entering retraining prior to moving west toward Pacific bases. During the same period, the nation continued to mobilize, train, and begin moving additional units filled with veterans and many new recruits for the upcoming final struggle with the Empire of the Rising Sun.

When Buddy Reynolds arrived at Camp Pendleton, he was assigned on 29 May to the Range Company, Headquarters Battalion, as officer in charge Pitts, at the marine training camp's rifle range. He continued supervising training as assistant officer in charge of the rifle range in the period 1–20 June, and finally as officer in charge of the rifle range, 21–30 June. He continued in service on the rifle range through October, while President Truman approved the Operation Downfall plan on 18 June, the first atomic bomb was tested on 16 July in southern New Mexico, and atomic bombs were dropped on Hiroshima and Nagasaki on 6 and 9 August, followed by the Japanese Empire's acceptance of surrender terms on 14 August and its formal surrender ceremony on the battleship *Missouri* on 2 September.

On 3 October, Reynolds was awarded the Purple Heart for "wounds received as a result of enemy action in the Asia-Pacific Area in 1945," while he was still on duty at the rifle range, and he continued to serve there until 7 November when he was given terminal leave, to return home pending release from active on 28 December 1945.

The Marine Corps released him to a general service unit in the 13th Reserve District, which he joined on 7 January 1946.

Now home from World War II, he returned to Salem, where his wife, Muriel, who had traveled with him and the 1941 football team to Honolulu, remained while he was overseas. They lived at 241 North High Street in Salem while he entered law school at Willamette, receiving his law degree in 1947.

Their first two children, son Pete and daughter Mary, were born in 1945 and 1946 while Reynolds was in law school. On 10 March 1948, while in inactive reserve status, he was awarded the Silver Star Medal with permanent citation for "conspicuous gallantry and intrepidity in action against Japanese forces on Iwo Jima, Volcano Islands, on 1 March 1945." On 27 September 1948, he received an appointment as a captain (permanent) in the Marine Corps Reserve, with rank from 19 July 1948. He accepted the appointment and executed the oath of office on 8 October.

In May 1949, the family moved to Astoria, Oregon, where he continued to practice as an attorney-at-law until he became a corporate attorney with Associated Building in Astoria in July 1952. In March 1955, he left Associated Building and again became self-employed as an attorney. While in Astoria, two more daughters were born: Muriel in 1951 and Deborah in 1960.

Their last known address in Astoria was the March 1955 address, 515 4th Street, before they again reported their home address to the Willamette Alumni Association in October 1970: 2209 Santa Rosa, Las Vegas, Nevada. His office address was 323 Las Vegas Boulevard South, Las Vegas, Nevada, 89101, when he died at the age of fifty-five on November 13, 1972, his death reported to the Willamette Alumni Association in March 1973.

CHAPTER EIGHTEEN

From Marine Corps Aviation
and Postwar Education

Two Distinguished Judges

TWICE LEFT BACK: ANOTHER CHAMPION AMONG MILLIONS OF UNSUNG HEROES

JUDGE CLARENCE WALDEN, WITH OUTSIZED NUMERAL 51 ON HIS JERSEY, STANDING IN THE third line next to Assistant Coach Howard Maple in the football team photograph, didn't graduate from Willamette—and didn't make the trip to Hawaii for "the voyage to paradise," or the "return from hell," an experience he referred to in the 1991 team reunion in Hawaii as playing the position on the football team of "left back." As he later explained in a letter, admittedly, his real passion in sports was the game of baseball.

Born on May 4, 1922, in a home on a dairy farm in Proebstel, Washington, he was the seventh of eight children of Norwegian immigrants, August and Caroline Wolden, who were married in Portland, Oregon, on January 28, 1905. The first four of their eight children were born before the family moved to Proebstel, an unincorporated community originally settled by a German family with the same last name. The doctor for each birth in Proebstel would drive from Vancouver ten miles in a Model T Ford to check on everybody and prepare the birth certificate. For reasons never explained or understood, the doctor spelled the Wolden name as "Walden," and Clarence and the three other children born on the dairy farm in Proebstel have carried the name ever since they were born. The post office was in the nearby small town of Orchards, so that was always listed as the place of birth on the certificates.

The grade school he attended was located one mile from home, and he walked to school every day, rain or shine. The school was two rooms with two teachers. The principal was Betty McKenna, whom he described as "a stocky Irish lady who loved baseball and was our coach"—with just enough boys for a team to play in the grade school league in Clark County. She groomed young Clarence to be a pitcher, since, as he said, "I had great control and never hit her during batting practice. She could hit like a boy but not run like a boy."

Betty McKenna's interest in developing his pitching skills unquestionably stimulated his growing interest in the game of baseball; earned him the nickname of "Whizzer" on his Little Mill Plain Union High School team, the Plainsmen, which upset the powerful Ridgefield baseball team in 1940, his senior year, and earned him the *Columbian* newspaper all-star honors as one of three pitchers on the Trico (tri-county) team that year. It was the first year the *Columbian*, with the aid of league coaches of both eastern and western baseball teams, named an all-star baseball team, after the newspaper had similarly selected all-star teams in football and basketball that same school year. Little Mill Plain Union High School was located between Vancouver and Camas, about five miles from the Columbia River.

His graduating class numbered twenty-two students that year. From his winning baseball performance in high school, it was off to Willamette University and another sterling pitching performance under the Bearcat baseball coach, athletic director, and former pitcher at Oregon Agricultural College, Roy Servais "Spec" Keene, who as a young man during World War I had ambitions to play professional baseball.

At Willamette in the spring and fall of 1941, where Clarence Walden played baseball in the spring and returned to play football in the fall, he made clear that his being the "blocking dummy left behind" when the team went to play in the Shrine Bowl football game in Hawaii made him angry enough to leave the university.

In 1942, still simmering over his football fate at season's end, he quit school and, on 26 June, enlisted in the navy volunteer reserve, V-5 program—a naval aviation cadet training program. From 13 July to October 1942 he was stationed at Boise, Idaho, in the cadet pilot training program flying Piper Cubs. From 10 October to 9 December, he was in aviation

Second Lieutenant Clarence Walden, USMC aviator, Naval Air Station Corpus Christi, December 1943. (*Source*: CWC)

cadet pre-flight school at St. Mary's College, where he played football on the junior varsity team. Then on to Pasco, Washington, from 30 December to 30 March 1943 for primary training in the bi-wing Stearman aircraft called "Yellow Perils" by naval aviators in World War II.

He took his intermediate training at Corpus Christi, Texas, from 4 April to 4 August 1943, where he received his commission as a second lieutenant in the Marine Corps. His final training was in twin-engine PBYs. He was then assigned to VMD-254 (Marine Photographic Squadron 254) at Mojave Marine Station, where he trained to fly as a photo pilot in PB4Ys, the navy version of the army air force's B-24 Liberator heavy bomber. The navy's designation for the B-24 was PB4Y-1, but the aircraft VMD-254 were to operate in the Pacific were special, long-range reconnaissance versions (PB4Y-1Ps) with two extra fuel tanks in the forward bomb bays and room for five or six powerful, high-resolution cameras in the aft bomb bays, the cameras electrically driven off the big aircraft's four engines' generators rather than by batteries.

In December 1943, the squadron was ordered to Espiritu Santo, a large island in the New Hebrides Archipelago—today the island nation of Vanuatu—in the South Pacific. Espiritu Santo was an island containing a large and growing staging base for the war in the Pacific theater, while also protecting the security of American, Australian, and New Zealand trade and supply lines. Second Lieutenant Clarence Walden was entering what he remembers as the most exciting time of his life, serving as a marine aviator and copilot on the crew of Major James R. Christensen, one of VMD-254's executive officers in World War II's Pacific theater.

The squadron's mission was little known, unsung, and deliberately underreported, with each sortie difficult, long, and hazardous. High-altitude photoreconnaissance was the primary mission, with each airplane normally carrying a twelve-man crew. The PB4Y-1Ps didn't fly in huge bombing formations as was the case for army air force B-24 Liberators flying in the European theater, where the bombers could provide defensive fire support for one another. Instead, reconnaissance and photo missions flew singly, in pairs, or perhaps in flights of four depending on the length of the mission, the photo target, enemy defenses, and other factors. They flew unarmed except for heavy .50-caliber machine guns to defend against enemy fighters, which included nose, belly, top, and tail turrets mounting twin .50s and right and left waist windows mounting single guns. There were no fighter escorts, and some of their photo missions were over the Japanese-occupied and most heavily defended bases in the entire theater. The most notable examples were the Japanese bases at Rabaul on the island of New Britain in the Solomon Islands, and in this instance, Truk lagoon and atoll at the eastern end of the western Pacific's Caroline Islands. During VMD-254's presence in the Pacific in the 1943–1944 period of the war, these two Japanese bastions unquestionably struck the most dread and highest heart rates in American aviators and crews assigned missions against them.

In the year Clarence Walden spent in the Pacific, most of his flights were squadron missions conducting squadron business out of Espiritu Santo, as a copilot for his squadron executive officer, who was also his aircraft commander, business such as supply, resupply, and unit and personnel movement as the squadron sometimes moved forward from Espiritu Santo to Guadalcanal and Bougainville in the Solomon Islands, and finally to the small island of Emirau, which the marines occupied unopposed in March 1944.

As to Clarence Walden's approximately five hundred hours of flying in the Pacific war, twelve missions were over enemy-held islands, and the longest was ten hours in duration. But there was far more to his story and the reasons for lifelong exciting thoughts and memories of his World War II experiences. For example, there was the photo mission over Truk—from which he was, again, "left back." But this time he wasn't angry that he was left behind when VMD-254's squadron commander, Lieutenant Colonel Edwin P. Pennebaker Jr., decided, because of Clarence Walden's inexperience, to pull him off the mission before it departed from Espiritu Santo and replace him with Captain Donald K. Kennedy, who would be Major James R. Christenson's copilot. Lieutenant Walden, like nearly all in his squadron, knew the mission would be dangerous.

After the flight crews left Espiritu Santo, Walden did Christensen's laundry, folded it neatly, and put it away, his way of saying good-bye. But Clarence Walden, the young lieutenant who would one day be a judge in an American city's court, soon learned, as did all the men in VMD-254, that their squadron's successful mission over Truk produced an almost immediate, dramatic, and lasting impact on the Pacific war and without a doubt saved thousands of lives on both sides while paving the way for a stunning defeat for the enemy in the western Pacific—and changing the course of the war against the Japanese Empire.

Truk Atoll, a drowned mountain range approximately 125 miles in circumference at the eastern end of the western Pacific's Caroline Islands, is 3,495 miles west of Pearl

A VMD-254 photograph of Marine Captain Don Kennedy's PB4Y-1 over Guadalcanal in 1944. Photograph by a crew member on another VMD-254 aircraft, Captain Don Sanders's plane. (Courtesy of John G. Bishop; original photo: USN)

Map of Truk Atoll. The x's and names in bold mark the location of Japanese ships sunk during Operation Hailstone, Task Force 58's 16–17 February 1944 attack on Truk Atoll. (*Source*: WOL)

Harbor, 565 miles southeast of Guam, and approximately 2,100 miles from both Tokyo and Manila. Truk, similar to Ulithi, is not a single island but a group of volcanic and coral formations surrounded by a coral atoll that encloses a thirty-nine-mile-wide lagoon with several deep-water passages to the ocean—a large and, until February 1944, safe lagoon and perfect fleet anchorage.

The Carolines were among two other island groups, the Gilberts and Marshalls, that were German colonies prior to World War I. Japan, allied with Germany's enemies in "the war to end all wars," took the three island groups from the Germans early in the war, and, as spoils of war, the League of Nations gave control of the three island groups to Japan by mandate. Eventual independence was the league's goal, but the Japanese had other plans. Defying the league, they secretly began to fortify the mandates, as they were soon called, and went to great lengths to keep their work secret. They strictly forbade charting and mapping by outsiders, and no unauthorized aircraft were permitted to fly over the area.

Prior to 4 February 1944, no American forces had ever flown over or photographed Truk. An attempt a year earlier by six Royal Australian Catalina bombers had failed. Happily, because of extremely poor conditions and thunderstorms, the slower, lower-flying Catalinas returned to base, never having seen Truk lagoon. Had they reached their target area, they would likely have all been shot down by a storm of antiaircraft fire and swarming Japanese fighters.

But this time circumstances would be different. Ordered by Vice Admiral Aubrey W. Fitch, U.S. Navy, commander Air Solomons on Guadalcanal, VMD-254's mission was to photograph the Japanese bastion in preparation for strikes by the Pacific Fleet's fast carriers. At the start of this attempt, troubles immediately appeared, and the prospect of failure again loomed.

The mission's plan, described in detail in the article "Photo Mission: Truk," by John G. Bishop Jr. in the January–February 1999 issue of *Naval History* magazine, was to send four aircraft from Espiritu Santo to Guadalcanal, then to the final staging base named Piva on northern Bougainville Island in the Solomons. Heavy rains and a 29 January runway test at Piva revealed that the big, heavily loaded aircraft, with extra fuel and ammunition loads, couldn't attain flying speed on the rain-softened volcanic sand underlying the perforated Marston matting runway. Lieutenant Colonel Pennebaker decided to try the new strip on the small island of Stirling in the Treasury Islands, recently cleared by New Zealanders. He was to lead three other aircraft flown by Major Christensen, Captain Edward J. Sanders, and Captain James Q. Yawn.

On 1 February, Pennebaker led the flight from Guadalcanal to Stirling, the planes carrying spare parts and a few mechanics that had to work long and hard to have the aircraft ready for the mission. Truk was slightly more than one thousand nautical miles distant, and pilots wanted every gallon of fuel they could carry. Before the first attempt early the morning of 2 February, a front moved in and heavy rain was falling. Pennebaker's airplane was grounded for a fuel leak before takeoff. The other three airplanes were scheduled for takeoff at 0300 hours, with Major Christensen the mission commander. Describing the preflight briefing, author John Bishop wrote in his article,

> there was total silence when Pennebaker said: "Anyone who doesn't want to go can stay behind and we'll replace him." Technical Sergeant John Perdue [a radar operator and gunner on Yawn's plane] remembers thinking, ". . . I wouldn't want to live with that the rest of my life!" Shortly before takeoff, the chaplain gave some of the crewmen the last rites.

To further complicate the mission, the Stirling runway ran the length of the island, with the takeoff end at a sheer cliff dropping two hundred feet straight down to the ocean. The heavily loaded aircraft were carrying 3,450 gallons of fuel, a full load of ammunition, and eleven crew members. The estimated gross weight was sixty-five thousand pounds, five thousand more than the recommended maximum takeoff gross weight. The airplanes were so overloaded they dropped out of sight leaving the runway at the cliff as they accelerated to flying speed. On this first attempt, the ground crews lost sight of the aircraft in the heavy rain as they rolled down the strip. Only engine sounds told them the planes were still airborne.

Four hours into the flight, Yawn's plane began losing power on one of the engines. The combination of reduced power and strong headwinds meant fuel might be insufficient to complete the mission, so Christensen decided to turn back. When they recovered at Piva, on Bougainville, Sanders's plane slid off the runway on landing, blew a tire, and went out of commission. With two airplanes remaining, they again departed from Stirling on Friday, 4 February, at 0300 hours. As soon as Christensen's plane disappeared over the cliff, the ground crew ran to the end of the runway to see whether their friends had made it. They were relieved to see the planes climbing away to the north just barely above the waves.

Three hours into the flight, a storm front they had to penetrate separated the two planes, requiring them to proceed independently. Additionally, in penetrating the storm, they had to contend with ice forming on their wings. Fortunately, the severe weather proved a blessing in disguise by screening their approach, and the navigation skills of Second Lieutenants Richard Starnes (Christensen's navigator) and Paul Dean (Yawn's navigator) got both planes to the target.

About two hours out from Truk, the two airplanes' crews were ordered to put on their oxygen masks as the aircraft commanders initiated climbs from the cruising altitude of ten thousand feet to an altitude that would give them the widest field of view possible with their cameras and put the most distance possible between them and Japanese fighters sure to come up and intercept them. Yawn's plane broke out of heavy clouds at twenty-two thousand feet, and crew members immediately sighted the target. He promptly radioed Christensen, who instructed him to circle in the clear so that they could rejoin and proceed to the target together. Unfortunately, neither crew ever spotted the other, and both had to proceed individually.

Christensen was first over the target, running in from the east at twenty-five thousand feet. Antiaircraft guns started firing from ship and shore batteries, but most of the Japanese had been caught napping. His crew counted only twelve bursts of antiaircraft fire, and their plane suffered no damage. The instant the photo run was completed, Christensen dove, turning south toward the front to elude any Japanese fighters. He returned safely to Piva after spending twenty-one minutes over the target. Yawn's experience would be far more exciting, as the enemy, from far below, was scrambling to react to the two large intruders.

What neither aircraft commander or crew was aware of when the guns on Truk opened fire were the eyes, ears, and subsequent actions of Japanese admiral Mineichi Koga of the Combined Fleet, who was strolling across the parade ground with a group of his aides in front of the huge base's headquarters on Moen Island as the ack-ack banged away. He immediately surmised what was in progress and began thinking while ignoring the excited chatter of his aides, who identified the planes as American, probably photoreconnaissance. He strode into his office, closed the door, and, after pausing briefly to think about what he must say and do, abruptly picked up his telephone. He was well aware of Japan's enemies' growing strength, boldness, and approach from the eastern Pacific. Part of the Combined Fleet had already departed Truk en route to the Palaus according to previous plans. The rest was to follow in the next few weeks. But Koga quickly reasoned that there could be no "next few weeks." As James E. Cox wrote in his article "Payback Time at Truk" in *Semper Fi* magazine in the summer of 2004, Koga "had to get his ships out of Truk. Now!"

Captain Yawn approached Truk from the east, starting his run on his planned flight path. Below, what seemed to be the entire Japanese fleet lay at anchor. There were ships of every kind crowding the lagoon. His crew counted two aircraft carriers, four battleships, and eleven cruisers, plus countless destroyers and numerous other types of ships. Hundreds of aircraft lined airstrips. By this time defenses had been alerted, and soon after their first photo run began, Staff Sergeant George Kneitz, in the belly turret, called out a Japanese

Zero below their aircraft. The Zero was shadowing them, making no move to attack—a commonly used Japanese air defense tactic preceding an antiaircraft barrage, in which the Japanese pilot, staying out of range of bomber defenses, was radioing more accurately the estimated target altitude to permit more effective fuse settings, gun elevation, and ranging by crews. Yawn instructed Kneitz to keep a close watch: "If he makes a move toward us, let him have it." The enemy plane disappeared just as the sky lit up with antiaircraft fire.

By the end of the first run, it became apparent to Yawn that the assigned area wasn't covered. He made the decision to turn and make a second run when all on board knew anti-aircraft fire would become more intense—and it did. Japanese gunners had bracketed the large target's altitude, and shells burst above and below their aircraft. They had been over the target thirty minutes when the second run ended. Yawn turned for home and dove to escape. The acceleration and turbulence during the dive was so violent that the buffeting briefly knocked Staff Sergeant Elmer Prokasky unconscious in the tail turret. As Yawn leveled off, Perdue, in the top turret, and Prokasky, conscious again, both reported sighting three Zeroes at five o'clock, slightly high, lining up for an attack on the big aircraft.

Yawn dove and accelerated again until just above the wave tops, a defensive tactic intended to complicate fighter attacks. If the pilot of a rapidly closing fighter from above and behind a wave-skimming aircraft of any type misjudges his closure rate and altitude above sea level, he can overshoot his target and become the victim—colliding with the ocean. The three Zeroes broke off the attack and disappeared.

With fighters and flak behind them, and oxygen discipline relaxed, Yawn added climb power and returned to the cruise altitude of ten thousand feet for the return home. But it wasn't over yet. Sergeant Joe Perry, in the nose turret, spotted a Japanese warship below them. The rest of Yawn's crew confirmed that it was a heavy cruiser steaming south at full speed. Yawn and the cruiser's captain must have seen each other at the same moment, because they both turned away from one another. The cruiser's captain immediately initiated a hard turn to port, undoubtedly believing the big reconnaissance aircraft would attack his ship with bombs. Yawn turned hard right (starboard), each reacting so quickly that neither fired a shot.

According to Yawn, two U.S. submarines and two PBY Catalinas, air-sea rescue aircraft, had been positioned near Truk to provide support in case any of the planes had to ditch—a morale booster for all the mission's crew members. Because the exposed film was so import-ant, intelligence officers had provided crews a code with which to send a radio message informing submarines and Catalinas of the ditching location. Yawn instead wisely used the code to report the cruiser's position, approximate speed, and heading and changed course once again to land on Bougainville.

Yawn's time en route was about two hours more than Christensen's. The mission leader's crew and others had been standing around waiting, some giving up hope of ever seeing their friends again. When the big, liver-colored plane came taxiing up, celebrations were in order, but after the debriefing, most of the crews went looking for some chow and sleep. Yawn's aircraft was a different matter. When mechanics inspected it after the 12.4-hour flight, they decided to change all four engines.

VMD-254's photographic laboratory on Bougainville developed the film immediately and made prints. They were taken to the squadron's mapping section where they were turned into a mosaic map. The section also made a 10 × 12 foot three-dimensional model of Truk based on the mosaic. It was in sections that could be assembled like a giant puzzle, and Commander Roswell Bolstad of the Coast and Geodetic Survey sent the model off to its secret destination.

After the Truk flight, Captain Kennedy, who replaced Lieutenant Walden when he was "left back" at Espiritu Santo, wrote a letter home to his wife, Eloise, on 5 February.

Once on our way, we were happy and as jolly as possible for we knew if this was our last ride we were going down smiling. Then, when we were successful and had gotten away with the "prize package," there was a general uproar. Chris [Major Christensen] and I were jumping up and down in our seats, screaming, singing, shaking hands and beating each other on the back. That was one of the happiest moments of our lives. The day of February 4, 1944, is one which I will always remember.

The Joint Chiefs of Staff in Washington had tentatively planned to commit five divisions against Truk in what would have been a brutal and costly amphibious campaign. But circumstances had changed. Truk had been the Japanese Combined Fleet's "home port" for operations in the south and southwest Pacific and a forward staging base to resupply and support Japanese garrisons on other islands, such as Eniwetok Atoll and Kwajalein, but now Truk had been unmasked by VMD-254. To counter the growing threat to the bastion other nations had labeled the Gibraltar of the Pacific, the Combined Fleet's Admiral Koga had already made his decision on learning of the squadron's high-altitude reconnaissance aircraft overhead and ordered his remaining major combatants to Palau in the northern Carolines—unfortunately for the Empire, the admiral, and his fleet, rendering the remaining forces assigned to the atoll even more vulnerable.

As soon as the Pacific Command in Pearl Harbor examined VMD-254's maps, Admiral Nimitz initiated Operation Hailstone, the attack on Truk. During the period 31 January–3 February, just prior to the squadron's launch to photograph Truk, two marine divisions landed and seized Kwajalein in the Marshall Islands, preparatory to an attack on Eniwetok.

In the meantime, four VMD-254 flight crews were scheduled for another Carolines photographic mission over the island of Ponape, 437 miles southeast of Truk, halfway between the lagoon and the attacking U.S. 5th Fleet. Christensen, this time with his normally assigned copilot, Lieutenant Clarence Walden, and the remaining three aircraft, commanded by Yawn, Kennedy, and Captain Sheffield Phelps, flew to Stirling. Yawn's crew flew the mission on 7 February but this time went alone. The entire mission went smoothly, and after landing at Bougainville, they settled down for a few days of rest. In the interim, within days after the Truk mission, a naval intelligence officer came looking for the crews at their Bougainville camp near Empress Augusta Bay, bringing a cold case of beer and a message: "Thanks for the cruiser."

On 16–17 February, just before Eniwetok was invaded on the 18th, Task Force 58, commanded by Vice Admiral Marc Mitscher—with 5 fleet aircraft carriers: *Enterprise* (CV-6), *Yorktown* (CV-10), *Essex* (CV-9), *Intrepid* (CV-11), and *Bunker Hill* (CV-17); 4 light carriers, *Belleau Wood* (CVL-24), *Cabot* (CVL-28), *Monterey* (CVL-26), and *Cowpens* (CVL-25); 7 battleships; 45 other warships; 10 submarines; and 587 airplanes—delivered a shattering blow from which Truk never recovered. The Japanese lost 3 cruisers, 4 destroyers, 3 auxiliary cruisers, 2 submarine tenders, 3 smaller warships, and 32 merchant ships—many of them said to be loaded with Japanese troops, most of which didn't survive—and 270 aircraft. Several of the Japanese ships were sunk by submarines or ships sealing off deepwater exits from the lagoon. The Americans lost forty killed and twenty-five aircraft, with crews from sixteen of those aircraft picked up by submarines or other navy ships.

It was the largest single day's loss for the Japanese during the war and foreclosed any opportunity for Japanese forces on Truk to support Eniwetok defenders. Three days later, Admiral Nimitz called the raid "a partial payback for Pearl Harbor." In a ceremony on Guadalcanal, on 18 April 1944, the second anniversary of the Doolittle Raid on Tokyo, and the day Task Force 58 was virtually destroying enemy forces on Truk, Lieutenant Colonel Pennebaker awarded Major Christensen and Captain Yawn the Distinguished Flying Cross, and each member of their crews was awarded an Air Medal.

The Japanese relocated about one hundred of their remaining aircraft from Rabaul to Truk. American carrier forces attacked again 29–30 April 1944 and destroyed most of them. The U.S. aircraft dropped ninety-two bombs over a twenty-nine-minute period to take out the Japanese planes. The April strikes found no shipping in Truk lagoon and were the last major attacks on Truk during the war.

Truk was bypassed and isolated by Allied (primarily U.S.) forces as they continued their advance toward Japan by invading other Pacific islands such as Guam, Saipan, Palau, Iwo Jima, and Okinawa. Cut off, the Japanese forces on Truk and other central Pacific islands ran low on food and faced starvation before Japan, on 14 August 1945, signaled their intent to surrender.

In December 1944, VMD-254 was transferred to the marine base in Kinston, North Carolina, for training in the Grumman F6F Hellcat fighter planes, preparing to be reassigned to carrier duty as photo pilots, while the Pacific war ground on inexorably toward a planned invasion of the Japanese homeland following the bloody Iwo Jima and Okinawa campaigns in the period 18 February–22 June 1945. The invasion plan, named Operation Downfall, approved by President Harry S. Truman on 18 June, with the first phase, Operation Olympic, originally scheduled for about 1 October but then pushed back one month, was fortunately interrupted by the dropping of atomic bombs on Hiroshima and Nagasaki on 6 and 9 August. The Japanese surrender, signed in Tokyo Bay on 2 September aboard the battleship *Missouri* (BB-83), formally ended the war. On 3 December 1945, Lieutenant Clarence Walden was relieved from active duty at Cherry Point, North Carolina.

On 1 April 2000, during a life of service of a far different kind, he wrote a letter to a friend he had known in high school, summarizing his World War II service. In the next to last paragraph, he wrote:

Medals awarded me were: American Campaign Medal, Asiatic-Pacific Campaign Medal with 1 bronze star, and the World War Victory Medal. As you can see I was no hero. War may be hell, but for me military duty was the most exciting experience of my life!

There was another brief Post-It note with the letter to his longtime good friend, and copied to this author—the nicknames he had been given over the years. The first was "Pee Wee" from grade through high school. The second was "Bill," given him by a former Willamette University football teammate and golfing buddy, Wally Olson. But the one given him by his wife while he was flying the F6F Hellcat at Kinston, a top-line navy fighter at the end of World War II, was "Buzz," the nickname that stuck with him, and of which he remains most proud. Her maiden name was Arlee Louise Steere, and they married on July 20, 1945, in Kinston, Lenoir County, North Carolina, with all his officer friends invited, just twenty-five days before the Japanese announced they would surrender. To this day, he is known by his close friends and associates as Buzz.

On returning from World War II, he enrolled in Oregon State University and graduated in 1950 with a bachelor of science degree. He later entered the McGeorge School of Law at the University of the Pacific, earning his law degree in 1965, and subsequently served as an attorney in California. Some years later, on being contacted by the Willamette Alumni Association in a survey, he asked to be associated with the Willamette class of 1945.

His oldest of three surviving children is Stephen Alan, born in 1945; next is Eric John, born in 1949; and the third is Lynn Ann (Walden) Davidson, who lives with her family in Woodland, not far from her father. Born on October 2, 1963, her initials, L. A. W., help describe both the judge and her loving family relationship to her father.

On July 31, 1982, he retired as a judge in the Yolo County Municipal Court, Department 2, Woodland, California. Though Woodland is a rapidly growing town fifteen miles northwest of Sacramento, it is now within the greater metropolitan area of Sacramento. Judge Walden remains actively employed at the age of ninety-two and until a few years ago was performing wedding ceremonies as one of two retired judges who call themselves the "Traveling Officiants." His happiness in his work was sadly interrupted by the loss of his wife, Arlee Louise, on February 6, 1986. But he has not slowed down.

The marriage ceremonies have continued, and he counts more than 2,500 to his credit since his appointment to the bench in January 1, 1960. He is justifiably proud of solemnizing that number of marriages between a man and a woman over a fifty-one-year period. His first ceremony was solemnized in the courtroom on March 4, 1960. In 2012, he officiated twenty-six marriages, and in 2013 he did thirteen, believing he would "continue to preside as Judge of the Court of Love as long as I'm 'presentable.'" Halfway through 2014 he officiated three weddings, the last being on June 21 in the Woodland Hotel in front of more than one hundred guests. Clearly, his work has been a mission of love and great joy, but in 2014 he said it was "time to hang up the old robe."

Judge Clarence Walden, though he saw himself as the blocking dummy "left back" when the Willamette Bearcats' traveling squad went to the Territory of Hawaii and played a

Judge Clarence Walden (retired) continues to take great pride and joy in his reputation as the "Marrying Judge." (*Source*: CWC)

football game against the University of Hawaii one day before the Japanese attack on Pearl Harbor, was inducted with all his teammates into the Willamette University Hall of Fame on September 13, 1997, including three others seen in the team photograph who didn't make the traveling squad. And though he didn't see himself as a hero, and was again "left back" on Espiritu Santo, he was indeed a hero, one of millions of unsung American heroes who were champions of the finest kind in life and victorious against the totalitarians who stalked the earth in the most destructive war in history.

JUDGE JAMES MARTIN FITZGERALD, A MAN DEEPLY AFFECTED BY HIS PEARL HARBOR EXPERIENCES

Third from the right end of the first row in the Bearcats' 1941 football team photograph is James Martin Fitzgerald, who at the end of his long, distinguished career would be known as the Honorable James M. Fitzgerald, a 1940 graduate of Jefferson High School in Portland, Oregon, former prewar member of the Oregon National Guard, 1940–1941, and a decorated marine radioman/ventral gunner flying as a crew member on a navy TBF torpedo bomber in the South Pacific during World War II.

James Fitzgerald, known by his close friends and 1941 Bearcat teammates throughout his life as Fitz, was born in Portland, Oregon, on October 7, 1920. During 1941 spring football practice at the University of Oregon, where he had a football scholarship, he was approached by Willamette University's head football coach Spec Keene. Keene was well known as a formidable coach and athletic director, and an outstanding salesman on behalf of any athletic endeavor he served. He promised Fitz a starting position on the Bearcats and a once-in-a-lifetime chance to sail to Hawaii. Already a member of the Army of the United States (National Guard) and an excellent athlete, Fitz became part of Spec Keene's dream of football glory in the Shrine Bowl against the Rainbow Warriors from the University of Hawaii, with the opportunity for further football games with the Rainbows on a home-and-home basis.

Like his Willamette teammates, Fitz suspected nothing of what he would face in the excitement of a dream come true before the team's fateful November 27 departure from San Francisco on the Matson Line's "Great White Ship," *Lurline*. Known by his teammates as the strong, rather silent type, he proved to be sharply observant and analytical when war came so abruptly and brutally to the island of Oahu that Sunday morning of December 7, 1941.

Yet within him there also dwelled a deep compassion that he voiced frequently the rest of his life, a compassion that came pouring out when he was confronted with the reality of the terrible wounds and ghastly burns inflicted on the Pearl Harbor survivors he struggled to assist on the *President Coolidge*'s voyage home beginning December 19 of that year. Assigned to support the 30 burn victims among the 125 total wounded on board the *Coolidge*, over time it became clear that they had marked him with painful memories. He gave voice to the victims, his painful memories, and continued to do so in the long, disastrous national nightmare that followed.

There can be little question that those memories were unremitting, deep, and abiding influences in his life. He spoke of those memories in almost hushed reverence in interviews seen on film after World War II, and unquestionably he carried them into the Marine Corps Reserve following his service in the National Guard when he reenlisted as a private in America's armed forces at the marine recruiting station in his hometown of Portland, Oregon, on 22 July 1942. He was beginning nearly four and a half years of service in marine aviation, service that went fifteen months past the Japanese Empire's surrender in Tokyo Bay in early September 1945—and nearly became a military career for him.

When he reenlisted in the armed forces in July, he had left civilian employment with the city of Portland fire department that same month, where he served as a fireman. On his enlistment application he stated that he had worked as a hoseman, who understood the use of ladders, hose, and first-aid equipment.

He entered recruit basic training at the recruit training depot, 8th Recruit Battalion, Class 3 b, Marine Corps Base San Diego, California, on 24 July, completed the course on 16 September, and was transferred to Aircraft Engineering Squadron 24, Air Base Group 2, at Naval Air Station San Diego on 10 October. From there he was assigned to the Marine Barracks School Detachment at Navy Training Base Great Lakes, Illinois, where he arrived on 13 October and entered sixteen weeks of Torpedoman School.

He was promoted to corporal on 8 February before completing the course on 15 February 1943. From Great Lakes he returned to San Diego and this time rejoined Aircraft

Engineering Squadron 21 at Naval Air Station San Diego, arriving 19 February. On 8 March, he was transferred to Engineering Squadron 38, Air Base Group 7, then to Aircraft Engineering Squadron 23, Air Base Group 2, on 20 March, one day following his promotion to sergeant. On the same date he joined Air Regulating Squadron 2 and would, after transferring for additional unit training with Marine Scout Bombing Squadron 232 (VMSB-232), Marine Air Group 23, be on his way to the southwest Pacific.

VMSB-232, having been equipped with Douglas Dauntless Dive-Bombers (SBD-5 models) flying combat missions out of Henderson Field (code name "Cactus") in the Solomon Island campaigns, had returned to MCAS El Toro in October 1942 to be reequipped with Grumman torpedo bombers, the TBF Avenger, and TBMs, virtually the same aircraft, but manufactured by General Motors. VMSB-232, Marine Air Group 23, was redesignated VMTB-232, Marine Air Group 11, after Fitz joined them at El Toro Marines and while the squadron was preparing for their overseas move into the southwest Pacific.

He left the continental United States with his squadron on 4 July 1943, on board the Dutch-built ship SS *Japara*, commissioned in Rotterdam, Holland, in 1939. Originally built to carry only twelve passengers, seized by the U.S. Coast Guard under the Ship Requisition Act of 6 June 1941 while in port in the United States, the *Japara* had been converted to a troopship earlier in 1943 to carry 1,600 men. The ship was sailing as part of a convoy escorted by navy combatants. Fitz and the men of VMTB-232 were bound for Turtle Bay Airfield on the island of Espiritu Santo in the New Hebrides, the squadron's first assigned overseas base. After conducting additional training for combat operations for a relatively brief period, the squadron moved to Munda Airfield on the island of New Georgia, north of Guadalcanal in the Solomon Island chain, in order to support Allied forces during the Bougainville landings in November 1943.

For the next few months, both VMTB-232 and 233 participated in strikes against the heavily defended but now isolated Japanese garrison at Rabaul, on the eastern tip of New Britain Island. On 20 December 1943, Fitz was transferred to VMTB-233. While still serving as a marine ordnance specialist supporting VMTB-232 flying operations, he continued to plan and harbor other ambitions—a determination to get into the fight as an Avenger crew member.

While performing duties in the squadron, he began working part time in the Seabees alongside a friend. The two began showing up and participating in squadron gunnery practices. Both squadrons had been taking heavy losses and badly needed skilled gunners on their aircraft, and he and his friend were eventually transferred into crew member positions, with Fitz transferring into VMTB-233, where he began flying familiarization and training missions as a crew member, initially a ventral gunner, and from there, in the months and years ahead, expanding his capabilities to become a radio/ventral gunner on the big, single-engine torpedo bomber.

Many years later, when he introduced his wife, Karin, to the term "ventral gunner," she didn't know what it meant. She had heard him describe the cramped space in which he worked in the belly of the TBF, aiming and firing the gun from the ventral position, a posi-

The Grumman TBF Avengers' lead aircraft provides a clear view of dorsal gunner position with the .30-caliber machine gun visible directly below the forward edge of the star insignia on the side of the aircraft. (*Source*: USN)

tion just forward of and underneath the airplane's tail. Karin finally got her chance to see what he had been describing in his wartime experiences when he took her to the Tillamook Air Museum in Oregon. When he enlisted in the marines, he was listed as five feet, eight inches tall, and she was stunned by the narrow confines that closed around him when he was flying in the TBF or TBM. All his missions were obviously dangerous; nevertheless, as soon as his squadron arrived on Espiritu Santo, where he observed the aircrews and planes in extensive practice and training for combat, was when he began thinking and planning—and probably scheming—to become an enlisted crew member on the big torpedo bombers.

Karin would describe the ventral gunner's space as resembling a coffin, and for good reason. It was a fact that to enter the space from inside the aircraft, the crew member had to remove his parachute—not a comforting thought when entering combat with its possibility of a sudden emergency—a parachute he might have to struggle to reach and put on. The gun was a single, swivel-mounted .30-caliber machine gun to protect the big, slow aircraft and its three-man crew (including him) from attack by Japanese fighters from below and to the rear.

He also described for her the startling effects of seeing bombs released from the bomb bay abruptly flash past and just below his gun position, falling away toward the target. Later, as he became more proficient in operating the radio on bombing runs and not under fighter attack, he sat on a folding bench facing forward to operate the radio.

The airplane, clearly designated a torpedo bomber, was less well known as a bomber, with a bomb bay that could deliver a torpedo, high-explosive bombs, or mines, and it carried forward-firing machine guns, permitting strafing attacks, plus flexible gun positions for aircraft defense. The large bomb bay allowed for one Bliss-Leavitt Mark 13 torpedo, 13 feet, 5 inches long, and 22.5 inches in diameter; a single two-thousand-pound bomb; or up to four five-hundred-pound bombs. Worse, there was only one set of controls on the aircraft and no access to the pilot's position from the rest of the plane.

Later in the war, at pilots' requests, the single .50-caliber nose gun was removed in favor of two wing-mounted .50-caliber guns to give more forward-firing power for defense and strafing. With a surface ceiling of thirty thousand feet and a range of one thousand miles, it was better than any previous American torpedo bomber. In spite of all its capability, it was the vision of an aircraft to remember but not to love.

Fitz's flight log in the South Pacific told his training and combat mission story, a story he would have to extract from his World War II records and have certified years later, in 1996, to receive decorations he had more than well deserved for years.

In January 1944, he flew his first eleven missions, with a total of 21.8 hours flying time, all in the TBF. Every single mission he flew with the same pilot and one other crew member, beginning in January all the way through March, a clear indication that the Marine Corps, like the navy and army air force, worked hard to establish and maintain aircrew integrity, and thus in-flight teamwork, efficiency under pressure, and overall combat crew effectiveness. Each mission in January provided some form of training for the new crew, with no combat target assigned that first month. However, Fitz's first mission on 13 January, with pilot Voyles and fellow crew member, Gilbert, was to participate in a search for a lost army air force DC-3 transport. His flight log didn't indicate whether the search was successful, a common practice in flight log entries unless the crew received specific feedback regarding confirmed search results.

Each log entry was a spreadsheet type of entry, in columns, with the month written in longhand at the top the page and "Date" specified down the left column. Next, in columns, were "Type of Machine"—each of the eleven flights was in the TBF; "Number of Machine," being a five-digit serial number; "Duration of Flight," in number of hours to one decimal place; "Character of Flight," with letter symbols to indicate the type of mission; the "Pilot," where the pilot's last name only was entered; and "Passengers." The TBF carried a crew of three men, thus in the passenger column was first listed the third crew member's last name only, with "self" in the same column. Finally, in the far right column, were "Remarks," where he could enter further explanations about each mission. There were twenty lines for flight log entries on each page of the log.

It's important to note that his logs imply a single aircraft striking each target, but that wasn't the case at all. Most combat missions that he and his pilots and fellow-crew members flew were multiaircraft strikes against the target he briefly described. The reader can be assured the TBFs and TBMs, with some exceptions, had fighter escorts on the great majority of their daylight strike missions, although he never mentions that fact.

In February, Fitz flew eleven more missions, totaling 29.4 hours, six in the TBM. His first, on 3 February 1944, was a 3.3-hour combat mission, a strike on Tobera Airfield, one in a complex of airfields defending the powerful Japanese bastion of Rabaul. On 11 February, his 3.1-hour mission was a strike on shipping in Karavia Harbor, Karavia Bay, New Britain, approximately nine miles south of Rabaul. On 12 February, his 3.1-hour mission was a strike on Lukunai Airfield, again close to Rabaul. To provide background and perspective on his first three combat missions and on some of Fitz's future missions, the following is a history of the fierce fighting involving major force commitments above, around, and on Rabaul beginning in February 1942.

Rabaul was one of two major ports in the Australian territory of New Guinea. Captured by the Japanese in February 1942, it was known as the "Pearl Harbor of the South Pacific." In early 1943 the harbor was well defended by 367 antiaircraft guns and five airfields. Two of those airfields, the Lakunai and Vunakanau Airfields, were prewar Australian strips. Rapopo, fourteen miles to the southeast, had become operational in December 1942 and included concrete runways and extensive support and maintenance facilities. In August 1943, the Japanese completed Tobera, another strip with concrete runways. The four fields had 166 protected revetments for bombers and 265 for fighters, with additional unprotected dispersal parking areas. The fifth airfield protecting Rabaul, Borpop, was completed in December 1942 and was across St. George's Channel on the island of New Ireland, approximately halfway north up the length of New Ireland toward the heavily defended base at Kavieng—at the north end of the island.

The Japanese carefully coordinated Rabaul's army and naval antiaircraft defenses, though the army operated 192 of the 367 antiaircraft guns and the navy 175. The naval guns defended Simpson Harbor, its shipping, and the three airfields of Tobera, Lakunai, and Vunakanau. The army units protected Rapopo Airfield and army installations and assisted the navy in defending Simpson Harbor. Extending defensive coverage was an effective early-warning radar system, reaching out ninety miles from Rabaul and extending further with additional radars on New Britain, New Ireland, and the Buka Islands. These three sets provided thirty to sixty minutes' early warning of an attack.

Beginning 12 October and extending through mid-November 1943, the Allies began a series of coordinated, heavy, and sustained land-based air and carrier-based raids against airfields and the harbor at Rabaul as part of Operation Cartwheel, a strategy intended to bypass the heavily defended base of Rabaul while at the same time defending the invasion of Bougainville against potentially damaging Japanese naval force attacks at night. Units of the U.S. 5th Air Force, the Royal Australian Air Force, and the Royal New Zealand Air Force, directed by the Allied air commander in the southwest Pacific area, General George Kenney, participated in the campaign. After the first raid of 349 aircraft, bad weather had blunted bombing, which resulted in a single raid by fifty Mitchell B-25 medium bombers on 18 October. Strikes resumed on 23 October, this time extending six days, and culminated in a large raid on 2 November.

While the heavy attacks on Rabaul were in progress, on 1 November, Admiral William F. Halsey's invasion force of fourteen thousand marines came ashore at Empress Augusta Bay, halfway up the west coast of Bougainville, beginning a campaign that would eventually involve 126,000 Allied troops from the United States, Australia, New Zealand, and the colony of Fiji, along with 728 aircraft—and last until the end of the war.

An undated close-up view of Simpson Harbor, Rabaul, New Britain. (*Source*: WOL)

In the 2 November raid, six squadrons of army air force P-38 Lightning fighters escorted nine squadrons of B-25s, totaling seventy-two bombers attacking antiaircraft defenses and Simpson Harbor with minimum-altitude strafing and bombing. Eight B-25s were shot down by antiaircraft guns or Japanese naval fighters, or crashed attempting to return to base. Among the lost crew members was Major Raymond H. Wilkins, in the 3rd (B-25) Attack Group, posthumously awarded the Medal of Honor for his leadership. The

Ninetieth Bombardment Squadron (M) during the 2 November 1943 attack on Simpson Harbor. (*Source*: USAAF)

Aircraft of the USAAF attacking Japanese ships in Simpson Harbor, 2 November 1943. The Japanese cruiser *Haguro* is in the foreground. Nine squadrons of B-25 medium bombers (seventy-two aircraft) and six squadrons of P-38 fighters (eighty aircraft) participated. Eight B-25s and nine P-38s were shot down during the raid or crashed attempting to return to base. (*Source*: USAAF)

eighty escorting P-38s lost nine aircraft, a measure of the fierce and effective Japanese air defense system at Rabaul.

While the raids were in progress, the Japanese navy, which had been conserving its forces for the past year, committed seven heavy cruisers, along with one light cruiser and four destroyers, from Truk Atoll to refuel in Simpson Harbor, intending to launch a night attack on the invasion force and its supporting ships in Empress Augusta Bay. Admiral William F. "Bull" Halsey, commander of the 5th Fleet and well known as a fiercely aggressive naval commander, knew of the Japanese navy's move toward the landing at Bougainville and their night-fighting capability and was deeply concerned because he hadn't the naval forces available to counter the Japanese heavy cruisers other than the carriers *Saratoga* and *Princeton*, and the destroyer screen with the transports. As a result, the admiral elected to risk his carriers in an early-morning attack on Simpson Harbor by the ninety-seven aircraft available on the carriers.

The reputation of Rabaul was well known among all the Allied army, navy, and marine aviators, who considered it a hornet's nest. Admiral Halsey later said the threat the Japanese cruisers at Rabaul posed to his landings at Bougainville was "the most desperate emergency that confronted me in my entire term as Commander, South Pacific." He confronted the emergency largely because significant naval units in his fleet had been detached to support the invasion of Tarawa in the Gilbert Islands, which was scheduled for 20 November.

Given the serious threat to the Bougainville landing, Halsey sent the two carriers under the command of Rear Admiral Frederick Sherman steaming north through the night until in range of Rabaul, then launched the daybreak raid on the base. Air-tasking orders to Allied air force units on Barakoma Airfield on recently captured Vella Lavella Island sent aircraft out to intercept the surface task group and provided some measure of air cover, while at Rabaul the carrier aircraft, approaching behind the cover of a weather front, drove home their attack. Launched from the carriers with Halsey's guidance that aircrews concentrate on damage to as many ships as possible rather than sinking a small number, the raid proved a huge success. One hour later, a follow-up raid by twenty-seven army air force B-24 Liberator heavy bombers of the 5th Air Force, escorted by fifty-eight P-38s, increased the damage caused by the carrier aircraft.

As a result of the raids, six of the cruisers were damaged, four heavily; three destroyers were lightly damaged; and most of the Japanese warships returned to Truk, ending the serious threat to the Bougainville landing. Aircraft losses in the raids were light.

An additional carrier force, Task Group 50.3, of the U.S. 5th Fleet, reached Halsey's operating area on 7 November. Composed of the carriers *Bunker Hill*, *Essex*, and *Independence*, under the command of Rear Admiral Alfred L. Montgomery, his task group and Sherman's Task Force 38 were ordered by Halsey to launch a double carrier strike against Rabaul on 11 November. One of the cruisers left behind in Simpson Harbor, the *Agano*, was torpedoed and heavily damaged in these attacks. The Japanese launched a series of counterattacks involving 120 aircraft against the U.S. carriers. But Task Force 38 had retired to the south, undetected after their attack. The counterstrike against Montgomery's force was intercepted and lost thirty-five planes, with no damage inflicted on Task Group 50.3.

In spite of the damage administered to the Japanese base at Rabaul in the fall of 1943, as Fitz, now based on Munda Airfield on the island of New Georgia, would soon learn personally, the heavily defended bastion remained a hornet's nest.

On 14 February 1944, the first acid test came for Fitz, a mine-sowing mission at Rabaul's Simpson Harbor, a mission launched from Torokina Airfield on Bougainville involving aircraft from both VMTB-232 and 233. The mission, consisting of twenty-four aircraft, both TBFs and TBMs, was disastrous. They had no fighter escorts. VMTB-232 launched eight aircraft in the first wave at 0030 hours. The second and third waves of eight aircraft each were from the 233rd, airborne at 0200 and 0325 hours, respectively. Approaching their target at night in three widely separated groups of eight, the big, slow, heavy, single-engine planes operating at 160 knots to drop their parachute mines—each weighing 1,600 pounds—presented the enemy the opportunity to come to full alert before, during, and after the first group struck.

The first group of eight over the target reportedly lost one aircraft. The commanding officer tried to radio the follow-on groups to turn back, but he couldn't make radio contact. The spacing between groups, one and a half hours apart, and the lower altitude of the entire strike force was too distant at low altitude to assure good communication. The second group, all TBFs, lost two airplanes. Flying at eight hundred feet over the water, the third group, also TBFs, was immediately found by searchlight and antiaircraft guns, and five aircraft were shot down. Eighteen men and a total of six aircraft from the 233rd were lost during the attack. Four of the eighteen men survived that night, but none of the four survived their captivity. One was murdered at Tunnel Hill; two died of starvation, disease, and medical neglect; and the fourth was murdered by the Japanese navy in April.

Additional tragedy occurred from missing-in-action status for twelve families and loved ones of men from four of the lost aircraft in the 233rd, three of which didn't return and were not observed to have been shot down or to have crashed en route on return or in the target area. Two of the aircraft were observed to have been shot down, one in flames in the center of Blanche Bay, east of Vulcan, and the second north of the northwest end of Lukanai Airfield; the other was observed to go down, but the crew was believed to possibly have survived. They were declared missing and later declared killed in action.

Returning 233rd crews reported laying sixteen mines and having sighted one enemy night fighter at a distance.

Table 2. Casualties in VMTB 232 and 233

		Type A/C	
BOYDEN, James W. USMCR, pilot	1st Lt.	TBF	MIA
PATRICKUS, Arthur J. USMC, radioman	PFC	TBF	MIA
PARDUN, Bernard C. USMCR, turret gunner	PFC	TBF	MIA
SHERMAN, Robert W. USMCR, pilot	1st Lt.	TBF	MIA
CASHMAN, William B. USMC, radioman	PFC	TBF	MIA
GREENE, James W., Jr. USMCR, turret gunner	Sgt.	TBF	MIA
FOWLER, James L. USMCR, pilot	1st Lt.	TBF	KIA*
PUDIL, John J. USMC, radioman	PFC	TBF	KIA
WHITE, Cecil M. USMCR, turret gunner	PFC	TBF	KIA
HATHWAY, Alonzo N. USMCR, pilot	1st Lt.	TBF	MIA
THOMPSON, Willie C. USMCR, radioman	PFC	TBF	MIA
EDWARDS, John J. USMC, turret gunner	Cpl.	TBF	MIA
CORNELIUS, Hugh L. USMC, pilot	1st Lt.	TBF	KIA**
ST. GERMAIN, Edwin D. USMCR, radioman	PFC	TBF	KIA
SLIPKAS, Edward M. USMC, turret gunner	S/Sgt.	TBF	KIA
BARTHOLF, John F., Jr. USMCR, pilot	Capt.	TBF	KIA***
LARGO, Raymond P. USMC, radioman	PFC	TBF	KIA
SULLIVAN, Joseph A., Jr. USMC, turret gunner	S/Sgt.	TBF	KIA

*Pilot and crew initially determined MIA and later declared KIA.
**Aircraft shot down in flames, center of Blanche Bay, east of Vulcan.
***Aircraft shot down north of northwest end of Lukanai Airfield.
All other MIAs subsequently declared KIA by the secretary of the navy one year later.

The stunning losses to VMTB-233 at Simpson Harbor at Rabaul, New Britain, on 14 February 1944 undoubtedly left a deep, sobering, and difficult impression on every member of Fitz's squadron, and especially Fitz, who had flown his first combat mission just eleven days earlier. Such are the combat missions that aircrew members in all services never forget as long as they live—in this instance, 37.5 percent of aircraft and their crews launched to strike.

On 15 February, in a 2.6-hour mission, Fitz flew with pilot Voyles and crew member Gilbert in aircraft number 24463 providing ground support to troops of New Zealand's 3rd Division and American troops fighting in the Battle of Green Islands. The battle to control the group of islands located between Bougainville and New Ireland had begun on 29 January and lasted until 27 February. Once secured, the Green Islands became the forward base for the U.S. South Pacific Combat Air Transport Command (SCAT) that supplied material and mail to combat soldiers and evacuated wounded. The Green Islands also became home for marine fighters and bombers that continued missions aimed at isolating the Japanese bases on Rabaul and Kavieng. The first commander of the SCAT base was naval Lieutenant Richard M. Nixon, who later became president of the United States.

On 17 February, Fitz participated in a vain attempt to strike shipping. Bad weather forced the mission aircraft to return to base. On 21 February, he was in a strike mission against gun emplacements at Lakunai Airfield, near Rabaul, and on 24 and 26 February he flew in strikes on Vunapope, in Rabaul, near the site of a well-known Catholic mission where the Japanese had interned approximately 350 missionaries—fathers, brothers, and sisters of numerous nationalities—who prior to the Japanese invasion and occupation of New Britain were providing religious counsel, services, and nursing care on New Britain, New Ireland, and other islands in the region. By the time VTBF-233 raided Vunapope, the missionaries had been forcibly moved by the Japanese or had surreptitiously removed themselves to safer locations. Eventually, the mission's buildings were completely razed by the relentless aerial assaults on Rabaul, and tragically two nuns were killed during the bombing raids. (The incredible story of the missionaries at Vunapope became the subject of intense study and investigation and, in its release on 14 November 2010, the subject of a well-known ninety-minute Australian television movie, *Sisters of War*.)

On 1 March, Fitz was promoted to staff sergeant, with little time to celebrate, and on 4 March, he was a crew member with his pilot, Voyles, and a substitute crew member, Carlis, on a 3.4-hour mission, bombing antiaircraft positions on Rabaul. Then, on 8 and 10 March, he flew with his normally assigned crew on brief 1.0- and 1.2-hour, successive ground-support missions for Allied troops on Bougainville. The crew was scheduled for a well-earned period of rest and recuperation (R & R), and on their 10 March Bougainville mission they landed their TBF number 47743 at Torokina Airfield on the island—two days after the Japanese shelled the airfield and destroyed a B-24 Liberator bomber and three fighters and damaged nineteen other aircraft. Later that day, they ferried TBF number 25327 to Guadalcanal, a 2.3-hour flight. The next day they flew the same plane 3.8 hours to Espiritu Santo. Fitz had flown five missions for a total of 11.7 hours in March, three of them combat missions, one against Rabaul, to add to seven others against the "hornet's nest" in February.

On 15 March, Fitz was off from "Buttons," the code name for Turtle Bay Airfield on Espiritu Santo, to Australia, flying three hours as a passenger in a SCAT army air force C-47 to La Tontouta—or Noumea Airfield—at Paita, New Caledonia in the New Hebrides, and on 17 March, he took two more hops totaling nine hours from Tontouta to Brisbane and then to Sydney, Australia, where he remained on R & R until 25 March. On his return trip to duty, he was a passenger on two flights in a navy PBM, two and six hours along the reverse course, first to Brisbane, then to Noumea, and from there on another SCAT C-47 to Buttons.

When Fitz returned to Espiritu from R & R, he entered retraining for the entire month of April, extending through 6 May to upgrade his capabilities and be integrated into a new crew—flying seventeen missions for a total of 33.8 hours in April and another 9.3 hours in May, before resuming combat missions. During that period he was transferred into the headquarters squadron of Marine Air Group 11, pending his reassignment and 3 May transfer to VMTB-232 as the squadron was preparing to move back into combat operations from Emirau Airfield on the island of the same name in the province of New Ireland.

Training missions on Espiritu Santo in April included familiarization, glide-bombing, low-level bombing, and antisubmarine bombing, interspersed with two missions searching for a lost army air force Mitchell B-25 medium bomber on 23 April, and three missions to the New Hebrides' Efate Island on 7, 14, and 18 April, working on unspecified problems and at the same time undoubtedly doing more "on-the-job training" to upgrade his own skills as a radioman/gunner.

Another mission involved an unspecified problem involving SBD dive-bombers, probably units of the two different types of aircraft flying on the same simulated strike mission. The seven missions and 9.3 hours in May, leading up to his resumption of combat missions on 11 May, included six glide-bombing missions and one mission to perfect division tactics. (A division was normally three aircraft.)

He flew the 11 May mission from Emirau Island's Inshore Airfield, a fighter strip and one of two airfields that had been under construction with many other supporting facilities on the island since 11 April. VMTB-232 had begun moving to Emirau from Espiritu Santo on 3 May. Also based on the airstrip were VMF-115 and VMF-211, both marine fighter squadrons flying F4U Corsairs. Famed marine fighter pilot Joe Foss was in VMF-115 the month of May, and the internationally famous pilot Charles Lindbergh flew four combat missions with Joe Foss and VMF-115 from Emirau in May while in the same month flying thirteen combat missions escorting TBFs with an F-4U squadron and strafing assigned ground targets while flying from Nissian Airfield on Green Isle and Emirau.

On 11 May his new pilot, Bradley; fellow crew member, Lockwood; and Fitz were on a bombing and strafing mission against coastal guns at a target named in his log as Namaracla, in which they dropped a two-thousand-pound bomb. On 13 May, they bombed and strafed another target he named as Rataual supply, dropping four five-hundred-pound incendiary bombs. On 18 May, they flew a strike mission against Lukatarange Plantation, dropping eight two-hundred-pound incendiary bombs. They returned to release a two-thousand-pound bomb on Tobero Airfield on Rabaul on 21 May and flew to Green Island Airfield for landing. The same day they returned to Emirau Airfield. On 26 May, they carried four five-hundred-pound bombs on a shipping reconnaissance mission in the area near the heavily defended Japanese base at Kavieng on the northern tip of New Ireland, a base that was also to be bypassed in Operation Cartwheel. His final combat mission was another strike mission against "hospital ridge," in heavily defended Rabaul, with four five-hundred-pound bombs.

Staff Sergeant James Fitzgerald was not home yet, and the war was far from over, but he had just completed his second "return from hell"—after 7 December 1941—when 27 May 1944 ended. He flew 29.0 hours in May for a total of 148.7 hours in the Avengers and battled his way into a hazard-filled crew position while overseas in a combat zone, and he volunteered time and time again to fly combat missions into the teeth of one of the most heavily defended Japanese target areas in the Pacific theater of operations—when not formally trained to be a ventral gunner, radio/gunner, or crew member on a torpedo bomber.

He remained in VTMB-232 on the Emirau Island Airfield, performing duties associated with his ordnance specialty in servicing the squadron, until 26 July 1944, when he was transferred to the Marine Air Group 11 headquarters squadron on Espiritu Santo, preparatory to his return to a new assignment in the continental United States. On 23 June, he received his promotion to technical sergeant. On 8 August, he departed for home, arriving 28 August on board the USS *Pastores* (AF-16), a stores ship, to join the Marine Fleet Air Wing Center in San Diego. Again, on his return, the *Pastores* sailed home in a convoy escorted by navy combatants. He returned from overseas credited with service in Espiritu Santo, New Hebrides; Bougainville, British Solomon Islands; Noumea, New Caledonia; the New Britain–New Ireland Areas; and Rabaul, New Guinea. He would later learn that the commander of VMTB-232 had granted him the authority to wear the Air Crew Insignia with three stars on his uniform.

In San Diego on 11 September, the Marine Corps notified him that he had been selected for a refresher course in aerial gunnery school and would be transferred effective 13 September to Marine Base Defense Air Group 43, Marine Corps Air Station El Centro, California, and was granted a thirty-day furlough en route, with five days of travel to Portland, Oregon, and orders to report for duty at his new station, not later than 0800 hours on 18 October 1944. At MCAS El Centro, he entered an extensive Bombardier and Air Gunners School, which included an additional course and resulted in an extensive increase in his technical capabilities. He scored well in all subjects: radio code; radio procedure; radio material; blinker; aircraft recognition; sighting (approximate speed); 3A2 trainer; .30-caliber browning automatic machine gun, 95; .50-caliber browning automatic machine gun, 98; malfunction range, 95; and air-to-air firing (1,084 rounds, 49 hits), with turret grades as follows: attitude 3.3, firing average 3.4, final turret grade 3.3, final mark 96.90.

His wife, Karin, remembered years later his telling her that when he returned from overseas, the Marine Corps began encouraging him to enter pilot training. Undoubtedly his consistently outstanding performance of duty, in or out of training courses, or in his duties and willingness to take on dramatically increased responsibilities—and profoundly hazardous duties and responsibilities—while continuing to provide excellent results in his work were the precise reasons such encouragement was given, and probably given to him before he left his combat assignment. He was being influenced toward a career beginning with flight training and a commission in the Marine Corps Reserve.

In a letter dated 13 December 1944, he submitted his application for flight training, sending it through medical and command channels to the commandant of the Marine

Corps, after he had previously been given medical examinations and was found to possess "the physical, temperamental, and flight aptitude qualifications for flight training." Records forwarded with his flight training application to the Marine Corps commandant from his commander stated, "Technical Sergeant Fitzgerald possesses to a marked degree officer-like qualities and is mentally, morally, and professionally qualified for commission in the U.S. Marine Corps, in the event of successful completion of the flight training course." The succeeding paragraph additionally stated, "Technical Sergeant Fitzgerald participated in action against the enemy as an aerial gunner at Bougainville, New Britain, New Ireland, and Rabaul. He has been awarded the Combat Aircrew Insignia with three (3) stars for bombing and strafing of enemy fortified ground installations." His commander forwarded the documents recommending approval of his application.

Pending expected approval of his application, which occurred on 5 February 1945, the Marine Corps prepared orders sending him for academic refresher training in the Marine Aviation Detachment, Navy Academic Refresher Unit, part of the navy's V-5 program, at Murray State Teachers College, Murray, Kentucky. He departed El Centro on 18 February with orders to report to the detachment commander not later than 22 February. After successfully completing the academic refresher course, he proceeded to Naval Aviation Pre–Flight School in Athens, Georgia, on 13 June, and then into an additional Pre–Flight School in Iowa City, Iowa, on 27 September 1945, just over three weeks after the signing of the Japanese Empire's surrender on board the battleship *Missouri* in Tokyo Bay.

On 23 November he transferred to the Headquarters Squadron, Marine Aviation Detachment, to begin primary flight training in the navy's Air Technical Training Center, Memphis (Millington), Tennessee, arriving 3 December to enter training. He successfully completed primary pilot training and on 19 April 1946 transferred to the Marine Base, Naval Air Training Base, Corpus Christi, Texas, for basic pilot training, which he successfully completed, and then transferred to the Aviation Detachment, Marine Base, Naval Air Training Base, Pensacola, Florida, on 21 August 1946, where he began work toward winning his marine aviator's wings of gold.

In the meantime, the U.S. government continued and accelerated the nation's demobilization, resulting in drastic reductions in the active-duty armed forces. That fall in 1946, as the character of his service was soon to change, Fitz made the decision to change the course of his life and accept a release from active duty in the Marine Corps. As it happened, on 7 December 1946, he was honorably discharged, five years to the day after, as a young twenty-one-year old Willamette University Bearcat football player, he stood witness on the island of Oahu, Hawaii, to the brutal Japanese attack on Pearl Harbor and was mobilized that day to do more than witness. Now, five years later, he had not only stood witness and participated in making history on Oahu but also completed his own World War II history, while in flight training, fully intending to continue his service to the nation.

When discharged at the age of twenty-six, he was authorized to wear the Good Conduct Medal with First Bar, Asiatic-Pacific Ribbon with three stars, American Theater Ribbon, Victory Medal Ribbon, the Honorable Service Lapel Button, and the Marine Corps Button.

He returned home upon being discharged and in 1947 reentered Willamette University as a student, this time passing up the game of football. On December 4 that year, he wrote a brief letter to the commandant of the Marine Corps requesting a transcript of his records involving his flight training with the corps, explaining that he had learned the university would allow credit toward graduation from some of the flight training courses. In a letter dated December 26, a staff officer in the corps' education section responded with a comprehensive summary of the courses requested and enclosed all his marine training courses and most of his experiences. He added, "It would be appreciated if you would advise us as to the amount of credit you may be awarded on the basis of your military training."

Fitz began his study of law in 1948 while completing his bachelor of arts requirements at the same time. While in Willamette to complete his work toward a law degree, he met Karin, the young lady with whom he fell in love, and they married on January 19, 1950. He graduated from Willamette with an LLB degree in May 1951.

As a lawyer and member of the Oregon Bar in Salem, Fitz obtained a fellowship at the University of Washington, hoping the graduate study would lead to a job in the State Department. Before starting the graduate work at the university, he and Karin decided to spend the summer in Ketchikan, Alaska, both working in the fishing industry. At summer's end, they returned to Seattle on a fishing boat, down the "Inside Passage." Fitz then started his year at the University of Washington.

While in graduate school, he received a job offer as assistant U.S. attorney in Ketchikan, and after completing his year of study, he left ten days after Karin gave birth to their first of four children, son Dennis James, on Father's Day in June 1952. Six weeks later, Karin and the baby joined Fitz in Ketchikan, where they lived from 1952 to 1954, before relocating permanently to Anchorage. Then came their first daughter, Denise Lyn, on New Year's Day, 1957; a second daughter, Debra Jo, also on New Year's Day, 1958; and then son Kevin T. Fitzgerald on March 17, 1960.

After moving to Anchorage, Alaska, where he continued to serve as assistant U.S. attorney from 1952 to 1956, he served as city attorney for the city of Anchorage from 1956 to 1959. When Alaska became a state in 1959, he served as legal counsel to the governor of Alaska and in the same year was appointed as its first commissioner of public safety. From 1959 to 1969, he was judge, Alaska Superior Court, 3rd Judicial District; then he served from 1969 to 1972 as presiding judge, Alaska Superior Court, 3rd Judicial District. From 1972 to 1974, he was an associate justice on the Alaska Supreme Court. On September 20, 1974, President Gerald Ford appointed him a U.S. district court judge for the district of Alaska. He was chief U.S. district court judge from 1984 to 1989. He became a senior U.S. district judge in 1989 and retired in 2006.

While in Anchorage, he contributed to the city and state in numerous community service capacities: Salvation Army advisory board member from 1962 to 1984 and chairman of the board, 1965–1966; Anchorage Parks and Recreation Board member, 1965–1976, and chairman in 1966; Anchorage Hockey Association member, director and president, 1965–1966; U.S. Ski Association director in 1972; Alaska Commission on Judicial Qualification, member and chairman, 1970–1971; and 9th Circuit District Judges Association member and president, 1983–1985.

He was always mindful of the important role Coach Spec Keene played in his life; proud of his awards and citations received from the university, his association with the 1941 Willamette football team, and his induction with the team into the Willamette University Athletic Hall of Fame; and the remainder of his life worked diligently to encourage and support the university and its law instructors' and professors' regular interaction with lawyers and judges in Anchorage, hoping to establish a college of law in Anchorage. He was also proud of his Irish heritage, his father, Thomas Fitzgerald, having been born in Ireland and become a naturalized U.S. citizen before marrying Marcella (Linderman) Fitzgerald.

During the period following the 1941 football team's fifty-year reunion in Hawaii, somehow, perhaps through some contacts at the reunion and recollections, Fitz began thinking of his service in the Marine Corps in World War II, wondering whether his combat missions in the TBF Avenger, which were particularly hazardous, had merited decorations he never received. Maybe he hadn't been recommended, or recommendations might have been forwarded and put aside or lost during the nation's rapid postwar demobilization beginning in 1945.

In 1994, after looking into law and regulatory requirements on marine decorations, he contacted Judge Harry Pregerson, a U.S. circuit judge in the 9th Circuit Court of Appeals in Woodland Hills, California, and asked whether he would inquire with the Marine Corps

Karin and James Fitzgerald at the Willamette Bearcats' 1991 Reunion, where they visited the Punchbowl National Cemetery, in Honolulu. (*Source*: KJC)

on his behalf to learn what might be done, if anything, to determine whether he had been nominated for any decorations, and, if not, whether he was eligible to receive appropriate decorations for his combat missions. Judge Pregerson pursued his query and, on March 8, 1995, after some exchanges by phone and correspondence, mailed Judge Fitzgerald's flight logbook to Colonel Fred Anthony, head of the corps' Military Awards Branch in Marine Corps headquarters in Washington, DC.

The flight log was carefully evaluated, and in a letter to Judge Pregerson dated May 2, 1996, Colonel Anthony stated that Judge Fitzgerald's flight log was certified to contain twenty-one qualifying (combat) missions in the period February 3 to May 27, 1944, and the commandant of the Marine Corps, General Charles C. Krulak, approved the award of three Air Medals. In the same letter, Colonel Anthony indicated that the ruling on the possible award of the Distinguished Flying Cross necessitated a review and determination by the Secretary of the Navy if a waiver of time restrictions prescribed by law for World War II decorations was warranted and to make recommendations to appropriate congressional committees. Colonel Anthony went on to say,

> *Due to the unknown procedures that may be established by the Congress of the United States in determining Judge Fitzgerald's entitlement to the Distinguished Flying Cross, we are unable to predict a completion date at this time. Accordingly, the aforementioned personal decoration, if approved, will be forwarded to you when received by this Headquarters.*

In the meantime, on the preceding April 19, General Kulak sent a memorandum to Secretary of the Navy John Dalton informing him that he had authorized the award of three Air Medals to Judge Fitzgerald, and "if his service had been recognized at that time [during World War II], it is my firm belief that his award [of the Distinguished Flying Cross] would have been approved. Therefore, I strongly recommend approval." He went on to say the citation and certificate for the Distinguished Flying Cross should be issued "for service from 11 to 26 May 1944."

On May 13, 1996, Colonel Anthony sent a letter to the Honorable Floyd Spence, chairman of the Committee on National Security, in which he explained that Judge Fitzgerald had been awarded three Air Medals, but the Secretary of the Navy "does not have the authority to waive the time limitation to award the Distinguished Flying Cross." He then explained,

> *It has been further determined that the award of the Distinguished Flying Cross to Judge Fitzgerald warrants approval on the merits and a waiver by law of the time restriction is recommended.*

Judge Fitzgerald received all four of the decorations he had clearly merited for fifty-two years. The citations accompanying the three Air Medals and the Distinguished Flying Cross read,

The President of the United States takes pleasure in presenting the AIR MEDAL (Gold Stars for the First through Third Awards) to

STAFF SERGEANT JAMES M. FITZGERALD

UNITED STATES MARINE CORPS RESERVE

For services set forth in the following

CITATION:

For meritorious achievement while participating in aerial flight while serving with Marine Scout Bombing Squadron 233 and Marine Torpedo Bombing Squadron 232 from 3 February to 26 May 1944. In the successful completion of these missions, Staff Sergeant Fitzgerald contributed materially to the success of United States efforts. By his superb airmanship, steadfast perseverance, and unselfish devotion to duty in the face of hazardous flying conditions, Staff Sergeant Fitzgerald reflected great credit upon himself and upheld the highest traditions of the Marine Corps and the United States Naval Service.

For the President

Signed: C. C. Kulak

Commandant of the Marine Corps

The President of the United States takes pleasure in presenting the DISTINGUISHED

FLYING CROSS *to*

STAFF SERGEANT JAMES M. FITZGERALD

UNITED STATES MARINE CORPS RESERVE

For service as set forth in the following CITATION:

For extraordinary achievement while participating in aerial flight with Marine Torpedo Bombing Squadron 232 from 11 to 26 May 1944. In the successful completion of these missions, Staff Sergeant Fitzgerald contributed materially to the success of United States efforts. By his undaunted courage, superb airmanship, and unyielding devotion to duty in the face of hazardous flying conditions, Staff Sergeant Fitzgerald reflected great credit upon himself and upheld the highest traditions of the Marine Corps and the United States Naval Service.

For the President,

Signed: C. C. Krulak

Commandant of the Marine Corps

During his final 1989–2006 period of service as a senior U.S. district judge, Fitz, Karin, his secretary, and law clerks necessarily traveled extensively in his performance of duties on appellate courts such as the 9th Circuit Court of Appeals, or in trying single and multi-court cases in such locations as the islands of Guam and Saipan in the great, wide Pacific Ocean, and in states such as Washington, Oregon, Idaho, California, and Arizona. It was travel that brought great joy along with hard work, because they were all able to see places, take tours, and do things they never would have otherwise been able to see and enjoy.

Judge James M. Fitzgerald died on April 3, 2011, while residing in a retirement community in Santa Rosa, California.

CHAPTER NINETEEN

A Marine's Safe Journey in the Pacific and His Teammate, a B-17G Copilot Shot Down over Berlin

A WORLD WAR II PACIFIC ODYSSEY

ANDREW "ANDY" ROGERS, A TACKLE ON THE 1941 BEARCATS TEAM, FOURTH FROM THE left in the back row in the team photograph, survived the Pacific war uninjured, though involved in some difficult and perilous missions in the Marine Corps—on the ground, at sea, and in the air. Like many others in colleges and universities all over the United States, Andy decided to seek entry into an officer candidate school (OCS), a ninety-day course, in one of the armed forces rather than wait to be drafted. OCS recruiters were frequenting the Willamette campus, and, though rejected by two other services, he was accepted on a medical waiver by a marine second lieutenant recruiter who reminded him that officers on Marine Corps stations elsewhere might refuse to abide by the waiver. Andy's World War II story was unforgettable, yet typical of what millions of Americans who quietly went into battle, endured, and survived the war.

When Andy completed Willamette graduation requirements in 1943 and was within a few weeks of his September ceremony, he received his letter ordering him to South Carolina for boot camp. From boot camp it was off to Quantico, Virginia, for OCS, thence to Camp Pendleton, California, where he was greeted with the surprising question, "Hadn't you left yet?" He was sent to a replacement training battalion in San Diego, and from there to another replacement training battalion on Oahu, Hawaii, which sent him to the 4th Marine Division on the island of Maui.

It was from Maui that he was reassigned to the 3rd Marine Division on the island of Guam where the 1944 battle to retake the island was still in progress, having begun with landings on both sides of the Orote Peninsula on the largest Japanese-held island in the Marianas on 21 July and lasting until 10 August. An early, prime objective was to cut off and isolate the airfield, which was more than halfway toward the west end of the peninsula.

Third Marine Division men break from a clearing through thick brush on Guam in pursuit of retreating Japanese. Leading them are General Sherman (medium) tanks. (*Source*: USMC)

By the time Andy arrived as a platoon leader, the Americans' divisions, the 3rd Marines, the army's 77th, and the 1st Provisional Marine Brigade, all landing on the west side of the island, had moved beyond the difficult and bloody battles over the beaches, cliffs, and reefs ringing the island, had turned ninety degrees left, and were in the mop-up phase of operations, moving to the northeast up the narrower part of the island. Nevertheless, the mop-up was not easy.

During the final phase of the campaign to completely clear the island, a decision was made to shoot at anything that moved, and Andy recalled they did. Finally, the 3rd Marines organized into a line of companies across the western half of the island, with their left flank moving up the west coast and their right flank linked up with units of the 77th Division, each rifleman approximately ten yards apart, stretching across the island to the 77th, intending to sweep through the remaining sectors toward Ritidian Point at the northwest end of the island and Pati Point on the northeast end. The plan didn't work well, as the sweep took them through jungle areas. In spite of the obstacles encountered, the island was finally declared secure on 10 August.

To make matters a bit more difficult for Andy, his company commander turned out to be the only commander with whom he ever clashed during the war. The officer was an alumnus of Portland, Oregon's Linfield College, a college the Willamette Bearcats played while Andy was at the university.

Prior to the American landings to retake Guam, the Japanese had based a large force of more than twenty-two thousand defenders on the island, and the Americans committed approximately thirty-six thousand troops against them. Total casualties were high, the Americans suffering 1,747 killed and 6,053 wounded, while the Japanese, fighting to the bitter end with numerous nighttime suicide counterattacks, lost more than 18,040 killed, with only 485 choosing to surrender.

Normally the Marine Corps engaged their men in combat operations about every six months. So it was back to school for Andy, this time having obtained a private pilot license in a government contract operation that paid for forty hours of flying for college credit before he left Willamette, and he volunteered for the marines' air observers training, their mission being, while airborne, to gather and report intelligence for the conduct of ground and naval combat operations. From additional training on Guam, he was to go with the 3rd Marine Division headquarters to take the island of Iwo Jima.

Again he was diverted temporarily, this time to attend aerial gunnery school at the navy base of Oahu's Barbers Point, while the aircraft carriers *Saratoga* (CV-3) and *Ranger* (CV-4) were training in Hawaiian waters for night combat operations. While at marine headquarters on Oahu, he encountered football teammate Second Lieutenant Marion Edward "Buddy" Reynolds, also a marine.

This time, after his training, Andy was redirected through Guam to Ulithi Atoll, an atoll composed of forty islets totaling 1.7 square miles of land area, surrounding a lagoon about twenty-two miles long and up to fifteen miles wide, located in the Caroline Islands, 360 miles southwest of Guam, 850 miles east of the Philippines, and 1,300 miles south of Tokyo.

The large, natural anchorage, with waters eighty to one hundred feet deep, could accommodate more than seven hundred ships and was being developed by the navy as a support base for major combat operations in the Pacific, including the planned invasions of Iwo Jima and Okinawa, and ultimately the home islands of Japan. Andy's new assignment was to the famed pre–World War II aircraft carrier *Saratoga* as a marine air observer and gunner flying in the ball turret of a TBF or TBM Avenger torpedo bomber in night operations, an always dangerous mission. But he was to learn it wasn't easy to find and get aboard the *Saratoga* at Ulithi. When he and one other air observer arrived in front of the Ulithi harbor master to be taken aboard the carrier, they asked, "Where's the carrier *Saratoga*?" His reply was unexpected: "Can you recognize her if you see her?" The response: "Yes." "Then get aboard a boat and keep going until you find her. There are over two thousand ships in this harbor, and I can't tell you where she is." So they went aboard a long boat and began motoring through the huge anchorage until they found her shortly before dark.

Saratoga had arrived at Ulithi on 7 February 1945 and sailed with Andy aboard three days later, accompanying the carrier *Enterprise* (CV-6) to form night-fighter Task Group 58.5/Night Carrier Division 7, with four other carrier task groups. *Saratoga's* air group consisted of fifty-three Hellcats with pilots trained as night fighters and seventeen Avengers, normally operated as torpedo bombers but carrying three-man crews capable of dropping high-explosive bombs, day or night, and defending themselves against fighters with one flexible, turret-mounted .50-caliber machine gun, facing rearward behind the pilot, and one .30-caliber machine gun mounted ventrally (under the tail), which was used to defend against enemy fighters attacking from below and to the rear.

After landing rehearsals with the marines at Tinian on 12 February, the large carrier force carried out diversionary strikes against the Japanese home islands on 16 and 17 February before the landings on Iwo Jima on the 19th. The strikes were massive, and they were the first carrier-based attacks on the home islands since the army air force's sixteen B-25s, led by Lieutenant Colonel Jimmy Doolittle, had launched from the carrier *Hornet* (CV-8), intending to strike Tokyo, on 18 April 1942.

During the ensuing two days beginning 16 February, more than 1,500 carrier-based aircraft, including dive-bombers, and hundreds of Japanese aircraft were in the air while the Americans were striking Tokyo. By the end of the 17th, more than five hundred Japanese planes, both on the ground and in the air, had been lost, and Japan's aircraft works were badly hit. The Americans lost eighty planes. *Saratoga* was assigned to provide fighter cover while the remaining carriers launched the strikes on Japan, but during the raids her fighters attacked two Japanese airfields.

The carrier forces refueled en route on 18 and 19 February, and on 21 February, *Saratoga* was detached with an escort of three destroyers to join the amphibious forces and carry out night patrols over Iwo Jima and night heckler missions over nearby Chichi Jima. As the carrier approached her planned operating area south of Iwo Jima at 1700 hours, six Japanese aircraft on a kamikaze mission, taking advantage of low cloud cover and the carrier's insufficient escort, scored five bomb hits on the carrier in three minutes, and three of the aircraft crashed on the *Saratoga*'s forward deck.

The flight deck forward was wrecked, her starboard side was holed twice, and large fires were started on her hangar deck, while she lost 123 of her crew dead or missing, with 192 wounded—many badly burned—and thirty-six of her aircraft destroyed. Another attack two hours later scored an additional bomb hit, further damaging her flight deck, although the kamikaze's aircraft bounced overboard. The fires were under control by 2015 hours, and the crew was able to recover one F4F Wildcat fighter, which came from another aircraft carrier, flown by a pilot who stubbornly refused to be waved off by the landing signals officer. The *Saratoga* was subsequently ordered to withdraw to Bremerton, Washington, for major repairs, and to Eniwetok Atoll en route, where she could hospitalize her wounded.

Andy Rogers's memories of his time in the Pacific theater were vivid and astoundingly accurate, particularly of the nights and days following his arrival on board *Saratoga* at Ulithi Atoll.

Before the kamikaze attack in the late afternoon of the 21st, one Avenger was scheduled to launch on a night mission, with a second backup in case the first had to abort. If Andy got airborne this day, it would be his first sortie in an Avenger. Standard operating procedure was to have the spare aircraft spotted on deck behind the primary aircraft, ready to launch if the primary had to abort the mission, and, as was often the case, Andy and the other observer flipped a coin to determine who would be in the spare aircraft. Andy won the toss and remained on deck in his plane's topside ball turret facing aft, ready to go, while the other launched. Unaccountably, an escorting destroyer fired on the aircraft that launched but missed, and the aircraft and his fellow observer with whom he had jousted proceeded on

USS *Saratoga* hit by a kamikaze, 21 February 1945. Andy Rogers was in the ball-turret gunner position in an Avenger torpedo bomber, on the aft end of the *Saratoga*, prepared to launch in the spare aircraft, if required, when she was struck on the ship's bow. (*Source*: USN)

their mission. Then, without warning, the first kamikaze seemed to appear out of nowhere and flashed low overhead, from behind Andy's aircraft while he was facing aft in his turret, and struck the forward flight deck, severely damaging the deck and setting fires. Two more kamikazes were on the way.

The Japanese aircraft were coming in deliberately low in the overcast skies, in a shallow descent, aligned with *Saratoga's* flight deck as though landing. Their approach was intended to avoid early recognition and the fierce barrage of the ship's array of antiaircraft guns massed alongside both sides of the flight deck. Had they approached from abeam either the starboard or the port side, the chances of successfully striking their target would have been considerably reduced by fierce defensive fire.

Andy, and undoubtedly the other two Avenger crew members, scrambled from their aircraft and raced for cover on what they considered the safest side of the flight deck, the port (left) side, to take cover in gun positions below flight deck level—still seventy feet above the water—and remained there throughout the attacks, as he remembered events. The *Saratoga* began listing, ultimately to approximately fifteen degrees to starboard. She was taking on water through her punctured hull. Meanwhile, on the forward flight and hangar decks, in spite of the repeated attacks, experienced damage-control officers, sailors, and firefighters battled to avoid catastrophic damage and put out the fires. Unknown to him, the crew was probably also activating pumps and counterflooding the port side to right the ship. Later, as *Saratoga* was departing the area through the support ships, Andy witnessed the recovery of one F4F fighter plane from one of the escort carriers, piloted by a man with whom he later became acquainted.

In the meantime, another tragedy was unfolding that he didn't witness but later learned of. Due to the attacks on the *Saratoga*, the marine air observer with whom he had jousted with a coin toss to man the spare aircraft on her flight deck had to recover with his aircraft and crew on the escort carrier *Bismarck Sea* (CVE-95), a much smaller escort carrier, a class of ship sometimes referred to as "jeep carriers," with a normal complement of twenty-seven planes. She had arrived off Iwo Jima on 16 February to support the amphibious landings and was providing typical missions in support of the invasion of that island, such as observation and spotting planes, photographic flights, combat air patrol over the beaches, antisubmarine patrols, and strike missions in direct support of troops.

The evening of 21 February, after she had recovered her aircraft, and apparently at least the one aircraft from the battered *Saratoga*, the *Bismarck Sea* also came under attack by kamikazes. In spite of heavy defensive gunfire, which downed one bomber, two kamikazes struck her, the first on the starboard side under the first 40 mm gun (aft), crashing through the hangar deck abeam of the after elevator. The crash knocked four torpedoes onto the hangar deck, parted the elevator cables, and damaged the after firefighting main.

The fire was nearly under control when the glow from the burning ship drew a second kamikaze, which also slammed into her just forward of the aft elevator well, exploding on impact. The attack killed or mortally wounded the entire firefighting party and destroyed the firefighting saltwater distribution system, thus preventing any further damage control. The violent explosion buckled bulkheads and collapsed the decks in the ammunition clipping rooms, adding fuel to the fire. The planes on the hangar deck added gasoline to the holocaust. Soon the flames raged out of control, and a variety of ordnance began to explode, so Captain J. L. Pratt shortly ordered the ship abandoned. In less than thirty minutes, all her surviving crew made it into the water. After many explosions and two hours of burning, the ship rolled over and sank.

The *Bismarck Sea* sank with the loss of 318 men. Three destroyers and three destroyer escorts rescued survivors over the next twelve hours, between them saving a total of 605 officers and men from her crew of 923. The destroyer-escort *Edmonds* (DE-406) directed the rescue operations, which resulted in saving 378 of the carrier's crew, including the commanding officer, in spite of darkness, heavy seas, and continuing air attacks. Thirty of the *Edmonds* own crew went over the side to bring the wounded and exhausted carrier men to safety. Andy Rogers was to learn that his fellow observer, who had wagered with a coin toss, had wagered his life. He did not survive the sinking of the *Bismarck Sea*—a difficult memory Andy continued to hold for the rest of his life.

He remained on the *Saratoga* until she arrived at Eniwetok, another major forward American naval base taken from the Japanese in February 1944, where the carrier offloaded her burn cases at the navy hospital. Shortly after arrival at the Eniwetok anchorage, he and the fighter pilot who recovered on the *Saratoga* on the 21st, and whom Andy had befriended because they were both relative strangers among the *Saratoga*'s crew, were playing cribbage to pass the time. The pilot jokingly commented, "If we just keep our mouths shut, we might end up in Bremerton." No such luck.

The ship's secretary, an officer responsible for personnel matters and other duties, soon told them they would have to rejoin their units and assume their regular duties, a not too devoutly wished outcome because it meant a return to Iwo Jima, where the fierce, bloody fighting was still in progress.

The *Saratoga* left for Bremerton, Washington, for repairs and arrived on 16 March, and Andy, unable to go directly back to his unit, went to Saipan by air, where he lined up a flight on a Canadian-built Catalina PB2Y-2 aircraft to Iwo Jima—a destination the pilot clearly wished to avoid. The aircraft was airborne about noon, but the pilot later decided he must reverse course and return to Saipan. His IFF (identification friend or foe) had failed, a relatively new combination transmitter and receiver that transmitted and received signals to identify other aircraft as friendly to avoid being targeted by their own defenses. First available in the American navy in late 1943 following its invention by the British in 1940, the new units, still suffering technical problems, were being installed in American ships, aircraft, and antiaircraft defenses.

On return to Saipan, the PBY flying boat landed on the water, and the pilot taxied toward the concrete ramp, where wheels were attached for towing the aircraft up. As the aircraft was being towed up the ramp, a wheel collapsed and punctured the plane's hull. So much for Andy's PBY flight back to Iwo Jima. Next, he and other air observers he met at the seaplane base, who had been ordered and wanted to go to Iwo Jima, learned of transportation via a destroyer the next morning. But that, too, didn't work out as well as Andy hoped.

As they approached the ship, they saw other marines already on board, lining her rails, and a major among them let the later arrivals know they had been outranked: "No more bunks available." So the accommodating destroyer crew gave them cots to set up. They were two days en route to Iwo Jima on a type of small, heavily armed, feisty naval combatant of less than two thousand tons, infamous in reputation for pitching and rolling, along with speed and the ability to turn rapidly. Andy and the other junior observers learned firsthand that cots were excellent platforms for pitching and rolling—and landing them unceremoniously onto the deck at any time night or day.

There had been several important objectives in taking this first piece of Japanese territory, Iwo Jima, but the primary goal was to provide a staging area for attacks on the empire's home islands. Once again, the Japanese fought to the death, with their garrison of approximately 22,000 suffering 21,844 killed and only 216 taken prisoner. Americans suffered 6,821 killed, 19,217 wounded, and 2 captured but recovered, from among more than 83,000 U.S. Marines, U.S. Navy corpsmen and others, and U.S. Army Air Force airmen and nurses.

By the time Andy arrived on Iwo Jima, the marines had fought their way off the beaches, and 760 of them from the 30,000 that came ashore the first day had actually cut Mt. Suribachi off from the northern part of the island by a near suicidal charge across the island. From that day forward, about forty thousand more Americans came ashore. But progress became an agonizingly slow, bitter, and costly fight as the Americans battled their way north and south through heavily fortified positions, which included a dense network of bunkers, hidden artillery positions, and eleven miles of interconnected underground tunnels. Before the island was finally declared secure on 26 March, the Americans had to capture and make operational the island's three airfields on the northern 80 percent of the island and clear and take Suribachi in the south.

Throughout the early days of the struggle to take the island, navy and marine aircraft, mainly from escort carriers similar to the *Bismarck Sea*, provided close air support for the marines, while naval gunfire and marine artillery such as 37 mm guns pinpointed and attacked the deeply dug in and heavily protected Japanese machine guns, artillery, and fighting positions hidden in caves throughout the island. On 6 March, army air force 15th Fighter Group P-51s began arriving on Field No. 1, the southernmost airfield and the first airfield readied to receive them, to gradually shift the close-support firepower to the army air force units. Later the P-51s would begin very long range escort of B-29s to their targets in the home islands.

When Andy arrived on Iwo Jima, he was able to go by vehicle overland to Field No. 1, where he eventually began flying a total of about twenty observation missions in marine OY-1 light aircraft, normally conducted at altitudes of 750 feet above the ground in support of continuing offensive operations to find and destroy remaining Japanese forces.

Happy warrior Andy Rogers beside his OY-1, "Twin Mags," at No. 1 Airfield on Iwo Jima. (*Source*: ARC)

Andy would learn in those twenty missions that the defenders of Suribachi wouldn't fire at the light aircraft supporting efforts to root out the enemy, because they knew that if they did, they would give away their gun positions and immediately receive incoming naval gunfire and attacks by close-support aircraft. While Andy was on the island, he witnessed the first emergency recovery of a B-29 Superfortress involved in continuing heavy bombing attacks on the Japanese home islands.

As he was leaving Iwo Jima for the last time to return once more to Guam, he passed by the cemetery where he saw what he remembered as approximately 6,500 wooden crosses marking the graves of America's fallen—a sobering sight, he said, of "so many buried marines," a sight he would never forget.

The invasion of Okinawa began five days after Iwo Jima was declared secure, a battle that lasted from 1 April to 22 June and would ultimately be far more costly than Iwo Jima—and result in another stunning encounter with a 1941 football teammate from Willamette University on the far-off Pacific island of Guam. His name? Ted Ogdahl, also a marine, who nearly lost his life on Okinawa.

While Andy and the entire 3rd Marine Division waited and trained on Guam for participation in Operation Downfall, the invasion of the Japanese home islands, a fellow marine lieutenant named Arnold Baker, who was a tent mate of Andy's while serving in division headquarters, told him of a wounded friend in the hospital and suggested that, since entertainment was limited, they take a bottle of liquor and a box of cigars to him. When they arrived to visit the wounded marine, Andy was astonished to see a badly wounded Ted Ogdahl, recovering from a bullet wound in his chest and back while Ted's unit had been attacking Japanese units on Okinawa. Ted had been evacuated from Okinawa's battlefields and had arrived in Guam's Anderson Field via airlift on 17 May, then was transported to the island's Field Hospital No. 103.

There was a phone in Andy and Arnold's tent, and not long after encountering Ted Ogdahl, Andy was surprised and pleased to learn from Arnold Baker that Chuck Furno was soon coming through Guam's Anderson Field in a military air transport aircraft on his way to his first combat assignment in a P-38 squadron in the Philippines. Ted Ogdahl, who had learned that Chuck was on his way from the States through Guam, gave him Baker's phone number and told Chuck that Andy was on the island. Ted wanted to make sure Chuck could visit with Andy too. Arnold had access to a jeep and was able to do what his wounded friend asked him to do so that Chuck Furno could briefly visit with another Bearcat teammate.

The movement of forces from Europe and the continental United States into the Pacific began in earnest following the surrender of Nazi Germany in early May. And while the growth of Allied military power in the Pacific continued, the training of forces already in place for Operation Downfall was beginning in earnest.

On Monday, 18 June 1945, in a meeting with the Joint Chiefs of Staff, President Harry S. Truman approved the plan for Operation Downfall after intense and prolonged agonizing over the expected casualties on both sides—while the huge buildup of an Allied invasion force continued with a massive movement of forces to the western Pacific. But behind the scenes, the development of the atomic bomb was nearing fruition, and President Truman was hoping the invasion could be avoided.

The plan for the first phase, Operation Olympic, envisioned seizing the southern half of Kyushu, holding in place, and then dropping up to nine atomic bombs behind the Japanese defending the beaches and on troop concentrations further inland if the Japanese, under continuing, relentless air and sea attacks, refused to surrender in the period prior to the invasion. On 16 July, at White Sands, not far from the town of Alamogordo, in southern New Mexico, the United States successfully tested its first atomic bomb and, with the president's approval, continued preparations to drop two atomic bombs, both preceded by ultimatums that contained unambiguously dire warnings if the Japanese government failed to accept Allied terms of surrender.

The first fell on Hiroshima from a B-29 Superfortress on 6 August, and after a brief pause, hoping the Japanese would act to avoid the next catastrophic blow, the second atomic bomb fell on Nagasaki on 9 August. Finally, after another agonizing wait, on 14 August word came that World War II was over. The Empire of Japan would surrender. On the island of Oahu, Hawaii, where two football teams had been stranded by the attack of 7 December 1941, a joyous, spontaneous celebration erupted, a celebration that, in fact, would span all the nations of the free world.

Andrew Rogers's Pacific odyssey, along with the journeys of millions more fighting men and women of the Allied nations, was nearing an end. Their lives had been spared the horror their leaders feared awaited them in the Japanese home islands. He and all the men from the 1941 San Jose State College and Willamette University football teams who were still on active duty were going home, a trip that in his case he would have to wait for and would take more time than he hoped.

The formal surrender of Japan was signed on 2 September 1945 on the deck of the battleship *Missouri* (BB-63) in Tokyo Bay, while Operation Magic Carpet, the post–World War II effort by the War Shipping Administration to repatriate more than eight million American military and civilian personnel from the European, Pacific, and China-Burma-India theaters, was already under way. Hundreds of Liberty and Victory ships and troop transports began returning soldiers from Europe in June 1945. Beginning in October 1945, more than 370 navy ships undertook repatriation duties in the Pacific. Warships such as aircraft carriers, battleships, hospital ships, and large numbers of assault transports participated. The European Magic Carpet Operation ended in February 1946, and the Pacific phase continued until September 1946.

Andy's fate? After he and other air observers realized they had accumulated only a small number of points under the Marine Corps' new point system used to determine an order of precedence for repatriation, they became creative, writing up recommendations for Air Medals for one another, hoping that each of five combat missions needed to obtain one Air Medal would add points sufficient to shorten their wait to return home. Their success was questionable, but Andy's wait finally ended when he was taken aboard the second famous World War II aircraft carrier named *Hornet* (CV-12), the namesake of the first *Hornet* (CV-8), which had carried the sixteen Doolittle raiders' B-25s to World War II glory from Naval Air Station Alameda for the 18 April 1942 raid on Tokyo. The first *Hornet* was sunk early the morning of 27 October 1942 in the Battle of Santa Cruz, northwest of the New Hebrides Islands.

The second *Hornet*, out of overhaul on 13 September 1945, immediately departed on the first of five trips she would take as part of Operation Magic Carpet. Andy, wishing to be mustered out of the corps in San Diego, where he would go to work for his brother making wooden crates for produce, didn't make land where he hoped and instead arrived in Bremerton, Washington, where he was asked, "Where do you want to muster out?" His reply remained unchanged, and the corps granted him paid transportation to San Diego, where he began his life anew as a civilian.

Many years later, on April 25, 1997, long after he had retired from a highly successful business career, Andy would learn that a long-serving, now-decommissioned aircraft carrier *Hornet* (CV-12) had been returned to her distinguished namesake's home port at Naval Air Station Alameda, given as a floating museum, where visitors could tour and become acquainted with her, and surviving Doolittle raiders could meet the public and attend reunions.

Andrew Rogers's business career, like his years in the Marine Corps, was clearly an odyssey covering many moves and job changes. From his brother's American box factory in El Centro, California, where he built boxes and then moved inside as a bookkeeper, it was off to Phoenix, where another brother was a foreman in a warehouse. From there he went to Flagstaff and worked at an employment office, while he reestablished and maintained contact with his former business professor at Willamette, who encouraged him to come to the Veterans Administration office in Seattle, which shortly the government closed down. Then it was San Francisco, to the office of the American Box Company, where he was hired in the town of Firebaugh in the San Joaquin Valley. The job paid too little, but the foreman hired him to make boxes with a machine, a job that turned out to be seasonal with the annual produce harvest.

After the season ended, he contacted the American Box Company headquarters in San Francisco and landed a job in their box factory in Yuma, Arizona. American Box Company then offered him a job as a lumberyard manager in the small town of Firebaugh, hired him, and he remained there one year. Following that experience, American Box bought a lumberyard in Vallejo, California, and he moved there, managing the lumberyard for seventeen years. While there, he became involved on his own in the construction business—primarily in the building of apartments, duplexes, and four-plexes—and stayed with it for twenty years, finally retiring in 1987.

He remained in contact with Willamette University's 1941 football team, attending activities honoring the team, such as when he and his wife, Dottie, went to the fiftieth-anniversary team reunion celebration in Honolulu's refurbished Moana Hotel in 1991, with all the reunion's many activities, and the team's induction into the Willamette Athletic Hall of Fame in 1997.

On June 29, 2017, Oregon's congressman Kurt Schrader, representing the state's 5th District, was given permission to rise and recognize Andrew Rogers in a brief talk from the floor of the nation's House of Representatives:

Mr. Speaker, I rise today to give special recognition to Andrew Rogers, the last surviving member of the heroic 1941 Willamette University Bearcats football team.

The 1941 season was a tremendous success for the team, going 8–2, capturing the Northwest Conference title. But we remember that Bearcats historic season for far more than just athletics.

At the end of the season, Willamette University was invited to play the University of Hawaii on December 6, 1941.

The following morning, the Japanese attack on Pearl Harbor began. Rogers, the team, and visiting Willamette supporters volunteered to guard the Punahou School for ten days while others helped with the injured.

After the attack on Pearl Harbor, Rogers volunteered to join the United States Marine Corps, where he served as an infantry platoon leader for the 3rd Marine Division throughout the Second World War. He served meritoriously during the final phase of the recapture of Guam, as well as during the Battle of Iwo Jima. Rogers reminds all Americans of the impact we can have when we step up in times of need. His military service during a dark, uncertain time in our history is another shining example of the Greatest Generation.

I am proud to share his story and offer this small piece of recognition for all that Andrew Rogers has done for this great country.

Under the devoted care of his daughter in the final years of his life, in mid-October 2017 Andrew Rogers had to be evacuated from his home in Napa, California, to the home of a relative in the small town of Woodside, California, in San Mateo County, near San Francisco, due to raging wildfires in California's Napa Valley. While there, he died on October 26 and was cremated, with his ashes to eventually be placed at Tulocay Cemetery in Napa.

A B-17G BOMBER PILOT: A QUIET RETURNING HERO AND EDUCATOR

Irving E. "Irv" Miller was born to Edward and Agnes Miller in Biron Village, a small community on the Wisconsin River in southeastern Wisconsin on February 7, 1918, and graduated from Lincoln High School in Manitowoc, Wisconsin. He came west and entered Willamette in August 1937, earned a bachelor of arts degree in business in 1938, was a backup halfback on the 1941 Bearcat team, remained through his senior year after returning from Hawaii, and enlisted in the army air force reserves. He was called to active duty on 17 September 1942 and served in enlisted status while he trained toward becoming a pilot and obtaining a commission.

During his enlisted status he went through basic and preflight training, officer candidate school, and primary, basic, and advanced pilot training—the latter in twin-engine Mitchell B-25s at Douglas Army Airfield in Arizona. He was commissioned a second lieutenant on 12 March 1944. From there he entered and completed transition as a copilot on a replace-

Irving E. Miller and his wife, Marcella, November 26, 1941, as he prepares to board the train for the voyage from San Francisco to the Bearcats' Shrine Bowl football game in Honolulu on December 6, 1941. *Wallulah* 1942. (*Source*: MOHLAWU)

ment crew in the three phases of combat crew training in B-17 heavy bombers. When his crew was formed and ready, and having been assigned to the 91st Bomb Group (H), at Bassingbourn Station No. 121, England, they ferried a B-17G across the Atlantic where they were further assigned to the 322nd Bomb Squadron in the late summer of 1944.

Miller was entering combat service with one of the most illustrious B-17 bombardment groups in World War II's 8th Air Force, the 91st, with its four squadrons, the 322nd, 323rd, 324th, and 401st Bombardment Squadrons (H). Their illustrious record flying B-17Fs and B-17Gs out of Bassingbourn, from 14 October 1942 through the end of April 1945, provides insight into the courage, dedication, valor, and enormous sacrifices of the American airmen prosecuting the daylight precision bombing campaigns over Europe. From 19 August 1942 through 25 June 1945, Bassingbourn served as headquarters for the 1st Combat Bombardment Wing of the 1st Bomb Division. The 91st Group was the 7th of an eventual forty-two heavy groups to deploy to England. Their group tail code was a "Triangle A." Its operational squadrons and fuselage codes were as follows:

322nd Bombardment Squadron (LG)

323rd Bombardment Squadron (OR)

324th Bombardment Squadron (DF)

401st Bombardment Squadron (LL)

The following online paragraph from the 91st's history explains the origin of the 91st's nickname, the "Ragged Irregulars," whose primary targets in the beginning were airfields, docks and harbor facilities, shipbuilding yards, and submarine pens.

A stark example of German antiaircraft defenses against B-17s of the 91st Bombardment Group (H) as they fly through intense flak over Hamm, Germany, 4 March 1943. (*Source*: USAAF)

The term "Ragged Irregulars" was tacked onto the men of the 91st because they had been shot up so badly (in the months following their arrival) they could not put up a full group into combat. They had to fill in on other units to make up a full group bombing formation. Hence the nickname was coined by the group commander.

Some of their early heaviest losses contributing to their nickname were in the raids on Hamm, Germany, 4 March 1943 (25 percent loss, Distinguished Unit Citation awarded after the war), and Bremen, Germany, 17 April 1943 (21 percent loss), where the Luftwaffe attacked with two hundred fighters.

They arrived in Europe early and in the years from November 1942 through April 1945 paid a staggering price. The group, in the beginning, was one of eleven in the 8th Air Force, flew 340 missions totaling 9,591 credited sorties, and lost a total of 197 aircraft missing in action, numbers exceeding those of any other group in the 8th, and losses roughly equivalent to four entire bomb groups and nearly half a squadron in both aircraft and crews. The 322nd lost forty-nine aircraft; the 323rd, fifty-five; the 324th, thirty-eight; and the 401st, fifty-five. They lost a total of 1,010 combat crewmen, with 887 killed and 123 missing in action. More than 960 crewmen became prisoners of war.

Their first mission was 7 November 1942 to the submarine docks at Brest, France. They lost their first two aircraft on 23 November 1942 on a mission against the U-boat pens at St. Nazaire, France. Their last mission was 25 April 1945 to Pilsen, Germany. The last plane lost, "Skunk Face II," was on 17 April 1945 during a mission to Dresden, Germany.

The group had the distinction of the highest number among all the 8th Air Force groups of enemy aircraft confirmed shot down: 420. They claimed an additional 127 damaged and 238 possible. Among their claims to fame, they were the first group to attack a target in the Ruhr on the 4 March 1943 mission to Hamm, and they led the famous Schweinfurt mission of 17 August 1943, a mission in which 230 aircraft from nine groups participated—189 attacked the target, and 36 were lost, including five of nine, the other four heavily damaged, from the 322nd Squadron—against 250–350 German fighters attacking in two waves, before and following bomb release. The final two claims to fame for the 91st were being the first bomb group to complete one hundred missions, on 5 January 1944, and being selected to test the first flak suits in March 1943.

Records do not tell the arrival date of the aircraft and crew that brought Second Lieutenant Irving E. Miller to Bassingbourn Station No. 121, but he undoubtedly arrived in September 1944, with the crew's pilot, because events were to eventually prove he was a copilot flying with First Lieutenant Howard L. Mitchell, pilot and aircraft commander flying on Mitchell's first of eighteen missions of a normally thirty-five-mission tour of duty, on 27 September of that year.

Crews deploying to Europe as replacements were formed as crews as they entered their training and went through three phases of combat crew training together to learn how to most efficiently operate together. The squadrons to which they were assigned generally went to great lengths to keep them together throughout their tours of duty. Their eighteenth mission, briefing no. 401 and mission no. 264 for the 322nd, on 5 December 1944, in aircraft no. 693 ended their time together.

The mission was to Berlin, the first time the 91st had been launched against Berlin since 21 June that year. The 91st was the lead group, Group A, with the 322nd furnishing thirteen crews for the high squadron in Group A, which was leading the division to the target. The Borgis Steel Works in the northwest suburbs was the primary and PFF (Pathfinder Force) target, a plant producing guns, shell casings, tank parts, and mines. The 322nd was flying B-17Gs, the latest model, which had been modified and improved, with a "chin [gun] turret" remotely controlled within the aircraft, and it carried the latest radar equipment, with crew training to do PFF bombing—all of which gained a consequent reduction of required crew members from ten to nine.

The 322nd, radio call sign LG (for "Lingers"), lost two aircraft that morning and nearly lost a third. Lead and low squadrons made short, visual runs, able to see the target briefly through broken clouds. The 322nd, the high squadron, bombed PFF, and results for all squadrons were unobserved. Antiaircraft fire was accurate for the high squadron only, consisting of both barrage and tracking fire. The following is a brief account from the 322nd's 5 December 1944 "dailies," summarizing some of what the squadron endured that morning:

Our aircraft #693, Lt. Mitchell, pilot, was last observed at 1058 hours, 5236N-1315E, with #1 propeller [left outboard] wind milling, 6 parachutes reported. Aircraft #360, Lt.

Blanton, pilot, was last seen at 5237N–1300E, at 1055 hours with #1 propeller feathered. No parachutes seen. Aircraft #234, Lt. Freer, pilot, was observed to have received a direct anti-aircraft hit in #3 engine [right, inboard engine]; last seen at 1104 hours in the target area. Four aircraft received major damage, five aircraft received minor damage, all due to anti-aircraft fire. Two crew members of aircraft #306, Lt. Smoley, pilot, were injured by flak, Sgt. Higdon, D. A., and Sgt. Nowicki, H. M., ball turret and waist gunner, respectively. This aircraft [was believed to have landed, away at Horton]. Three members of Flight Officer Rosch's crew, Flight Officer Alexander, Geo, navigator, Sgt. Larson, togglier [bombardier], and Sgt. Faulkner, R. H., engineer, bailed out over the target, misunderstanding the pilot's order to "stand by to bail out," the aircraft was hit by anti-aircraft fire just at bombs away, losing #1 and #2 engines [both engines on the left side] and damaging the control surfaces. This aircraft landed safely at base upon return.

The windmilling propeller on aircraft no. 693, most probably caused by flak damage, foretold Lieutenant Mitchell's order to bail out. When an engine fails or is shot out, the propeller almost invariably continues to turn, driven by the airspeed and airflow as the aircraft continues to fly, but one or more additional steps must be taken to avoid loss of the aircraft. The engine's big, three-bladed propeller must be "feathered," accomplished by electrically activating a hopefully undamaged motor within the large engine, which "feathers"—streamlines—the three blades in the aircraft's slipstream. If the attempts to feather the propeller fail, the huge blades continue to windmill, acting like three large barn doors, creating enormous drag on the aircraft. The inevitable results are decreasing airspeed, progressively increasing power required by the other three engines while speed continues to decrease, continuing loss of altitude just to maintain safe flying speed, and the virtual impossibility of safe return to base, even if every effort is made to reduce aircraft weight. The likelihood of engine overheat and failure on one or more of the remaining three engines increases as maximum power attempts to slow or level the descent.

The nine crew members on aircraft no. 693 prior to bailout were First Lieutenant Howard L. Mitchell, pilot; Second Lieutenant Irving E. Miller, copilot; First Lieutenant Thomas H. Rieker, navigator; Staff Sergeant Eugene L. Boutier, bombardier; Technical Sergeant George W. Caudell, top turret gunner; Staff Sergeant Trennie L. Lee, bottom turret gunner; Technical Sergeant Ralph J. Fugatt, radio operator; Staff Sergeant Frank E. Schnurstein, waist gunner; and Staff Sergeant Gilbert L. Elliott, tail gunner.

All were carried as missing in action until April 1945, when the 322nd learned that three of their number were prisoners of war: Irving E. Miller, George W. Caudell, and Ralph J. Fugatt. On the same list of POWs in April was Second Lieutenant Ralph J. Blanton, the pilot of the second aircraft lost on 5 December 1944: no. 360.

Beginning on 12 May 1945, after Germany's surrender and lasting three days, the 322nd flew eight, ten, and six crews, respectively, on "Revival" missions under the command of Brigadier General William Milton Gross, 1st Combat Wing Commander at Bassingbourn.

In that period, the 322nd participated in the evacuation of 2,032 POWs from Stalag Luft No. 1 at Barth, Germany. Many of the men evacuated were formerly assigned to squadrons of the 91st Group.

On 26 May 1945, Operation Home Run began, the redeployment of the 322nd Squadron to the United States, with four crews flying the first leg across the North Atlantic route. They were to reconstitute with the 91st in the days, weeks, and months ahead, moving and training toward the Pacific for participation in Operation Downfall, the invasion of the Japanese home islands—which fortunately was history that never occurred.

Years later, the former copilot on aircraft no. 693, Irving E. Miller, in relating his wartime experiences to Irene Reeves, who served with him when Miller was superintendent of schools in Jefferson, Oregon, in the period 1 July 1952–30 June 1970, provided his last, stark insight into the great risks the young American airmen of the World War II generation faced in Europe.

His plane was just a thousand feet above the ground when, undoubtedly the last able to leave the aircraft, he managed to bail out, breaking his upper arm while struggling to leave. Everyone in the nine-man crew managed to bail out, with the exception of the tail gunner, who went down with the plane.

Miller made his way to a German farmhouse. They let him sleep in their barn overnight; however, they apparently turned him in. The next morning the Gestapo came and got him. There were other prisoners, and they marched them through the village. He said the prisoners were more afraid of the villagers than they were of the soldiers because the previous night the Royal Air Force had heavily bombed the area, and the townspeople were up in arms and very threatening.

He went several days before the Germans set his broken arm. He said he had heard many times that if the German doctors knew they were pilots, they would amputate their arms. However, they did set his arm, putting a pin in to hold it. As an aside, Irene added, "Irv always wanted everything to go along on an even keel. He became very much a part of the community. I have only pleasant memories of our years together at the Jefferson High School. I know his family will miss him, and I am glad I was able to attend Irv and Marcella's 50th wedding anniversary in 1990."

On returning from World War II, his decorations and awards included the World War II Service Lapel Button, the World War II Victory Medal, the American Campaign Medal, the Air Medal, the Purple Heart Medal, the POW Medal, and the European-African Middle Eastern Campaign Medal with one Bronze Service Star. He was released from active duty on 10 November 1945 and entered a life of service in education.

He returned to Willamette University for additional education and graduated with his degree in business in 1946.

In 1957, he obtained a master's degree in education from Stanford University and entered a distinguished career as a superintendent of schools in Oregon for thirty-two years, working in Wheeler, Jefferson, Mt. Angel, and Gaston. In June 1970, he left his superintendent's position at Jefferson, Oregon, to become the superintendent at Mt. Angel's new John F. Kennedy High School, and he remained in Mt. Angel after his retirement from education administration in Oregon. He was a member of the Confederation of Oregon School Administrators and the president of the Oregon Association of Secondary School Principals.

He and Marcella raised three children, a son, Stephen, born May 11, 1945; a daughter, Marilyn Lucas, born November 8, 1946; and their youngest, a son, Ross, born July 3, 1951. Irving Miller died in the Benedictine Sisters' Nursing Home in Mt. Angel at the age of seventy-five on July 8, 1993, following his and Marcella's 1991 attendance of the 1941 Bearcat football team's fiftieth anniversary reunion at the Moana Hotel in Honolulu, Hawaii.

Chapter Twenty

Vancouver High School Classmates
and the Trappers' 1939 Football Teammates

Into the Pacific Theater as a P-38 Pilot

Kenneth W. Jacobson and Charles Sam "Chuck" Furno had teammates, class-mates, and more in common when they both went to play on Coach Roy "Spec" Keene's 1940 Willamette Bearcats football team, aiming for Hawaii. As the April 1931 photograph of the two in the Central Elementary School's fourth grade class depicts, they quite literally grew up together. Whereas Ken Jacobson had been born of Swedish parents in Vancouver, Chuck was the second child of Charles and Gladys Furno, Italian immigrants. Later, it became clear that both young men loved the game of football, and like all other players on the Willamette and San Jose State teams in the fall of 1941, they wanted to play well to ensure they would go with the Bearcats to play in the Shrine Bowl in Honolulu Stadium on Saturday, December 6.

What's more, they wanted to stay with the game of football, play more seasons, develop better skills, and maybe in Ken's case—though not a serious consideration—one day be a candidate drafted for a professional team. Over the years, the two classmates maintained a lasting friendship, augmented by Willamette team reunions, pleasant memories found in the university's alumni association, and the nearly always strong, loyalty-driven attachments found on championship collegiate football teams. As time passed following their journey to Hawaii and back, their paths gradually diverged, except for a one-year period in 1946–1947 when they once again were teammates on another championship Bearcat football team. During World War II, they went in opposite directions, Ken Jacobson toward the war in Europe, and Chuck Furno into the far reaches of the Pacific theater of operations.

A little-known fact of Chuck Furno's life at Willamette was his membership in the Sigma Chi fraternity, an organization founded in 1855 at the University of Miami (Ohio) based on the ideals and principles of friendship, justice, and learning, ideals and principles he carried throughout his life.

Charles S. Furno, halfback on the 1941
Willamette University Bearcats' football team.
(*Source*: MOHLAWU)

He was the small, self-demanding, quick-starting, swivel-hipped sophomore halfback who, though fast, tough, and mercurial, was more prone to injury in the large and growing iron man's virtually sixty-minute game of that era—and an injured knee had kept him out of the one Shrine Bowl game in his life in which he had the opportunity to play. Perhaps Coach Keene was keeping him out of the game so that his knee could further heal and be ready for the game against San Jose State College on 16 December, one of two other planned games that never occurred due to the Japanese attack on Pearl Harbor. After all, Willamette had been defeated by San Jose State College in the fall of 1940. They would be tough again this fall in Honolulu.

It was the attack that changed every American's life and immediately thrust both football teams and all who accompanied them headlong into war. But the one and perhaps most stunning disappointment in his life would never hold Chuck Furno back. Never. It simply temporarily redirected his life back into the fight.

After returning from his life-changing voyage to Hawaii and back, like Ken Jacobson and Marshall Barbour, he individually went to Portland and took a battery of tests administered by the army air force reserves to learn whether he was qualified to enter officer training. He successfully passed all his tests and was told to return to Willamette and remain in school until he was called to active duty. He completed his 1941–1942 academic year and returned for the next year, again playing on Spec Keene's 1942 Bearcats' team. In a somewhat abbreviated season of nearly all conference games, he, Ken, and several others from the 1941 Northwest Conference championship team had the pleasure of again capturing the mantle of champions. He again won his varsity letter in football—his third.

When the army air force called him to active duty on 4 March 1943, he entered the reserves—the Army of the United States—as an enlisted man in Nebraska, then went to Montana State College in Bozeman, Montana, where he studied academic subjects for four months. From there he went to Santa Ana, California, where, having entered the aviation cadet program, he was in pre–flight school for two months and one week. While there he took other academic courses, including code, aircraft recognition, and gunnery. He then traveled to Visalia, California, where he completed primary flying training in two and a quarter months and flew sixty-five hours in the PT-22 trainer, the same type of primary trainer flown by teammate Marshall Barbour. Primary pilot training prepared him for basic flying training at Marana Field, near Tucson, Arizona, where he flew an additional seventy hours in BT-13s and AT-6s in two and a half months.

From Marana he traveled to advanced pilot school at Williams Field just outside Phoenix, Arizona, where in two and a quarter months he flew an additional ninety hours in AT-6s, which included formation flying, air-to-air combat maneuvering, and air-to-ground weapons delivery maneuvers. On graduation from advanced flying training, he received his pilot's wings, was commissioned a second lieutenant in the army air force reserves, and entered active duty as a commissioned officer on 23 May 1944.

From Williams Field he went to George Field, a short distance from Victorville, California, about seventy-five miles from Los Angeles, to enter a fighter transition school in the P-39, where he flew thirty hours in two months while studying emergency procedures. At the same location he completed fixed gunnery school in two more months, flying an additional twenty-five hours in AT-6s.

Those graduates who performed at or near the top of their classes were sent on to become two-engine fighter pilots. He was next assigned to a P-38 training base to complete his transition to the two-engine fighter in which he would fly combat in the Pacific theater of operations. He was preparing to fly a technologically highly advanced World War II fighter-bomber which the Germans came to know as the "fork-tailed devil": two engined, well known for its long range and fighting capability, twin tailed, and demanding of its pilot in ways few people could ever know or understand. One sole pilot at its controls, with quick hands and sharp hand-eye coordination, flies the aircraft for often long, difficult hours, high or low level, in weather on instruments—or at night—with every sensor in his body required to maintain three-dimensional situational awareness: eyes, ears, a keen sense of smell, taste, and touch, wed to instantaneous judgment, decisions, skill, and the right actions to support and save teammates, aircraft, and oneself.

In May 1945, almost a month after President Franklin D. Roosevelt died in Warm Springs, Georgia, and shortly after Nazi Germany surrendered on 8 May, Chuck Furno left the continental United States and flew as a passenger in military transport aircraft in a series of long flights, island-hopping from the West Coast, through Hickam Field or the Honolulu Airport on Oahu, then to Wake Island and Guam, bound for the Philippines on the island of Mindinao. En route the military aircraft transporting him to the Philippines took him to Anderson Field on the island of Guam.

Chuck had previously kept in contact by phone—and probably by correspondence—with teammate Ted Ogdahl, who was a lieutenant and infantry platoon leader in the marines and, unknown to Chuck, had been seriously wounded on 12 May in the battle for Okinawa. His wounds were so serious that he was hurriedly evacuated by military medical aircraft to Navy Hospital No. 103 on Guam and arrived on 17 May. Ted was visited in the hospital by another friend, a marine lieutenant in the 3rd Marine Division named Arnold Baker.

In an astonishing turn of events, Ted Ogdahl would learn that Arnold was a tent mate of Andy Rogers, another Bearcat teammate of Ted's on the 1941 team. He learned of the mutual acquaintance with Arnold and Andy in the headquarters company of the 3rd Marine Division when Arnold came to visit him, with Andy in tow, to bring him a bottle of liquor and a box of cigars. The visit and totally unexpected meeting between the two football teammates was a happy surprise and would lead to one more pleasant surprise—this one for Chuck Furno while he was traveling into war in the Philippines.

Ted, who was aware Chuck was going to be en route through Guam to his assignment, gave Arnold Baker Chuck's phone number and asked him to call Chuck to ensure he knew that Ted and Andy Rogers were on Guam and to stop by and visit both of them. (It's highly probable that Ted also specifically requested Arnold not to divulge that he had been wounded, not knowing whether Ted's family had yet been notified by the Marine Corps.)

Undoubtedly, when the three teammates met in Navy Hospital No. 103 on Guam with the assistance of Arnold Baker and the jeep he was authorized to have at his disposal, there was considerable excitement and no small amount of joy. But there was probably something else tempering the happy reunion in the midst of war.

By then, Andy was a well-traveled marine lieutenant who'd had his scrapes in war. Earlier he had been a platoon leader on Guam in the summer of 1944 during mop-up operations in the latter stages of the battle to retake the island. Later, after training to be a flight observer—intelligence gatherer—in Hawaii, he was prepared to launch off the deck of the aircraft carrier *Saratoga* (CV-3) as a crew member on a spare TBM Avenger on possibly his first mission, a 19 February 1945 night-bombing and intelligence-gathering flight near Iwo Jima. While the crew waited, seated in their aircraft toward the stern of the carrier observing scheduled launches, the carrier was struck by kamikazes—and then later, after the severely damaged carrier limped back to Eniwetok, he returned to action, flying as an observer from an Iwo Jima airfield in light aircraft during March of that bloody ground campaign.

Chuck, Ted, and Andy were three men among many of those on the two collegiate football teams and millions of others who were far from home and learned the bitterly harsh meaning and impact of World War II. What's more, Chuck likely knew, and both Arnold and Andy (and probably Ted) knew, that the American armed forces in the Pacific were clearly building up for a planned invasion of the Japanese homeland. Given the ferocity and suicidal nature of Japanese resistance on land, at sea, and in the air, in the Iwo Jima and Okinawa campaigns, the prospect of such an event was not comforting.

The truth was, high in the national command authority in Washington, DC, the planned invasion was a fact, as was a massive movement of forces to the Pacific theater, including redeployment of combat forces from Europe that were already retraining for the Pacific and the planned invasion, code-named Operation Downfall—before the German surrender that same month of May.

As explained in more detail in Andy Rogers's story above, "A World War II Pacific Odyssey," movement of forces from Europe and the continental United States into the Pacific began in earnest following the surrender of Nazi Germany in early May. And while the growth of Allied military power in the Pacific continued, the training of forces already in place for Operation Downfall was increasing.

Unknown to the three former Bearcats during their brief reunion on Guam, the chiefs of staff of the American armed services, their allies, and President Harry S. Truman were already wrestling with the plan and the staggering magnitude of the undertaking and risks of Operation Downfall. They were entering the decision phase with intense, prolonged agonizing over expected casualties on both sides, while the buildup of an Allied invasion force continued with a massive movement of forces to the western Pacific. At the same time, behind the scenes, the development of the atomic bomb was nearing fruition, and President Truman was hoping the invasion could be avoided.

Preceding Chuck Furno's May 1945 arrival on the island of Mindinao, the character of the war in the Philippines had changed dramatically since General Douglas MacArthur waded ashore on the island of Leyte on 20 October 1944 and proclaimed, "I have returned." The Leyte landings marked the beginning of the end of Japan's devastating rule in the Philippines and the island territories and nations of the southwest Pacific.

The bloody Leyte campaign lasted until 31 December of that year, and the Americans lost 3,504 killed and suffered 12,080 wounded, their Philippine allies lost an undetermined number, and the Japanese lost an estimated 49,000 killed and 389 captured. During the Leyte campaign, the only other Allies to suffer any losses were the Australians, who lost thirty dead and sixty-four wounded when a Japanese kamikaze crashed into the heavy cruiser HMAS *Australia* in October during the Battle of Leyte Gulf.

Though the battles for Leyte and Leyte Gulf had sharply reduced Japanese air units and combat capability by approximately 50 percent, their increasingly desperate situation in the Philippines and in the south and southwest Pacific by October 1944 had caused the empire's militarists to accelerate the forming of "special attack," or kamikaze (suicide), units, clearly indicating a new and dangerous form of warfare. Thus the P-38 air-to-air fighter and fighter-bomber combat missions Chuck Furno was about to enter remained extremely hazardous. The enemy was still present in force with a new, dangerously aggressive, suicidal form of land-based and seaborne air warfare to match their already suicidal land warfare—while every Allied airborne mission of any type was always plagued by the unexpected, particularly if pilots and crews were not adequately trained and prepared for what they might face.

American forces, under General MacArthur's command and strategic guidance, landed on the main island of Luzon on 9 January 1945. The final battle for the island had begun and would still be in progress at the end of the war.

Charles Furno's P-38, Philippines, Maret Field, Zamboanga City, island of Mindinao, May 1945, where he joined the 67th Fighter Squadron "Fighting Cocks." (*Source*: JLC)

But the strategic plan to defeat the Japanese and drive them from the Philippines envisioned something decidedly different. Once Leyte was retaken, the Americans were to move their main effort northward, onto Luzon, while the Americans and their Philippine allies cleared the southern Philippine archipelago, and the Americans, Australians, British, and Dutch turned their attention to Malaysia and the large former Dutch East Indies' island of Borneo.

The first step began in January 1945 when MacArthur issued orders for the start of preplanned operations to recapture the entire southern Philippine archipelago from the Japanese, all code-named Victor, regardless of which forces were to participate in the several phases of the campaign. By the time Chuck Furno arrived on Maret Field in May to join the 67th Fighter Squadron's "Fighting Cocks," the final part of MacArthur's strategic plan for the Philippines and the south and southwest Pacific was already in motion.

While the Philippine archipelago was being cleared, American forces invaded Palawan Island in the Calamian Group, landing at Puerto Princesa the first day at the narrow waist of Palawan—a long, narrow island with its southern end lying approximately 375 miles west-northwest of Mindinao's Zamboanga City. Palawan Island is oriented southwest to northeast, roughly paralleling Mindinao and pointing directly at the north end of Mindoro Island and Manila on the southwest end of the main island of Luzon, where administrative control of Palawan was vested.

The campaign to seize all of Palawan ended on 22 April 1945, clearing the way to further expand the already-opened new airfield and base for rapidly growing air forces near Puerto Princesa to support the Allies' thrust into the south and southwest Pacific. From Palawan and Puerto Princesa, Americans could move to seize the entire Zamboanga Peninsula, further secure the expanding Maret Field, and at the same time begin to interdict movements of Japanese forces attempting to move from Indochina and Malaysia into the Philippines—while striking against Japanese-held oil fields on Borneo.

By the time Chuck Furno joined the 67th Fighter Squadron in May, the final, major Allied campaign of World War II, against the large Dutch East Indies island of Borneo, had begun on 1 May and would last until 21 July. His work, which would be in the P-38L, would go on afterward, in fighting near Borneo, which for him continued until 9 August. But he wouldn't be flying out of Zamboanga's Maret Field against targets in and around Borneo. Instead, the 67th Fighter Squadron was already forward-based at the Puerto Princesa Airfield on the Philippines' Palawan Island; it had been there since April and was now under the command of the 347th Fighter Group.

The Borneo campaign was the final World War II campaign to which the 13th Air Force's 347th Fighter Group, at Puerto Princesa, was assigned. The XIII Fighter Command base at the airfield provided the living, command, and operational environments in which Chuck Furno would fly his combat missions.

The huge Allied effort involved the forces of Australia, the United States, the United Kingdom, and the Netherlands, with landings on Tarakan Island on the northeast coast at the mouth of the Sesajap River by Australia's 26th Brigade. The 13th's units included five squadrons of B-25s from the 42nd Bombardment Group, with another 5th Air Force B-25 bombardment group attached, the 38th; the 5th Bombardment Group (B-24s) and their four squadrons, flying from Samar Island; another B-24 bombardment group, the 307th, composed of four squadrons, the 868th Bombardment Squadron, SB-24 low-altitude radar bomber for maritime surveillance patrols; the 347th Fighter Group, with the 67th, 68th, and 339th Fighter Squadrons, flying out of Palawan Island in P-38s; the 419th Night-Fighter Squadron (P-61s), flying from Palawan and Zamboanga; and the 4th Reconnaissance Group (F-5s [P-38s reconnaissance-equipped] and B-25s), with the 17th Photographic Reconnaissance Detachment, operating out of Palawan.

All this was just the beginning of a massive air warfare capability that included land-based and carrier-based marine and navy aircraft, with a squadron of marines flying out of Zamboanga, plus heavy air commitments by the Royal Australian Air Force and American naval forces, including carriers.

The P-38L's armament was four .50-caliber machine guns with a total of one thousand rounds of armor-piercing incendiary (API) rounds and one 20 mm cannon; it could deliver one-thousand-pound bombs and 165-gallon napalm tanks and carry two three-hundred-gallon drop tanks to add fuel and range. The new P-38Ls were equipped with two Allison V-17105, 1,475 hp engines on a maximum gross weight aircraft of 21,600 pounds that could reach a top speed of 666 miles per hour.

Second Lieutenant Furno undoubtedly had to fly one or more area orientation missions to better prepare him for the missions to come: high-speed, low-angle attack missions, strafing different types of targets through defenders' unseen and potentially deadly small-arms and automatic weapons fire, with his machine guns and cannon firing from shallow dive angles of five to fifteen degrees with bottoming pullout altitudes at one hundred feet or less;

high-speed, low-level skip-bomb missions to deliver 165-gallon napalm bombs from altitudes of one hundred to two hundred feet; other missions at medium altitudes, seven to ten thousand feet, some in difficult to bad weather; dive-bomb missions in which he and flight members approached the target through flak, rolling in over targets at sixteen thousand feet for forty-five-degree dives through intense automatic weapons fire and flak to release one-thousand-pound bombs; and missions with takeoffs or landings at night for long-range, early morning or late afternoon strikes, or on early morning dawn or dusk patrols to cover and protect his home base. During the Borneo campaign, he regularly flew in some of the longest fighter missions in World War II—a characteristic of the 13th Air Forces' operations in the island-hopping campaigns of the Pacific theater, in which Lightnings were known to fly 1,900 to 2,100 statute miles.

Missions from Puerto Princesa in support of the Battle of Tarakan and operating areas near Brunei involved ranges to target areas of four hundred to six hundred miles, and 350–450 miles in missions over North Borneo.

The assigned combat mission for the 347th Fighter Group on 21 May 1945 typified the operations the 67th Fighter Squadron flew out of Puerto Princesa in the last three months of the war. On 20 May, Field Order No. 158 for Mission No. 347-11 came via a secret message from the Far East Air Force's assistant chief of staff, Intelligence, through XIII Fighter Command to the 347th, where at each level of command additional tasking details were added specifying how many aircraft from the group's three squadrons would participate, the name of the target and type of mission, weapons loads, takeoff time, and time on target. In this instance, crews flying the mission were briefed to expect an attack on the target by B-25 medium bombers at 1100 hours, just ahead of the 347th P-38s' arrival over the target area.

The day's mission routine typically began the day prior to the mission, with aircraft maintenance and ordnance personnel working through the night to ready, fuel, and load the aircraft with the ordnance ordered for the mission. At the same time, supporting organizations were made aware of pertinent details needed by those units to support the coming mission, such as control tower, medical, fire and rescue, and radar units up and ready. Mission planning also began the day before, with crews probably wakened four hours prior to takeoff in order to have breakfast and receive the pre-mission weather, intelligence, and operations briefings beginning two hours before takeoff.

The day following the attack, a mission report was sent back up the chain of command to the Far East Air Force detailing results in a standard format.

On 21 May, the 67th's mission report stated that eight P-38s from the 67th, and eleven P-38s from the 68th, fire-bombed Serla, Northwest Borneo. They were airborne at 0855 hours and were over the target from 1105 to 1145 after two hours and ten minutes en route to the target area. Their weapons load included one 165-gallon napalm bomb on the centerline of each aircraft and full loads of .50-caliber and 20 mm ammunition. Once over the target, they waited while the B-25s completed their bomb runs, then began their attacks, south to north, divided into two groups against two target areas containing specific targets and bombing from minimum altitude. One target was an area of gun positions, identified undoubtedly in reconnaissance photographs and map coordinates. Six bombs hit in the gun position target area, "burning a good sized building," from which white smoke rose to one thousand feet. Eight bombs hit in the second target area, "with several fires, with black and white smoke to 3,000 feet." Three bombs hit in another target area, starting several fires. Strafing runs were made on two oil storage tanks in another specified target area, leaving them burning with "brownish [smoke], white liquid coming from pipe lines," and six build-ings were strafed and left burning. All nineteen aircraft returned safely at 1330 hours, a four-hour-and-thirty-five-minute mission from liftoff to touchdown.

Pilots provided the foregoing results in post-mission debriefings to operations supervisors and intelligence personnel, which were part of standard operating procedures on all combat missions. During all such debriefings, pilots' responsibilities included relating to intelligence and operations supervisors any potentially useful observations of enemy activity or possible targets. For the mission on 21 May, pilots reported sightings of "gun positions including 1 dugout with net covering in area 8310 not identified [the number is a map coordinate]." At 1230 hours on the return flight they observed "five small native boats through a break in the clouds at Balabac Island, headed along the east coast. No activity noted at Serla. Buildings in good condition and well kept, except for barracks at 7708 which looked damaged."

In the remarks section of the report, pilots said they "did not see B-25s which were scheduled to hit in same general area at 1100. Heard garbled radio message from them, which indicated B-25s were leaving target." They had seen no enemy aircraft and conse-quently encountered no combat in the air. However, they did observe two puffs of white smoke—flak—fired from an unknown position and burst at one thousand feet over the water, labeling the antiaircraft fire as inaccurate.

The mission report included bombs dropped and ammunition expended: "18 × 165 gal-lon Napalm fire bombs, white phosphorous fused in target area, 1 × 165 gallon Napalm fire bomb, white phosphorous fused jettisoned." Ammunition expended: "Caliber .50—16,530 rounds" and "20 MM—2,100 rounds."

By the time pilots' debriefings were complete, the day had been long and intensely demanding for each pilot, both physically and emotionally, lasting from nine to ten hours. For Second Lieutenant Charles Furno, when he began flying combat missions, he could normally expect a mission cycle of one every three days, a cycle that in a combat environment could place enormous pressure and stress on any individual.

On 22 May, the 347th sent nine P-38s from the 67th and four from the 68th to fire-bomb Tarakan in support of ground troops, mission length four and a half hours. On 24 May, a fifteen-plane firebomb mission launched for Tarakan again, eight from the 67th, seven from the 68th, but weather caused the mission to divert to their secondary target, Malinau Village, Borneo.

On 28 May, the 347th sent thirty-seven P-38s on a strafing mission against antiaircraft positions on Balikpapan, Borneo, nine from the 67th, thirteen from the 68th, and fifteen from the 339th, as part of a major strike mission that included B-24s and B-25s. All 347th aircraft returned safely.

During the first ten days of June, the 67th sent six P-38Ls, considered the "best of the breed," on a firebomb and strafing mission at Brunei Town, a coastal town on the northwest side of Borneo, a low-level mission at one hundred feet or less, carrying 165-gallon tanks of napalm and a full load of .50-caliber machine-gun and 20 mm cannon rounds.

In the remaining days through 10 June, the 67th flew five two-plane air cover missions for an Allied convoy in Brunei Bay in the Borneo area. Then came three more flights of two each flying cover over an Allied convoy in the Balabac Straight, two in a dawn patrol over Puerto Princesa, a strafing mission of eight aircraft to destroy hidden enemy aircraft, and three more flights of four aircraft providing cover to the Allied convoy in the Balabac Straight, a total of twenty-eight more missions.

On 10 June, the Australian 9th Division, plus additional units of their 26th Brigade, landed on the northwest side of Borneo, near Brunei, and fanned out up and down the west coast with three brigades to begin driving Japanese forces into coastal enclaves where they could be trapped and systematically reduced. The battle for Borneo lasted until 1 August, while the Battle of Balikpapan lasted from 1 to 21 July and likewise involved virtually the same 13th Air Force air order of battle.

As the fighting in the Borneo campaign wound down in late July and the first few days of August, Chuck Furno was with the 67th Fighter Squadron's air echelon (aircraft, crews, and maintenance personnel only) at Puerto Princesa, while the 13th Air Force began preparing to shift the direction of their air effort toward Luzon, where pockets of Japanese units continued fighting. One of the first steps toward Luzon was the 67th's deployment to Laoag City Airfield in far northern Luzon, arriving 9 August, the day the atomic bomb was dropped on Nagasaki, Japan, the second of the two war-ending strikes on the Japanese homeland. On the 15th of August, the 14th in Hawaii and the United States, the Japanese announced their surrender. While at Laoag City, Chuck retained the additional duties of squadron finance officer.

Now came the wait for his return home. He wasted no time in preparing himself for what he intended to do after the war, but he had arrived in the Philippines late and knew his wait would be longer than many others. In the 67th he had begun playing baseball on the army air force's team that won the service championship of the Philippines. His participation on the baseball team permitted him to travel more extensively in the island nation after hostilities ended, while maintaining his athletic skills and physical fitness.

When the 67th's deployment to Laoag City was extended, he was transferred back to Zamboanga and joined the 70th Fighter Squadron, "The White Knights" of the 18th Fighter Group, on 21 August, seven days after the Japanese had announced their surrender. The previous April, the 70th had been operating out of a base on Mindoro Island before moving to Zamboanga's Maret Field. The squadron's aircraft flew into Maret Field, while the rest of the 70th's men and equipment were moved the first week of May by convoy on the Victory Ship SS *John Alden*.

After the move was complete and the unit was prepared to renew flight operations in their new location, history recording resumed for the period 26 May to 25 June, with personnel strengths reported for the period in two categories, flying and ground. Flying personnel were forty-eight officers and four flight officers (pilots who were enlisted men carrying the grade of flight officer). Ground personnel were three hundred enlisted men and eleven officers, with a net increase of one flying officer and a net decrease in ground personnel of twenty-seven enlisted men. Actually at Zamboanga were 57 officers and 239 enlisted men, with the rest on various duties elsewhere or on leave in the United States.

Aircraft in the squadron's inventory at the end of the period were twenty-six P-38Ls, all but one P-38L-5s—the latest model—and one C-47A. The new 70th Squadron commander as of 5 June was Captain Robert D. Wallace. The history also summarized missions flown in June, identifying eleven in and around the island of Borneo, while Charles Furno had been flying out of Puerto Princesa on Palawan.

Following the end of hostilities in August, a slowdown in 70th Fighter Squadron activity began immediately. The 9th of August had marked their last combat missions. Continuing in September, emphasis shifted to search missions and local patrols, six search and the remainder local patrols and training new pilots, for a total of twenty-four missions dispatched and twenty-three completed, with a total of sixty-three of sixty-seven sorties completed, a dramatic reduction in the pace of flying activity. (A sortie is flown by one aircraft on one mission.)

On 23 September, Charles Furno was appointed to replace the 70th's squadron adjutant, First Lieutenant Chester E. Knoer. Among his duties as the 70th Squadron adjutant, he was required to write the squadron's war diary, a monthly summary in the unit's history of

Chuck Furno in the cockpit of his P-38L, ready to start his engines, probably Laoag, Luzon, Philippines, after hostilities ended in August 1945. (*Source*: JLC)

personnel-oriented activities, and on 5 October 1945 he completed and signed a one-page entry covering the period 1 September through 30 September 1945:

No awards came through during the month, but three officers received promotions.

A diary for the month proves that little happened from day to day. On the 2nd peace terms were signed, and alert flights were begun. Nothing else of merit happens until the 6th when the enlisted men threw a dance in their new day room. Its success was due largely to the efforts of Staff Sergeant William Yoakum. The 7th brought good news in the form of General Orders awarding the unit two additional battle stars. This made twenty-one more enlisted men eligible for return to good old Uncle Sugar Able. The next day the squadron joined other units in the group to bring a third dimension to the Philippine Victory Parade in Zamobanga. The 9th brought news of JOHN F. BOEYE, HOWARD A. LINN and HARRY L. SWAN being promoted to captain as of August 27th, s.o. 259 FEAF. The 10th gave us all some laughs when a U.S.O. show appeared at the group theater. On the following day 1st Lts. Byron G. Fagg, James R. Geier, George E. Holcomb, Roger F. White, Frank J. Gallagher and Alexander B. Colbath, Jr., departed for the States, having been relieved of duty as of the 8th. On the 14th, sixty-four enlisted men started the happy journey back home. These were all high point men, and those over thirty-eight years of age. That same afternoon a list of 76 names of men with 80 points or more was published. These men were to have left the following week. On the 15th the enlisted men held another dance in their day room. Word was received on the 17th that the squadron was authorized the Borneo star which made twenty-one more enlisted men eligible to go home. The list was posted the following day. Also on the 17th Master Sergeant Billy C. Simpson was made First Sergeant per Special Order No. 88. A definite lull set in for the next few days in which nothing of notice occurred. On the 21st Lt. HINES taxied into our Piggy-Back plane, and washed out both planes. The 29th was a banner day for our officers. The new club was opened that evening, and it got pretty drunk out. Things were mighty quiet in the officers' area the next day. The 30th brought news that Captains Sylvester C. Shaughnessy, and Paul P. Stobricke, and 1st Lts. Glen E. Noble, and Arthur C. Cannon were on a list to go home. 1st Lt. Chester E. Knoer left a few days previous. The month ended with the group opening its new radio stations.

Thus ends the historical month of September 1945. It will go down in history as the month that brought to a formal close the greatest war that man has ever known. We all pray that it has brought to a close the last war that mankind will ever see. A realist would say that this was wishful thinking, but it is no doubt the heartfelt wish of every man who has seen, lived and fought in this of all wars. Before another squadron monthly history is written almost all the combat veterans of the unit will be gone or on their way. We have all had a great experience and it's the hope of each man for the other that he have as much success as a civilian as we all did as a unit in helping to win this war. Thus we go back to the peace that we feel is justly deserved.

CHARLES S. FURNO

2nd Lt, Air Corps

The 70th remained at Maret Field outside Zamboanga, Mindinao, until the squadron was ordered to move north, taking Chuck Furno back to Laoag City's airfield beginning 12 October. The move, directed by the 18th Fighter Group commander, was complete on 31 October, when thirty-seven officers and ninety-six enlisted constituted the squadron's total manpower. As soon as the squadron aircraft arrived at Laoag, patrol missions over the Japanese-held island of Formosa began. (Today, Formosa is Taiwan.) As officers and men continued their exodus for home, the amount of flying decreased. Nevertheless, patrol missions over Formosa were to prove interesting.

No sooner did the 70th arrive at the Laoag City airfield than the patrol missions over Formosa began. On 13 October, the 70th sent eight aircraft, two flights of four each, on what was described as a fighter cover mission. The first takeoff was at 1145, and the flight of four was "on station" over the island from 1300 to 1430, authorized to fly at altitudes between 2,500 and 10,000 feet. The second flight was airborne at 1300 hours, on station from 1405 until 1640, authorized altitudes from "deck" (just above ground level) to 10,000 feet.

They carried no bombs, but they did carry two thousand rounds of .50 caliber and 150 rounds of 20 mm for self-protection (if needed). In the debriefing, pilots reported observing eight-four single-engine airplanes at Karoabe airdrome, but no activity. Two other airfields and one seaplane base and their levels of activity were described by the pilots. Work was being done on aircraft at one of the fields, and the airplanes appeared serviceable. At another airfield, the description was simply "activity on ground." At the fourth airfield, pilots observed "seaplanes in water and land planes in revetments." The fighter cover missions were gathering intelligence while ensuring, as much as possible, that there was no activity indicating impending hostile action, that day or in the future. All eight aircraft landed, having expended no ammunition.

On 14 October, the 70th Squadron sent ten aircraft over Formosa, two flights of four and one flight of two, again carrying defensive ammunition loads only. This time pilots sighted aircraft on the ground in fourteen different locations, noting that at one location an aircraft with "black cross insignia" was on the field, and at another airfield there were ten C-47s with Chinese markings.

On 15 October, eleven aircraft were sent in two flights of four and one flight of three. Observations of ground activity were reported as the same as the previous day, although observations of a PB4Y (navy) and a C-46 (army) aircraft over the island prompted a closer look. Again, defensive weapons loads were taken, and no rounds were expended.

The next day the 70th dispatched four aircraft, with pilots observing Japanese airplanes at Teyohara Field that "appeared to have original red insignia repainted dark green." At Tonseki Field, one C-47 with Chinese markings was observed flown off the field sometime between 1100 and 1215 hours. Weather permitting, the pattern of one flight of four aircraft continued through 21 October.

As reported by the commander, Captain Robert D. Wallace, in his 5 November report to the 18th Fighter Group,

The most interesting missions of the month were undoubtedly the patrol missions over the island of Formosa . . . in the period 14 October 1945 thru . . . 21 October 1945. . . . Activity over the once strongly fortified Japanese base was nil but the pilots enjoyed flying the missions so they would have an opportunity of taking a sight-seeing tour, from the air, around the island of Formosa.

On the 14th one P-38 snafued and had to land at Matsuyama Airfield, situated in the north central part of Formosa. 1st Lt. R.H. SEYTER was the pilot of the aircraft, and he remained in Taihoku, the large city near the airfield, until the 19th at which time our C-47 escorted by four P-38s took two mechanics to Matsuyama to repair the snafued airplane. Also in the C-47 besides the two mechanics were six pilots who went along for the ride. Thus, including the men in the C-47 and those who flew P-38s, there was a total of seventeen men when they all landed at Matsuyama. Before the snafued plane could be repaired and flown off the field the weather decided to close in at the field for a couple of days and forced the entire party to remain until the 21st. During the short time spent in Formosa by the seventeen men they reported they had a few strange experiences while there.

Immediately upon debarking from the airplanes, Japanese officers and men came forward to offer their hospitality and assistance to the Americans. There was plenty of bowing, saluting and smiling on the part of the Japanese, which could probably be contributed partly to the Allies complete victory over their empire and also in part that our men arrived at Matsuyama armed to the teeth. However the Japanese extended all the kindnesses that they knew how to toward our men. A bus was chartered to transport the men from the air base into town and thence on to the hotel that was a furnished quarters for two days and nights spent there. The men were a bit dumbfounded when they had to take off their shoes before entering into any of the houses. Also experienced some difficulties in sitting on the floor to eat their food with chopsticks. The food was good and everyone soon had the situation well in hand and enjoying it all.

It was learned that the Chinese are placing occupation troops on Formosa and that most of the people there have a dislike for the Chinese troops. The people believe the Chinese will plunder and loot everything they can on the island, taking what they want and giving nothing in return for it.

The seventeen men that made the trip, not knowing what to expect when they arrived there, were very well pleased with the outcome and are looking forward to the next time they may have an opportunity to return to the island of Formosa and observe more of the oriental customs.

Total missions and sorties for October were 16 dispatched, 14 completed, and the number of sorties dispatched 59, with 51 completed.

Captain Wallace ended his October report with these words:

The month of October ended with the squadron looking forward to a much better month of November. We are all pleased to be at Laoag now that the move is completed and are looking forward to building a new squadron area and continue making the 70th Fighter Squadron one of the best outfits in this theater.

Captain Wallace's hopes for the squadron's future would not come to pass. Flying dwindled further in November. In the meantime, with the end of all patrol and top cover missions, flying stopped entirely, while officers and enlisted with sufficient points were returning home. The 70th remained at Laoag for garrison duty until inactivated on 26 December 1945.

Unquestionably, as the flying wound down and the men departed, many were wondering what would become of these formidable and beautiful flying machines that they had trained in, flown missions in, and returned safely to home base in so many times. Some of the same thoughts undoubtedly crossed the minds of the men who maintained and repaired the 70th's P-38s. In wars fought thousands of miles from the continental United States, the inevitable question would arise: "How do we take these marvelous machines home?"

The answer was a sad memory Charles Furno was to carry with him nearly the rest of his life: the scrapping and burying of their P-38s on the island from where he had flown a few of his missions.

For a fighter pilot to observe or learn that this wonderful machine that he's flown, risked his life in and had his life saved by, fought for his country in, guarded and saved others' lives with, become so confident in, accustomed to, comfortable in, recognizing its near-unbelievable intricacies and qualities, there can be little else but some deep measure of buried sadness if he sees or hears of its burial. It is a strange and powerful emotion and mixed feelings to survive combat, to watch others you have known be killed or to learn they simply disappeared, never to be seen again, and then to learn that these magnificently designed machines are being buried along with your friends and comrades in arms. It's akin to a ship's captain and crew who have been forced to abandon their ship, watching helplessly as she slowly slips beneath the ocean's surface to plunge into depths that swallow her forever, taking some shipmates with her.

As did a number of his Willamette teammates who arrived and served in the Pacific late in the war, Chuck and the men of the 70th Fighter Squadron returned home primarily in Operation Magic Carpet, on a ship, in his case as a first lieutenant, arriving in the continental United States in April 1946. He was relieved from active duty on 24 April, during the nation's rapid demobilization, and departed on terminal leave 13 May through 18 June. His separation from the army air force reserves was at the Fort Lewis Separation Center, Washington, effective 30 July.

He had earned a World War II Service Lapel Button, a World War II Victory Medal, and authorizations to wear a Navy Commendation Ribbon and a Marine Corps Medal for services rendered at Pearl Harbor while a civilian.

After the war, Charles Furno returned to Willamette and again earned a varsity letter on Willamette's 1946 Bearcats football team, his fourth, as he, Ken Jacobson, Marv Goodman, Bill Reder, Paul Cookingham, and Pat White—all December 1941 Hawaii veterans—played their last game for the Willamette University Bearcats on Thursday,

Charles Furno's 1947 graduation photograph, from the *Wallulah*. (*Source*: MOHLAWU)

Thanksgiving Day, November 28, 1946, against Whitman College in Walla Walla, Washington. They were completing their last season, in which the Bearcats again won their Northwest Conference championship.

He earned his degree in physical education, graduating in 1947. While there he met and married Zephne "Zip" Given, who attended Willamette but didn't complete her degree work, though she remained affiliated with the class of 1949. After a few months teaching in Hermiston, Oregon, he and Zip returned to his hometown of Vancouver, Washington, in April 1949, where he was hired as a high school teacher and shortly thereafter as an assistant football coach by Vancouver High School.

They had two daughters: Susan Powell, born December 23, 1950, and who now resides in Hillsboro, Oregon, and Janet Leffler, born December 10, 1953, and now resides in Kalama, Washington, approximately thirty miles north of Vancouver.

In 1954, he was named head football coach at Vancouver High School, and in 1958 he coached the Trappers to an undefeated season. He taught history and coached football at Vancouver High School for fourteen years where he had an impressive record of eighty-four wins and only thirty-five losses, and while coaching and teaching at the high school, he obtained a master's degree in business from the University of Oregon in 1957. He left teaching and coaching in 1967 and became supervisor of secondary physical education, health, and athletics in the Vancouver School District, remaining in that position until he retired in 1979.

Soon after arriving at Vancouver High School, he joined and remained active in the U.S. Army Reserves, qualified to fly army helicopters, and beginning in 1961 he trained army aviators in helicopter flying techniques. He retired from the reserves as a lieutenant colonel and received a letter from the Office of the Adjutant General, Department of the Army, dated 9 December 1980, placing him on the retired list effective 1 February 1981.

For thirty years, thousands of youths in Clark County were affected directly or indirectly by Chuck Furno, in part through the TODAY Foundation (The Organization Dedicated to Athletics and Youth), which in 2000 inducted him into their Hall of Fame. Over the years he remained in close contact with former students and athletes who played under his supervision as his reputation continued to flourish. In 2004, Coach Furno was inducted into the National High School Football Coaches Hall of Fame. On February 9, 2005, he received Recognition for Lifetime Service by the National Football Foundation.

His players and students tell of his legacy best. He had a magnetic, entirely genuine presence about him. "Chuck earned the respect of his players and students, and in return he respected them," said Roy Sandberg in October 2006. "He has a jovial way about him. He's short in stature and long in character and personality. Students and fellow-teachers had tremendous respect for him as a human being." He remained in touch with those students, attending class reunions and meeting ex-Trapper athletes for breakfast regularly. Like all his high school classmates, he exemplified the best of the millions of an entire generation of Americans who did their duty and sacrificed like none other in the most destructive war in history.

Photographs of lieutenant and soon to be teacher and coach Charles Furno, beside or in the cockpit of his P-38, "Lady Louise," tell his story well. With a mischievous smile, his eyes

Coach Chuck Furno at age ninety-one, in his Pontiac G-6 sports car in Vancouver, Washington. (*Source*: CSFFC)

twinkling, brimming with confidence and quiet determination, he is ready for the flight, no matter how long it takes or who or what he might face. Never quit.

He was proud of his four varsity football letters, his service in the armed forces, and his induction into Willamette's Athletic Hall of Fame with his 1941 football teammates, while he and Zephne remained proudly active in the 1941 Bearcat football team and Willamette Alumni Association reunions. He never forgot his Spec Keene Scholarship to play football at Willamette University and Spec Keene's role in his life.

Zephne and Charles Furno celebrated their fiftieth anniversary on March 26, 1998. Born on February 1, 1921, in Vancouver, he died peacefully in his sleep in his hometown on March 17, 2013.

ONTO AN ISLAND IN THE SOUTH ATLANTIC

Ken Jacobson, born in Vancouver on September 19, 1921, remembered that his parents, who immigrated from Sweden, were not particularly enamored of the game of football. They were intense, hardworking, and no-nonsense parents and didn't attend his games during either high school or university seasons. But Ken wasn't noticeably affected by their seeming lack of interest. Strong, willful, tough, and outgoing, he was at once gregarious while charting his own course, and he didn't hesitate a moment to keep a photographic record of his life's journey, especially the voyages to Oahu and back that year.

A clear indication of his strong sense of independence, determination, and self-reliance was the quiet use of his personal camera to take photographs in downtown Honolulu after

Ken Jacobson in the 1941 team photograph. Below left is Ted Ogdahl, and to the right is Jim Burgess. (*Source*: MOHLAWU)

the Japanese attack on Pearl Harbor, when strict martial law and military government had been imposed, along with some supposedly equally strong censorship. He, as did to a lesser degree San Jose State College's Victor Albert "Bert" Robinson, continued the use of his camera while homeward bound in a highly classified, navy-combatant-escorted movement of the two passenger-carrying former luxury liners through submarine-infested waters in the first evacuation convoy from Hawaii following the Japanese attack.

Each ship, having arrived in Honolulu from Manila in the Philippines, on 16 December 1941, had taken on approximately four hundred additional passengers each, mostly women and children, a few of them made widows and orphans by the attack, plus 180 severely wounded survivors of Pearl Harbor, 125 on the SS *President Coolidge*, 55 on the U.S. Army transport *Hugh L. Scott*. The convoy, with each ship converted in part to a hospital ship, had been hastily planned and directed, almost frantically and chaotically cobbled together, and loaded with additional passengers following the Japanese attack. The unorganized American military response to evacuation orders had been compounded by their inability to locate the Japanese strike fleet, made worse by the fact that Hawaii's citizenry were still plagued with fear and rampant rumors of a possible landing by Japanese troops.

Aboard the overcrowded *Coolidge*, sailing in company with the *Scott* from 19 to 25 December, Ken continued taking stunning photographs of some of his teammates and both passenger-carrying vessels, including their passage beneath the Golden Gate Bridge on Christmas morning 1941, plus the naval escorts—the cruiser USS *Detroit* (CL-8), the destroyer *Cummings* (DD-365), and one of *Detroit*'s catapult-launched SOC-1 bi-wing scout float planes—on the return voyage. Then, seventy-one years later, through his grandson via marriage, he generously donated electronic copies to the Willamette University Archives, which would help tell the team's powerful story in this book, *Scrimmage for War*.

He did in fact, like his Vancouver High School classmate Chuck Furno, stay with the game of football, playing the Bearcats' somewhat abbreviated 1942 season, then returning to the game after World War II at Willamette to play his senior year in the fall of 1946. After graduation in 1947, it was on to other sports as coach, teacher, and athletic director at the then-small Dallas, Oregon, High School, where he remained in the field of education for thirty-six years.

When the Bearcats returned home from the Territory of Hawaii, many of his teammates faced being drafted soon after the next semester began, but he hadn't yet registered for the draft. Instead of opting for the navy V-12 program, a college training program already under consideration at Willamette, designed to supplement the force of navy and marine commissioned officers during World War II, Ken joined the army air force reserves during the spring of 1942 and awaited the call to active duty. In the meantime, a number of his teammates elected to enter the V-12 program, and between 1 July 1943 and 30 June 1946, the program grew to more than 125,000 men at 131 colleges and universities in the United States.

Individually, in the spring of 1942, Ken and teammates Chuck Furno and Marshall Barbour, who also joined the army air force, went to Portland, Oregon, and took batteries of tests, which they all passed. When they were informed of their success and acceptance, they were each told to go back to Willamette and continue in school until called to active duty.

During the spring and summer before the 1942 Bearcats' football season and his entry into the army air force reserves, he went back to Vancouver and found a job building government housing to support the explosive, early growth of the shipbuilding industry in the area. His fiancée and high school sweetheart, Velda Fetis, had found work as a secretary in a local steamship company, and he moved there temporarily to work, enabling them to find and pay rent on an apartment. As the Willamette fall semester approached, Coach Keene found a job for both Velda and Ken, and they returned to Salem—then, impelled in part by his coming call to active duty in the army air force, decided to get married.

He married Velda on September 11 that year, and they took their honeymoon on the Oregon coast. They returned to Salem in time for him to enter school and begin football practice, while she went to work in her new job. Ken returned to his starting position at quarterback and blocking back under Coach Keene and played Willamette's somewhat abbreviated 1942 football season, as did a significant number of men from the 1941 team, including Chuck Furno, Cece Conner, Tony Fraiola as assistant coach, Ted Ogdahl as team captain, George Constable, Pat White, David Kelly, Allan Barrett, and Andrew Rogers.

Called to active duty in March 1943, he took Velda back to Vancouver by train, where she could remain with her parents while he reported to duty in Lincoln, Nebraska; was sent to Drake University for officer training; and went on to pre–flight training at Santa Ana Army Air Base at the Western Flying Training Command, California. There were no runways or aircraft there, and he underwent nine weeks of pre–flight training and a battery of tests to determine whether he was qualified to be a pilot, navigator, bombardier, mechanic, or some other duty. He was found to be qualified for pilot training; however, while there, he contracted a severe ear infection and was hospitalized. He went from Santa Ana to primary pilot training at the army's contract flying school at Gary Field, four miles northwest of Blythe, California, and had no difficulty soloing in the Boeing-Stearman PT-17 Kaydet biplane, going from there into basic flying training in Bakersfield, California.

While in the Gary Field contract school, where his instructor was a civilian crop-dusting pilot, once he soloed, he was to pay a price for lack of supervision by his instructor pilot. He recalled he hardly ever saw his instructor after he soloed and "didn't know what he was doing simply flying around by himself." Nor was he being adequately prepared for the next phase of his training in a newer, faster, more demanding low-wing monoplane in a deliberately more demanding wartime military flying training program.

His flying in the army's Vultee-built BT-13 trainer, the Valiant, in Bakersfield was limited, and he never soloed, under advice of his instructor. He was told he might be successful if he was "washed back" to the next class, but his instructor implied that he and others flying with him faced an increased risk should he continue in flying training. His instructor wrote a letter to the training group commander, recommending he not continue, and Ken was subsequently given orders to report to the radio communications technical school at Scott Army Airfield, Illinois, which had been one of thirty-two air service training camps established after the United States' entry into World War I in April 1917.

The rapidly changing structure and missions the army air force was undergoing at the outset of World War II resulted in Scott Field's becoming a headquarters for various technical schools moved to Scott. After 1940, the primary wartime mission of Scott was to train skilled radio operators and maintainers, to produce, as the radio school's slogan proclaimed, "the best damned radio operators in the world." When Ken arrived, he was unaware that Scott's radio school would become something of a "Communications University of the Army Air Forces" and would expand during the war to fill about forty-six large school buildings on base. From this course, many specialized radio and communications courses evolved, and the schools would graduate 77,370 radio operators/mechanics who flew in aircraft carrying multiple crew members and operated command-and-control communications from the ground and in the air in every theater of the war—and were often referred to as the "eyes and ears of the army air forces."

Velda went with him to Scott for the seven- to eight-month school he entered in January 1944. While there he received a letter from the Chicago Bears professional football organization asking him to come try out for the team. In his reply, he informed them that he was on active duty and couldn't accept their invitation, whereupon they wrote back asking that he contact them after he was released from active duty.

The war in Europe was beginning to wind down when Ken and five other men were ordered to South America, to an island in the Fernando de Noronha Archipelago, a chain of twenty-one islands 221 miles off the northeast coast of Brazil. There they were to build a radio-magnetic direction-finding station, with necessary communications available to provide emergency steering to a safe landing should aircraft crews become lost redeploying aircraft flying across the Atlantic from the European theater through Africa. The aircraft were heading for the continental United States or, much farther, to the distant Pacific theater during the buildup to invade Japan. The six were on duty on the island with their radio directional site operating for about six months when the Japanese surrendered. He recalled, "Fortunately, I remember we only had to provide an emergency steer to one aircraft in that six-month period."

On his return to the United States, the Chicago Bears again expressed interest in him, and he signed a contract with them, but he decided instead to use the Serviceman's Readjustment Act of 1944—known as the G.I. Bill—and return to Willamette in 1946 to complete his education. He also returned to the Bearcats football team in the summer, as did Chuck Furno, Paul Cookingham, Marv Goodman, Bill Reder, and Pat White from the 1941 team, but football, like everything else, had changed during the war.

The man-in-motion single wing of Willamette's Spec Keene years had given way to the faster double-wing attack, and when Ken, now weighing two hundred pounds, tried out at fullback, the Bearcats' coach, Walt Erickson, moved him from the backfield to the line, at tackle. In spite of Willamette's three years' "time out" from collegiate competition, the Bearcats went 6–2–1 and again won the Pacific Northwest Conference championship and the Paul Bunyan Ax, the conference trophy.

Ken Jacobson's graduation photograph, 1947 *Wallulah*. (*Source*: MOHLAWU)

Given credit for his time in training at Drake University during the war, he was able to graduate from Willamette in 1947, earning his degree in business administration. From there it was into education, coaching athletics, teaching, and administration at Dallas High School in the Polk County town of Dallas, Oregon, a small town fifteen miles west of Salem and Willamette University. There he and Velda remained, raising a family, while he continued working at Dallas High School.

But his entry into education didn't come easy. When he left the army air force, he had joined the ranks of millions coming home who had no experience in the field of education and no training in coaching or teaching, and he had to find a job and a place where he and Velda could live. To qualify him to teach, he was advised to take three courses: Oregon School Law, Oregon History, and Primary/Secondary Education. With his degree from Willamette and the three courses to bolster what he considered inadequate preparation, he was able to sign a contract with Dallas High School to teach the ninth grade, but with a few additional responsibilities: he was to coach junior varsity basketball, track, wrestling, and tennis, none of which he felt qualified to coach.

Beyond being presented with those additional duties in his contract, the school lacked an adequate gymnasium for basketball or wrestling. What's more, there was no track for a track team for six years. A suitable track had to come a piece at a time, like almost everything else, with hurdles, pole vault, and high-jump and broad-jump pits for training and conditioning—and he had no experience in any of these sports except some in tennis, since he and Velda had become reasonably good players during high school and won a tournament in doubles. But he had never coached tennis.

And wrestling? Zero experience. His young wrestling team members taught him. So Ken Jacobson set about being a builder, and he became an extraordinary builder. He learned as he taught and built where there was little or nothing. And he kept building and improving the rest of his career in education while the town of Dallas grew.

As for basketball, he and the army air force men on their island in the Atlantic had played pickup games of one-on-one and two-on-two in basketball during the war, a good way to pass the time on islands where little recreation was available, but hardly sufficient to qualify him to coach the game in interscholastic competition. In due time, however, that too would change. He would learn, and fast. He was a self-starting, hardworking, natural athlete with the personality, self-discipline, and drive to push himself while urging and motivating young people to learn and achieve.

He and his team had success in the junior varsity basketball league in Dallas, and he coached the JVs for five years before being relieved of that responsibility. But for that first year, it was Tuesday and Friday in basketball and wrestling on Thursdays. There were thirteen different weight categories in wrestling, and even there, in spite of his being coached by his young wrestlers, two or three of his boys made it into the state tournament that first year.

For the next wrestling season, he was pleased to be relieved from coaching wrestling and seeing one of the school's janitors, who was a good man and had been a former professional wrestler, hired as the wrestling coach. For in the background, Ken had voluntarily returned to his favorite game, football, and in 1948 he was co-coach on the varsity with the high school's head coach. He then became head coach, and his football team won its first league championship in 1950—the same year as the JV basketball team's first championship, in a season where the young team practiced and played home games in a small gymnasium in a Dallas grade school.

One of the school's students who was interested in track made a pole-vault pit, a runway, and a box for the pole to start track on the school's baseball field. Ken went to a man who manufactured track-and-field equipment to continue building and providing the necessary equipment, such as hurdles, to fully develop what was needed for a track team. The result was the young team's first track championship in 1950.

The school hadn't a suitable football field, either, so he laid out a field that included a track, but it had no lights. Polk County let them use their lighted field for games a mile distant from the school and the practice field he developed, but soon the county had to discontinue its loan of the lighted field, causing them to return to the one he had marked out to practice and play games. The school eventually installed lights, resulting finally in the full development of the home football field where he had become head coach while becoming ever-more deeply involved in fund-raising, through ticket sales, concessions, and other activities, to support and improve the teams and their athletic facilities at Dallas High School— duties normally assigned to an athletic director and his staff. He was clearly developing the skills necessary to become the Dallas High School athletic and activities director.

In 1953, Dallas High School, having relocated from its old academy building to a new location, opened its new basketball gymnasium with a head coach and the former JV players Ken had coached. In 1955, he coached the football team into the finals of the state play-offs, but they lost. He remained successful and highly regarded as the head football coach for fifteen years. In May 1960, he completed work earning a master's degree in education from Oregon State. After fifteen years coaching varsity football, Ken moved into the position of athletic and activities director while coaching the varsity track team one more year, for a total of sixteen years.

Throughout the thirty-six years he worked for the Orange and Black Dallas High School Dragons until his retirement in 1983, the town's population was fluctuating but overall continued to increase, requiring the school to compete at various levels with different schools in the state's athletic organization, but overall gradually increasing its level of interscholastic competition to a larger 4A school, though the number of students in the school was considerably below those of the schools they were competing against. Throughout the entire period, Ken and the school's administrators were able to hire dedicated, successful athletic coaches who continued to add strength and prestige to Dallas High School's athletic programs.

Following his retirement from Dallas High School, he remained active in the 1941 Bearcat football team's reunions, was inducted into the Willamette University Hall of Fame with the entire Bearcat team in 1997, and participated in the making of videotaped interviews and in the making of the year 2000 National Football League (NFL) Films video about the Bearcats' voyage to Hawaii, their football game on December 6, their prompt mobilization following the Japanese attack, their ten days' guard duty at Punahou

Ken Jacobson, Earl Hampton, and Chuck Furno at a 2011 reunion at Willamette University. (*Source*: KJC)

School, and their return home on the *Coolidge*, a video broadcast on ESPN and subsequently released on a DVD in February 2006.

On October 17, 2003, Ken spoke to the Willamette football team regarding the experiences of the 1941 team at Pearl Harbor. On November 5, 2007, he was inducted into the Dallas High School Athletic Hall of Fame. His childhood sweetheart and wife, Velda, died on January 5, 2010. They had raised a family of three children: two sons, both married—Steve K. Jacobson, of Salem, with his wife Barbara, and Eric R. Jacobson, with wife Cindy—and daughter, Jill A. Zatwarnicki, with her husband Bill.

Apparently in good health, Ken passed away suddenly on September 29, 2015. At the time of his death, he was residing in his independent-living apartment in the retirement community in Dallas, Oregon. In October 2013, the community had joyously rewarded Ken and two other World War II veterans in a very special ceremony and send-off.

HONOR FLIGHT TO THE NATIONAL WORLD WAR II MEMORIAL

On December 7, 2013, teammate Andrew Rogers, who was residing in Napa, California, at that time, made a point of phoning Ken Jacobson in Dallas, Oregon. At the time of Andy's call, they were the two surviving men from the journey to the Territory of Hawaii and back, where they had played in the Shrine Bowl and witnessed the Japanese attack on Pearl Harbor, a journey that began in Salem, Oregon, on November 26 that fateful year.

Shortly before Andrew called him, the World War II marine veteran of the Pacific campaigns was unaware of Honor Flights, their purposes, or their significance. Ken had served in the army air force and in the final months of World War II was sent the opposite direction during the war—to a small island in a chain of islands in the Atlantic, 221 miles northeast of Brazil. In recent years Ken had become aware of Honor Flights because they had taken root in Oregon in 2010. He had taken the journey to visit the World War II Memorial in Washington, DC, in October 2013.

But during the December 7 phone conversation, it's unlikely that either of them spoke of another surviving team member, Clarence Walden, a former marine aviator and Pacific veteran who, in his words, played the position of "left back" on the team more than sixty-two years earlier. Though in the 1941 team photograph, and thus inducted in the 1997 Willamette University Athletic Hall of Fame class, he wasn't selected to go with the team as a twenty-eighth Bearcat on the 1941 traveling squad and didn't finish his education at Willamette. He instead completed his undergraduate work at Oregon State College in 1950. Judge Clarence Walden is long retired from the bench in Woodland, California, but remains vital and occasionally joyfully active as the "marrying judge" in Woodland.

The first notification of a possible Honor Flight came to Ken Jacobson in June 2013. The purpose of Honor Flights is to take as many World War II veterans as possible to Washington to see the memorials honoring their actions in the war. The possibility became a reality for Ken, and the Dallas Retirement Village in Dallas, Oregon, where Ken and two other World War II veterans had lived for several years, sponsored the three, plus two guardians, for an Honor Flight to Washington, DC, over the weekend ending on Sunday, October 20, 2013.

Photograph taken during Ken Jacobson's Honor Flight to the World War II Memorial, Washington, DC, October 19, 2013. (*Source*: KJC)

Honor Flight of Oregon, serving veterans in Clackamas, Marion, Polk, Tillamook, and Yamhill Counties, is part of the Honor Flight Network, the national nonprofit organization founded in 2005.

As reporter Aaron Newton of the *Polk County Itemizer-Observer* wrote for the June 23 and 25 issues, "The Honor Flight Network, born in 2006 from similar programs in Ohio and North Carolina, has exploded in acclaim and fervor in recent years." For the Dallas Retirement Village, this would be their first direct involvement in the program. Sue Lamb, development director for the Dallas Retirement Foundation, partnered with Southern Oregon Honor Flight in Roseburg to get seats for Ken, ninety-two; Art Mosher, ninety-one; and Virgil Trick, ninety-six. Two more of the Dallas residents had been on Honor Flights, but their experiences were before they became residents in the retirement village. Sue later pointed out, "A lot of people here are from that era. I've been getting calls from people to put their name on the list. . . . Time being what it is, we need to keep moving on this." She added, "If it's successful, we're going to be purchasing, on an ongoing basis, two seats on each flight to send at least one vet from here and one guardian from here." At the time, there were seventy World War II veterans in the Dallas Retirement Village.

The June announcement caused a fund-raising scramble. With the $1,000 required per veteran raised by the Dallas Retirement Village, they would be flown to visit the World War II Memorial in the nation's capital—their memorial, which for nearly fifty-five years many veterans of World War II had only hoped would someday be built, somewhere.

The whirlwind trip lasted fifty-three hours. Ken, Art, and Virgil made the once-in-a-lifetime journey along with forty-six other veterans from across Oregon. The village held a grand send-off for the three on October 17, complete with a color guard, numerous guests, and some patriotic songs to stir pleasant memories for their trip before their short drive to Portland the day before the flight. They stayed at an airport motel and had a 4:00 a.m. get-up to make their flight. The flight left Portland at 6:30 a.m. Friday and landed at Dulles International Airport outside of DC nearly six hours later. They visited the memorial on Saturday and returned home exhausted on Sunday, but they brought with them memories that hopefully helped them know without question that they were deeply admired and respected by a grateful nation for all they had done and given in their lives of sacrifice so many years ago, and in all the years to follow.

At their layover in Chicago and the final stop in Washington, there were raucous crowds mirroring the reception when the Beatles first came to the United States, said Brenda Berry-Kendall, life enrichment coordinator at the village. "The guys were kind of embarrassed because of the grandeur," she said. "I couldn't believe how thunderous the crowd was in Chicago. A young, twelve-year-old girl shook Virgil Trick's hand and said, 'Thank you for saving our country.'"

His response to her? "I just did my part."

But sadness also briefly became a traveling companion in Chicago when the trip for one veteran from Yamhill County, Oregon, was his last. He died while a family member was with him. The family member made funeral arrangements for him from Chicago. As in World War II, life and life's battles and journeys would go on. And so did the trip to Washington, DC. Art Mosher added another observation about the loss: "I thought that was kind of symbolic of our group. Us veterans are going."

Ken Jacobson had previously come to Washington, DC, but the World War II Memorial didn't exist on that first visit. In October 2013, he carried clear memories away from the memorial. He described the visit in his typically modest, understated manner as "impressive." He noted that there was a section of the memorial dedicated to each state, and "the guys really appreciated it." "A group of high school kids from Oregon wanted to help, raised their own money and went along."

The veterans were taken to the Elks Club for dinner, each one given an American flag, and while there were treated to a "mail call." The surprise "mail call" was a re-creation of an almost daily ritual for America's men and women serving all over the world during the war, where they waited anxiously to hear their names called by mail clerks or others in unit administrative positions and be handed letters or packages from home. For Honor Flights, the volunteers who help plan, coordinate, and manage each flight contact children, other family members, and friends in advance to ask them to write letters to hand to their veterans at "mail call." They are touching moments to remember.

It is most fitting that Ken Jacobson had the opportunity to represent the 1941 Willamette University Bearcats football team on his visit to the National World War II Memorial, although it's doubtful he viewed his visit as meriting such significance. He was far too modest to make such an assumption. Nevertheless, his and the San Jose State team's journey was more than remarkable, and rightly, though slowly, it has become legend, especially at

Willamette University, where the Bearcats of that year were inducted into the University's Athletic Hall of Fame.

They sailed to the Territory of Hawaii in the last days of November 1941 to enjoy an island that few, if any, of the fifty-two players had ever seen, each team to play two football games and return home for Christmas. He carried his personal camera and recorded his team's voyage to paradise, a voyage none would ever forget. They played only one of two games scheduled and lost.

Then came the shattering December 7 attack on Pearl Harbor and many other targets on Oahu by 350 Japanese naval aircraft launched in two waves from six aircraft carriers escorted by two battleships, two cruisers, ten destroyers, and three scout submarines, supported by twenty-seven more submarines—igniting the final and disastrous Pacific Ocean conflagration of World War II. At first, they were witnesses only; then they were mobilized under martial law and asked to dig trenches and firing positions, string barbed wire, stand guard, and possibly help defend with their lives the island to which they had come merely to play football. Draftees with no draft call. Unsuspecting involuntary volunteers.

They were fun-loving, casual observers quite literally pressed into service by the declaration of martial law on the afternoon of 7 December; given orders for duty; handed rifles, bayonets, and other military uniform items; and pressed into military and police service with no prior warning and little or no experience. With the twenty-five San Jose State Spartans, they willingly took up arms and served through twelve puzzling, confusing, chaotic days and blacked-out nights, wondering when and how they would return home and trying to communicate with families at home (and with Oahu's civilian and military population), while at the same time wondering whether the Japanese would follow up the shattering air attacks by landing troops on the island.

While the twenty-five San Jose State Spartans mobilized to assist the Honolulu Police Department—including three who had watched in stunned disbelief from a hillside as the USS *Oklahoma* capsized in a harbor filled with burning ships and oil-fed flames—all were drilled and given instructions by the police, with most assigned to ride in patrol cars; help enforce blackouts; assist the FBI and police in rounding up Japanese, German, and Italian aliens; guard key installations; and assist in sentry duty at Punahou School.

In the meantime, the Willamette University players stood sentry duty around the clock for ten days on the long perimeter of Punahou School, providing security for the Army Engineers and hundreds of construction workers and other civilian employees who, acting under martial law and contingency plans, had taken control of the school's entire campus.

Then, with two hours' notice, came the two teams' abrupt December 19 departure on the SS *President Coolidge*, in convoy with the U.S. Army transport, *General Hugh L. Scott*, escorted by the cruiser USS *Detroit* and the destroyer USS *Cummings*, and, through the first night outbound, the destroyer USS *Reid*, in an unforgettable seven-day voyage to San Francisco. Seven of the Spartans chose to stay behind and continue their service with the Honolulu Police Department, while the team's co-captain at the last minute talked one more of his teammates out of staying behind and Coach Roy Keene refused to allow well-intended, more permanent volunteer service from Willamette team members until they first consulted with their parents.

The two teams' voyage home was a wrenching, unforgettable trip through waters patrolled by Japanese submarines, after rumors and news reports were already filled with stories of submarine attacks in Hawaiian and West Coast waters. They were sailing on an overcrowded former luxury liner carrying 125 severely wounded Pearl Harbor survivors, including thirty burn victims, with attending doctors, nurses, and corpsmen, plus medical supplies suitable for a small hospital, as well as approximately four hundred other evacuees, including women and children abruptly ordered home, with some of them having lost husbands and fathers during the attack. Similar but smaller passenger loads were added to the *Scott*. All had been added to a virtually full passenger load on both ships, which had arrived in Honolulu from the Philippines on Wednesday the 16th, with all now required to wear or carry life vests at all times. Once on board and under way came the sobering call to lifeboat stations for able-bodied passengers, with no-holds-barred briefings on the threat that lay ahead.

For the football players and crew members that volunteered to give up better quarters to the wounded, they were billeted in steerage for the voyage home. As part of the arrangements for the voyage, the football players were asked to, and gladly did, assist and help comfort the wounded. They also were prepared and, if necessary, ready to assist the doctors, nurses, medics, and ship's crew in moving the wounded, women, and children to lifeboats if successfully attacked by a submarine and directed to "abandon ship." There were tense, fear-filled periods broken up by the good humor of the wounded and young men who at times struggled with their own emotions, yet loved to make others smile and laugh. There were movies, dancing, singing, and the U.S.-bound gift of two young panda bears from China that helped make the voyage home more palatable.

Daily zigzagging, watching scout planes launch and recover from the *Detroit* morning and afternoon when weather was suitable to search ahead for telltale signs of submarines, ships, or aircraft, as ships' officers and crew using binoculars—and wary passengers using eyesight primarily—scanned the ocean's surface for the same purpose. A submarine warning that heightened concerns but proved false didn't help to reduce fears less than forty-eight hours from home, in spite of an early Christmas party on Christmas Eve. Rough seas, squalls, sharply reduced visibility, dim and distant lights, and early morning fog were combined with the comfort of friendly aircraft overhead as they drew closer to home.

Last came early Christmas morning and the joyous passage beneath the Golden Gate Bridge into San Francisco Harbor and the incredible, totally unexpected, yet carefully secured, muffled, and secretive, welcome by the city's people and the ever curious, demanding press in the rush to get safely home. And for the two football contingents, there was the delayed disembarkation as they watched and waited in deference to the wounded, women, and children—and the scramble to get through reporters and on the way home. For all those headed to Salem, Oregon, there was a rush to board the ferry to Oakland for the overnight train ride home—and to quietly talk and reflect on the past month as they rolled north.

In so many ways, Ken's life, and the lives of his football teammates, symbolized the nature of all who served among a whole generation born before the Great Depression and, with their mothers, fathers, brothers, and sisters, struggled through it—then found themselves, as citizen soldiers, thrust into the most destructive war in human history. But their initiation and greeting in the era of the "New Totalitarians" had been more than different. They were there, in paradise, then in hell, among the igniters of bright lights in a whole generation of bright lights who did in fact save their country, and indeed Western civilization.

It is a grand story and facts of life far more than legend.

PHOTOGRAPHIC CREDIT ABBREVIATIONS

ABMC	American Battle Monuments Commission
ARC	Andrew Rogers Collection
CSFFC	Charles S. Furno Family Collection
CWC	Clarence Walden Collection
ESPNDF	ESPN documentary film
HAA	*Honolulu Star-Bulletin* newspaper, courtesy of the *Honolulu Advertiser* Archives
IJN	Imperial Japanese Navy
JBC	John Barbour Collection
JLC	Janet Leffler Collection, daughter of Charles S. Furno
KCC	Kathy Carver Collection, daughter of Victor A. Robinson
KJC	Kenneth Jacobson Collection
LCC	Leah Conner Collection
MNC	Matson Navigation Company
MOHLAWU	Mark O. Hatfield Library Archives, Willamette University
NA	National Archives
NAPR	National Archives Pacific Region
NHHC	Naval History and Heritage Command
NMF	Norwegian Merchant Fleet
NPSAM	National Park Service, *Arizona* Memorial
NPSSFMML	National Park Service, San Francisco Maritime Museum and National Historical Park Library
OSULSCA	Oregon State University Library Special Collections and Archives
PSA	Punahou School Archives
SJSULA	San Jose State University Library Archives
UDML	University of Detroit Mercy Library, photographic digital image from the Fr. Edward J. Dowling, S.J., Marine Historical Collection
USA	U.S. Army
USAAF	U.S. Army Air Force

USACE	U.S. Army Corps of Engineers photo collection
USAF	U.S. Air Force
USASC	U.S. Army Signal Corps
USMC	U.S. Marine Corps and VMF-224
USN	U.S. Navy
WOL	Wikipedia online
WPA	*West Point Atlas: A Short Military History of World War I*

Bibliography

Interviews with the Author
Fitzgerald, Karin
Furno, Charles
Galvin, John
Hadley, Shirley (McKay)
Hampton, Earl
Jacobson, Kenneth W.
O'Brien, Daniel H.
Peterson, Alice
Rogers, Andrew
Walden, Clarence

Books
Allen, Gwenfread. *Hawaii's War Years, 1941–45*. Honolulu: University of Hawaii Press, 1950.

Blair, Clay. *The Forgotten War*. New York: Doubleday, 1987.

De Chant, John A. *Devilbirds: The Story of USMC Aviation in WWII*. New York: Harper, 1947.

Gatke, Robert Moulton. *Chronicles of Willamette: The Pioneer University of the West*. Portland, OR: Binfords & Mort, 1942.

Giangreco, D. M. *Hell to Pay: Operation Downfall and the Invasion of Japan, 1945–47*. Annapolis, MD: Naval Institute Press, 2009.

Goldstein, Donald M., and Katherine V. Dillon *The Pacific War Papers: Japanese Documents of World War II*. Washington, DC: Potomac Books, 2004.

La Torre. San Jose State College Annual, 1942. San Jose, CA.

Leaming, Jack. *From 6-S-7*. Las Vegas, NV, 1998.

Lippincott, Benjamin E., historian, 13th Air Force. *From Fiji through the Philippines with the Thirteenth Air Force*. San Angelo, TX: Newsfoto Publishing, Date Unknown.

McWilliams, Bill. *Sunday in Hell: Pearl Harbor Minute by Minute*. New York: E-Reads, 2011.

Prange, Gordon W., Donald M. Goldstein, and Katherine V. Dillon. *At Dawn We Slept: The Untold Story of Pearl Harbor*. New York: McGraw-Hill, 1981.

Sherrod, Robert. *History of Marine Corps Aviation in World War II*. Washington, DC: Combat Forces Press, 1952.

Stone, Peter. *The Lady and the President: The Life and Loss of the S.S.* President Coolidge. Victoria, Australia: Oceans Enterprises, 1997.

Wallulah, Willamette University Annual, 1942. Salem, OR.

Wallulah, Willamette University Annual, 1943. Salem, OR.

Wallulah, Willamette University Annual, 1944. Salem, OR.

Wallulah, Willamette University Annual, 1947. Salem, OR.

West Point Atlas: A Short Military History of World War I. West Point, NY: Department of Military Art and
Engineering, 1954.
West Point Atlas of American Wars. Vol. 2, *1900–1953*. New York: Praeger, 1959.
Willmott, H. P. *Pearl Harbor*. London: Cassell, 2001.

BOOKLETS
Dodge, Charlotte Peabody. *Punahou: The War Years, 1941–1945*. Honolulu, HI: Punahou School, 1945.
Ships in Gray: The Story of Matson in World War II. San Francisco, 1949.

ARTICLES
"10,000 Miles of 'Waiting' for Jap Subs." *San Francisco Chronicle*, San Francisco, CA, 27 December 1941.
"A Message from Chairman of Annual Shrine Event." *Honolulu Star-Bulletin*, Honolulu, HI, 6 December
1941.
"A Veteran Says: 'I Want to Go Back to China and Fight'; Home and Business Lost." *San Francisco Chronicle*,
San Francisco, CA, 26 December 1941.
"Army Issues a Partial List of the Honolulu Evacuees." *San Francisco Chronicle*, San Francisco, CA, 27 Decem-
ber 1941.
"Bearcat Gridders Arrive Here Today." *Oregon Statesman*, Salem, OR, 26 December 1941.
"Bearcats Run Wild." *Honolulu Star-Bulletin*, Honolulu, HI, 6 December 1941.
Bishop, John. "Photo Mission: Truk." *Naval History*, January/February 1999. (Copy courtesy of Judge Clarence
Walden.)
Brachman, Bob. "San Jose Home from Hawaii." *San Francisco Examiner*, San Francisco, CA, 26 December
1941.
"Brief Facts on Willamette U for Island Fans." *Honolulu Star-Bulletin*, Honolulu, HI, 6 December 1941.
Bucher, Ric. "Spartans Settle for Tie." *San Jose Mercury News*, San Jose, CA, 17 November 1991.
Burgess, Emma. "Spartans to Take on Hawaii." *Spartan Daily*, San Jose State University, San Jose, CA, 14
November 1991.
"'Cat Gridders Off for Hawaii This Morning." *Oregon Statesman*, Salem, OR, 26 November 1941.
"'Cats Vie with Airmen Tonight in Season's Grid Opener Here." *Oregon Statesman*, Salem, OR, 19 September
1941.
Chapin, John C. "The 4th Marine Division in World War II." United States Marine Corps History Division,
Quantico, VA, undated.
"Children Tell More Details of Hawaii Raid." *San Francisco Examiner*, San Francisco, CA, 27 December 1941.
"Coast Gridders to Arrive Today." *Honolulu Advertiser*, Honolulu, HI, 3 December 1941.
"Coast Teams Arrive to Play Hawaii." *Honolulu Advertiser*, Honolulu, HI, 4 December 1941.
"Complete Shrine Program for Annual Big Spectacle." *Honolulu Star-Bulletin*, Honolulu, HI, 6 December
1941.
"Convoy Brings Hawaii Victims to Bay City." *Oregon Statesman*, Salem, OR, 26 December 1941.
Cox, James A. "Payback Time at Truk." *Semper Fi* magazine, Marine Corps League, Merrifield, VA, Summer
2004.
"Do Not Pass! Waterfront Placed under Heavy Guard." *San Francisco Chronicle*, San Francisco, CA, 26 Decem-
ber 1941.
Douquet, Anne. "1941 SJSU Football Players Recall Severity, Pain of Pearl Harbor." *Spartan Daily*, San Jose
State University, San Jose, CA, 18 November 1991.
English, Reid. "Bearcat Players Recall Infamous Day." *Statesman Journal*, Salem, OR, 7 December 1991.
———. "Defense Lifts Willamette, 34–21." *Statesman Journal*, Salem, OR, 29 September 1991.
———. "Willamette Inducts First Members to Its Hall." *Statesman Journal*, Salem, OR, 30 September 1991.
"Evacuees Tell of Jap Raid on Hawaii." *San Francisco Call-Bulletin*, San Francisco, CA, 27 December 1941.
"First Shrine Game Was Suggested by Late M. A. Nicoll." *Honolulu Star-Bulletin*, Honolulu, HI, 6 December
1941.
"Four Spartan Grid Members Receive All-Coast Honors." *Spartan Daily*, San Jose State College, San Jose,
CA, 22 December 1941.

"Gene Stewart:" *Oregon Statesman*, Salem, OR, 27 December 1941.

"Golden Raiders Survey Honolulu Scenery Today." *Spartan Daily*, San Jose State College, San Jose, CA, 3 December 1941.

"Great Homecomings." *Honolulu Star-Bulletin*, Honolulu, HI, 6 December 1941.

"Gridders Safe; Former Spartan Relates Arrival in Honolulu." *Spartan Daily*, San Jose State College, San Jose, CA, 11 December 1941.

"Gridders Tell Experiences." *Willamette Collegian*, Willamette University, Salem, OR, 23 January 1942.

"Gridders to Tell of Island Attack." *Spartan Daily*, San Jose State College, San Jose, CA, 14 January 1942.

"Gridmen Unreported in Honolulu Crisis; Games Are Indefinite." *Spartan Daily*, San Jose State College, San Jose, CA, 8 December 1941.

"Group Returns on US Convoy, Coach Advises." *Oregon Statesman*, Salem, OR, 26 December 1941.

"Hawaii vs. Willamette." *Honolulu Star-Bulletin*, Honolulu, HI, 6 December 1941.

"Hawaii Wounded in S.F." *San Francisco Call-Bulletin*, San Francisco, CA, 26 December 1941.

"Hawaii Wounded in S.F., Evacuee Ships Escorted by U.S. Planes." *San Francisco Call Bulletin*, 26 December 1941.

"Hawaiian Trip Filled with Action." *Willamette Collegian*, Willamette University, Salem, OR, 10 January 1942.

"Here's the Civilian List of Those Back from Islands." *San Francisco Chronicle*, San Francisco, CA, 27 December 1941.

Holly, Hazel. "Women Volunteers Acclaimed for Work with Evacuees." *San Francisco Examiner*, San Francisco, CA, 27 December 1941.

Hop, Loi'i Leong. "Teams' Arrival Marks 22nd Annual Invasion by Mainland Elevens." *Honolulu Star-Bulletin*, Honolulu, HI, 3 December 1941.

———. "Willamette's Short High Passes May Whip Hawaii." *Honolulu Star-Bulletin*, Honolulu, HI, 4 December 1941.

Hruby, Dan. "San Jose's War Story." *San Jose Mercury News*, San Jose, California, 16 November 1991.

"Hundreds of Women and Children Start on Trains for Their Homes." *San Francisco Chronicle*, San Francisco, CA, 27 December 1941.

"'I Thought It Was Just a Sham Battle.'" *San Francisco Chronicle*, San Francisco, CA, 26 December 1941.

"Irving E. Miller." Obituary, *Statesman Journal*, Salem, OR, 10 July 1993.

"Jap Sub Pack on Coast Disappears; Attacks Halt." *San Francisco Examiner*, San Francisco, CA, 27 December 1941.

Lenn, Earnest. "Ships with Hawaii Injured Reach S.F." *San Francisco Examiner*, 26 December 1941.

Lieser, Gil. "Willamette Celebrates Centenary." *Honolulu Star-Bulletin*, Honolulu, HI, 6 December 1941.

Lynn, Capi. "Bearcats Start with Bang." *Statesman Journal*, Salem, OR, 14 September 1997.

Marqua, Frank. "Witnesses to History." *Press Democrat*, Santa Rosa, CA, 6 December 2011.

Maves, Norm, Jr. "Rendezvous at Pearl Harbor: A Grim, Personal Encounter with History." *The Oregonian*, Portland, OR, 7 December 1998.

McQueen, Red. "Hoomaliamali." *Honolulu Advertiser*, Honolulu, HI, 6 December 1941.

Meisler, Dan. "Film Will Highlight Football War Story." *Statesman Journal*, Salem, OR, 25 July 2000.

"Miss Jack Tells Group of Hawaii." *Willamette Collegian*, Willamette University, Salem, OR, 10 January 1942.

Mitsukado, Andrew. "Hawaii Favored over Willamette." *Honolulu Advertiser*, Honolulu, HI, 6 December 1941.

———. "Rambling Around." *Honolulu Advertiser*, Honolulu, HI, 4 December 1941.

"Named for Hawaii Trip, 27 Cat Grid Kids Grin, Rally Slated Wednesday." *Oregon Statesman*, Salem, OR, 25 November 1941.

"No Decision until Dec. 9." *Honolulu Star-Bulletin*, Honolulu, HI, 4 December 1941.

"Obituary: T. Theodore 'Ted' Ogdahl." *Statesman Journal*, Salem, OR, 30 July 1988.

"Official Program—Shrine Game." *Honolulu Star-Bulletin*, Honolulu, HI, 6 December 1941.

Pearce, Dick. "Young Evacuees Tell of Attack on Hawaii." *San Francisco Examiner*, San Francisco, CA, 26 December 1941.

"Pearl Harbor Recalled." *The Oregonian*, Portland, OR, 7 December 1981.

"Pineapple Bowl." *Honolulu Star-Bulletin*, Honolulu, HI, 6 December 1941.

"Play by Play Account of UH-Willamette Game." *Honolulu Advertiser*, Honolulu, HI, 7 December 1941.

"Player Numbers, Willamette, UH Jerseys." *Honolulu Star-Bulletin*, Honolulu, HI, 6 December 1941.

Postrel, Ban. "Surprise of Pearl Harbor Forever Changed Willamette Athletes." *Statesman Journal*, Salem, OR, 7 December 1997.

"Rainbows Have But One Setback in Regular Race." *Honolulu Star-Bulletin*, Honolulu, HI, 6 December 1941.

Reeves, Irene. "Irving E. Miller Remembered." *Jefferson, OR (Marion Co.) Review*, 5 August 1995.

"Return of Football Team Still Unsettled, Coach Ben Winkelman Says in Telephone Conversation." *Spartan Daily*, San Jose State College, San Jose, CA, 19 December 1941.

"Salem Welcomes Home Willamette Party." *Oregon Statesman*, Salem, OR, 27 December 1941.

"San Jose State Football Team Given Tribute by Secretary of the U.S. Navy." *Spartan Daily*, San Jose State College, San Jose, CA, 13 January 1942.

"San Jose State Football Team Stranded in Honolulu." *San Jose Mercury Herald*, San Jose, CA, 8 December 1941.

"Scalping Doesn't Worry Stew; Accepts Chemawa Job." *Willamette Collegian*, Willamette University, Salem, OR, 23 January 1942.

"Senator McKay: Reveals His Reactions." *Oregon Statesman*, Salem, OR, 27 December 1941.

Silverman, Milton. "Isle Evacuees Mix Sorrow with Elation." *San Francisco Chronicle*, San Francisco, CA, 26 December 1941.

Silverton, Milton. "Isle Evacuees Mix Sorrow with Elation." *San Francisco Chronicle*, San Francisco, CA, 26 December 1941.

Snow, Charlotte. "Team Spirit Improves with Age." *Statesman Journal*, Salem, OR, 29 September 1991.

"Spartan Grid Team Returns from War." *San Jose Mercury Herald*, San Jose, CA, 26 December 1941.

"Spartan Team in Surprise Return from Hawaii." *San Jose Mercury Herald*, San Jose, CA, 26 December 1941.

"Spartans Hold Practice with Opponents." *Spartan Daily*, San Jose Stage College, San Jose, CA, 1 December 1941.

"Spartans Lose to Moffett, 22–13," *Spartan Daily*, San Jose Stage College, San Jose, CA, 27 November 1941.

"Spartan's Team Reported Assigned to Police Duty in Honolulu." *Spartan Daily*, San Jose Stage College, San Jose, CA, 9 December 1941.

"Spec Keene." *Oregon Statesman*, Salem, OR, 27 December 1941.

"Spec Phones WU Party Works on Isle." *Willamette Collegian*, Willamette University, Salem, OR, 12 December 1941.

"State Gridders Make Last Home Appearance Tonight; Former Spartan Stars to Play for Flyers." *Spartan Daily*, San Jose Stage College, San Jose, CA, 26 November 1941.

"Stranded Footballers Still Unreported in Hawaiian Islands." *Spartan Daily*, San Jose Stage College, San Jose, CA, 10 December 1941.

"Team Tours Pearl Harbor—50 Years Later." *Statesman Journal*, Salem, OR, 7 December 1991.

Terrell, John U. "Hawaii's Wounded Arrive Here." *San Francisco Chronicle*, San Francisco, CA, 26 December 1941.

———. "War Comes to the Coast . . . Ambulances Pick Up the Injured as Crowds Mill around Seeking Relatives." *San Francisco Chronicle*, San Francisco, CA, 26 December 1941.

"The Biggest Game for the Biggest Cause." *Honolulu Advertiser*, Honolulu, HI, 3 December 1941.

"The Women: They Tell Experiences." *Oregon Statesman*, Salem, OR, 27 December 1941.

Tillman, Barret. "The Mustangs of Iwo." *Air Force Magazine*, Arlington, VA, April 2013.

"Tom Taylor Writes, Describes Trip to Honolulu." *Spartan Daily*, San Jose Stage College, San Jose, CA, 12 December 1941.

"U. of Hawaii Roster." *Honolulu Star-Bulletin*, Honolulu, HI, 6 December 1941.

"University of Hawaii Downs Willamette 20–6." *Honolulu Advertiser*, Honolulu, HI, 8 December 1941.

"Versatile Players on Bearcat '11.'" *Honolulu Star-Bulletin*, Honolulu, HI, 6 December 1941.

"Welcome Home Parties Fete Shirley McKay." *Willamette Collegian*, Willamette University, Salem, OR, 10 January 1942.

"Willamette Leads Colleges on Offensive." *Honolulu Star-Bulletin*, Honolulu, HI, 3 December 1941.

"Willamette Roster." *Honolulu Star-Bulletin*, Honolulu, HI, 6 December 1941.

MAGAZINES
Air Force Magazine, vol. 96, no. 4, p. 74. Arlington, VA, April 2013.

NEWSPAPERS
Honolulu Star-Bulletin, Honolulu, HI, 3 December 1941.
Honolulu Star-Bulletin, Honolulu, HI, 4 December 1941.
Honolulu Star-Bulletin, Honolulu, HI, 6 December 1941.
Oregon Statesman, Salem, OR, 19 September 1941.
Oregon Statesman, Salem, OR, 25 November 1941.
Oregon Statesman, Salem, OR, 26 November 1941.
Oregon Statesman, Salem, OR, 25 December 1941.
Oregon Statesman, Salem, OR, 26 December 1941.
Oregon Statesman, Salem, OR, 27 December 1941.
San Francisco Chronicle, San Francisco, CA, 26 December 1941.
San Francisco Chronicle, San Francisco, CA, 27 December 1941.
San Francisco Examiner, San Francisco, CA, 26 December 1941.
San Francisco Examiner, San Francisco, CA, 27 December 1941.
San Jose Mercury Herald, San Jose, CA, 8 December 1941.
San Jose Mercury Herald, San Jose, CA, 26 December 1941.
San Jose Mercury News, San Jose, CA, 16 November 1991.
San Jose Mercury News, San Jose, CA, 17 November 1991.
San Jose News, San Jose, CA, 13 January 1942.
Spartan Daily, San Jose State College, San Jose, CA, 26 November 1941.
Spartan Daily, San Jose State College, San Jose, CA, 27 November 1941.
Spartan Daily, San Jose State College, San Jose, CA, 1 December 1941.
Spartan Daily, San Jose State College, San Jose, CA, 3 December 1941.
Spartan Daily, San Jose State College, San Jose, CA, 8 December 1941.
Spartan Daily, San Jose State College, San Jose, CA, 9 December 1941.
Spartan Daily, San Jose State College, San Jose, CA, 10 December 1941.
Spartan Daily, San Jose State College, San Jose, CA, 11 December 1941.
Spartan Daily, San Jose State College, San Jose, CA, 12 December 1941.
Spartan Daily, San Jose State College, San Jose, CA, 19 December 1941.
Spartan Daily, San Jose State College, San Jose, CA, 13 January 1942.
Spartan Daily, San Jose State College, San Jose, CA, 14 January 1942.
Spartan Daily, San Jose State University, San Jose, CA, 14 November 1991.
Spartan Daily, San Jose State University, San Jose, CA, 18 November 1991.
Statesman Journal, Salem, OR, 7 December 1981.
Statesman Journal, Salem, OR, 7 December 1991.
Statesman Journal, Salem, OR, 7 December 1997.
Statesman Journal, Salem, OR, 25 July 2000.
The Honolulu Advertiser, Honolulu, HI, 3 December 1941.
The Honolulu Advertiser, Honolulu, HI, 4 December 1941.
The Honolulu Advertiser, Honolulu, HI, 6 December 1941.
The Honolulu Advertiser, Honolulu, HI, 7 December 1941.
The Oregonian, Portland, OR, 7 December 1998.
The San Francisco Call-Bulletin, San Francisco, CA, 26 December 1941.
The San Francisco Call-Bulletin, San Francisco, CA, 27 December 1941.
Willamette Collegian, Willamette University, Salem, OR, 22 September 1941.
Willamette Collegian, Willamette University, Salem, OR, 12 December 1941.
Willamette Collegian, Willamette University, Salem, OR, 10 January 1942.
Willamette Collegian, Willamette University, Salem, OR, 23 January 1942.

ACTION REPORTS
USS *Argonne* (AP-4), 28 January 1942.

SHIPS' DECK LOGS
Aircraft Carrier USS *Enterprise* (CV-6)
Battleship USS *Maryland* (BB-46)
Battleship USS *Tennessee* (BB-43)
Cruiser USS *Detroit* (CL-8)
Cruiser USS *Louisville* (CA-28)
Cruiser USS *Phoenix* (CL-46)
Cruiser USS *St. Louis* (CL-49)
Destroyer USS *Cummings* (DD-369)
Destroyer USS *Cushing* (DD-376)
Destroyer USS *Preston* (DD-377)
Destroyer USS *Preston* (DD-379)
Destroyer USS *Reid* (DD-365)
Destroyer USS *Smith* (DD-376)

LETTERS
Knox, William Franklin, Secretary of the Navy. Letter to Carl Sumner Knopf, President, Willamette University, 7 January 1942. (Courtesy of Willamette University Archives, Salem, OR.)
Knox, William Franklin, Secretary of the Navy. Letter to Theodore W. McQuarrie, President, San Jose State College, 7 January 1942, as printed in the *San Jose News*, 13 January 1942. (Courtesy of San Jose State University Archives and the San Jose Public Library, San Jose, CA.)

NATIONAL ARCHIVES' MILITARY RECORDS
Barbour, Marshall Hall, USAAFR
Conner, Gilbert Cecil, USMCR
Fitzgerald, James Martin, USMCR
Furno, Charles Sam, USAAFR
Miller, Irving E., USAAFR
Ogdahl, Tillman Theodore, USMCR
Reynolds, Marion Edward, USMCR

VIDEOS
1941 Willamette Football Feature, ESPN, 12 February 2006.
1941 Willamette Football Team, Willamette University, date unknown.

UNPUBLISHED SOURCES
251st Coast Artillery War Diary, 7 December 1941.
Bloch, C.C. Memorandum for Commander-in-Chief (Pacific Fleet), 15 December 1941.
Facts and factual excerpts from the preface of the book *Cameras over the Pacific*, a history of VMD-254 by John Bishop. (Courtesy of Judge Clarence Walden.)
Frucht, Max M. Memo to the Commandant, 14th Naval District: Honolulu, T.H., 15 December 1941. National Archives.
———. Press Release for 17 December 1941. National Archives.
"Furno Press Release—8.1.06." Vancouver Hilton Hotel, Vancouver, WA, 12 October 2006.
Knox, Frank. Directive to Chief of Naval Operations. "Evacuation Plan for Dependents of Navy Personnel from the Outlying Bases." October 31, 1941.
Logan, Margaret C. "Convoy Nurse." Undated, written recollections of a Red Cross Nurse, Honolulu, T.H., University of Hawaii Special Collections.
Seamon, R. M., Major, USMCR, Operations Officer. Undated Aircraft Crew List in Marine Photographic Squadron Two Fifty Four. (Courtesy of Clarence Walden.)

Walden, Clarence. Personal letter to a close friend describing and commenting on his World War II military experiences, April 1, 2000.

Walden, Clarence. Personal letter to the author providing additional background and perspective on his life and World War II military experience, March 5, 2013.

Online Primary Sources

4th Marine Division History. https://www.marines.mil/Portals/59/Publications/The%204th%20Marine%20 Division%20in%20World%20War%20II%20%20PCN%2019000412800.pdf.

15th Air Force, 5th Bomb Wing. http://www.15thaf.org/5th_BW.

91st Division American Expeditionary Force, World War I. http://www.newrivernotes.com/topical_ books_1918_worldwar1_storyof_91st_division.htm.

301st Bombardment Group (H). http://www.301bg.com.

321st Bombardment Group (M), Historical Archive Chronologies, February–August 1944, as pertains particularly to 448th Bombardment Squadron (M) and Lieutenant Marshall Hall Barbour (copilot, then pilot). http://www.warwingsart.com/12thAirForce/321history.html.

322nd Dailies from 1943—91st Bomb Group (H), as pertains to Irving E. Miller, B-17G (copilot). http:// www.91stbombgroup.com/Dailies/322nd1944.html.

322nd Dailies from 1944—91st Bomb Group (H), as pertains to Irving E. Miller, B-17G copilot. http:// www.91stbombgroup.com/Dailies/322nd1944.html.

322nd Dailies from 1945—91st Bomb Group (H), as pertains to Irving E. Miller, B-17G (copilot). http:// www.91stbombgroup.com/Dailies/322nd1944.html.

"1941 Ryan PT-22 Recruit." http://www.youtube.com/watch?v=3RVeBMhVPRw.

"Athletics: Football, Willamette University." Salem, OR. http://www.willamette.edu/athletics/teams/football/ pearl_harbor/index.php.

"Athletics: Hall of Fame Coach—Ted Ogdahl/Willamette University." http://www.willamette.edu/athletics/ hof/coaches/bios/ogdahl_ted.php.

"BTO, PFF, OBOE, H2S, H2X, MICKEY—Enter the Mystical World of Radar Navigational Bombing." http://www.398th.org/FlakNews/Articles/Laufer_Radar.html.

Battle Stations Fan Site. "Operation Hailstone (Raid on Truk)." http://battlestations.eu/index.php/en/our -encyclopedia/naval-battles/144-operation-hailstone.

DD-365 DANFS History (Destroyer USS *Cummings*). http://www.hazegray.org/danfs/destroy/dd365txt.htm.

DANFS History. "*Bismarck Sea.*" http://www.history.navy.mil/danfs/b6/bismarck-sea-i.htm.

DANFS. "USS *Louisville* (CA-28)." http://www.ibiblio.org/hyperwar/USN/ships/dafs/CA/ca28.html.

Demirel, Evin. "Razorback Football—Ben Winkelman." http://thesportsseer.com/tag/ben-winkelman.

Erickson, Ruth. "Oral Histories of the Pearl Harbor Attack: Lieutenant Ruth Erickson, NC, USN." http:// www.history.navy.mil/faqs/faq66-3b.htm.

"FDR Chat 29." Address of the President on the Fall of Rome, June 25, 1944. http://www.mhric.org/fdr/ chat29.html.

Hackett, Bob, and Sander Kingsepp. "Sensuikan!" Japanese Submarines: Tabular Record of Movements (TROMs). http://www.combinedfleet.com/sensuikan.htm.

Hickam Air Force Base Public Affairs. "Account of 38th Reconnaissance Squadron." December 1997. http:// www.hawaiischoolreports.com/history/wwiimilitary.htm.

HyperWar, USSBS. "Campaigns of the Pacific War, Chapter 13: The Iwo Jima Campaign." http://www.ibiblio .org/hyperwar/AAF/USSBS/PTO-Campaigns/USSBS-PTO-13.html.

Marqua, Frank. "Witnesses to History." *Press Democrat*, Santa Rosa, CA, 6 December 2011. http://www .pressdemocrat.com/article/20111206/SPORTS/111209658?SPSID=29304&SPID=2290&DB_OEM_ ID=5600&p=all&tc=pgall&tc=ar.

"Matson Line I." online. http://cruiselinehistory.com/tag/matson-line.

"Pearl Harbor Remembered: Oregonians and the Attack on Pearl Harbor." Oregon State Archives. http:// arcweb.sos.state.or.us/pages/exhibits/pearl/football.htm.

"Pearl Harbor Remembered: Oregonians and the Attack on Pearl Harbor." Oregon State Archives. http:// arcweb.sos.state.or.us/pages/exhibits/pearl/team.htm.

"Police School at SJSC." http://justicestudies.sjsu.edu/wp-content/uploads/2012/01/JS_75_Years_of_Excel
     lence.pdf.
"Punahou School: Cooke Hall Celebrates Centennial." Punahou School, Honolulu, HI. http://www.punahou
     .edu/page.cfm?p=2143.
Results of the American Pacific Submarine Campaign of World War II. http://www.navy.mil/navydata/cno/n87/
     history/pac-campaign.html.
Razorback Football—Ben Winkelman. "'The Fiercest Tackler Ever Developed in the South': The Story of
     Arkansas' First NFL Player." *Sports Seer.* http://thesportsseer.com/tag/ben-winkelman.
Salem History. "Douglas McKay." http://www.salemhistory.net/people/douglas_mckay.htm.
Sealift in World War II. GlobalSecurity.org. http://www.globalsecurity.org/military/systems/ship/sealift-ww2.htm.
"Secretary Knox Lauds Local Football Men." *San Jose News,* San Jose, CA, 12 January 1942. http://news
     .google.com/newspapers?nid=1977&dat=19420112&id=tXUiAAAAIBAJ&sjid=vKsFAAAAIBAJ
     &pg=6128,1011689.
"Seventy-Five Years of Progress: An Historical Sketch of the Southern Pacific, 1869–1944." http://cprr.org/
     Museum/SP_1869-1944/index.html.
Steele, J. M., and S. S. Isquith. "USS *Utah.*" 15 December 1941. http://www.history.navy.mil/docs/wwii/pearl/
     ph94.htm.
"Troopships of World War II." http://www.skylighters.org/troopships/libertyships.html.
"The University of Chicago History, Amos Alonzo Stagg." http://athletics.uchicago.edu/history/history-stagg
     .htm.
"Unsung Battle: Fighting at Funafuti Atoll Played an Important Role in World War II." http://www.leather
     neck.com/forums/showthread.php?15213-Unsung-battle-Fighting-at-Funafuti-Atoll-played-an-import
     ant-role-in-World-War-II.
USS *Arizona* Memorial. "The First Casualties." 22 December 2004. http://www.nps.gov/archive/usar/phcas.html.
"USS *Reid* 369 History." http://ussreid369.org/History.htm.
"USS *Reid* (DD-369)." Destroyer Photo Index DD-369 USS *Reid,* NavSource. http://www.navsource.org/
     archives/05/369.htm.
"USS *Saratoga*—CV-3—World War II—Aircraft Carrier—US Navy." http://militaryhistory.about.com/od/
     worldwariiwarships/p/World-War-Ii-Uss-Saratoga-Cv-3.htm.
"VMF224—Tutuila, Samoa." http://vmf224cenpac.homestead.com/VMF224-TutuilaSamoa.html.
Warbird Alley. "Stinson L-5 Sentinel." http://en.wikipedia.org/wiki/Stinson_L-5_Sentinel.
Wikipedia. "Bell P-39 Airacobra." online. http://en.wikipedia.org/wiki/Bell_P-39_Airacobra.
Wikipedia. "Bassingbourn Barracks." http://en.wikipedia.org/wiki/Bassingbourn_Barracks.
Wikipedia. "Amos Alonzo Stagg." online. http://en.wikipedia.org/wiki/Amos_Alonzo_Stagg.
Wikipedia. "Battle of Guam (1944)." http://en.wikipedia.org/wiki/Battle_of_Guam_(1944).
Wikipedia. "Battle of Iwo Jima." http://en.wikipedia.org/wiki/Battle_of_Iwo_Jima.
Wikipedia. "Battle of Kwajalein." http://en.wikipedia.org/wiki/Battle_of_Kwajalein.
Wikipedia. "Battle of Okinawa." http://en.wikipedia.org/wiki/Battle_of_Okinawa.
Wikipedia. "Boeing B-17 Flying Fortress." http://en.wikipedia.org/wiki/Boeing_B-17_Flying_Fortress.
Wikipedia. "Bombing of Tokyo." http://en.wikipedia.org/wiki/Bombing_of_Tokyo.
Wikipedia. "Borneo Campaign 9 (1945)." http://en.wikipedia.org/wiki/Borneo_campaign_(1945).
Wikipedia. "Chuichi Nagumo." http://en.wikipedia.org/wiki/Chuichi_Nagumo.
Wikipedia. "Death of Isoroku Yamamoto." http://en.wikipedia.org/wiki/Death_of_Isoroku_Yamamoto.
Wikipedia. "Douglas McKay." http://en.wikipedia.org/wiki/Douglas_McKay.
Wikipedia. "Eagle Pass Army Airfield." http://en.wikipedia.org/wiki/Eagle_Pass_Army_Airfield.
Wikipedia. "Eighth Air Force." http://en.wikipedia.org/wiki/Eighth_Air_Force.
Wikipedia. "Gaudo Airfield." http://en.wikipedia.org/wiki/Gaudo_Airfield.
Wikipedia. "Glenn Scobey Warner." http://en.wikipedia.org/wiki/Glenn_Scobey_Warner.
Wikipedia. "Grumman TBF Avenger." http://en.wikipedia.org/wiki/Grumman_TBF_Avenger.
Wikipedia. "Hawaii Warriors." http://en.wikipedia.org/wiki/Hawaii_Warriors_football.
Wikipedia. "History of Douglas Municipal Airport, AZ" (during World War II when it was a flying train-
     ing base, including aircraft flown in primary, basic, and advanced flying training, the latter in Mitchell
     B-25s). http://en.wikipedia.org/wiki/Douglas_Municipal_Airport_(Arizona).

Wikipedia. "Identification Friend or Foe." http://en.wikipedia.org/wiki/Identification_friend_or_foe.

Wikipedia. "Liberty Ship." http://en.wikipedia.org/wiki/Liberty_ship.

Wikipedia. "List of Ships of the United States Army," as pertains to the USAT *Puebla*. http://en.wikipedia.org/wiki/List_of_ships_of_the_United_States_Army.

Wikipedia. "Naval Air Station Alameda." http://en.wikipedia.org/wiki/Naval_Air_Station_Alameda.

Wikipedia. "North American B-25 Mitchell." http://en.wikipedia.org/wiki/North_American_B-25_Mitchell.

Wikipedia. "Operation Dragoon." http://en.wikipedia.org/wiki/Operation_Dragoon.

Wikipedia. "Operation Hailstone." http://en.wikipedia.org/wiki/Operation_Hailstone.

Wikipedia. "Operation Magic Carpet." http://en.wikipedia.org/wiki/Operation_Magic_Carpet.

Wikipedia. "Operation Shingle." http://en.wikipedia.org/wiki/Operation_Shingle.

Wikipedia. "Punahou School." http://en.wikipedia.org/wiki/Punahou_School.

Wikipedia. "Saint-Raphael, Var." http://en.wikipedia.org/wiki/Saint-Rapha%E2%88%9A%C2%B4l,_Var.

Wikipedia. "San Jose State Spartans Football." http://en.wikipedia.org/wiki/San_Jose_State_Spartans_football.

Wikipedia. "Santa Ana Army Air Base." http://en.wikipedia.org/wiki/Santa_Ana_Army_Air_Base.

Wikipedia. "Scott Air Force Base." http://en.wikipedia.org/wiki/Scott_Air_Force_Base.

Wikipedia. "Solenzara Air Base." http://en.wikipedia.org/wiki/Solenzara_Air_Base.

Wikipedia. "Spec Keene." http://en.wikipedia.org/wiki/Spec_Keene.

Wikipedia. "Stinson L-5 Sentinel." http://en.wikipedia.org/wiki/Stinson_L-5_Sentinel.

Wikipedia. "SS *Lurline* (1932)." http://en.wikipedia.org/wiki/SS_Lurline_(1932).

Wikipedia. "SS *President Coolidge*." http://en.wikipedia.org/wiki/SS_President_Coolidge.

Wikipedia. "Ulithi." http://en.wikipedia.org/wiki/Ulithi.

Wikipedia. "United States Marine Corps Aviation." http://en.wikipedia.org/wiki/United_States_Marine_Corps_Aviation.

Wikipedia. "US People—Knox, William Franklin, Secretary of the Navy, 1940–1944." http://www.history.navy.mil/photos/pers-us/uspers-k/f-knox.htm.

Wikipedia. "USS *Bismarck Sea* (CVE-95)." http://en.wikipedia.org/wiki/USS_Bismarck_Sea_(CVE-95).

Wikipedia. "USS *Edmonds* (DE-406)." http://en.wikipedia.org/wiki/USS_Edmonds_(DE-406).

Wikipedia. "USS *Hugh L. Scott* (AP-43)." http://en.wikipedia.org/wiki/USS_Hugh_L._Scott_(AP-43).

Wikipedia. "USS *Louisville* (CA-28)." http://en.wikipedia.org/wiki/USS_Louisville_(CA-28).

Wikipedia. "USS *Saratoga* (CV-3)." http://en.wikipedia.org/wiki/USS_Saratoga_(CV-3).

Wikipedia. "V-12 Navy College Training Program." http://en.wikipedia.org/wiki/V-12_Navy_College_Training_Program.

Wikipedia. "Victory Ship." http://en.wikipedia.org/wiki/Victory_ship.

Wikipedia. "Willamette Bearcats." http://en.wikipedia.org/wiki/Willamette_Bearcats.

Wilson, Tom. "When Willamette Went to War." 9 December 2003. http://d3football.com/landing/index.

OTHER ONLINE SOURCES

"About Punahou School." Punahou School, Honolulu, HI. http://www.punahou.edu/page.cfm?p=1538.

"Commander, Cruiser Division Organization, 1 May 1945." Hyperwar. http://www.ibiblio.org/hyperwar/USN/OOB/PacFleet/Org-450501/index.html.

"Guide to the Pearl Harbor Collection." Willamette University Archives. http://nwda-db.wsulibs.wsu.edu/ark:/80444/xv38610#administrative_info.

Waymark. "Sweetland Field circa 1940s." Photograph No. 1387, Ben Maxwell Collection, Salem Public Library Historic Photograph Collections. http://www.waymarking.com/gallery/image.aspx?f=1&guid=3aca180a-a4f9-473d-97ee-7dd86d136096.

Wikipedia. "3rd Air Division." http://en.wikipedia.org/wiki/3d_Air_Division.

Wikipedia. "Eighth Air Force." http://en.wikipedia.org/wiki/Eighth_Air_Force.

Wikipedia. "McCulloch Stadium." Willamette University, Salem, OR. http://en.wikipedia.org/wiki/McCulloch_Stadium.

Wikipedia. "Moi'li'ili Field." http://en.wikipedia.org/wiki/Moiliili_Field.

Wikipedia. "Oregon." http://en.wikipedia.org/wiki/Oregon.

ACKNOWLEDGMENTS

WHILE RESEARCHING THE PEARL HARBOR HISTORY, *SUNDAY IN HELL*, I AGAIN LEARNED how history becomes a writer's teacher and sometimes leads a historian in an unexpected, completely circular path, where surprises wait—and another history can jump off one page in a newspaper or magazine clipping. As Bill O'Reilly said in narrating the television series *Legends and Lies*, "News is the first draft of history."

In the first instance, in 1992, I began researching and writing history with a lengthy, seven-year, 1,144-page book centered on the United States Military Academy during the Korean War. The intense work led through the inside of West Point's infamous 1951 cheating incident, the subsequent destruction that year of the army's nationally ranked varsity football team, and its astonishing rebuilding and *A Return to Glory* in the 1953 season. That was the year the Cadets' Army team returned to the national rankings, at no. 14, after the last whistle in the season's last game signaled their victory over Navy.

The cheating incident literally became a national scandal, followed by an inspired 1953 team filled with sophomore sensations and sterling team leaders, the Academy's 1954 seniors, both classes more than eager to lift Army's—and the Corps of Cadets'—flagging gridiron spirits.

But it was in the lead-up to that inspiring football season, through research, in an article from an Army magazine mailed to me by McPherson Conner, class of 1952, and memories of my first summer at West Point, that I stumbled upon an event half a world away, the final battle for a Korean War outpost named Pork Chop Hill, a bitter, bloody five-day battle few had heard of or remembered. The battle had been obscured primarily because famed military historian SLA Marshall published a book titled *Pork Chop Hill*, a history of the 16–18 April 1953 battle, on which a 1959 movie by the same name had been based, starring Gregory Peck.

The bloody 6–11 July 1953 battle for the outpost ended sixteen days prior to the signing of the Korean War truce, was extremely controversial in the minds of its survivors and many historians, and cost 243 American lives, while 916 more were wounded. Among those killed in action were two men in the class of 1952 who had been in the 4th New Cadet Company, the company I was in as a plebe (freshman) my first summer at West Point. The two first classmen (seniors) graduated the following spring. (Their classmate McPherson Conner had fought in the July battle too and was grievously wounded, ending his army career.)

The two men killed in action were Lieutenants Richard Thomas Shea Jr., the 4th New Cadet Company commander the summer of 1951, Army's record-setting track team captain, a World War II army enlistee, a gifted artist and cartoonist as a cadet, married, and his wife was pregnant with a son he never saw; and Richard George Inman, the son of the Vincennes, Indiana, High School football coach, a "walk-on" to the Army football team, and who struggled long and hard to make the varsity until the cheating incident gave him his chance to do what he always wanted to do—win the Army lettermen's Major A in football. Dick Inman was a high hurdler on the Army track team with Dick Shea in the April 1952 Penn Relays, where the Army team captain won the two-mile championship the third year in a row, and Dick Inman's high-hurdle shuttle relay team won the college division championship. Dick Inman was also an intense idealist and a serious poet who had won second place in a nationwide university and college poetry contest. What's more, when he was killed in action the night of 6–7 July 1953, back home in Indiana, his wife of four months was helping him write his first book, and he had already been in contact with Wernher von Braun, by letter, intent on entering the army's burgeoning rocket and space program on returning from the Korean War.

From that little-known, bitter July battle, the story of these two marvelous young men, and the gentle, but most welcome push by McPherson Conner, came my second major history, *On Hallowed Ground: The Last Battle for Pork Chop Hill.*

And now, Pearl Harbor has done the same for researchers and university and college officials who have repeatedly helped this author uncover far more facts about another inspiring story of football and war. Like the story of the July 1953 battle for Pork Chop Hill, the inspiration for this book was found scattered and almost buried in newspaper clippings; in San Francisco, Honolulu, Hawaii University, and state archives; in Willamette University and Oregon state archives; in San Jose State College archives; in a brief, twelve-minute glimpse in a 2000 ESPN broadcast; and in a brief, narrated video and 2006 DVD about the Willamette team.

No more. A quotation by the famed Alaska-centered historian Steven C. Levi, sent with emails from Gina Bardi, the reference librarian at the San Francisco Maritime National Historical Park Research Center, yields one important perspective, but not the only view. "History . . . is not a re-creation of the past. It's an assessment of the past based on documents provided by people in archives and museums who will answer your letters." The list of those who would answer writers' queries is today much longer than letters only. Sources now include phone, emails, social media, interviews, and personal and online visits to libraries and museums using powerful search engines, just to name a few.

The existence of this long-ago story was first written about by reporters in brief news pieces in San Francisco; Salem, Oregon; San Jose, California; Seattle and Puget Sound newspapers in Washington State; and Honolulu newspapers leading up to November 27, 1941, when the Willamette Bearcats and San Jose State Spartans left San Francisco, bound for Honolulu, on the famed "Great White Matson Liner," SS *Lurline*, to play a series of round-robin charity football games, beginning with Willamette's December 6 Shrine Bowl game against the University of Hawaii Rainbows for the benefit of the Shriners' Hospital in Honolulu. Then would come San Jose State and Hawaii on the 13th, to benefit the Honolulu police, and finally the two stateside teams would play each other at Honolulu Stadium on December 16 to help defray the costs of the trip to Hawaii.

The story resurfaced in the period after the Japanese December 7 attack on Pearl Harbor after the first evacuation convoy from Hawaii arrived in San Francisco on Christmas Day 1941. Crew members on the SS *President Coolidge* spoke to a number of reporters of their experiences on the last leg of their journey from Manila, Philippines, to and from Honolulu, and finally home. A lovely lady in the San Francisco Library, Marti Goddard, sent me a large collection of newspaper clippings about the ship's arrival that Christmas Day when I was early in the lengthy research for the Pearl Harbor history.

Among all the reporting of the unnamed ship's arrival were references to the two football teams on board. The ship's name was deliberately withheld from news stories on arrival in San Francisco due to tight security measures involving ship movements imposed immediately after the attack on Pearl Harbor. Then began the far more intense research, through all means at my disposal to begin the long-distance effort, in university libraries, archives, and athletic departments at Willamette, San Jose State, and the University of Hawaii, the Oregon State University Archives, and then alumni associations, to expand and deepen my research—to become a book that would hopefully tell the whole story.

This has been an incredible, educational journey in time, distance, and never-ending curiosity. Without all these wonderful people, whose names follow, I could never have completed the journey. First and foremost must come six close family members—my beautiful wife of more than sixty years, Veronica Eileen (Ronnie), whom our family lost to Alzheimer's disease on All Saints' Day, November 1, 2015, and my beautiful new wife, Anna Marie Bates, who agreed to marry me on October 15, 2016, in Las Vegas, Nevada, and granted me the privilege of sharing the rest of our lives together. Ronnie's and my three children, Kathleen Mendenhall, Mary Ann Villet, our son Bill IV (and their families), and a marvelous Christian lady, Mary F. Smith, who is now a true member of our family and equally important in our lives, plus our agent, Stuart M. Miller, and his wife, Charlotte.

Stu is a literary and talent agent and proud former member of the Marine Corps with fifty years in the literary and entertainment industries, and he has assisted, encouraged, and inspired Veronica and me for more than ten years. In the last five years he has represented us in finding publishers and negotiating our last two book contracts.

My wife, Ronnie, and I met Stu at the Roosevelt Hotel cocktail lounge in Hollywood the unforgettable night of November 29, 2005, the night before we attended the premiere of the movie *Code Breakers*—which was based on our first book, *A Return to Glory*—in the great, old Paramount Theater, next door to the studio where the film classic *Sunset Boulevard* was produced.

There is yet one more story about this book I must place before all readers. In the telling, please note that this book is dedicated to both Veronica and Anna, while my first book, *A Return to Glory*, self-published with the aid of a second mortgage on our home, was dedicated to Veronica only. She was the first grand inspiration in my life. We married one day after I graduated from West Point. I was still twenty-one, and she was one month from eighteen years.

She stood by me all the way through the sometimes truly difficult three careers, the first twenty-seven and a half years on active duty in the air force, and nearly four thousand hours of flying in jet trainers and fighter-bombers, the latter spanning our emotional family parting as I went off to war in Vietnam on November 14, 1965, a thirty-two-year-old father of three, ages nine, five, and three, left in her loving care under the ever-present question all wives and children in military families face in war: "Will he come home to us safely?"

With that life came twenty-six moves to fourteen states in the continental United States, and two accompanied years in the Republic of Korea in 1979–1981, where in October 1979 an international crisis and internal upheaval erupted, causing a firefight between Republic of Korea army units a scant five hundred yards from our quarters and just outside Yongsan Army Garrison in Seoul.

Then it was eight and a half years in the defense industry, first in New Hampshire and then California, and finally twenty-three years trying late in life to become an author of military history, all after we retired from the air force at Nellis Air Force Base, Las Vegas, Nevada, on February 1, 1983. Through it all, my beautiful wife (too many times to count) lifted me up to continue and complete what I set out to do. Then, just as we seemed to be closing in on completing this final book toward the end of 2014, my wife was struck by dementia. It came on ever so slowly but abruptly accelerated in the last ten days of November. It was devastating and nearly overwhelmed us because I had been slow to react.

In casting about for help, I was referred to an agency that helped us struggle through the first month into mid-January 2015, when our two daughters stepped in for a month and ten days, respectively, coming to our home to assist, and we were able hire a God-sent professional caregiver, Mary F. Smith. In the meantime, on January 2, I had to send one of the most painful messages of my life to numerous people who had helped me over a four-year period of research, telling them it was probable that I could never complete *Scrimmage for War*.

Finally, slowly, ever so slowly, in late February 2015, thanks to our entire family's encouragement and support, many softly spoken prayers, and the marvelous Christian caregiver and her training, I was able, as time permitted, to begin work again. Finally, on July 20, I sent another message to all who had been so understanding and encouraging after the stunning communication of January 2. Who were they?

David Rigsby, Willamette University athletic director and associate dean of campus life and now associate vice president for advancement, who gave me an invaluable introduction to this story and followed up with unrelenting encouragement; Lawrence Fan, San Jose State athletics media relations director; James C. Booth, formerly head of the Willamette University graduate association's alumni and parent relations; and Mary McRobinson, university archivist, Mark O. Hatfield Library, Willamette University, all four of whom I called on repeatedly to assist with information essential to obtain interviews, add to the research finds, and tell the two 1941 football teams' stories. Mary McRobinson's assistant archivist, Veronica Aguilar Ramos, who also contributed time and energy to the project, answering my requests for assistance; Bonnie Montgomery, historian and researcher, San Jose, California, who opened the door to the San Jose State University archives, obtained wonderful materials, and took photographs to tell the stories of Kenneth C. Bailey, the only player from either team killed in action during World War II, and the memorial chapel his grieving parents inspired, which was built and dedicated on the San Jose State campus; Mr. Donald Gill, reader services librarian at the U.S. Merchant Marine Academy, who provided invaluable information about "The Little Pearl Harbor" disaster in Bari, Italy, on December 2, 1943; Phillippa Wray, membership officer in the American Air Museum in the United Kingdom, who turned me toward the American Battle Monuments Commission website to find Kenneth C. Bailey's name and other key pieces of information; F. Clifton Berry Jr., FCB Associates LLC, a friend of many years, whose company worked with the American Battle Monuments Commission and who so graciously pointed me toward three marvelous and moving online photographs of the Sicily-Rome American Cemetery, Nettuno, Italy, in completing the story of the tragic loss of San Jose State's Kenneth C. Bailey and provided additional, stunning photographs of the 91st "Wild West Division" in action during World War I; Kenneth W. Jacobson, the 1941 Willamette University football team member and quarterback whose multiple interviews and stunning photographs taken throughout the team's journey to and from Honolulu, with the assistance of his grandson by marriage, Hal Ganley, brought his team's story to life, with gentle understated wisdom for all of us, as did the photographs by Victor Albert "Bert" Robinson, 1947 graduate of San Jose State, star right halfback on the Spartans' 1941 and 1946 teams and a fifty-one mission veteran B-17 pilot and aircraft commander in the 418th Bombardment Squadron (H), 301st Bombardment Group, in the 15th Air Force; Bert's wonderful, devoted daughter, Kathy Carver, our "adopted little sister," who worked tirelessly, contributing everything she could to her father's story and this project; John M. Barbour, son of Marshall Hall Barbour, who contributed a treasure trove of information about his father's World War II service and greatly enhanced with unit combat and base photographs and histories from the 448th Bombardment Squadron (M), 321st Bombardment Group, in Italy and Corsica in the Mediterranean theater of operations, 1944, with the assistance of Mrs. Lynn O. Gamma of the Air Force Historical Research Agency; and additional post–World War II inputs by Valerie Howell, district tutor in Woodburn, Oregon, and former Las Vegas resident; and Ms. Barbara Bannister at Woodburn High School, Oregon, who sent excerpts from high school annuals that provided excellent background on his service in the field of education in Woodburn; Janet Leffler and Susan Powell, daughters of Charles S. Furno of Vancouver, Washington. Janet graciously provided virtually all the information about his World War II career as a P-38L pilot and much about his life afterward, with additional information coming from a former student, Robert Lee Cone, and players on the Vancouver High School football teams he coached; Irene Reeves of Jefferson, Oregon, who wrote a small piece titled "Irving E. Miller Remembered" in the *Jefferson, Oregon Review* on August 5, 1995, a remembrance that opened other doors to telling the story of Irving Miller's service and sacrifice as a prisoner of war in the 322nd Squadron of the famed 91st Bombardment Group (H), a B-17 group stationed at Bassingbourn, United Kingdom. Mrs. Karin Fitzgerald, wife of the late federal judge James Fitzgerald who proudly served his memory by providing a comprehensive summary of their lives together as he progressed in administering the rule of law as a state then federal judge, as well as much of his World War II service; Kara Newcomer and Beth Crumley, both extremely knowledgeable and devoted women in the Marine Corps History Division were absolutely invaluable in explaining and helping me understand, find, and complete the World War II records of service of Willamette team members who joined and served in the Marine Corps: Ted Ogdahl, Andrew Rogers, Marion "Buddy" Reynolds, James Fitzgerald, Clarence Walden, and Cecil Conner. James Cartwright, University of Hawaii archivist, who provided some outstanding Honolulu Stadium and 1941 Shrine Bowl Game action photographs and other photographs pertinent to the two teams' presence on Oahu. Carlyn Tani and Mari-jo Hirata at Punahou School, who provided an outstanding World War II Punahou School history pamphlet, which contains some marvelous photographs used in this work. Bobbie Conner, niece of Cecil Gilbert Conner, who gave invaluable background information and a delightful photograph of Cecil, proudly wearing his marine uniform, and his sister, Bobbie's mother, as young people during World War II. Michael A. Dicianna, volunteer student archivist, Oregon State University Library, who did a magnificent job of finding, compiling, and sending photographs and numerous other items about Coach Roy S. "Spec" Keene, the head coach of the 1941 Willamette Bearcats, and James Douglas McKay, the then state senator from Salem, Oregon, who provided outstanding leadership to the entire Bearcat team during a trying period of their young lives. Both men graduated from Oregon Agricultural College (now Oregon State University), served in France in World War I, and returned to active duty in the continental United States during World War II. Journalist and author Frank Marqua of the Santa Rosa, California, *Press Democrat*, who graciously shared research information and provided important contact information for additional research, plus some fascinating related vignettes. Janet Baker and Marcia Poehl, reference librarians, and Dianna Clark, office assistant/administration, all three from the Salem, Oregon, Public Library, and from whom I seemed to endlessly request research assistance—and Brian Wood, Photovision Co., for the Salem Public Library Historic Photograph Collection, who provided a 1940 vintage aerial photograph of Willamette's Sweetland Field Stadium. And late in the research effort, beginning August 12, 2014, email and phone contact with a seriously ill Carolyn Moore, the daughter of Elaine and Gordon Moore, who so graciously provided wonderfully delightful vignettes about her father and mother's journey to Oahu and back, and their activities at Punahou School while the Willamette football team was temporarily stranded on the island. Others I would be remiss in failing to express my deep and sincere thanks for their assistance are Charles Dunham, Corvallis Public Library; Jennifer Xochihua, Grant High School (Portland, Oregon) Library assistant; Kari Gordon, Roseburg High School, Oregon, media assistant; Gina Bardi, reference librarian, National

Park Service Maritime Museum and Library, for the beautiful 1930s on-board photographs of the SS *President Coolidge* found in chapter 2; and the National Personnel Records Center, St. Louis, Missouri. And there are more.

I had wonderful interviews with ten people, five of them surviving Willamette team members, and one from San Jose State. Now there is only one remaining from the Willamette team: the "twice left back" Honorable Clarence Walden, the wonderful "marrying judge" who retired from the bench on July 31, 1982, and proudly continued to serve by marrying young people, performing more than 2,500 ceremonies over a fifty-year period. He was a World War II veteran with incredible stories of life's good works and achievements as a "citizen soldier" who has left indelible stories in the sands of time and, with his teammates, is a legend no more.

And, finally, a fairy-tale ending involving Anna Marie (Bates) McWilliams, the second beautiful lady to whom this book is dedicated. We met online June 11, 2016, and married on October 15, and we met as a direct result of this book.

In the mid-1950s, Anna had attended San Jose State College for three years before deciding that she wanted to travel and entered training and became a Pan American Airways stewardess. While attending San Jose State, her lasting beauty, inside and out, was clearly evident. She was a cheerleader for the football team and had been named the college's Centennial Homecoming Queen. While a Pan Am stewardess, she met and married an extraordinarily fine gentleman named Vane Quentin Bates Jr., who graduated in the same 1955 West Point class that I did but was commissioned and entered the Army Corps of Engineers while I was commissioned in the air force. Quentin and I had never been acquainted while at the academy.

He and Anna met in Hawaii, quite literally by colliding on surfboards, and he exited the army after three years to become outstandingly successful in business in the international world of elevators. They lived forty-four years of their fifty-five together in Littleton, Colorado, where they raised their three children, before he retired and they relocated to Orem, Utah.

On June 22, 2013, Anna lost Quentin Bates to an abrupt, massive heart attack, one day after they celebrated their fifty-fifth wedding anniversary. At the time, Anna's daughter Christy Kirkland was living with her husband, Scott, in Orem, near three of their four children, two of whom have families; her son Jim Bates was in Salt Lake City; and her son Steve Bates was in San Clemente, California, with his wife, Noelle, and their three children.

On June 11, 2016, someone—whom Anna doesn't recall—sent her a web address that briefly described the story in this book, a story she had never heard while attending San Jose State for three years, and where she had been closely associated with the college's football team. She decided to forward the web address to the class of 1955 forum, which is essentially a large, class internet "chat room" I had elected not to join due to time limitations resulting from my research and writing. She asked class members and their survivors, including widows, via email, "Does anyone in the class have knowledge of this story?" Since I wasn't a member of the 1955 forum, I didn't see her internet query.

I was still living in Las Vegas, Nevada, at the time, as was one other West Point class-mate, Tom Sims, who happened to be our class webmaster—and had painstakingly over the years developed an extensive book-related, personal website for Ronnie and me. Tom knew I'd written this book and simply forwarded a copy of Anna's query to me. I promptly answered Anna's email, with words to the effect, "Yes, I know about this story. I wrote a book about it."

Thus began the fairy-tale meeting, caused by this book, *Scrimmage for War*. Anna's three grown children, and three of her grandchildren, plus my youngest daughter, Mary Ann Villet of Boise, Idaho, and Veronica's wonderful caregiver, Fran Smith, of Las Vegas, Nevada, were among thirty-one family and friends who attended the wedding ceremony, as were Tom Sims and his wife, Susan, on October 15, 2016, in the home that Veronica and I had lived in for more than twenty years.

INDEX